# THE LOS ANGELES OLD-TIME RADIO SCHEDULE BOOK

VOLUME 3

1946·1954

KEITH D. LEE

*The Los Angeles Old-Time Radio Schedule Book — Volume 3, 1946-1954*

Published in the USA by:
BearManor Media
PO Box 1129
Duncan, Oklahoma 73534-1129
*www.bearmanormedia.com*

ISBN 978-1-59393-239-8

Printed in the United States of America.
Book design by Brian Pearce | Red Jacket Press.

# TABLE OF CONTENTS

# INTRODUCTION

This series of books are a listing of national and local Los Angeles-based OTR shows from Fall, 1929 through Summer, 1954, in an easy-to-read grid format. Each section lists the OTR shows that were playing during that particular calendar season in that particular OTR year. The shows that are listed were on the four major OTR networks (Blue/ABC, CBS, MBS, and NBC) and their local Los Angeles affiliates from 8AM to 11PM Monday through Sunday.

In reading any of the sample chapters, please note the following:

Each cell in the grid represents a fifteen minute block of time.

Each blank cell means that the preceding show is still on. I deferred from using quotation marks because it looked too unreadable.

A slash between the names of two or more daily shows either in the same cell or adjoining cells signifies that those shows shared that timeslot on intermittant days for each week during that particular calendar season. In the case of weekly shows, a slash signifies that the shows shared the same timeslot for part of that particular calendar season.

Such generic show titles as "Songs," "Music," "News," "Public Affairs," "Sports," and "Talk" and any combination thereof are used. In the case of a daily show, such a generic title signifies the type of show on during the week. In the case of a weekly show, the networks or their affiliated stations couldn't find a sponsor for that timeslot and filled it with a generic show of music, talk, etc.

The information printed has been thoroughly checked for absolute correctness based on the OTR sources that still exist; contradictions and errors in them notwithstanding.

The book is the summation of one year of research using the following sources:

JJ's Radio Logs: *http://www.jjonz.us/RadioLogs/*

*The New York Old-Time-Radio Schedule Book, Volumes 1-3*
by Keith D. Lee. BearManor Media, OK, 2011.

Because there aren't very many OTR sources anymore, and many of them contradict one another, many thanks are necessary to JJ for allowing me access to his wonderfully entertaining and informative Radio Log Web Page. Hopefully, this will inspire the next generations to research even more into the history of OTR.

# LISTINGS FOR 1946

## EVENING — WINTER, 1946

*Sunday*

| | ABC | CBS | MBS | NBC |
|---|---|---|---|---|
| *5pm* | The Ford Sunday Evening Hour | The Marlin Hurt and Beulah Show | A. L. Alexander's Mediation Board | The Charlie McCarthy Show |
| *5:15* | | | | |
| *5:30* | | A Man Named Jordan | Don't Be a Sucker | The Fred Allen Show |
| *5:45* | | Ned Calmer, news (5:55PM) | Gabriel Heatter, news | |
| *6pm* | Walter Winchell's Jergens Journal | Request Performance | Exploring the Unknown | The Manhattan Merry-Go-Round |
| *6:15* | Louella Parsons, gossip | | | |
| *6:30* | Listen to La Guardia | The Texaco Star Theater, James Melton | Double or Nothing | The American Album of Familiar Music |
| *6:45* | Jimmy Fidler, gossip | | | |
| *7pm* | The Theater Guild of the Air | Take It or Leave It | Freedom of Opportunity | The Hour of Charm |
| *7:15* | | | | |
| *7:30* | | The Baby Snooks Show | What's the Name of That Song | Meet Me at Parky's |
| *7:45* | | | | |
| *8pm* | Playhouse Favorites | Crime Doctor | The Human Adventure | The Great Gildersleeve |
| *8:15* | | Surprise Theater (8:25 PM) | | |
| *8:30* | The Quiz Kids | Blondie | Walter Winchell's Jergens Journal | The Standard Symphony Hour |
| *8:45* | | | The Rave of the Week | |
| *9pm* | Sam Hayes, news | The Adventures of the Thin Man | Glenn Hardy, news | |
| *9:15* | Report to the People | | Rex Miller, news | |
| *9:30* | Eastside Serenade | Romance of the Ranchos | Film Comments | The Lucky Strike Program, Jack Benny |
| *9:45* | | | Ed Thorgersen, sports | |
| *10pm* | Hit Tunes | The Ten o'Clock Wire | Leave It to Mike | The Richfield Reporter |
| *10:15* | Public Affairs | Dr. Sterling, health | | The Chapel Quartet |
| *10:30* | Freddy Martin Orchestra | Dance Orchestra | Music | Inside the News |
| *10:45* | | | | Show Time |

| EVENING — WINTER, 1946 | | | | |
|---|---|---|---|---|
| *Monday* | | | | |
| ABC | CBS | MBS | NBC | |
| Terry and the Pirates | Knox Manning, news | Sam Hayes, news | H. V. Kaltenborn, news | *5pm* |
| Dick Tracy | Through a Woman's Eyes | The Adventures of Superman | News | *5:15* |
| Jack Armstrong, the All-American Boy | Harry W. Flannery, news | Captain Midnight | The Voice of Firestone | *5:30* |
| News | Truman Bradley, news | Tom Mix and His Ralston Straightshooters | | *5:45* |
| Time and Tide | The Lux Radio Theater | Gabriel Heatter, news | Tonight at Hoagy's | *6pm* |
| | | Real Stories from Real Life | | *6:15* |
| Forever Tops | | Spotlight Bands | Information, Please | *6:30* |
| | | | | *6:45* |
| Jimmy Gleason's Diner | The Lady Esther Screen Guild Theater | This Land is Mine | The Carnation Contented Hour | *7pm* |
| | | Music | | *7:15* |
| Your CIO | The Bob Hawk Show | The Lone Ranger | Dr. I. Q., the Mental Banker | *7:30* |
| Strings | | | | *7:45* |
| Lum and Abner | The Jack Kirkwood Show | Michael Shayne, Private Detective | The Chesterfield Supper Club | *8pm* |
| Hedda Hopper, gossip | The Jack Smith Show | | Fleetwood Lawton, news | *8:15* |
| The Fat Man | Joanie's Tea Room | Sherlock Holmes | The Cavalcade of America | *8:30* |
| | Carroll Alcott, news (8:55 PM) | | | *8:45* |
| I Deal in Crime | The Whistler | Glenn Hardy, news | The Bell Telephone Hour | *9pm* |
| | | Rex Miller, news | | *9:15* |
| Symposium | Vox Pop | The Inside of Sports | Young Artist's Contest | *9:30* |
| Swoon | | Henry J. Taylor, news | | *9:45* |
| Relax | The Ten o'Clock Wire | Bulldog Drummond | The Richfield Reporter | *10pm* |
| News | Dr. Fisher, health | | The Frank Parker Show | *10:15* |
| Raymond Gram Swing, news | The Symphonette | The Johnson Family | Inside the News | *10:30* |
| Rainbow Rendezvous | | So the Story Goes | Show Time | *10:45* |

| EVENING — WINTER, 1946 | | | | |
|---|---|---|---|---|
| *Tuesday* | | | | |
| | ABC | CBS | MBS | NBC |
| *5pm* | Terry and the Pirates | Kurt Manning, news | Sam Hayes, news | News |
| *5:15* | Dick Tracy | Through a Woman's Eyes | The Adventures of Superman | News |
| *5:30* | Jack Armstrong, the All-American Boy | Harry W. Flannery, news | Captain Midnight | A Date with Judy |
| *5:45* | News | Truman Bradley, news | Tom Mix and His Ralston Straightshooters | |
| *6pm* | Guy Lombardo Orchestra | Inner Sanctum Mysteries | Gabriel Heatter, news | Amos 'n' Andy |
| *6:15* | | | Real Stories from Real Life | |
| *6:30* | The Story of a Star | This is My Best | The American Forum of the Air | Fibber McGee and Molly |
| *6:45* | | | | |
| *7pm* | Jones and I | Bob Crosby Orchestra | | The Pepsodent Show, Bob Hope |
| *7:15* | | | Upton Close, news | |
| *7:30* | Hoosier Hop | Melodies America Loves | Red Ryder | The Raleigh Cigarette Program, Red Skelton |
| *7:45* | | | | |
| *8pm* | Lum and Abner | The Jack Kirkwood Show | The Count of Monte Cristo | The Chesterfield Supper Club |
| *8:15* | Ed Sullivan Entertains | The Jack Smith Show | | Fleetwood Lawton, news |
| *8:30* | The Alan Young Show | Theater of Romance | The Falcon | The Johnny Desmond Follies |
| *8:45* | | Carroll Alcott, news (8:55 PM) | | |
| *9pm* | Dark Venture | Big Town | Glenn Hardy, news | The Bullocks Show |
| *9:15* | | | James Crowley, news | |
| *9:30* | Murder Will Out | Tapestries of Life | The Inside of Sports | The American Way |
| *9:45* | | | The Feeling is Mutual | |
| *10pm* | Relax | The Ten o'Clock Wire | Fulton Lewis Jr., news | The Richfield Reporter |
| *10:15* | News | Dr. Sterling, health | News | Miss Information |
| *10:30* | Raymond Gram Swing, news | Congress Speaks | Sing, America Sing | Inside the News |
| *10:45* | The Doctors Talk It Over | Behind the Scenes at CBS | So the Story Goes | Show Time |

| EVENING — WINTER, 1946 | | | | |
|---|---|---|---|---|
| *Wednesday* | | | | |
| ABC | CBS | MBS | NBC | |
| Terry and the Pirates | Kurt Manning, news | Sam Hayes, news | H. V. Kaltenborn, news | *5pm* |
| Dick Tracy | Through a Woman's Eyes | The Adventures of Superman | News | *5:15* |
| Jack Armstrong, the All-American Boy | Harry W. Flannery, news | Captain Midnight | The Voice of the Nation | *5:30* |
| News | Truman Bradley, news | Tom Mix and His Ralston Straightshooters | Elmer Patterson, news | *5:45* |
| The Golden Gate Quartet | Songs By Sinatra | Gabriel Heatter, news | Time to Smile, Eddie Cantor | *6pm* |
| | | Real Stories from Real Life | | *6:15* |
| So You Want to Lead a Band | Maisie | Spotlight Bands | Mr. District Attorney | *6:30* |
| | | | | *6:45* |
| Talk | Great Moments in Music | The Whisper Men | Kay Kyser's College of Musical Knowledge | *7pm* |
| News | | | | *7:15* |
| Boston Blackie | The N-K Musical Showroom, Andrew Sisters | The Lone Ranger | | *7:30* |
| | | | | *7:45* |
| Lum and Abner | The Jack Kirkwood Show | The Main Line | The Chesterfield Supper Club | *8pm* |
| Elmer Davis, news | The Jack Smith Show | | Fleetwood Lawton, news | *8:15* |
| The Fishing and Hunting Club | Dr. Christian | The Fresh Up Show, Bert Lahr | The Penguin Room, Hildegarde | *8:30* |
| | Carroll Alcott, news (8:55 PM) | | | *8:45* |
| News | The Jack Carson Show | Glenn Hardy, news | Mr. and Mrs. North | *9pm* |
| Music | | Rex Miller, news | | *9:15* |
| Spade Cooley Orchestra | The Adventures of Ellery Queen | The Inside of Sports | The Skippy Hollywood Theater | *9:30* |
| | | Spike Jones Orchestra | | *9:45* |
| Relax | The Ten o'Clock Wire | Fulton Lewis Jr., news | The Richfield Reporter | *10pm* |
| News | Dr. Fisher, health | Music | Music | *10:15* |
| Raymond Gram Swing, news | The Symphonette | The Johnson Family | Inside the News | *10:30* |
| Freddy Martin Orchestra | | So the Story Goes | Show Time | *10:45* |

# EVENING — WINTER, 1946

*Thursday*

| | ABC | CBS | MBS | NBC |
|---|---|---|---|---|
| *5pm* | Terry and the Pirates | Knox Manning, news | Sam Hayes, news | News |
| *5:15* | Dick Tracy | Through a Woman's Eyes | The Adventures of Superman | News |
| *5:30* | Jack Armstrong, the All-American Boy | Harry W. Flannery, news | Captain Midnight | The Voice of a Nation |
| *5:45* | News | Truman Bradley, news | Tom Mix and His Ralston Straightshooters | Elmer Patterson, news |
| *6pm* | The Hobby Hour | Music Millions Love | Gabriel Heatter, news | The Kraft Music Hall, Bing Crosby |
| *6:15* | Retribution | | Real Stories from Real Life | |
| *6:30* | Detect and Collect | Hobby Lobby | The Treasure Hour of Song | The Bob Burns Show |
| *6:45* | | | | |
| *7pm* | Curtain Time | Island Venture | You Make the News | Abbott and Costello |
| *7:15* | | | | |
| *7:30* | Jobs for G.I.s | The Powder Box Theater | Red Ryder | The Rudy Vallee Show |
| *7:45* | | | | |
| *8pm* | Lum and Abner | The Jack Kirkwood Show | The Theater of Famous Radio Players | The Chesterfield Supper Club |
| *8:15* | Earl Godwin, news | The Jack Smith Show | | Fleetwood Lawton, news |
| *8:30* | America's Town Meeting of the Air | The FBI in Peace and War | Rogue's Gallery | Maxwell House Coffee Time, Burns and Allen |
| *8:45* | | Carroll Alcott, news (8:55 PM) | | |
| *9pm* | | Suspense | Glenn Hardy, news | The Birdseye Open House, Dinah Shore |
| *9:15* | | | James Crowley, news | |
| *9:30* | Mystery House | The Citizen's Forum | The Inside of Sports | Noah Webster Says |
| *9:45* | | | News | |
| *10pm* | Cal Tinney, news | The Ten o'Clock Wire | Fulton Lewis Jr., news | The Richfield Reporter |
| *10:15* | Charlie Chan | Dr. Sterling, health | News | Mayor Bowron, comment |
| *10:30* | Raymond Gram Swing, news | Sports | Music | Inside the News |
| *10:45* | Freddy Martin Orchestra | Organ Recital | So the Story Goes | Show Time |

| EVENING — WINTER, 1946 | | | | |
|---|---|---|---|---|
| *Friday* | | | | |
| ABC | CBS | MBS | NBC | |
| Terry and the Pirates | Knox Manning, news | Sam Hayes, news | H. V. Kaltenborn, news | *5pm* |
| Dick Tracy | Through a Woman's Eyes | The Adventures of Superman | News | *5:15* |
| Jack Armstrong, the All-American Boy | Harry W. Flannery, news | Captain Midnight | The Voice of a Nation | *5:30* |
| News | Truman Bradley, news | Tom Mix and His Ralston Straightshooters | Elmer Patterson, news | *5:45* |
| Famous Jury Trials | The Ginny Simms Show | Gabriel Heatter, news | People Are Funny | *6pm* |
| | | Real Stories from Real Life | | *6:15* |
| The Sheriff | Those Websters | Spotlight Bands | Waltz Time | *6:30* |
| | | | | *6:45* |
| Madison Square Garden Boxing | The Durante - Moore Show | This Land is Mine | The Molle' Mystery Theater | *7pm* |
| | | Music | | *7:15* |
| | Pabst Blue Ribbon Time, Danny Kaye | The Lone Ranger | The Colgate Sports Newsreel, Bill Stern | *7:30* |
| | | | Cabbages and Kings | *7:45* |
| Woody Herman Orchestra | The Jack Kirkwood Show | The Drew Show | The Chesterfield Supper Club | *8pm* |
| | The Jack Smith Show | | Fleetwood Lawton, news | *8:15* |
| This is Your FBI | It Pays to Be Ignorant | So You Think You Know Music | Duffy's Tavern | *8:30* |
| | Carroll Alcott, news (8:55 PM) | | | *8:45* |
| News and Views | The Aldrich Family | Glenn Hardy, news | The Night Editor | *9pm* |
| | | Rex Miller, news | Latin Serenade | *9:15* |
| Spade Cooley Orchestra | Kate Smith Sings | The Inside of Sports | The Haunting Hour | *9:30* |
| | | Henry J. Taylor, news | | *9:45* |
| Cal Tinney, news | The Ten o'Clock Wire | Fulton Lewis Jr., news | The Richfield Reporter | *10pm* |
| News | Dr. Fisher, health | News | The Frank Parker Show | *10:15* |
| Raymond Gram Swing, news | The Symphonette | The Johnson Family | Inside the News | *10:30* |
| Freddy Martin Orchestra | | So the Story Goes | Show Time | *10:45* |

| EVENING — WINTER, 1946 | | | | |
|---|---|---|---|---|
| *Saturday* | | | | |
| | ABC | CBS | MBS | NBC |
| *5pm* | Music | The Voice of the Moment | News | The RCA Victor Show |
| *5:15* | Here's Morgan | Talk | The Canary Pet Shop | |
| *5:30* | News | Harry W. Flannery, news | Music | News |
| *5:45* | Harry Wismer, sports | Henry Garred, news | | Elmer Patterson, news |
| *6pm* | Musical Playground | Hollywood Preview | Leave It to the Girls | The National Barn Dance |
| *6:15* | | | | |
| *6:30* | Boston Symphony Orchestra | That's a Good Idea | Break the Bank | Can You Top This |
| *6:45* | | Saturday Night Serenade | | |
| *7pm* | | | The Quiz of Two Cities | The Judy Canova Show |
| *7:15* | | The Continental Celebrity Club, Jackie Kelk | | |
| *7:30* | Dick Tracy | | Red Ryder | Grand Ole Opry |
| *7:45* | | The Story Teller | | |
| *8pm* | Your CIO | The Dick Haymes Show | The Chicago Theater of the Air | Truth or Consequences |
| *8:15* | Design for Death | | | |
| *8:30* | Win, Place or Show | The Mayor of the Town | | The Life of Riley |
| *8:45* | | Carroll Alcott, news (8:55 PM) | | |
| *9pm* | Gangbusters | Your Hit Parade | Glenn Hardy, news | The Adventures of Bill Lance |
| *9:15* | | | News | |
| *9:30* | The Green Hornet | | Dance Orchestra | The Family Party |
| *9:45* | | Don't You Believe It | The Frank Parker Show | |
| *10pm* | Dance Orchestra | The Ten o'Clock Wire | Music | |
| *10:15* | | The Hollywood Barn Dance | | |
| *10:30* | Freddy Martin Orchestra | | | News |
| *10:45* | | Music | | Show Time |

## DAYTIME — WINTER, 1946

*Sunday*

| | ABC | CBS | MBS | NBC |
|---|---|---|---|---|
| *8am* | News | News and Views | The Wesley League | The Eternal Light |
| *8:15* | Music | | | |
| *8:30* | The Hour of Faith | Invitation to Learning | The Voice of Prophecy | News Roundup |
| *8:45* | | | | News |
| *9am* | It Happened During the Week | The Salt Lake Tabernacle Choir | The Pilgrim Hour | The University of Chicago Round Table |
| *9:15* | News | | | |
| *9:30* | Stradivari Orchestra | Transatlantic Call | The Lutheran Hour | Echoes and Encores |
| *9:45* | | | | |
| *10am* | John B. Kennedy, news | Brothers' Blood | Glenn Hardy, news | Layman's Views of the News |
| *10:15* | Orson Welles, comment | | Commander Scott | The Home Town Parade |
| *10:30* | Sammy Kaye's Sunday Serenade | News | Sweetheart Time | Musical Milestones |
| *10:45* | | Edward R. Murrow, news | | Modern Music |
| *11am* | Washington Inside and Out | The Radio Reader's Digest | The Band Concert | Harvest of Stars |
| *11:15* | General Junius Pierce, comment | | | |
| *11:30* | National Vespers | Hollywood Star Time | News | The Westinghouse Program, John C. Thomas |
| *11:45* | | | Music | |
| *12pm* | Elmer Davis, news | New York Philharmonic Orchestra | Broadway News | The Sheaffer Parade |
| *12:15* | Galen Drake, talk | | Ilka Chase, talk | |
| *12:30* | News | | Vera Holly Sings | One Man's Family |
| *12:45* | Dusty Records | | | |
| *1pm* | Darts for Dough | | Murder is My Hobby | The National Hour |
| *1:15* | | | | |
| *1:30* | Mary Small's Revue | The Electric Hour, Nelson Eddy | True Detective Mysteries | These Make History |

## DAYTIME — WINTER, 1946

*Monday-Friday*

| ABC | CBS | MBS | NBC | |
|---|---|---|---|---|
| The Breakfast Club | The Johnny Murray Show | Arthur Gaeth, news | Fred Waring Orchestra | *8am* |
| | Valiant Lady | News | | *8:15* |
| | The Light of the World | Take It Easy Time | Dr. Paul | *8:30* |
| | Aunt Jenny's Real Life Stories | Victor Lindlahr, health | David Harum | *8:45* |
| Glamor Manor, Cliff Arquette | Kate Smith Speaks | William Lang, news | Edward Jorgenson, news | *9am* |
| | Big Sister | The Coke Club, Morton Downey | Larry Smith, news | *9:15* |
| Breakfast at Sardi's | The Romance of Helen Trent | Time Out | News | *9:30* |
| | Our Gal Sunday | The Mystery Chef | Ronnie Mansfield, songs | *9:45* |
| Tony Morse, news | Life Can Be Beautiful | Glenn Hardy, news | Mirandy | *10am* |
| Between the Bookends | Ma Perkins | Something to Talk About | What You Say | *10:15* |
| My True Story | Young Dr. Malone | Music | The Hollywood Fan Magazine | *10:30* |
| | The Road of Life | The John J. Anthony Program | Pioneers / Art Baker's Notebook | *10:45* |
| H. R. Baukhage, news | The Second Mrs. Burton | Cedric Foster, news | The Guiding Light | *11am* |
| Ethel and Albert | Perry Mason | Music | Today's Children | *11:15* |
| One Woman's Opinion | Rosemary | Queen for a Day | The Woman in White | *11:30* |
| Almanac | Tena and Tim | | Masquerade | *11:45* |
| Al Pearce and His Gang | Try 'n' Find Me | Broadway News | The Farm Reporter | *12pm* |
| | News | The Johnson Family | Ma Perkins | *12:15* |
| Ladies Be Seated | Talk | Mild and Mellow | Pepper Young's Family | *12:30* |
| | Bachelor's Children | | The Right to Happiness | *12:45* |
| The Jack Berch Show | House Party | Frolics | Mary Noble, Backstage Wife | *1pm* |
| The Radio Parade | | Bill Hays' Bible Reading | Stella Dallas | *1:15* |
| News | The Strange Romance of Evelyn Winters | This Changing World | Lorenzo Jones | *1:30* |

## DAYTIME — WINTER, 1946

*Sunday*

| | ABC | CBS | MBS | NBC |
|---|---|---|---|---|
| *1:45* | | | | Music |
| *2pm* | Musical Bouquet | The Prudential Family Hour | The Shadow | NBC Symphony Orchestra |
| *2:15* | | | | |
| *2:30* | Counterspy | Gene Autry's Melody Ranch | Quick as a Flash | |
| *2:45* | | William L. Shirer, news | | |
| *3pm* | The Radio Hall of Fame | The Adventures of Ozzie and Harriet | The Return of Nick Carter | The Catholic Hour |
| *3:15* | | | | |
| *3:30* | Phil Davis' Sunday Party | Money on the Line | Cedric Foster, news | News |
| *3:45* | | | Fulton Lewis Jr., news | The Melody Parade |
| *4pm* | Drew Pearson, news | The Hope Chest | The Better Half | The Lucky Strike Program, Jack Benny |
| *4:15* | Don Gardiner, news | | | |
| *4:30* | The Hollywood Music Hall | Answer Auction | Rhythm | The Fitch Bandwagon |
| *4:45* | | | | |

# DAYTIME — WINTER, 1946

*Monday-Friday*

| ABC | CBS | MBS | NBC | |
|---|---|---|---|---|
| Hymns of All Churches | Background for Living | Tello-Test Quiz | Young Widder Brown | *1:45* |
| What's Doing Ladies | The American School of the Air | Smile Time | When a Girl Marries | *2pm* |
| | | Lois and January, songs | Portia Faces Life | *2:15* |
| John B. Kennedy, news | Meet the Missus | The Bill Gwinn Show | Just Plain Bill | *2:30* |
| Spotlight | | | Front Page Farrell | *2:45* |
| Bride and Groom | The Housewives' Protective League | Philip Keyne Gordon, news | The Road of Life | *3pm* |
| | | Nancy Young, talk | Joyce Jordan, MD | *3:15* |
| The Frances Scully Show | Talk / Jimmy Carroll Sings | | Aunt Mary | *3:30* |
| General Junius Pierce, comment | The World Today | Elsa Maxwell, news | A Woman of America | *3:45* |
| Taylor Grant, news | Easy Aces | Fulton Lewis Jr., news | One Woman's Secret | *4pm* |
| Raymond Gram Swing, news | Music | Rex Miller, news | News of the World | *4:15* |
| Constance Bennett, comment | Talk and Music / Open House / The American Melody Hour / | Erskine Johnson, gossip | Art Baker's Notebook | *4:30* |
| Hop Harrigan | Mr. Keen, Tracer of Lost Persons | Talk and Music | | *4:45* |

# DAYTIME — WINTER, 1946

*Saturday*

| | ABC | CBS | MBS | NBC |
|---|---|---|---|---|
| *8am* | The March of Dimes | Let's Pretend | Larry Meiser, news | G.I.'s Abroad |
| *8:15* | Mirandy | | Bill's Wax Shop | Jamboree |
| *8:30* | Wake Up and Smile | The Billie Burke Show | The Land of the Lost | Smilin' Ed's Buster Brown Gang |
| *8:45* | | | | |
| *9am* | Galen Drake, talk | The Armstrong Theater of Today | The House of Mystery | News |
| *9:15* | Club Time | | | Music |
| *9:30* | The American Farmer | Stars Over Hollywood | Snow Villiage Sketches | |
| *9:45* | Betty Moore, talk | | | |
| *10am* | Symphonies for Youth | Grand Central Station | Glenn Hardy, news | The National Farm and Home Hour |
| *10:15* | | | Health Talk | |
| *10:30* | Allen Prescott, news | Crime Photographer | The Clinic Forum | The Veterans Advisor |
| *10:45* | Music | | | Traffic Tribunal |
| *11am* | The Metropolitan Opera | Mary Lee Taylor, cooking | Thirty Seconds to Go | Let's Laugh Ladies |
| *11:15* | | | Don McGrane Orchestra | |
| *11:30* | | Give and Take | Opry House Matinee, Edward Arnold | The Baxters |
| *11:45* | | | | The Stars Parade |
| *12pm* | | Assignment Home | Broadway News | The Farm Reporter |
| *12:15* | | | Music | The American World |
| *12:30* | | The Three B's | | Home is What You Make It |
| *12:45* | | | The Round Towner | |
| *1pm* | | The Martin Block Show | You Were There | Doctors Look Ahead |
| *1:15* | | | Felix DeCola Orchestra | |
| *1:30* | | Meet the Missus | Tune Session | Piano Recital |
| *1:45* | | | Horse Racing | |

## DAYTIME — WINTER, 1946

*Saturday*

| | ABC | CBS | MBS | NBC |
|---|---|---|---|---|
| *2pm* | Serenade | Philadelphia Symphony Orchestra | Sports Roundup | Out of the Deep |
| *2:15* | | | | |
| *2:30* | Tea and Crumpets | | Music | John W. Vandercook, news |
| *2:45* | | | | Tin Pan Alley |
| *3pm* | News and Views | | Cleveland Symphony Orchestra | Our Foreign Policy |
| *3:15* | | The People's Platform | | |
| *3:30* | Chester Bowles, comment | | Hawaii Calls | March Tempo |
| *3:45* | Labor USA | The World Today | | |
| *4pm* | Music | The Textron Theater | | The Stars of Tomorrow |
| *4:15* | The American Way | | | |
| *4:30* | Songs | The First Nighter Program | Judy Lang, songs | Name Your Music |
| *4:45* | Johnson and Massey, news | | I Was a Convict | |

## EVENING — SPRING, 1946

*Sunday*

| | ABC | CBS | MBS | NBC |
|---|---|---|---|---|
| *5pm* | The Ford Sunday Evening Hour | Calamity Jane / | A. L. Alexander's Mediation Board | The Charlie McCarthy Show |
| *5:15* | | The Amazing Mrs. Danberry | | |
| *5:30* | | A Man Named Jordan | Don't Be a Sucker | The Fred Allen Show |
| *5:45* | | Ned Calmer, news (5:55 PM) | Gabriel Heatter, news | |
| *6pm* | Walter Winchell's Jergens Journal | Request Performance | Exploring the Unknown | The Manhattan Merry-Go-Round |
| *6:15* | Louella Parsons, gossip | | | |
| *6:30* | Listen to La Guardia | The Texaco Star Theater, James Melton | Double or Nothing | The American Album of Familiar Music |
| *6:45* | Jimmy Fidler, gossip | | | |
| *7pm* | The Theater Guild of the Air | Take It or Leave It | Freedom of Opportunity | The Hour of Charm |
| *7:15* | | | | |
| *7:30* | | The Baby Snooks Show | What's the Name of That Song | Meet Me at Parky's |
| *7:45* | | | | |
| *8pm* | Enchantment | Crime Doctor | Twenty Questions | The Great Gildersleeve |
| *8:15* | | Surprise Theater (8:25 PM) | | |
| *8:30* | The Quiz Kids | Blondie | Walter Winchell's Jergens Journal | The Standard Symphony Hour |
| *8:45* | | | The Rave of the Week | |
| *9pm* | Sam Hayes, news | The Adventures of the Thin Man | Glenn Hardy, news | |
| *9:15* | Report to the People | | Rex Miller, news | |
| *9:30* | Eastside Serenade | Romance of the Ranchos | Ed Thorgersen, sports | The Lucky Strike Program, Jack Benny |
| *9:45* | | | Public Affairs | |
| *10pm* | Hit Tunes | The Ten o'Clock Wire | Spotlight Revue | The Richfield Reporter |
| *10:15* | Orson Welles, comment | America Speaks | | The Chapel Quartet |
| *10:30* | Freddy Martin Orchestra | Time for Reason | Meet the Press | Inside the News |
| *10:45* | | News | | Show Time |

## EVENING — SPRING, 1946

*Monday*

| ABC | CBS | MBS | NBC | |
|---|---|---|---|---|
| Terry and the Pirates | Knox Manning, news | Sam Hayes, news | H. V. Kaltenborn, news | *5pm* |
| Dick Tracy | Through a Woman's Eyes | The Adventures of Superman | News | *5:15* |
| Jack Armstrong, the All-American Boy | Harry W. Flannery, news | Captain Midnight | The Voice of Firestone | *5:30* |
| Tennessee Jed | Truman Bradley, news | Tom Mix and His Ralston Straightshooters | | *5:45* |
| The Lone Ranger | The Lux Radio Theater | Gabriel Heatter, news | Tonight at Hoagy's | *6pm* |
| | | Real Stories from Real Life | | *6:15* |
| Forever Tops | | Spotlight Bands | Information, Please | *6:30* |
| | | | | *6:45* |
| The Bill Thompson Show | The Lady Esther Screen Guild Theater | Bulldog Drummond | The Carnation Contented Hour | *7pm* |
| | | | | *7:15* |
| Question for America | The Bob Hawk Show | The Cisco Kid | Dr. I. Q., the Mental Banker | *7:30* |
| | | | | *7:45* |
| Lum and Abner | The Lanny Ross Show | Michael Shayne, Private Detective | The Chesterfield Supper Club | *8pm* |
| Hedda Hopper, gossip | The Jack Smith Show | | Fleetwood Lawton, news | *8:15* |
| The Fat Man | Joanie's Tea Room | Sherlock Holmes | The Cavalcade of America | *8:30* |
| | Carroll Alcott, news (8:55 PM) | | | *8:45* |
| Famous Jury Trials | The Whistler | Glenn Hardy, news | The Bell Telephone Hour | *9pm* |
| | | Rex Miller, news | | *9:15* |
| Fiesta Grande | Vox Pop | The Inside of Sports | Young Artist's Contest | *9:30* |
| | | Henry J. Taylor, news | | *9:45* |
| Cal Tinney, news | The Ten o'Clock Wire | Fulton Lewis Jr., news | The Richfield Reporter | *10pm* |
| News | The Bill Bryan Trio | News | Music | *10:15* |
| Raymond Gram Swing, news | Flight | Sing, America Sing | Inside the News | *10:30* |
| Rainbow Rendezvous | | So the Story Goes | Show Time | *10:45* |

## EVENING — SPRING, 1946

*Tuesday*

| | ABC | CBS | MBS | NBC |
|---|---|---|---|---|
| *5pm* | Terry and the Pirates | Kurt Manning, news | Sam Hayes, news | News |
| *5:15* | Dick Tracy | Through a Woman's Eyes | The Adventures of Superman | News |
| *5:30* | Jack Armstrong, the All-American Boy | Harry W. Flannery, news | Captain Midnight | A Date with Judy |
| *5:45* | Tennessee Jed | Truman Bradley, news | Tom Mix and His Ralston Straightshooters | |
| *6pm* | Ray Henie, news | Inner Sanctum Mysteries | Gabriel Heatter, news | Amos 'n' Andy |
| *6:15* | The Eugenia Baird Show | | Real Stories from Real Life | |
| *6:30* | The Story of a Star | This is My Best | The American Forum of the Air | Fibber McGee and Molly |
| *6:45* | | | | |
| *7pm* | Concert Time | Casey, Crime Photographer | | The Pepsodent Show, Bob Hope |
| *7:15* | | | Upton Close, news | |
| *7:30* | Hoosier Hop | Melodies America Loves | Red Ryder | The Raleigh Cigarette Program, Red Skelton |
| *7:45* | Public Affairs | | | |
| *8pm* | Lum and Abner | The Lanny Ross Show | The Count of Monte Cristo | The Chesterfield Supper Club |
| *8:15* | Ed Sullivan Entertains | The Jack Smith Show | | Fleetwood Lawton, news |
| *8:30* | Dark Venture | Theater of Romance | The Falcon | The Johnny Desmond Follies |
| *8:45* | | Carroll Alcott, news (8:55PM) | | |
| *9pm* | Bob Wills and the Texas Playboys | Big Town | Glenn Hardy, news | The Bullocks Show |
| *9:15* | | | James Crowley, news | |
| *9:30* | Murder Will Out | Tapestries of Life | The Inside of Sports | The American Way |
| *9:45* | | | Public Affairs | |
| *10pm* | Cal Tinney, news | The Ten o'Clock Wire | Fulton Lewis Jr., news | The Richfield Reporter |
| *10:15* | News | The Bill Bryan Trio | News | Miss Information |
| *10:30* | Raymond Gram Swing, news | Open Hearing | Sing, America Sing | Inside the News |
| *10:45* | The Doctors Talk It Over | Behind the Scenes at CBS | So the Story Goes | Show Time |

## EVENING — SPRING, 1946

*Wednesday*

| ABC | CBS | MBS | NBC | |
|---|---|---|---|---|
| Terry and the Pirates | Kurt Manning, news | Sam Hayes, news | H. V. Kaltenborn, news | *5pm* |
| Dick Tracy | Through a Woman's Eyes | The Adventures of Superman | News | *5:15* |
| Jack Armstrong, the All-American Boy | Harry W. Flannery, news | Captain Midnight | Casa Cugat | *5:30* |
| Tennessee Jed | Truman Bradley, news | Tom Mix and His Ralston Straightshooters | Elmer Patterson, news | *5:45* |
| The Lone Ranger | Songs By Sinatra | Gabriel Heatter, news | Time to Smile, Eddie Cantor | *6pm* |
| | | Real Stories from Real Life | | *6:15* |
| So You Want to Lead a Band | Bob Crosby Orchestra | Spotlight Bands | Mr. District Attorney | *6:30* |
| | | | | *6:45* |
| The Anderson Family | Great Moments in Music | Nick Carter, Master Detective | Kay Kyser's College of Musical Knowledge | *7pm* |
| | | | | *7:15* |
| Boston Blackie | Holiday for Music, Curt Massey | The Cisco Kid | | *7:30* |
| | | | | *7:45* |
| Lum and Abner | The Lanny Ross Show | The Main Line | The Chesterfield Supper Club | *8pm* |
| Don Hollenbeck, news | The Jack Smith Show | | Fleetwood Lawton, news | *8:15* |
| The Fishing and Hunting Club | Dr. Christian | The Fresh Up Show, Bert Lahr | The Penguin Room, Hildegarde | *8:30* |
| | Carroll Alcott, news (8:55 PM) | | | *8:45* |
| Men's Magazine | The Jack Carson Show | Glenn Hardy, news | Mr. and Mrs. North | *9pm* |
| Fool's Money | | Rex Miller, news | | *9:15* |
| The Weird Circle | The Adventures of Ellery Queen | The Inside of Sports | The Skippy Hollywood Theater | *9:30* |
| | | Dance Orchestra | | *9:45* |
| Cal Tinney, news | The Ten o'Clock Wire | Fulton Lewis Jr., news | The Richfield Reporter | *10pm* |
| News | The Bill Bryan Trio | Organ Recital | Music | *10:15* |
| Raymond Gram Swing, news | The Symphonette | Sing, America Sing | Inside the News | *10:30* |
| Freddy Martin Orchestra | | So the Story Goes | Show Time | *10:45* |

## EVENING — SPRING, 1946

*Thursday*

| | ABC | CBS | MBS | NBC |
|---|---|---|---|---|
| *5pm* | Terry and the Pirates | Knox Manning, news | Sam Hayes, news | News |
| *5:15* | Dick Tracy | Through a Woman's Eyes | The Adventures of Superman | News |
| *5:30* | Jack Armstrong, the All-American Boy | Harry W. Flannery, news | Captain Midnight | Casa Cugat |
| *5:45* | Tennessee Jed | Truman Bradley, news | Tom Mix and His Ralston Straightshooters | Elmer Patterson, news |
| *6pm* | The Hobby Hour | Music Millions Love | Gabriel Heatter, news | The Kraft Music Hall, Bing Crosby |
| *6:15* | Retribution | | Real Stories from Real Life | |
| *6:30* | Detect and Collect | Hobby Lobby | The Treasure Hour of Song | The Bob Burns Show |
| *6:45* | | | | |
| *7pm* | Curtain Time | Island Venture | You Make the News | Abbott and Costello |
| *7:15* | | | | |
| *7:30* | Here's Morgan | The KNX Theater | Red Ryder | The Rudy Vallee Show |
| *7:45* | Design for Death | | | |
| *8pm* | Lum and Abner | The Lanny Ross Show | The Theater of Famous Radio Players | The Chesterfield Supper Club |
| *8:15* | Earl Godwin, news | The Jack Smith Show | | Fleetwood Lawton, news |
| *8:30* | America's Town Meeting of the Air | The FBI in Peace and War | Rogue's Gallery | Maxwell House Coffee Time, Burns and Allen |
| *8:45* | | Carroll Alcott, news (8:55PM) | | |
| *9pm* | | Suspense | Glenn Hardy, news | The Birdseye Open House, Dinah Shore |
| *9:15* | | | James Crowley, news | |
| *9:30* | Mystery House | The Citizen's Forum | The Inside of Sports | Noah Webster Says |
| *9:45* | | | The King Cole Trio | |
| *10pm* | Cal Tinney, news | The Ten o'Clock Wire | Fulton Lewis Jr., news | The Richfield Reporter |
| *10:15* | News | The Bill Bryan Trio | News | Mayor Bowron, comment |
| *10:30* | Raymond Gram Swing, news | Talk | Sing, America Sing | Inside the News |
| *10:45* | Freddy Martin Orchestra | Sports | So the Story Goes | Show Time |

## EVENING — SPRING, 1946

*Friday*

| ABC | CBS | MBS | NBC | |
|---|---|---|---|---|
| Terry and the Pirates | Knox Manning, news | Sam Hayes, news | H. V. Kaltenborn, news | *5pm* |
| Dick Tracy | Through a Woman's Eyes | The Adventures of Superman | News | *5:15* |
| Jack Armstrong, the All-American Boy | Harry W. Flannery, news | Captain Midnight | Casa Cugat | *5:30* |
| Tennessee Jed | Truman Bradley, news | Tom Mix and His Ralston Straightshooters | Elmer Patterson, news | *5:45* |
| The Lone Ranger | Holiday and Company | Gabriel Heatter, news | People Are Funny | *6pm* |
| | | Real Stories from Real Life | | *6:15* |
| The Sheriff | The Jimmy Durante Show | Spotlight Bands | Waltz Time | *6:30* |
| | | | | *6:45* |
| Madison Square Garden Boxing | Pabst Blue Ribbon Time, Danny Kaye | Public Affairs | The Molle Mystery Theater | *7pm* |
| | | Notes | | *7:15* |
| | Maisie | The Cisco Kid | The Colgate Sports Newsreel, Bill Stern | *7:30* |
| | | | Cabbages and Kings | *7:45* |
| Woody Herman Orchestra | The Lanny Ross Show | Melody Tours | The Chesterfield Supper Club | *8pm* |
| | The Jack Smith Show | | Fleetwood Lawton, news | *8:15* |
| This is Your FBI | The Ginny Simms Show | The Carrington Playhouse | Duffy's Tavern | *8:30* |
| | Carroll Alcott, news (8:55PM) | | | *8:45* |
| The Alan Young Show | The Aldrich Family | Glenn Hardy, news | The Night Editor | *9pm* |
| | | Rex Miller, news | Latin Serenade | *9:15* |
| Music | Kate Smith Sings | The Inside of Sports | The Haunting Hour | *9:30* |
| | | Henry J. Taylor, news | | *9:45* |
| Cal Tinney, news | The Ten o'Clock Wire | Fulton Lewis Jr., news | The Richfield Reporter | *10pm* |
| News | The Bill Bryan Trio | News | Fiesta | *10:15* |
| Raymond Gram Swing, news | The Symphonette | Sing, America Sing | Inside the News | *10:30* |
| Freddy Martin Orchestra | | So the Story Goes | Show Time | *10:45* |

## EVENING — SPRING, 1946

*Saturday*

| | ABC | CBS | MBS | NBC |
|---|---|---|---|---|
| *5pm* | Songs | The Voice of the Moment | News | The RCA Victor Show |
| *5:15* | Music with an Appeal | Talk | The Canary Pet Shop | |
| *5:30* | News | Harry W. Flannery, news | The Harry Savoy Show | News |
| *5:45* | Harry Wismer, sports | Bob Garred, news | | Elmer Patterson, news |
| *6pm* | Musical Playground | Hollywood Preview | Leave It to the Girls | The National Barn Dance |
| *6:15* | | | | |
| *6:30* | Boston Symphony Orchestra | That's a Good Idea | Hi Pop | Can You Top This |
| *6:45* | | Saturday Night Serenade | | |
| *7pm* | | | The Quiz of Two Cities | The Judy Canova Show |
| *7:15* | | The Continental Celebrity Club, Jackie Kelk | | |
| *7:30* | Hayloft Hoedown | | Red Ryder | Grand Ole Opry |
| *7:45* | | The Story Teller | | |
| *8pm* | Dick Tracy | The Dick Haymes Show | The Better Half | Truth or Consequences |
| *8:15* | | | | |
| *8:30* | Win, Place or Show | The Mayor of the Town | The Avenger | The Life of Riley |
| *8:45* | | Carroll Alcott, news (8:55PM) | | |
| *9pm* | Gangbusters | Your Hit Parade | Glenn Hardy, news | The Adventures of Bill Lance |
| *9:15* | | | News | |
| *9:30* | The Green Hornet | | Music | Stars of Tomorrow |
| *9:45* | | Don't You Believe It | The Frank Parker Show | |
| *10pm* | Dance Orchestra | The Ten o'Clock Wire | Music | |
| *10:15* | | The Hollywood Barn Dance | | |
| *10:30* | Freddy Martin Orchestra | | The Chicago Theater of the Air | News |
| *10:45* | | Talk | | Show Time |

## DAYTIME — SPRING, 1946

*Sunday*

| | ABC | CBS | MBS | NBC |
|---|---|---|---|---|
| *8am* | Songs | Wings Over Jordan | The Pro Art Quartet | The Eternal Light |
| *8:15* | Music | | | |
| *8:30* | The Hour of Faith | The Salt Lake Tabernacle Choir | The Voice of Prophecy | News Roundup |
| *8:45* | | | | News |
| *9am* | It Happened During the Week | Invitation to Learning | The Pilgrim Hour | The University of Chicago Round Table |
| *9:15* | Gillespie's Garden Guide | | | |
| *9:30* | Stradivari Orchestra | Transatlantic Call | The Lutheran Hour | Echoes and Encores |
| *9:45* | | | | |
| *10am* | Cliff Edwards, news | The People's Platform | Glenn Hardy, news | Layman's Views of the News |
| *10:15* | General Junius Pierce, comment | | Commander Scott | The Home Town Parade |
| *10:30* | Sammy Kaye's Sunday Serenade | News | Sweetheart Time | Musical Milestones |
| *10:45* | | Edward R. Murrow, news | | Modern Music |
| *11am* | Washington Inside and Out | The Radio Reader's Digest | The Band Concert | Harvest of Stars |
| *11:15* | News | | | |
| *11:30* | National Vespers | Hollywood Star Time | News | The Westinghouse Program, John C. Thomas |
| *11:45* | | | The World Tomorrow | |
| *12pm* | Don Hollenbeck, news | New York Philharmonic Orchestra | Broadway News | The Sheaffer Parade |
| *12:15* | Galen Drake, talk | | Ilka Chase, talk | |
| *12:30* | News | | Vera Holly Sings | One Man's Family |
| *12:45* | Sports | | | |
| *1pm* | Darts for Dough | | Murder is My Hobby | The National Hour |
| *1:15* | | | | |
| *1:30* | Warriors of Peace | The Electric Hour, Nelson Eddy | True Detective Mysteries | These Make History |

## DAYTIME — SPRING, 1946

*Monday-Friday*

| ABC | CBS | MBS | NBC | |
|---|---|---|---|---|
| The Breakfast Club | The Johnny Murray Show | Arthur Gaeth, news | Fred Waring Orchestra | *8am* |
| | Valiant Lady | News | | *8:15* |
| | The Light of the World | Take It Easy Time | Dr. Paul | *8:30* |
| | Aunt Jenny's Real Life Stories | Victor Lindlahr, health | David Harum | *8:45* |
| Glamor Manor, Cliff Arquette | Kate Smith Speaks | William Lang, news | Edward Jorgenson, news | *9am* |
| | Big Sister | The Coke Club, Morton Downey | Music | *9:15* |
| Breakfast at Sardi's | The Romance of Helen Trent | Time Out | News | *9:30* |
| | Our Gal Sunday | The Mystery Chef | Ladies Day | *9:45* |
| Tony Morse, news | Life Can Be Beautiful | Glenn Hardy, news | Music | *10am* |
| Between the Bookends | Ma Perkins | Talk and Music | What You Say | *10:15* |
| My True Story | Young Dr. Malone | | The Hollywood Fan Magazine | *10:30* |
| | The Road of Life | The John J. Anthony Program | Pioneers / Art Baker's Notebook | *10:45* |
| H. R. Baukhage, news | The Second Mrs. Burton | Cedric Foster, news | The Guiding Light | *11am* |
| Ethel and Albert | Perry Mason | Music | Today's Children | *11:15* |
| One Woman's Opinion | Rosemary | Queen for a Day | The Woman in White | *11:30* |
| News | Tena and Tim | | Masquerade | *11:45* |
| Al Pearce and His Gang | Neighbors, Irene Beasley | Broadway News | The Farm Reporter | *12pm* |
| | News | The Johnson Family | Ma Perkins | *12:15* |
| Ladies Be Seated | Talk | Mild and Mellow | Pepper Young's Family | *12:30* |
| | Bachelor's Children | | The Right to Happiness | *12:45* |
| The Jack Berch Show | House Party | Here's Howe | Mary Noble, Backstage Wife | *1pm* |
| Find Me | | Bill Hays' Bible Reading | Stella Dallas | *1:15* |
| The Frances Scully Show | The Strange Romance of Evelyn Winters | George Olsen Orchestra | Lorenzo Jones | *1:30* |

## DAYTIME — SPRING, 1946

*Sunday*

| | ABC | CBS | MBS | NBC |
|---|---|---|---|---|
| *1:45* | | | | Music |
| *2pm* | The Court of Missing Heirs | The Prudential Family Hour | The Shadow | NBC Symphony Orchestra |
| *2:15* | | | | |
| *2:30* | Counterspy | Gene Autry's Melody Ranch | Quick as a Flash | |
| *2:45* | | William L. Shirer, news | | |
| *3pm* | The Radio Hall of Fame | The Adventures of Ozzie and Harriet | Those Websters | The Catholic Hour |
| *3:15* | | | | |
| *3:30* | Phil Davis' Sunday Party | The Hope Chest | Cedric Foster, news | For the Family |
| *3:45* | | | Quentin Reynolds, news | The Melody Parade |
| *4pm* | Drew Pearson, news | Money on the Line | This Changing World | The Lucky Strike Program, Jack Benny |
| *4:15* | Don Gardiner, news | | Quaker City Serenade | |
| *4:30* | The Hollywood Music Hall | The Western Show | Open House | The Fitch Bandwagon |
| *4:45* | | | | |

## DAYTIME — SPRING, 1946

*Monday-Friday*

| ABC | CBS | MBS | NBC | |
|---|---|---|---|---|
| Hymns of All Churches | Background for Living | Tello-Test Quiz | Young Widder Brown | *1:45* |
| What's Doing Ladies | The American School of the Air | This Changing World | When a Girl Marries | *2pm* |
| | | Smile Time | Portia Faces Life | *2:15* |
| John B. Kennedy, news | Meet the Missus | The Bill Gwinn Show | Just Plain Bill | *2:30* |
| George Fisher, gossip | | | Front Page Farrell | *2:45* |
| Bride and Groom | The Housewives' Protective League | Philip Keyne Gordon, news | The Road of Life | *3pm* |
| | | Nancy Young, talk | Joyce Jordan, MD | *3:15* |
| Music | Talk / Jimmy Carroll Sings | | Aunt Mary | *3:30* |
| Constance Bennett, comment | The World Today | Elsa Maxwell, news | A Woman of America | *3:45* |
| Taylor Grant, news | Easy Aces | Fulton Lewis Jr., news | One Woman's Secret | *4pm* |
| Raymond Gram Swing, news | Music | Rex Miller, news | News of the World | *4:15* |
| News | Talk and Music / The American Melody Hour / | Erskine Johnson, gossip | Art Baker's Notebook | *4:30* |
| Hop Harrigan | Mr. Keen, Tracer of Lost Persons | Lois and January, songs | | *4:45* |

## DAYTIME — SPRING, 1946

*Saturday*

| | ABC | CBS | MBS | NBC |
|---|---|---|---|---|
| *8am* | Treasury Salute | Let's Pretend | Larry Meiser, news | The American Cancer Society |
| *8:15* | Mirandy | | Bill's Wax Shop | |
| *8:30* | Wake Up and Smile | The Billie Burke Show | The Land of the Lost | Smilin' Ed's Buster Brown Gang |
| *8:45* | | | | |
| *9am* | Galen Drake, talk | The Armstrong Theater of Today | The House of Mystery | News and Views |
| *9:15* | Club Time | | | |
| *9:30* | Notes from My Diary | Stars Over Hollywood | Snow Villiage Sketches | |
| *9:45* | | | | Ladies' Day |
| *10am* | The American Farmer | Grand Central Station | Glenn Hardy, news | The National Farm and Home Hour |
| *10:15* | | | Al Williams, news | |
| *10:30* | The Museum of Modern Music | County Fair | The Clinic Forum | The Veterans Advisor |
| *10:45* | | | | Traffic Tribunal |
| *11am* | Chicago Serenade | Mary Lee Taylor, cooking | Thirty Seconds to Go | Let's Laugh Ladies |
| *11:15* | | | Don McGrane Orchestra | |
| *11:30* | Hilltoppers Music | Give and Take | Opry House Matinee, Edward Arnold | The Baxters |
| *11:45* | Melodies to Remember | | | The Parade of Stars |
| *12pm* | Taylor Made Melodies | Assignment Home | Broadway News | The Farm Reporter |
| *12:15* | | | The Round Towner | The American World |
| *12:30* | | The Three B's | Men of Vision | Home is What You Make It |
| *12:45* | | | The Round Towner | |
| *1pm* | A Date with the Duke | The Martin Block Show | Horse Racing | Doctors Look Ahead |
| *1:15* | | | You Were There | |
| *1:30* | Roundup Time | Meet the Missus | Music | The Camera Clinic |
| *1:45* | | | Policing L.A. | |

## DAYTIME — SPRING, 1946

*Saturday*

| | ABC | CBS | MBS | NBC |
|---|---|---|---|---|
| *2pm* | The Saturday Concert | Philadelphia Symphony Orchestra | Zeke Manners Variety | Phone Again, Finnegan |
| *2:15* | | | The Pulse of the City | |
| *2:30* | | | Los Angeles Symphony Orchestra | John W. Vandercook, news |
| *2:45* | | | | Tin Pan Alley |
| *3pm* | The American Cancer Society | Cross-Section USA | Cleveland Symphony Orchestra | On the Scouting Trail |
| *3:15* | The Christian Science Monitor | American Portrait | | |
| *3:30* | Chester Bowles, comment | | | March Tempo |
| *3:45* | Labor USA | The World Today | | |
| *4pm* | The Voice of Business | The Academy Award Theater | Hawaii Calls | Our Foreign Policy |
| *4:15* | The American Way | | | |
| *4:30* | Teen Town | Listen to a Love Song, Tony Martin | Judy Lang, songs | Name Your Music |
| *4:45* | | | I Was a Convict | |

## EVENING — SUMMER, 1946

*Sunday*

| | ABC | CBS | MBS | NBC |
|---|---|---|---|---|
| *5pm* | Walter Winchell's Jergens Journal | Meet Corliss Archer | The Northwestern Reviewing Stand | The Manhattan Merry-Go-Round |
| *5:15* | Louella Parsons, gossip | | | |
| *5:30* | Jimmy Fidler, gossip | The Texaco Star Theater, James Melton | Special Investigator | The American Album of Familiar Music |
| *5:45* | Policewoman | Ned Calmer, news (5:55PM) | News | |
| *6pm* | The Hour of Mystery | Take It or Leave It | Exploring the Unknown | The Hour of Charm |
| *6:15* | | | | |
| *6:30* | | Make Music | Double or Nothing | Rhapsody in Rhythm |
| *6:45* | | | | |
| *7pm* | Warriors of Peace | Crime Doctor | Mystery is My Hobby | Ask Another |
| *7:15* | | | | |
| *7:30* | Stump the Authors | Blondie | What's the Name of That Song | The Standard Symphony Hour |
| *7:45* | | | | |
| *8pm* | Enchantment | That is a Good Idea | Twenty Questions | |
| *8:15* | | Brainstorm | | |
| *8:30* | The Quiz Kids | Defense | Walter Winchell's Jergens Journal | The RCA Victor Show |
| *8:45* | | | Sheila Graham, gossip | |
| *9pm* | Sam Hayes, news | A Man Called Jordan | Glenn Hardy, news | The Shining Hour |
| *9:15* | Report to the People | | Rex Miller, news | |
| *9:30* | Eastside Serenade | Romance of the Ranchos | Private Showing | The Sealtest Village Store, Arden and Haley |
| *9:45* | | | | |
| *10pm* | Hit Tunes | The Ten o'Clock Wire | Spotlight Revue | The Richfield Reporter |
| *10:15* | Orson Welles, comment | The University Explorer | | The Chapel Quartet |
| *10:30* | Freddy Martin Orchestra | America Speaks | Music | Inside the News |
| *10:45* | | Time for Reason | So the Story Goes | Show Time |

## EVENING — SUMMER, 1946

*Monday*

| ABC | CBS | MBS | NBC | |
|---|---|---|---|---|
| Terry and the Pirates | Kiss and Make Up, Milton Berle | Sam Hayes, news | H. V. Kaltenborn, news | *5pm* |
| Tennessee Jed | | The Adventures of Superman | News | *5:15* |
| Dick Tracy | The Jack Kirkwood Show | Captain Midnight | The Music Festival | *5:30* |
| News | | Tom Mix and His Ralston Straightshooters | | *5:45* |
| Question for America | The Lady Esther Screen Guild Theater | Gabriel Heatter, news | The Carnation Contented Hour | *6pm* |
| | | Real Stories from Real Life | | *6:15* |
| Forever Tops | The Bob Hawk Show | Spotlight Bands | Dr. I. Q., the Mental Banker | *6:30* |
| | | | | *6:45* |
| The Lone Ranger | Patti Clayton, songs | Bulldog Drummond | The Chesterfield Supper Club | *7pm* |
| | Skyline Roof, Gordon MacRae | | Fleetwood Lawton, news | *7:15* |
| Music | Free for All | The Cisco Kid | The University of Chicago Round Table | *7:30* |
| | | | | *7:45* |
| Lum and Abner | Jack of All Trades | Michael Shayne, Private Detective | The Bell Telephone Hour | *8pm* |
| Ed Sullivan's Pipelines | | | | *8:15* |
| The Fat Man | Forever Ernest | The Casebook of Gregory Hood | The Voice of Firestone | *8:30* |
| | Carroll Alcott, news (8:55PM) | | | *8:45* |
| I Deal in Crime | The Whistler | Glenn Hardy, news | Tonight at Hoagy's | *9pm* |
| | | Rex Miller, news | | *9:15* |
| Boston Blackie | Music | The Inside of Sports | The Hollywood Bowl | *9:30* |
| | The Bill Bryan Trio | Henry J. Taylor, news | | *9:45* |
| Sports | The Ten o'Clock Wire | Fulton Lewis Jr., news | The Richfield Reporter | *10pm* |
| News | Bob Elson Interviews | News | Music | *10:15* |
| Elmer Davis, news | The Symphonette | Sing, America Sing | Inside the News | *10:30* |
| Rainbow Rendezvous | | So the Story Goes | Show Time | *10:45* |

## EVENING — SUMMER, 1946

*Tuesday*

| | ABC | CBS | MBS | NBC |
|---|---|---|---|---|
| *5pm* | Terry and the Pirates | Arthur Godfrey Talent Scouts | Sam Hayes, news | News |
| *5:15* | Tennessee Jed | | The Adventures of Superman | News |
| *5:30* | Dick Tracy | Encore Theater | Captain Midnight | A Date with Judy |
| *5:45* | News | | Tom Mix and His Ralston Straightshooters | |
| *6pm* | The Music Festival | Nite Life | Gabriel Heatter, news | A Man Called X |
| *6:15* | | | Real Stories from Real Life | |
| *6:30* | Between the Bookends | This is My Best | The American Forum of the Air | An Evening with Romberg |
| *6:45* | Report | | | |
| *7pm* | From There | Patti Clayton, songs | | The Chesterfield Supper Club |
| *7:15* | | Skyline Roof, Gordon MacRae | Upton Close, news | Fleetwood Lawton, news |
| *7:30* | So You Want to Lead a Band | Theater of Romance | Red Ryder | The Johnny Desmond Follies |
| *7:45* | | | | |
| *8pm* | Lum and Abner | Big Town | The Count of Monte Cristo | Dunninger, the Mentalist |
| *8:15* | The Kenny Baker Show | | | |
| *8:30* | Dark Venture | What I Say | The Falcon | Fred Waring Orchestra |
| *8:45* | | Ona Munson, comment | | |
| *9pm* | Retribution | Get the Story | Glenn Hardy, news | The Bullocks Show |
| *9:15* | | | James Crowley, news | |
| *9:30* | Philo Vance | Tapestries of Life | The Inside of Sports | Forum |
| *9:45* | | The Bill Bryan Trio | Music | |
| *10pm* | Sports | The Ten o'Clock Wire | Fulton Lewis Jr., news | The Richfield Reporter |
| *10:15* | News | Bob Elson Interviews | News | Miss Information |
| *10:30* | Elmer Davis, news | Music | Sing, America Sing | Inside the News |
| *10:45* | The Doctors Talk It Over | | So the Story Goes | Show Time |

## EVENING — SUMMER, 1946

*Wednesday*

| ABC | CBS | MBS | NBC | |
|---|---|---|---|---|
| Terry and the Pirates | Sad Sack | Sam Hayes, news | H. V. Kaltenborn, news | *5pm* |
| Tennessee Jed | | The Adventures of Superman | News | *5:15* |
| Dick Tracy | Bob Crosby Orchestra | Captain Midnight | Casa Cugat | *5:30* |
| News | | Tom Mix and His Ralston Straightshooters | Elmer Patterson, news | *5:45* |
| Sports Review | The Academy Award Theater | Gabriel Heatter, news | Kay Kyser's, College of Musical Knowledge | *6pm* |
| | | Real Stories from Real Life | | *6:15* |
| Listen to La Guardia | Holiday for Music, Curt Massey | Spotlight Bands | | *6:30* |
| | | | | *6:45* |
| The Lone Ranger | Patti Clayton, songs | The Return of Nick Carter | The Chesterfield Supper Club | *7pm* |
| | Skyline Roof, Gordon MacRae | | Fleetwood Lawton, news | *7:15* |
| The Anderson Family | Dr. Christian | The Cisco Kid | The Penguin Room, Hildegarde | *7:30* |
| | | | | *7:45* |
| Lum and Abner | Fiesta | The Main Line | Mr. and Mrs. North | *8pm* |
| Don Hollenbeck, news | | | | *8:15* |
| The Fishing and Hunting Club | The Adventures of Ellery Queen | The Beatrice Kay Show | McGarry and the Mouse | *8:30* |
| | | | | *8:45* |
| The Hobby Hour | Miss Sherlock | Glenn Hardy, news | Mr. District Attorney | *9pm* |
| Fool's Money | | Rex Miller, news | | *9:15* |
| The Weird Circle | Music | The Inside of Sports | The Skippy Hollywood Theater | *9:30* |
| | The Bill Bryan Trio | News | | *9:45* |
| Sports | The Ten o'Clock Wire | Fulton Lewis Jr., news | The Richfield Reporter | *10pm* |
| News | Bob Elson Interviews | News | Music | *10:15* |
| Raymond Gram Swing, news | The Symphonette | Sing, America Sing | Inside the News | *10:30* |
| Freddy Martin Orchestra | | So the Story Goes | Show Time | *10:45* |

## EVENING — SUMMER, 1946

*Thursday*

| | ABC | CBS | MBS | NBC |
|---|---|---|---|---|
| *5pm* | Terry and the Pirates | The 10-2-4 Musical Ranch | Sam Hayes, news | News |
| *5:15* | Tennessee Jed | | The Adventures of Superman | News |
| *5:30* | Dick Tracy | Hobby Lobby | Captain Midnight | Casa Cugat |
| *5:45* | News | | Tom Mix and His Ralston Straightshooters | Elmer Patterson, news |
| *6pm* | Public Affairs | That's Life | Gabriel Heatter, news | The Camel Caravan, Vaughn Monroe |
| *6:15* | The P. T. A. | | Real Stories from Real Life | |
| *6:30* | Detect and Collect | Phone Again Finnegan | By Popular Demand | The Fifth Horsemen |
| *6:45* | | | | |
| *7pm* | Harry Kogen Orchestra | Patty Clayton, songs | California Melodies | The Chesterfield Supper Club |
| *7:15* | | Skyline Roof, Gordon MacRae | | Fleetwood Lawton, news |
| *7:30* | Beach Party | Sound Off | Red Ryder | Music |
| *7:45* | Design for Death | | | |
| *8pm* | Lum and Abner | Suspense | Tommy Dorsey Orchestra | Meredith Wilson Orchestra |
| *8:15* | Earl Godiwin, news | | | |
| *8:30* | America's Town Meeting of the Air | It Couldn't Happen | Vic and Sade | Noah Webster Says |
| *8:45* | | The Ghost Walks | | |
| *9pm* | | The Dick Haymes Show | Glenn Hardy, news | The Kraft Music Hall, Edward Norton |
| *9:15* | | | James Crowley, news | |
| *9:30* | Mystery House | The Citizen's Forum | The Inside of Sports | The National Concert |
| *9:45* | | The Bill Bryan Trio | Music | |
| *10pm* | Sports | The Ten o'Clock Wire | Fulton Lewis Jr., news | The Richfield Reporter |
| *10:15* | News | Bob Elson Interviews | News | Mayor Bowron, comment |
| *10:30* | Raymond Gram Swing, news | Sports | Sing, America Sing | Inside the News |
| *10:45* | Freddy Martin Orchestra | Organ Recital | So the Story Goes | Show Time |

## EVENING — SUMMER, 1946

*Friday*

| ABC | CBS | MBS | NBC | |
|---|---|---|---|---|
| Terry and the Pirates | It Pays to Be Ignorant | Sam Hayes, news | H. V. Kaltenborn, news | *5pm* |
| Tennessee Jed | | The Adventures of Superman | News | *5:15* |
| Dick Tracy | Wayne King Orchestra | Captain Midnight | Casa Cugat | *5:30* |
| News | | Tom Mix and His Ralston Straightshooters | Elmer Patterson, news | *5:45* |
| The Court of Missing Heirs | The Mercury Summer Theater | Gabriel Heatter, news | The Molle' Mystery Theater | *6pm* |
| | | Real Stories from Real Life | | *6:15* |
| The Sheriff | Hawk Durango | Spotlight Bands | The Colgate Sports Newsreel, Bill Stern | *6:30* |
| | | | Cabbages and Kings | *6:45* |
| Madison Square Garden Boxing | Patty Clayton, songs | Spotlite | The Chesterfield Supper Club | *7pm* |
| | Skyline Roof, Gordon MacRae | | Fleetwood Lawton, news | *7:15* |
| | Tommy Riggs and Betty Lou | The Cisco Kid | The King's Men | *7:30* |
| | | | Mystery | *7:45* |
| The Adventures of Sam Spade | The Aldrich Family | Meet the Press | The Night Editor | *8pm* |
| | | | Latin Serenade | *8:15* |
| This is Your FBI | Sweeney and March | The Carrington Playhouse | People Are Funny | *8:30* |
| | | | | *8:45* |
| Break the Bank | The Westerners | Glenn Hardy, news | Waltz Time | *9pm* |
| | | Rex Miller, news | | *9:15* |
| News Roundup | Music | The Inside of Sports | Murder at Midnight | *9:30* |
| | The Bill Bryan Trio | Henry J. Taylor, news | | *9:45* |
| Sports | The Ten o'Clock Wire | Fulton Lewis Jr., news | The Richfield Reporter | *10pm* |
| News | Bob Elson Interviews | News | Fiesta | *10:15* |
| Raymond Gram Swing, news | The Symphonette | Sing, America Sing | Inside the News | *10:30* |
| Freddy Martin Orchestra | | So the Story Goes | Show Time | *10:45* |

## EVENING — SUMMER, 1946

*Saturday*

| | ABC | CBS | MBS | NBC |
|---|---|---|---|---|
| *5pm* | Music | The Voice of the Moment | News | Sports |
| *5:15* | News | City Beat | Sports | News |
| *5:30* | Boston Symphony Orchestra | Reports | The Harry Savoy Show | News |
| *5:45* | | Serenade | | Elmer Patterson, news |
| *6pm* | | | The Chicago Theater of the Air | Music |
| *6:15* | | | | |
| *6:30* | Live in Peace | Oklahoma Roundup | | Grand Ole Opry |
| *6:45* | | | | |
| *7pm* | We, the Guilty | Hollywood Star Time | The Quiz of Two Cities | No Happy Ending |
| *7:15* | | | | |
| *7:30* | Win, Place and Show | The Danny O'Neill Show | Red Ryder | Our Foreign Service |
| *7:45* | | | | |
| *8pm* | Famous Jury Trails | Your Hit Parade | Leave It to the Girls | The Adventures of Bill Lance |
| *8:15* | | | | |
| *8:30* | The Lone Ranger | | The Play Shop | The National Barn Dance |
| *8:45* | | Listen to a Love Song, Tony Martin | | |
| *9pm* | Gangbusters | | | Can You Top This |
| *9:15* | | Don't You Believe It | Caravan | |
| *9:30* | The Green Hornet | The Story Teller | | Conquest |
| *9:45* | | Music | The Frank Parker Show | |
| *10pm* | Dance Orchestra | The Ten o'Clock Wire | Music | News |
| *10:15* | | The Hollywood Barn Dance | | The Late Date |
| *10:30* | Freddy Martin Orchestra | | | Sports |
| *10:45* | | Cross Section | | Show Time |

## DAYTIME — SUMMER, 1946

*Sunday*

| | ABC | CBS | MBS | NBC |
|---|---|---|---|---|
| *8am* | Around the World | Invitation to Learning | The Pilgrim Hour | The Eternal Light |
| *8:15* | | | | |
| *8:30* | The Hour of Faith | Yours, Sincerely | The Lutheran Hour | Echoes and Encores |
| *8:45* | | | | |
| *9am* | It Happened During the Week | The People's Platform | The Voice of Prophecy | News and Views |
| *9:15* | Gillespie's Garden Guide | | | |
| *9:30* | Sunday Strings | News | Sweetheart Time | |
| *9:45* | | Howard K. Smith, news | The Voice of Bert Howell | |
| *10am* | Washington Inside and Out | Assignment Home | Glenn Hardy, news | Musical Milestones |
| *10:15* | News | | Commander Scott | Modern Music |
| *10:30* | Sammy Kaye's Sunday Serenade | News | Vera Holly Sings | Harvest of Stars |
| *10:45* | | Edward R. Murrow, news | | |
| *11am* | News | Columbia Symphony Orchestra | The Band Concert | The Sheaffer Parade |
| *11:15* | National Vespers | | | |
| *11:30* | | | News | One Man's Family |
| *11:45* | The Church of Wildwood | | The World Tomorrow | |
| *12pm* | Don Hollenbeck, news | The Columbia Workshop | Broadway News | The National Hour |
| *12:15* | The Vagabonds Quartet | | Ilka Chase, talk | |
| *12:30* | Down Your Alley | The Electric Summer Hour | True Detective Mysteries | These Make History |
| *12:45* | | | | News |
| *1pm* | Darts for Dough | The Prudential Family Hour | Under Arrest | NBC Symphony Orchestra |
| *1:15* | | | | |
| *1:30* | Counterspy | John Henry Faulk, comment | The Abbott Mysteries | |

## DAYTIME — SUMMER, 1946

*Monday-Friday*

| ABC | CBS | MBS | NBC | |
|---|---|---|---|---|
| The Breakfast Club | Kate Smith Speaks | Arthur Gaeth, news | Fred Waring Orchestra | *8am* |
| | Aunt Jenny's True Life Stories | News | | *8:15* |
| | The Romance of Helen Trent | Take It Easy Time | Lone Journey | *8:30* |
| | Our Gal Sunday | Victor Lindlahr, health | David Harum | *8:45* |
| Glamor Manor, Kenny Baker | Big Sister | Talk | Edward Jorgenson, news | *9am* |
| | Ma Perkins | The Coke Club, Morton Downey | For You | *9:15* |
| Breakfast at Sardi's | Young Dr. Malone | Talk and Music | News | *9:30* |
| | The Road of Life | | Talk | *9:45* |
| Tony Morse, news | The Second Mrs. Burton | Glenn Hardy, news | The Guiding Light | *10am* |
| Between the Bookends | Perry Mason | Talk | Today's Children | *10:15* |
| My True Story | News | Queen for a Day | The Women in White | *10:30* |
| | Tena and Tim | | Masquerade | *10:45* |
| H. R. Baukhage, news | Variety | Smile Time | Life Can Be Beautiful | *11am* |
| Ethel and Albert | | Zeke Manners Variety | Ma Perkins | *11:15* |
| Club Time / Listening Post | Talk | Be Beautiful | Pepper Young's Family | *11:30* |
| Talk | Bachelor's Children | | The Right to Happiness | *11:45* |
| News | House Party | Broadway News | The Farm Reporter | *12pm* |
| Talk / Clliff Edwards, songs | | The Johnson Family | Stella Dallas | *12:15* |
| Ladies Be Seated | The Strange Romance of Evelyn Winters | Variety Musicale | Lorenzo Jones | *12:30* |
| | Rosemary | | Young Widder Brown | *12:45* |
| The Jack Berch Show | Knox Manning, news | Jack Hill, news | When a Girl Marries | *1pm* |
| Find Me | The Johnny Murray Show | Bill Hays' Bible Reading | Stella Dallas | *1:15* |
| Hollywood and Vine | Meet the Missus | Mild and Mellow | Just Plain Bill | *1:30* |

## DAYTIME — SUMMER, 1946

*Sunday*

| | ABC | CBS | MBS | NBC |
|---|---|---|---|---|
| *1:45* | | William L. Shirer, news | | |
| *2pm* | Phil Davis' Sunday Party | The Silver Theater | Those Websters | The Catholic Hour |
| *2:15* | | | | |
| *2:30* | The Eugenia Baird Show | Music | Music | Sincerely Yours |
| *2:45* | | | | |
| *3pm* | Drew Pearson, news | Gene Autry's Melody Ranch | Let's Go to the Opera | The Fabulous Dr. Tweedy |
| *3:15* | Don Gardiner, news | | | |
| *3:30* | The Radio Hall of Fame | The Western Show | The Star Show | Rogue's Gallery |
| *3:45* | | | | |
| *4pm* | The Ford Festival of American Music | Richard Lawless | A. L. Alexander's Mediaton Board | AlexTempleton Time |
| *4:15* | | | | |
| *4:30* | | Money on the Line | Open House | Tommy Dorsey Orchestra |
| *4:45* | | | | |

| DAYTIME — SUMMER, 1946 | | | | |
|---|---|---|---|---|
| *Monday-Friday* | | | | |
| ABC | CBS | MBS | NBC | |
| Hymns of All Churches | | | Front Page Farrell | *1:45* |
| What's Doing Ladies | Valiant Lady | Once Over Lighlty | The Road of Life | *2pm* |
| | The Light of the World | The John J. Anthony Program | Joyce Jordan, MD | *2:15* |
| John B. Kennedy, news | Background for Living | The Bill Gwinn Show | Aunt Mary | *2:30* |
| George Fisher, gossip | News | | Dr. Paul | *2:45* |
| Bride and Groom | The Housewives' Protective League | Philip Keyne Gordon, news | One Woman's Secret | *3pm* |
| | | Nancy Young, talk | News of the World / | *3:15* |
| Club Time | Talk and Music / The American Melody Hour / | | The Song Star | *3:30* |
| The Frances Scully Show | Mr. Keen, Tracer of Lost Persons | The Sea Hound | What You Say | *3:45* |
| Taylor Grant, news | News | Fulton Lewis Jr., news | Ladies Day | *4pm* |
| Raymond Gram Swing, news | Barbara Tate, talk | Rex Miller, news | The Hollywood Fan Magazine | *4:15* |
| Music | Henry W. Flannery, news | Erskine Johnson, gossip | Art Baker's Notebook | *4:30* |
| Alvin Wilder, news | Henry Gerrard, news | Music | | *4:45* |

## DAYTIME — SUMMER, 1946

*Saturday*

| | ABC | CBS | MBS | NBC |
|---|---|---|---|---|
| *8am* | Treasury Salute | The Armstrong Theater of Today | News and Views | Platter Party (7:45AM) |
| *8:15* | Wake Up and Smile | | | Play Ball |
| *8:30* | | Stars Over Hollywood | Music | Smilin' Ed's Buster Brown Gang |
| *8:45* | | | | |
| *9am* | The Buddy Weed Trio | Grand Central Station | | The National Farm and Home Hour |
| *9:15* | The Brown Dots Quartet | | | |
| *9:30* | Mirandy | County Fair | | The Veterans Advisor |
| *9:45* | Ladies' Day | | | Traffic Tribunal |
| *10am* | The American Farmer | Mary Lee Taylor, cooking | Glenn Hardy, news | The Kitchen |
| *10:15* | | | Music | News |
| *10:30* | The Playground | Give and Take | The Clinic Forum | The Baxters |
| *10:45* | | | | Nature Sketches |
| *11am* | The Piano Playhouse | Let's Pretend | | Date a Star |
| *11:15* | | | Zeke Manners Variety | Meet the Author |
| *11:30* | Roundup Time | The Billie Burke Show | Jamboree | Let's Laugh Ladies |
| *11:45* | | | | |
| *12pm* | Saturday Date with the Duke | Horse Racing | Broadway News | The Farm Reporter |
| *12:15* | | | The Round Towner | |
| *12:30* | | Chicagoans Orchestra | Melodies | The Schools are Yours |
| *12:45* | | | Freedom of Opportunity | You Were There |
| *1pm* | The Saturday Concert | Of Men and Books | Thirty Seconds to Go | Music |
| *1:15* | | Adventures in Science | | |
| *1:30* | | Meet the Missus | Coke Session | The Camera Clinic |
| *1:45* | | | Policing L.A. | |

| DAYTIME — SUMMER, 1946 | | | | |
|---|---|---|---|---|
| *Saturday* | | | | |
| | ABC | CBS | MBS | NBC |
| *2pm* | | The Song Shop | Mind Your Manners | Home is Where You Make It |
| *2:15* | | American Portrait | The Pulse of the City | |
| *2:30* | Paul Porter, talk | | Author Meets the Critics | Sports |
| *2:45* | Labor USA | The World Today | | Edward Tomlinson, news |
| *3pm* | The Voice of Business | St. Louis Municipal Opera | | Our Foreign Policy |
| *3:15* | News | | | |
| *3:30* | Junior Junction | Treasury Bandstand | Showcase | Curtain Time |
| *3:45* | | | I Was a Convict | |
| *4pm* | The American Way | The D. Gayle Show | Serenade | Ladies Day |
| *4:15* | Sports | | | |
| *4:30* | Serenade | Harry W. Flannery, news | Juvenile Jury | Name Your Music |
| *4:45* | | Henry Gerard, news | | |

## EVENING — FALL, 1946

*Sunday*

| | ABC | CBS | MBS | NBC |
|---|---|---|---|---|
| *5pm* | Paul Whiteman Orchestra | Public Affairs | A. L. Alexander's Mediation Board | The Charlie McCarthy Show |
| *5:15* | | | | |
| *5:30* | The Clock | | Special Investigator | The Fred Allen Show |
| *5:45* | | News | News | |
| *6pm* | Walter Winchell's Jergens Journal | The Campbell Room, Hildegarde | Exploring the Unknown | The Manhattan Merry-Go-Round |
| *6:15* | Louella Parsons, gossip | | | |
| *6:30* | Jimmy Fidler, gossip | The Eddie Bracken Show | Double or Nothing | The American Album of Familiar Music |
| *6:45* | Police Woman | | | |
| *7pm* | The Theater Guild of the Air | Take It or Leave It | A Brighter Tomorrow | The Bickersons |
| *7:15* | | | | |
| *7:30* | | Kate Smith Sings | What's the Name of That Song | Meet Me at Parky's |
| *7:45* | | | | |
| *8pm* | Enchantment | Crime Doctor | Twenty Questions | The Bob Burns Show |
| *8:15* | | News (8:25PM) | | |
| *8:30* | Tales of Willie Piper | Blondie | Walter Winchell's Jergens Journal | The Standard Symphony Hour |
| *8:45* | | | Sheila Graham, gossip | |
| *9pm* | Sam Hayes, news | The Adventures of Sam Spade | Glenn Hardy, news | |
| *9:15* | Report to the People | | Rex Miller, news | |
| *9:30* | Eastside Serenade | Romance of the Ranchos | Public Affairs | The Lucky Strike Program, Jack Benny |
| *9:45* | | | Music | |
| *10pm* | Music | The Ten o'Clock Wire | | The Richfield Reporter |
| *10:15* | | The University Explorer | News | Music |
| *10:30* | Freddy Martin Orchestra | America Speaks | Music | Inside the News |
| *10:45* | | Money Talk | So the Story Goes | Show Time |

## EVENING — FALL, 1946

*Monday*

| ABC | CBS | MBS | NBC | |
|---|---|---|---|---|
| Terry and the Pirates | Front Page Feature | News | Life with Crosby | *5pm* |
| Dick Tracy | Revue | The Adventures of Superman | News | *5:15* |
| Jack Armstrong, the All-American Boy | Harry W. Flannery, news | Captain Midnight | The Voice of Firestone | *5:30* |
| News | Henry Garred, news | Tom Mix and His Ralston Straightshooters | | *5:45* |
| Stump the Authors | The Lux Radio Theater | Gabriel Heatter, news | Touchdown Tips | *6pm* |
| | | The Barry Wood Show | | *6:15* |
| Johnny Olsen's Rumpus Room | | Spotlight Bands | The Victor Borge Show | *6:30* |
| | | | | *6:45* |
| The Lone Ranger | The Lady Esther Screen Guild Theater | Bulldog Drummond | The Carnation Contented Hour | *7pm* |
| | | | | *7:15* |
| The Sons of the Pioneers | The Bob Hawk Show | The Cisco Kid | Dr. I. Q., the Mental Banker | *7:30* |
| Music | | | | *7:45* |
| Lum and Abner | Lowell Thomas, news | Richard Davis | The Chesterfield Supper Club | *8pm* |
| Earl Godwin, news | The Jack Smith Show | | Fleetwood Lawton, news | *8:15* |
| The Fat Man | Joanie's Tea Room | The Casebook of Gregory Hood | The Cavalcade of America | *8:30* |
| | Carroll Alcott, news (8:55PM) | | | *8:45* |
| The Doctors Talk It Over | The Whistler | Glenn Hardy, news | The Bell Telephone Hour | *9pm* |
| The Joe Mooney Quartet | | Rex Miller, news | | *9:15* |
| Boston Blackie | Inner Sanctum Mysteries | The Inside of Sports | The Hollywood Bowl Auditions | *9:30* |
| | | Henry J. Taylor, news | | *9:45* |
| Sports | The Ten o'Clock Wire | Fulton Lewis Jr., news | The Richfield Reporter | *10pm* |
| News | Bob Elson Interviews | News | Music | *10:15* |
| Elmer Davis, news | The Symphonette | Sing, America Sing | Inside the News | *10:30* |
| Rainbow Rendezvous | | So the Story Goes | Show Time | *10:45* |

| EVENING — FALL, 1946 | | | | |
|---|---|---|---|---|
| *Tuesday* | | | | |
| | ABC | CBS | MBS | NBC |
| *5pm* | Terry and the Pirates | Front Page Feature | News | Feature Wire |
| *5:15* | Dick Tracy | Revue | The Adventures of Superman | News |
| *5:30* | Jack Armstrong, the All-American Boy | Harry W. Flannery, news | Captain Midnight | A Date with Judy |
| *5:45* | News | Henry Garred, news | Tom Mix and His Ralston Straightshooters | |
| *6pm* | Earl Godwin, news | Vox Pop | Gabriel Heatter, news | Amos 'n' Andy |
| *6:15* | Public Affairs | | News | |
| *6:30* | Boston Symphony Orchestra | Hollywood Players | The American Forum of the Air | Fibber McGee and Molly |
| *6:45* | | | | |
| *7pm* | | The Woman's Forum | | The Pepsodent Show, Bob Hope |
| *7:15* | | | Upton Close, news | |
| *7:30* | Music Preferred | Melodies America Loves | Red Ryder | The Raleigh Cigarette Program, Red Skelton |
| *7:45* | News | | | |
| *8pm* | Lum and Abner | Lowell Thomas, news | The Count of Monte Cristo | The Chesterfield Supper Club |
| *8:15* | News | The Jack Smith Show | | Fleetwood Lawton, news |
| *8:30* | Dark Venture | The Mel Blanc Show | The Falcon | The Rudy Vallee Show |
| *8:45* | | Carroll Alcott, news (8:55PM) | | |
| *9pm* | Retribution | Big Town | Glenn Hardy, news | Favorite Story |
| *9:15* | | | James Crowley, news | |
| *9:30* | The Anderson Family | Tapestries of Life | The Inside of Sports | Murder at Midnight |
| *9:45* | | Facts and Fantasies | Public Affairs | |
| *10pm* | Sports | The Ten o'Clock Wire | Fulton Lewis Jr., news | The Richfield Reporter |
| *10:15* | News | Bob Elson Interviews | News | Madison 2345, Times Information |
| *10:30* | Elmer Davis, news | Open Hearing | Sing, America Sing | Inside the News |
| *10:45* | Freddy Martin Orchestra | | So the Story Goes | Show Time |

## EVENING — FALL, 1946

*Wednesday*

| ABC | CBS | MBS | NBC | |
|---|---|---|---|---|
| Terry and the Pirates | Front Page Feature | News | Life with Crosby | *5pm* |
| Dick Tracy | Revue | The Adventures of Superman | News | *5:15* |
| Jack Armstrong, the All-American Boy | Harry W. Flannery, news | Captain Midnight | Casa Cugat | *5:30* |
| News | Henry Garred, news | Tom Mix and His Ralston Straightshooters | Elmer Patterson, news | *5:45* |
| So You Want to Lead a Band | Songs By Sinatra | Gabriel Heatter, news | Duffy's Tavern | *6pm* |
| | | The Barry Wood Show | | *6:15* |
| Pot o' Gold | The Ford Show, Dinah Shore | Spotlight Bands | The Skippy Hollywood Theater | *6:30* |
| | | | | *6:45* |
| The Lone Ranger | The Academy Award Theater | Michael Shayne, Private Detective | The Fabulous Dr. Tweedy | *7pm* |
| | | | | *7:15* |
| The Sons of the Pioneers | Information, Please | The Cisco Kid | Kay Kyser's College of Musical Knowledge | *7:30* |
| Music / Public Affairs | | | | *7:45* |
| Lum and Abner | Lowell Thomas, news | The Main Line | The Chesterfield Supper Club | *8pm* |
| Listen to LaGuardia | The Jack Smith Show | | Fleetwood Lawton, news | *8:15* |
| The Fishing and Hunting Club | Dr. Christian | It's Up to Youth | The Great Gildersleeve | *8:30* |
| | Carroll Alcott, news (8:55PM) | | | *8:45* |
| Philco Radio Time, Bing Crosby | The Jack Carson Show | Glenn Hardy, news | Mr. and Mrs. North | *9pm* |
| | | Rex Miller, news | | *9:15* |
| The Henry Morgan Show | The Adventures of Ellery Queen | The Inside of Sports | Mr. District Attorney | *9:30* |
| | | Public Affairs | | *9:45* |
| Sports | The Ten o'Clock Wire | Fulton Lewis Jr., news | The Richfield Reporter | *10pm* |
| News | Bob Elson Interviews | News | Music | *10:15* |
| Raymond Gram Swing, news | The Symphonette | Sing, America Sing | Inside the News | *10:30* |
| Freddy Martin Orchestra | | So the Story Goes | Show Time | *10:45* |

## EVENING — FALL, 1946

*Thursday*

| | ABC | CBS | MBS | NBC |
|---|---|---|---|---|
| *5pm* | Terry and the Pirates | Front Page Feature | News | News |
| *5:15* | Dick Tracy | Revue | The Adventures of Superman | News |
| *5:30* | Jack Armstrong, the All-American Boy | Harry W. Flannery, news | Captain Midnight | Casa Cugat |
| *5:45* | News | Henry Garred, news | Tom Mix and His Ralston Straightshooters | Elmer Patterson, news |
| *6pm* | Public Affairs | The Dick Haymes Show | Gabriel Heatter, news | The Kraft Music Hall, Edward Horton |
| *6:15* | | | News | |
| *6:30* | Real Story | Casey, Crime Photographer | By Popular Demand | A Day in the Life of Dennis Day |
| *6:45* | America's Town Meeting of the Air | | | |
| *7pm* | | The Radio Reader's Digest | Grid Roundup | Abbott and Costello |
| *7:15* | | | Paul Schilssler, news | |
| *7:30* | | Phone Again Finnegan | Red Ryder | Pabst Blue Ribbon Time, Eddie Cantor |
| *7:45* | Monitor Views | | | |
| *8pm* | Lum and Abner | Lowell Thomas, news | Sound Off | The Chesterfield Supper Club |
| *8:15* | Serenade | The Jack Smith Show | | Fleetwood Lawton, news |
| *8:30* | Take It From There | The FBI in Peace and War | California Melodies | The Aldrich Family |
| *8:45* | | Carroll Alcott, news (8:55PM) | | |
| *9pm* | Fantasy Melody | Suspense | Glenn Hardy, news | Maxwell House Coffee Time, Burns and Allen |
| *9:15* | | | James Crowley, news | |
| *9:30* | Strange Wills | Ford Sterling, news | The Inside of Sports | Noah Webster Says |
| *9:45* | | Fact or Fantasy | Public Affairs | |
| *10pm* | Sports | The Ten o'Clock Wire | Fulton Lewis Jr., news | The Richfield Reporter |
| *10:15* | News | Bob Elson Interviews | News | Mayor Bowron, comment |
| *10:30* | Raymond Gram Swing, news | Music | Sing, America Sing | Inside the News |
| *10:45* | Freddy Martin Orchestra | Organ Recital | So the Story Goes | Show Time |

## EVENING — FALL, 1946

*Friday*

| ABC | CBS | MBS | NBC | |
|---|---|---|---|---|
| Terry and the Pirates | Front Page Feature | News | Life with Crosby | *5pm* |
| Dick Tracy | Revue | The Adventures of Superman | News | *5:15* |
| Jack Armstrong, the All-American Boy | Harry W. Flannery, news | Captain Midnight | Casa Cugat | *5:30* |
| News | Henry Garred, news | Tom Mix and His Ralston Straightshooters | Elmer Patterson, news | *5:45* |
| Music By Adlam | The Ginny Simms Show | Gabriel Heatter, news | People Are Funny | *6pm* |
| | | The Barry Wood Show | | *6:15* |
| The Sheriff | The Jimmy Durante Show | Spotlight Bands | Waltz Time | *6:30* |
| | | | | *6:45* |
| Madison Square Garden Boxing | It Pays to Be Ignorant | Spotlight on America | The Molle' Mystery Theater | *7pm* |
| | | | | *7:15* |
| | Maisie | The Cisco Kid | The Colgate Sports Newsreel, Bill Stern | *7:30* |
| | | | Cabbages and Kings | *7:45* |
| The Court of Missing Heirs | Lowell Thomas, news | Let George Do It | The Chesterfield Supper Club | *8pm* |
| | The Jack Smith Show | | Fleetwood Lawton, news | *8:15* |
| This is Your FBI | The Marie Wilson Show | The Burl Ives Show | The Alan Young Show | *8:30* |
| | Carroll Alcott, news (8:55 PM) | Public Affairs | | *8:45* |
| Break the Bank | The Baby Snooks Show | Glenn Hardy, news | The King's Men | *9pm* |
| | | Rex Miller, news | Latin Serenade | *9:15* |
| News Roundup | The Adventures of the Thin Man | The Inside of Sports | Murder at Midnight | *9:30* |
| | | Henry J. Taylor, news | | *9:45* |
| Sports | The Ten o'Clock Wire | Fulton Lewis Jr., news | The Richfield Reporter | *10pm* |
| News | Bob Elson Interviews | News | Music | *10:15* |
| Raymond Gram Swing, news | The Symphonette | Sing, America Sing | Inside the News | *10:30* |
| Freddy Martin Orchestra | | So the Story Goes | Show Time | *10:45* |

| EVENING — FALL, 1946 | | | | |
|---|---|---|---|---|
| *Saturday* | | | | |
| | ABC | CBS | MBS | NBC |
| *5pm* | Paul Porter, talk | Front Page Feature | News | Sports |
| *5:15* | American Radio | Sports | Music | News |
| *5:30* | What's the Score | Harry W. Flannery, news | Hawaii Calls | Madison 2345, Times Information |
| *5:45* | News | Henry Garred, news | | Elmer Patterson, news |
| *6pm* | Labor USA | The Camel Caravan, Vaughn Monroe | Author Meets the Critics | The Roy Rogers Show |
| *6:15* | The Voice of Business | | | |
| *6:30* | Holiday for Music, Curt Massey | It Couldn't Happen Here | Meet the Press | Can You Top This |
| *6:45* | | Saturday Night Serenade | | |
| *7pm* | Famous Jury Trials | | The Quiz of Two Cities | The Judy Canova Show |
| *7:15* | | This is Hollywood | | |
| *7:30* | I Deal in Crime | | Red Ryder | Grand Ole Opry |
| *7:45* | | The Story Teller | | |
| *8pm* | Sherlock Holmes | Hollywood Star Time | Love Story Theater | Truth or Consequences |
| *8:15* | | | | |
| *8:30* | The Lone Ranger | The Mayor of the Town | Juvenile Jury | The Life of Riley |
| *8:45* | | Carroll Alcott, news (8:55PM) | | |
| *9pm* | Gangbusters | Your Hit Parade | Glenn Hardy, news | The Pleasure Parade |
| *9:15* | | | Caravan | Cabbages and Kings |
| *9:30* | The Green Hornet | | Leave It to the Girls | Conquest |
| *9:45* | | Don't You Believe It | | |
| *10pm* | Music | The Ten o'Clock Wire | The Chicago Theater of the Air | News |
| *10:15* | | The Hollywood Barn Dance | | Public Affairs |
| *10:30* | Freddy Martin Orchestra | | | The Sealtest Village Store, Arden ahd Haley |
| *10:45* | | Talk | | |

## DAYTIME — FALL, 1946

*Sunday*

| | ABC | CBS | MBS | NBC |
|---|---|---|---|---|
| *8am* | Message of Israel | Wings Over Jordan | Dr. Talbot Choir | The Bible Hour |
| *8:15* | | | | The Old Hymnal |
| *8:30* | The Hour of Faith | The Salt Lake Tabernacle Choir | The Voice of Prophecy | The Eternal Light |
| *8:45* | | | | |
| *9am* | It Happened During the Week | Invitation to Learning | The Pilgrim Hour | The L.A. Times Funnies |
| *9:15* | Washington Inside and Out | | | |
| *9:30* | Sunday Strings | Yours, Sincerely | The Lutheran Hour | Echoes and Encores |
| *9:45* | | | | |
| *10am* | News | The People's Platform | Glenn Hardy, news | Sports |
| *10:15* | Sports Quiz | | Commander Scott | The Home Town Parade |
| *10:30* | Sammy Kaye's Sunday Serenade | News | Sweetheart Time | The University of Chicago Round Table |
| *10:45* | | Howard K. Smith, news | | |
| *11am* | Warriors of Peace | Public Affairs | The Crime Cases of Warden Lawes | The RCA Victor Show |
| *11:15* | | On Wings of Song | The Band Concert | |
| *11:30* | National Vespers | Stradivari Orchestra | Bill Cunningham, news | Harvest of Stars |
| *11:45* | | | The Canary Pet Shop | |
| *12pm* | Danger, Dr. Danfield | New York Philharmonic Orchestra | Broadway News | The Sheaffer Parade |
| *12:15* | | | Freedom of Opportunity | |
| *12:30* | The Cadets Quartet | | Susan Kent, talk | One Man's Family |
| *12:45* | Samuel Pettengill, news | | | |
| *1pm* | Are These Our Children | | The House of Mystery | The Quiz Kids |
| *1:15* | | | | |
| *1:30* | Music | The Hour of Charm | True Detective Mysteries | These Make History |
| *1:45* | | | | News |

## DAYTIME — FALL, 1946

*Monday-Friday*

| ABC | CBS | MBS | NBC | |
|---|---|---|---|---|
| The Breakfast Club | The Johnny Murray Show | Arthur Gaeth, news | Fred Waring Orchestra | *8am* |
| | News | News | | *8:15* |
| | Grand Slam | News | The Jack Berch Show | *8:30* |
| | Rosemary | Victor Lindlahr, health | David Harum | *8:45* |
| Glamor Manor, Kenny Baker | Kate Smith Speaks | Talk | Edward Jorgenson, news | *9am* |
| | Aunt Jenny's True Life Stories | The Coke Club, Morton Downey | Ladies' Day | *9:15* |
| Breakfast at Sardi's | The Romance of Helen Trent | Time Out | News | *9:30* |
| | Our Gal Sunday | | | *9:45* |
| Tony Morse, news | Big Sister | Glenn Hardy, news | For You | *10am* |
| Between the Bookends | Ma Perkins | Norma Dixon, talk | Private Wire | *10:15* |
| My True Story | Young Dr. Malone | Life Stories | What You Say | *10:30* |
| | The Road of Life | The Bill Gwinn Show | Joyce Jordan, MD | *10:45* |
| Hymns of All Churches | The Second Mrs. Burton | | The Guiding Light | *11am* |
| H. R. Baukhage, news | Perry Mason | Smile Time | Today's Children | *11:15* |
| Club Time / Listening Post | Lone Journey | Queen for a Day | The Woman in White | *11:30* |
| News | Radio Backstage | | Masquerade | *11:45* |
| News | Surprise Party | Broadway News | The Farm Reporter | *12pm* |
| Cliff Edwards, songs | The Bill Byron Trio | The Johnson Family | Ma Perkins | *12:15* |
| Find Me | Knox Manning, news | Mild and Mellow | Pepper Young's Family | *12:30* |
| The Frank Parker Show | Something to Talk About | | The Right to Happiness | *12:45* |
| Meet Me in Manhattan | House Party | Louise Massey, songs | Mary Noble, Backstage Wife | *1pm* |
| | | Music | Stella Dallas | *1:15* |
| Walter Kiernan, news | The Strange Romance of Evelyn Winters | | Lorenzo Jones | *1:30* |
| Ethel and Albert | Background for Living | | Young Widder Brown | *1:45* |

## DAYTIME — FALL, 1946

*Sunday*

| | ABC | CBS | MBS | NBC |
|---|---|---|---|---|
| *2pm* | Darts for Dough | The Prudential Family Hour | The Shadow | NBC Symphony Orchestra |
| *2:15* | | | | |
| *2:30* | Counterspy | The Hoagy Carmichael Show | Quick as a Flash | |
| *2:45* | | William L. Shirer, news | | |
| *3pm* | Phil Davis' Sunday Party | The Adventures of Ozzie and Harriet | Those Websters | The Catholic Hour |
| *3:15* | | | | |
| *3:30* | Wayne King Orchestra | The Hope Chest | The Return of Nick Carter | Sincerely Yours |
| *3:45* | | | | The Melody Parade |
| *4pm* | Drew Pearson, news | Gene Autry's Melody Ranch | Where and When | The Lucky Strike Program, Jack Benny |
| *4:15* | Don Gardiner, news | | | |
| *4:30* | The Hollywood Music Hall | The Western Show | The Northwestern Reviewing Stand | The Phil Harris - Alice Faye Show |
| *4:45* | | | | |

# DAYTIME — FALL, 1946

*Monday-Friday*

| ABC | CBS | MBS | NBC | |
|---|---|---|---|---|
| What's Doing Ladies | The American School of the Air | Tell Your Neighbor | When a Girl Marries | *2pm* |
| | | The John J. Anthony Program | Portia Faces Life | *2:15* |
| Bride and Groom | Meet the Missus | Heart's Desire | Just Plain Bill | *2:30* |
| | | | Front Page Farrell | *2:45* |
| Ladies Be Seated | The Housewives' Protective League | Philip Keyne Gordon, news | The Road of Life | *3pm* |
| | | Nancy Young, talk | Life Can Be Beautiful | *3:15* |
| Alvin Wilder, news | In My Opinion | | Aunt Mary | *3:30* |
| The Frances Scully Show | The World Today | Music You Love | Dr. Paul | *3:45* |
| Taylor Grant, news | Talk / Hawk Larabee | Fulton Lewis Jr., news | One Woman's Secret | *4pm* |
| Raymond Gram Swing, news | | Rex Miller, news | News of the World | *4:15* |
| Hits and Encores | Talk and Music / The American Melody Hour / | Erskine Johnson, gossip | Art Baker's Notebook | *4:30* |
| Tennessee Jed | Mr. Keen, Tracer of Lost Persons | Buck Rogers of the 25th Century | | *4:45* |

## DAYTIME — FALL, 1946

*Saturday*

| | ABC | CBS | MBS | NBC |
|---|---|---|---|---|
| *8am* | Treasury Salute | Let's Pretend | News and Views | For You |
| *8:15* | Wake Up and Smile | | | For Children |
| *8:30* | | Give and Take | | Smilin' Ed's Buster Brown Gang |
| *8:45* | | | The Quaker City Serenade | |
| *9am* | Judy Thompson, talk | The Armstrong Theater of Today | Judy and Jill | News |
| *9:15* | Mirandy | | | Consumer Time |
| *9:30* | The American Farmer | Stars Over Hollywood | Music | Meet the Author |
| *9:45* | | | | The Kitchen |
| *10am* | To Live in Peace | Grand Central Station | Glenn Hardy, news | The National Farm and Home Hour |
| *10:15* | | | Sonia Heine, comment | |
| *10:30* | Sports | County Fair | The Clinic Forum | Sports |
| *10:45* | | | | |
| *11am* | | Mary Lee Taylor, cooking | | |
| *11:15* | | | | |
| *11:30* | | Sports | Jamboree | |
| *11:45* | | | | |
| *12pm* | | | Broadway News | |
| *12:15* | | | The Kenny Baker Show | |
| *12:30* | | | The Round Towner | |
| *12:45* | | | News | |
| *1pm* | | | Thirty Seconds to Go | |
| *1:15* | | | Sports | |
| *1:30* | The Treasury Show | | Teen Session | |
| *1:45* | | | Policing L.A. | |

## DAYTIME — FALL, 1946

*Saturday*

| | ABC | CBS | MBS | NBC |
|---|---|---|---|---|
| *2pm* | News | Syncopation Piece | Grid Forecast | |
| *2:15* | Sports | | Sports | |
| *2:30* | | Columbia's Country Journal | | Edward Tomlinson, news |
| *2:45* | | | | The King Cole Trio |
| *3pm* | | The Song Shop | | Name Your Music |
| *3:15* | | The Columbia Workshop | | |
| *3:30* | | | | On the Scouting Trail |
| *3:45* | | The World Today | | |
| *4pm* | | Sweeney and March | | Our Foreign Policy |
| *4:15* | | | | |
| *4:30* | The Piano Playhouse | The Los Angeles Story | | Curtain Time |
| *4:45* | The Buddy Weed Trio | The Voice of the Moment | | |

# LISTINGS FOR 1947

## EVENING — WINTER, 1947

*Sunday*

| | ABC | CBS | MBS | NBC |
|---|---|---|---|---|
| *5pm* | Detroit Symphony Orchestra | Music | News and Views | The Charlie McCarthy Show |
| *5:15* | | | | |
| *5:30* | | A Man Named Jordan | Special Investigator | The Fred Allen Show |
| *5:45* | | | Stars and Spotlight | |
| *6pm* | Walter Winchell's Jergens Journal | The Campbell Room, Hildegarde | Exploring the Unknown | The Manhattan Merry-Go-Round |
| *6:15* | Louella Parsons, gossip | | | |
| *6:30* | Jimmy Fidler, gossip | The Eddie Bracken Show | Double or Nothing | The American Album of Familiar Music |
| *6:45* | Police Woman | | | |
| *7pm* | The Theater Guild of the Air | Take It or Leave It | A Brighter Tomorrow | The Bickersons |
| *7:15* | | | | |
| *7:30* | | Kate Smith Sings | The Mysterious Traveler | Meet Me at Parky's |
| *7:45* | | | | |
| *8pm* | Pat Novak for Hire | Crime Doctor | Twenty Questions | The Bob Burns Show |
| *8:15* | | News (8:25PM) | | |
| *8:30* | The Clock | Blondie | Walter Winchell's Jergens Journal | The Standard Symphony Hour |
| *8:45* | | | Sheila Graham, gossip | |
| *9pm* | News | The Adventures of Sam Spade | Glenn Hardy, news | |
| *9:15* | Report to the People | | Rex Miller, news | |
| *9:30* | Eastside Serenade | Romance of the Ranchos | Cleveland Symphony Orchestra | The Lucky Strike Program, Jack Benny |
| *9:45* | | | | |
| *10pm* | Music | The Ten o'Clock Wire | | The Richfield Reporter |
| *10:15* | | The University Explorer | | |
| *10:30* | Freddy Martin Orchestra | Time for Reason | News | Inside the News |
| *10:45* | | America Speaks | Bill Cunningham, news | Melody Time |

## EVENING — WINTER, 1947

*Monday*

| ABC | CBS | MBS | NBC | |
|---|---|---|---|---|
| Terry and the Pirates | Front Page Feature | News | Feature Wire | *5pm* |
| Sky King | Revue | The Adventures of Superman | News | *5:15* |
| Jack Armstrong, the All-American Boy | Harry W. Flannery, news | Captain Midnight | The Voice of Firestone | *5:30* |
| News | Henry Garred, news | Tom Mix and His Ralston Straightshooters | | *5:45* |
| Music By Adlam | The Lux Radio Theater | Gabriel Heatter, news | The American Way | *6pm* |
| | | Real Stories from Real Life | | *6:15* |
| So You Want to Lead a Band | | Guy Lombardo Orchestra | The Victor Borge Show | *6:30* |
| | | | | *6:45* |
| The Lone Ranger | The Lady Esther Screen Guild Theater | McGarry and the Mouse | The Carnation Contented Hour | *7pm* |
| | | | | *7:15* |
| Sherlock Holmes | The Bob Hawk Show | The Cisco Kid | Dr. I. Q., the Mental Banker | *7:30* |
| | | | | *7:45* |
| Lum and Abner | Lowell Thomas, news | Richard Davis | The Chesterfield Supper Club | *8pm* |
| News | The Jack Smith Show | | Fleetwood Lawton, news | *8:15* |
| The Atwater-Kent Radio Auditions | Joanie's Tea Room | The Casebook of Gregory Hood | The Cavalcade of America | *8:30* |
| | Carroll Alcott, news (8:55PM) | | | *8:45* |
| The Doctors Talk It Over | The Whistler | Glenn Hardy, news | The Bell Telephone Hour | *9pm* |
| Prevention Preferred | | Mel Ventner, news | | *9:15* |
| The Court of Missing Heirs | Inner Sanctum Mysteries | The Inside of Sports | The Hollywood Bowl Auditions | *9:30* |
| | | Henry J. Taylor, news | | *9:45* |
| Sports | The Ten o'Clock Wire | Fulton Lewis Jr., news | The Richfield Reporter | *10pm* |
| News | Bob Elson Interviews | News | The Barry Wood Show | *10:15* |
| Elmer Davis, news | The Symphonette | Sing, America Sing | Inside the News | *10:30* |
| Rainbow Rendezvous | | Tapestries | Melody Time | *10:45* |

| EVENING — WINTER, 1947 | | | | |
|---|---|---|---|---|
| *Tuesday* | | | | |
| | ABC | CBS | MBS | NBC |
| *5pm* | Terry and the Pirates | Front Page Feature | News | Feature Wire |
| *5:15* | Sky King | Revue | The Adventures of Superman | News |
| *5:30* | Jack Armstrong, the All-American Boy | Harry W. Flannery, news | Captain Midnight | A Date with Judy |
| *5:45* | News | Henry Garred, news | Tom Mix and His Ralston Straightshooters | |
| *6pm* | Pronounce It | Vox Pop | Gabriel Heatter, news | Amos 'n' Andy |
| *6:15* | | | Real Stories from Real Life | |
| *6:30* | Boston Symphony Orchestra | One World Flight | The American Forum of the Air | Fibber McGee and Molly |
| *6:45* | | | | |
| *7pm* | | The Woman's Forum | | The Pepsodent Show, Bob Hope |
| *7:15* | | | Upton Close, news | |
| *7:30* | The Sons of the Pioneers | Melodies America Loves | Red Ryder | The Raleigh Cigarette Program, Red Skelton |
| *7:45* | News | | | |
| *8pm* | Lum and Abner | Lowell Thomas, news | The Count of Monte Cristo | The Chesterfield Supper Club |
| *8:15* | Earl Godwin, news | The Jack Smith Show | | Fleetwood Lawton, news |
| *8:30* | Dark Venture | The Mel Blanc Show | The Falcon | The Rudy Vallee Show |
| *8:45* | | Carroll Alcott, news (8:55PM) | | |
| *9pm* | Retribution | Big Town | Glenn Hardy, news | Favorite Story |
| *9:15* | | | James Crowley, news | |
| *9:30* | Music / Public Affairs | Tapestries of Life | The Inside of Sports | The Pleasure Parade |
| *9:45* | | | Music | Tuttle Time |
| *10pm* | Sports | The Ten o'Clock Wire | Fulton Lewis Jr., news | The Richfield Reporter |
| *10:15* | News | Bob Elson Interviews | News | Madison 2345, Times Information |
| *10:30* | Elmer Davis, news | Open Hearing | Sing, America Sing | Inside the News |
| *10:45* | Freddy Martin Orchestra | | Music | Melody Time |

## EVENING — WINTER, 1947

*Wednesday*

| ABC | CBS | MBS | NBC | |
|---|---|---|---|---|
| Terry and the Pirates | Front Page Feature | News | Feature Wire | *5pm* |
| Sky King | Revue | The Adventures of Superman | News | *5:15* |
| Jack Armstrong, the All-American Boy | Harry W. Flannery, news | Captain Midnight | Casa Cugat | *5:30* |
| News | Henry Garred, news | Tom Mix and His Ralston Straightshooters | Elmer Patterson, news | *5:45* |
| The Arliene Frances Show | Songs By Sinatra | Gabriel Heatter, news | Duffy's Tavern | *6pm* |
| | | Real Stories from Real Life | | *6:15* |
| Pot o' Gold | The Ford Show, Dinah Shore | Bulldog Drummond | The Skippy Hollywood Theater | *6:30* |
| | | | | *6:45* |
| The Lone Ranger | Hollywood Players | Scotland Yard's Inspector Burke | The Fabulous Dr. Tweedy | *7pm* |
| | | | | *7:15* |
| The Sons of the Pioneers | Information, Please | The Cisco Kid | Kay Kyser's College of Musical Knowledge | *7:30* |
| The Skip Farrell Show | | | | *7:45* |
| Lum and Abner | Lowell Thomas, news | What's the Name of That Song | The Chesterfield Supper Club | *8pm* |
| Feature Page | The Jack Smith Show | | Fleetwood Lawton, news | *8:15* |
| Tales of Willie Piper | Dr. Christian | It's Up to Youth | The Great Gildersleeve | *8:30* |
| | Carroll Alcott, news (8:55PM) | | | *8:45* |
| Philco Radio Time, Bing Crosby | The Jack Carson Show | Glenn Hardy, news | A Day in the Life of Dennis Day | *9pm* |
| | | Mel Ventner, news | | *9:15* |
| The Henry Morgan Show | The Adventures of Ellery Queen | The Inside of Sports | Mr. District Attorney | *9:30* |
| | | Music | | *9:45* |
| Sports | The Ten o'Clock Wire | Fulton Lewis Jr., news | The Richfield Reporter | *10pm* |
| News | Bob Elson Interviews | News | The Barry Wood Show | *10:15* |
| Hits and Encores | The Symphonette | Sing, America Sing | Inside the News | *10:30* |
| Freddy Martin Orchestra | | Veteran Information | Melody Time | *10:45* |

## EVENING — WINTER, 1947

*Thursday*

| | ABC | CBS | MBS | NBC |
|---|---|---|---|---|
| *5pm* | Terry and the Pirates | Front Page Feature | News | Feature Wire |
| *5:15* | Sky King | Revue | The Adventures of Superman | News |
| *5:30* | Jack Armstrong, the All-American Boy | Harry W. Flannery, news | Captain Midnight | Casa Cugat |
| *5:45* | News | Henry Garred, news | Tom Mix and His Ralston Straightshooters | Elmer Patterson, news |
| *6pm* | Music | The Dick Haymes Show | Gabriel Heatter, news | The Kraft Music Hall, Eddie Foy |
| *6:15* | | | Real Stories from Real Life | |
| *6:30* | Real Story | Casey, Crime Photographer | The Treasure Hour of Song | Grand Marquee |
| *6:45* | America's Town Meeting of the Air | | | |
| *7pm* | | The Radio Reader's Digest | The Fishing and Hunting Club | Abbott and Costello |
| *7:15* | | | | |
| *7:30* | | Phone Again Finnegan | Red Ryder | Pabst Blue Ribbon Time, Eddie Cantor |
| *7:45* | Monitor Views | | | |
| *8pm* | Lum and Abner | Lowell Thomas, news | The Fishing and Hunting Club | The Chesterfield Supper Club |
| *8:15* | Feature Page | The Jack Smith Show | | Fleetwood Lawton, news |
| *8:30* | That Was the Year | The FBI in Peace and War | California Melodies | The Aldrich Family |
| *8:45* | | Carroll Alcott, news (8:55PM) | | |
| *9pm* | World Security Workshop | Suspense | Glenn Hardy, news | Maxwell House Coffee Time, Burns and Allen |
| *9:15* | | | James Crowley, news | |
| *9:30* | Music | Ford Sterling, news | The Inside of Sports | Noah Webster Says |
| *9:45* | | The Hobby Hour | Music | |
| *10pm* | Sports | The Ten o'Clock Wire | Fulton Lewis Jr., news | The Richfield Reporter |
| *10:15* | News | Bob Elson Interviews | News | Mayor Bowron, comment |
| *10:30* | Elmer Davis, news | Sweeney and March | Sing, America Sing | Inside the News |
| *10:45* | Freddy Martin Orchestra | | Music | Melody Time |

# EVENING — WINTER, 1947

*Friday*

| ABC | CBS | MBS | NBC | |
|---|---|---|---|---|
| Terry and the Pirates | Front Page Feature | News | Feature Wire | *5pm* |
| Sky King | Revue | The Adventures of Superman | News | *5:15* |
| Jack Armstrong, the All-American Boy | Harry W. Flannery, news | Captain Midnight | Casa Cugat | *5:30* |
| News | Henry Garred, news | Tom Mix and His Ralston Straightshooters | Elmer Patterson, news | *5:45* |
| The Fat Man | The Ginny Simms Show | Gabriel Heatter, news | People Are Funny | *6pm* |
| | | Real Stories from Real Life | | *6:15* |
| The Sheriff | The Jimmy Durante Show | The Crime Club | Waltz Time | *6:30* |
| | | | | *6:45* |
| Madison Square Garden Boxing | It Pays to Be Ignorant | Spotlight on America | The Hank McCune Show | *7pm* |
| | | | | *7:15* |
| | Maisie | The Cisco Kid | The Colgate Sports Newsreel, Bill Stern | *7:30* |
| | | | Cabbages and Kings | *7:45* |
| The Green Hornet | Lowell Thomas, news | Let George Do It | The Chesterfield Supper Club | *8pm* |
| | The Jack Smith Show | | Fleetwood Lawton, news | *8:15* |
| This is Your FBI | The Marie Wilson Show | The Burl Ives Show | The Alan Young Show | *8:30* |
| | Carroll Alcott, news (8:55PM) | California Caravan | | *8:45* |
| Break the Bank | The Baby Snooks Show | Glenn Hardy, news | The King's Men | *9pm* |
| | | Mel Ventner, news | Latin Serenade | *9:15* |
| A Tune, A Play and a Girl | The Adventures of the Thin Man | The Inside of Sports | The Molle' Mystery Theater | *9:30* |
| | | Henry J. Taylor, news | | *9:45* |
| Sports | The Ten o'Clock Wire | Fulton Lewis Jr., news | The Richfield Reporter | *10pm* |
| News | Bob Elson Interviews | News | The Barry Wood Show | *10:15* |
| Elmer Davis, news | The Symphonette | Sing, America Sing | Inside the News | *10:30* |
| Freddy Martin Orchestra | | Music | Melody Time | *10:45* |

# EVENING — WINTER, 1947

*Saturday*

| | ABC | CBS | MBS | NBC |
|---|---|---|---|---|
| *5pm* | The Piano Playhouse | Front Page Feature | News | The Wizard of Odds |
| *5:15* | American Radio | Sports | The Christian Science Monitor | News |
| *5:30* | What's the Score | Harry W. Flannery, news | Scramby Amby | Madison 2345, Times Information |
| *5:45* | News | Henry Garred, news | | Elmer Patterson, news |
| *6pm* | Melodies | The Camel Caravan, Vaughn Monroe | Author Meets the Critics | The Roy Rogers Show |
| *6:15* | | | | |
| *6:30* | Holiday for Music, Curt Massey | It Couldn't Happen Here | Meet the Press | Can You Top This |
| *6:45* | | Saturday Night Serenade | | |
| *7pm* | Famous Jury Trials | | The Quiz of Two Cities | The Judy Canova Show |
| *7:15* | | This is Hollywood | | |
| *7:30* | I Deal in Crime | | Red Ryder | Grand Ole Opry |
| *7:45* | | The Ghost That Walks | | |
| *8pm* | Murder at Midnight | Hollywood Star Time | Boston Blackie | Truth or Consequences |
| *8:15* | | | | |
| *8:30* | The Lone Ranger | The Mayor of the Town | Love Story Theater | The Life of Riley |
| *8:45* | | Carroll Alcott, news (8:55PM) | | |
| *9pm* | Gangbusters | Your Hit Parade | Glenn Hardy, news | Mystery is My Hobby |
| *9:15* | | | Holly House | |
| *9:30* | Murder and Mr. Malone | | Leave It to the Girls | Conquest |
| *9:45* | | The Jean Sablon Show | | |
| *10pm* | Music | The Ten o'Clock Wire | The Chicago Theater of the Air | News |
| *10:15* | | The Hollywood Barn Dance | | For the Family |
| *10:30* | Freddy Martin Orchestra | | | The Sealtest Village Store, Arden ahd Haley |
| *10:45* | | Talk | | |

## DAYTIME — WINTER, 1947

*Sunday*

| | ABC | CBS | MBS | NBC |
|---|---|---|---|---|
| *8am* | Message of Israel | Wings Over Jordan | Dr. Talbot Choir | The Bible Hour |
| *8:15* | | | | The Old Hymnal |
| *8:30* | The Hour of Faith | The Salt Lake Tabernacle Choir | The Voice of Prophecy | The L. A. Times Funnies |
| *8:45* | | | | |
| *9am* | It Happened During the Week | Invitation to Learning | The Pilgrim Hour | The Eternal Light |
| *9:15* | Washington Inside and Out | | | |
| *9:30* | Sunday Strings | Yours, Sincerely | The Lutheran Hour | Echoes and Encores |
| *9:45* | | | | |
| *10am* | News | The People's Platform | Glenn Hardy, news | Sports |
| *10:15* | Sports Quiz | | Commander Scott | The Home Town Parade |
| *10:30* | Sammy Kaye's Sunday Serenade | News | Juvenile Jury | The University of Chicago Round Table |
| *10:45* | | Howard K. Smith, news | | |
| *11am* | Warriors of Peace | The Weekly News Review | The Crime Cases of Warden Lawes | The RCA Victor Show |
| *11:15* | | | The Band Concert | |
| *11:30* | National Vespers | Once Upon a Tune | | Harvest of Stars |
| *11:45* | | | The Canary Pet Shop | |
| *12pm* | Danger, Dr. Danfield | New York Philharmonic Orchestra | Broadway News | The Sheaffer Parade |
| *12:15* | | | Freedom of Opportunity | |
| *12:30* | The Honey Dreamers | | Susan Kent, talk | One Man's Family |
| *12:45* | Samuel Pettengill, news | | | |
| *1pm* | Are These Our Children | | The House of Mystery | The Quiz Kids |
| *1:15* | | | | |
| *1:30* | Valley of the Shadow | The Hour of Charm | True Detective Mysteries | These Make History |

## DAYTIME — WINTER, 1947

*Monday-Friday*

| ABC | CBS | MBS | NBC | |
|---|---|---|---|---|
| The Breakfast Club | The Johnny Murray Show | Cecil Brown, news | Fred Waring Orchestra | *8am* |
| | News | The Editor's Diary | | *8:15* |
| | Grand Slam | News | The Jack Berch Show | *8:30* |
| | Rosemary | Victor Lindlahr, health | Lora Lawton | *8:45* |
| Glamor Manor, Kenny Baker | Kate Smith Speaks | Talk | Edward Jorgenson, news | *9am* |
| | Aunt Jenny's True Life Stories | The Coke Club, Morton Downey | Ladies' Day | *9:15* |
| Breakfast at Sardi's | The Romance of Helen Trent | Music | | *9:30* |
| | Our Gal Sunday | | | *9:45* |
| Galen Drake, talk | Big Sister | Glenn Hardy, news | | *10am* |
| Between the Bookends | Ma Perkins | Norma Dixon, talk | What You Say | *10:15* |
| My True Story | Young Dr. Malone | The Ben Alexander Show | | *10:30* |
| | The Road of Life | | Joyce Jordan, MD | *10:45* |
| Hymns of All Churches | The Second Mrs. Burton | Talk and Music | Today's Children | *11am* |
| H. R. Baukhage, news | Perry Mason | Smile Time | The Woman in White | *11:15* |
| Club Time / Listening Post | Lone Journey | Queen for a Day | Masquerade | *11:30* |
| The Frank Parker Show | Rose of My Dreams | | The Light of the World | *11:45* |
| News | Surprise Party | Broadway News | The Farm Reporter | *12pm* |
| Cliff Edwards, songs | Melody Trail | The Johnson Family | Ma Perkins | *12:15* |
| Edwin C. Hill, news | Knox Manning, news | Louise Massey, songs | Pepper Young's Family | *12:30* |
| Dorothy Dix, news | Something to Talk About | Music | The Right to Happiness | *12:45* |
| Charm School | House Party | Checkerboard | Mary Noble, Backstage Wife | *1pm* |
| Studio Tour | | Music / Jackie Hill, talk | Stella Dallas | *1:15* |
| Walter Kiernan, news | The Strange Romance of Evelyn Winters | Music | Lorenzo Jones | *1:30* |

## DAYTIME — WINTER, 1947

*Sunday*

| | ABC | CBS | MBS | NBC |
|---|---|---|---|---|
| *1:45* | | | | News |
| *2pm* | Darts for Dough | The Prudential Family Hour | The Shadow | NBC Symphony Orchestra |
| *2:15* | | | | |
| *2:30* | Counterspy | The Hoagy Carmichael Show | Quick as a Flash | |
| *2:45* | | William L. Shirer, news | | |
| *3pm* | Phil Davis' Sunday Party | The Adventures of Ozzie and Harriet | Those Websters | The Catholic Hour |
| *3:15* | | | | |
| *3:30* | Wayne King Orchestra | The Hope Chest | Nick Carter, Master Detective | Sincerely Yours |
| *3:45* | | | | The Melody Parade |
| *4pm* | Drew Pearson, news | Gene Autry's Melody Ranch | I Was a Convict | The Lucky Strike Program, Jack Benny |
| *4:15* | Don Gardiner, news | | | |
| *4:30* | The Hollywood Music Hall | The Western Show | The Northwestern Reviewing Stand | The Phil Harris - Alice Faye Show |
| *4:45* | | | | |

## DAYTIME — WINTER, 1947

*Monday-Friday*

| ABC | CBS | MBS | NBC | |
|---|---|---|---|---|
| Ethel and Albert | Background for Living | | Young Widder Brown | *1:45* |
| What's Doing Ladies | The American School of the Air | The Bill Gwinn Show | When a Girl Marries | *2pm* |
| | | | Portia Faces Life | *2:15* |
| Bride and Groom | Meet the Missus | Heart's Desire | Just Plain Bill | *2:30* |
| | | | Front Page Farrell | *2:45* |
| Ladies Be Seated | The Housewives' Protective League | Music | The Road of Life | *3pm* |
| | | Nancy Young, talk | Life Can Be Beautiful | *3:15* |
| News | In My Opinion | | Aunt Mary | *3:30* |
| The Frances Scully Show | The World Today | Music You Love | Dr. Paul | *3:45* |
| Taylor Grant, news | Music / The Plainsman | Fulton Lewis Jr., news | One Woman's Secret | *4pm* |
| Alvin Wilder, news | | Rex Miller, news | News of the World | *4:15* |
| Dick Tracy | Talk and Music / The American Melody Hour / | Erskine Johnson, gossip | Art Baker's Notebook | *4:30* |
| Tennessee Jed | Mr. Keen, Tracer of Lost Persons | Buck Rogers of the 25th Century | | *4:45* |

## DAYTIME — WINTER, 1947

*Saturday*

| | ABC | CBS | MBS | NBC |
|---|---|---|---|---|
| *8am* | Sagebrush | Let's Pretend | News | The Coffee Concert |
| *8:15* | | | Melodies | Jump-Jump and the Ice Queen |
| *8:30* | | The Adventurer's Club | | Smilin' Ed's Buster Brown Gang |
| *8:45* | | | Say It With Music | |
| *9am* | Judy Thompson, talk | The Armstrong Theater of Today | Music | Young America Speaks |
| *9:15* | Mirandy | | | By Request |
| *9:30* | The American Farmer | Stars Over Hollywood | Flight of the Past | Meet the Author |
| *9:45* | | | | The Kitchen |
| *10am* | American Radio | Grand Central Station | Glenn Hardy, news | The National Farm and Home Hour |
| *10:15* | Tell Me Doctor | | Sonia Heine, comment | |
| *10:30* | Fascinating Rhythm | County Fair | Symphony of Youth | The Veterans Advisor |
| *10:45* | | | | The Christian Science Monitor |
| *11am* | The Metropolitan Opera | Mary Lee Taylor, cooking | | Teen Timers |
| *11:15* | | | | |
| *11:30* | | Adventures in Science | This is Jazz | The Baxters |
| *11:45* | | Of Men and Books | | Bob Houston, songs |
| *12pm* | | Cross-Section USA | Broadway News | The Farm Reporter |
| *12:15* | | | The Kenny Baker Show | The Man on the Farm |
| *12:30* | | The Record Shop | The Round Towner | |
| *12:45* | | | The Veteran's Voice | Easy Listening |
| *1pm* | | Meet the Missus | Los Angeles Symphony Orchestra | Doctors, Then and Now |
| *1:15* | | | | |
| *1:30* | | Free for All | Horse Racing | Home is What You Make It |
| *1:45* | | | Policing L.A. | |

| DAYTIME — WINTER, 1947 | | | | |
|---|---|---|---|---|
| *Saturday* | | | | |
| | ABC | CBS | MBS | NBC |
| *2pm* | | Philadelphia Symphony Orchestra | For Your Approval | News |
| *2:15* | | | | Songs By Snooky |
| *2:30* | Tea and Crumpets | | The Clinic Forum | Edward Tomlinson, news |
| *2:45* | | | | The King Cole Trio |
| *3pm* | Junior Junction | The Song Shop | Bands and Bonds | Name Your Music |
| *3:15* | | The Columbia Workshop | | |
| *3:30* | The Teenage Advisor | | The World of Music | On the Scouting Trail |
| *3:45* | Labor USA | The World Today | | |
| *4pm* | The Year in Business | The Garden Gate | Hawaii Calls | Our Foreign Policy |
| *4:15* | Highland Swing | | | |
| *4:30* | The Music Library | The Los Angeles Story | Music | Curtain Time |
| *4:45* | | On Wings of Song | Ken Barton, comment | |

| EVENING — SPRING, 1947 | | | | |
|---|---|---|---|---|
| *Sunday* | | | | |
| | ABC | CBS | MBS | NBC |
| *5pm* | Detroit Symphony Orchestra | The City | A. L. Alexander's Mediation Board | The Charlie McCarthy Show |
| *5:15* | | | | |
| *5:30* | | A Man Named Jordan | Lawyer Q | The Fred Allen Show |
| *5:45* | | | Stars and Spotlight | |
| *6pm* | Walter Winchell's Jergens Journal | Meet Corliss Archer | Exploring the Unknown | The Manhattan Merry-Go-Round |
| *6:15* | Louella Parsons, gossip | | | |
| *6:30* | Jimmy Fidler, gossip | The Texaco StarTheater, Tony Martin | Double or Nothing | The American Album of Familiar Music |
| *6:45* | Police Woman | | | |
| *7pm* | The Theater Guild of the Air | Take It or Leave It | A Brighter Tomorrow | The Bickersons |
| *7:15* | | | | |
| *7:30* | | Kate Smith Sings | The Girls | The Play's the Thing |
| *7:45* | | | | |
| *8pm* | Drew Pearson, news | Crime Doctor | Twenty Questions | The Bob Burns Show |
| *8:15* | Don Gardiner, news | News (8:25PM) | | |
| *8:30* | The Green Hornet | Blondie | Walter Winchell's Jergens Journal | The Standard Symphony Hour |
| *8:45* | | | Sheila Graham, gossip | |
| *9pm* | Pat Novak for Hire | The Adventures of Sam Spade | Glenn Hardy, news | |
| *9:15* | | | Rex Miller, news | |
| *9:30* | Eastside Serenade | Romance of the Ranchos | The Chicago Theater of the Air | The Lucky Strike Program, Jack Benny |
| *9:45* | | | | |
| *10pm* | Music | The Ten o'Clock Wire | | The Richfield Reporter |
| *10:15* | | The University Explorer | | Music |
| *10:30* | Freddy Martin Orchestra | Time for Reason | The Treasury Department | Inside the News |
| *10:45* | | The California Legislature | Music | Melody Time |

## EVENING — SPRING, 1947

*Monday*

| ABC | CBS | MBS | NBC | |
|---|---|---|---|---|
| Terry and The Pirates | Front Page Feature | Hop Harrigan | Feature Wire | *5pm* |
| Sky King | Tom Hanlon, news | The Adventures of Superman | News | *5:15* |
| Jack Armstrong, the All-American Boy | Harry W. Flannery, news | Captain Midnight | The Voice of Firestone | *5:30* |
| News | Henry Garred, news | Tom Mix and His Ralston Straightshooters | | *5:45* |
| Treasury Agent | The Lux Radio Theater | Gabriel Heatter, news | The American Way | *6pm* |
| | | Real Stories from Real Life | | *6:15* |
| So You Want to Lead a Band | | Guy Lombardo Orchestra | The Victor Borge Show | *6:30* |
| | | | | *6:45* |
| The Lone Ranger | The Lady Esther Screen Guild Theater | Scotland Yard's Inspector Burke | The Carnation Contented Hour | *7pm* |
| | | | | *7:15* |
| Sherlock Holmes | The Bob Hawk Show | The Cisco Kid | Dr. I. Q., the Mental Banker | *7:30* |
| | | | | *7:45* |
| Lum and Abner | Lowell Thomas, news | Richard Davis | The Chesterfield Supper Club | *8pm* |
| News | The Jack Smith Show | | Fleetwood Lawton, news | *8:15* |
| The Clock | Joanie's Tea Room | The Casebook of Gregory Hood | The Cavalcade of America | *8:30* |
| | Carroll Alcott, news (8:55PM) | | | *8:45* |
| The Doctors Talk It Over | The Whistler | Glenn Hardy, news | The Bell Telephone Hour | *9pm* |
| Report to the People | | Mel Ventner, news | | *9:15* |
| Music | Inner Sanctum Mysteries | The Inside of Sports | The Hollywood Bowl Auditions | *9:30* |
| | | Henry J. Taylor, news | | *9:45* |
| Sports | The Ten o'Clock Wire | Fulton Lewis Jr., news | The Richfield Reporter | *10pm* |
| News | Bob Elson Interviews | News | The Barry Wood Show | *10:15* |
| Elmer Davis, news | The Symphonette | The Peter Potter Show | Inside the News | *10:30* |
| Rainbow Rendezvous | | | Melody Time | *10:45* |

## EVENING — SPRING, 1947

*Tuesday*

| | ABC | CBS | MBS | NBC |
|---|---|---|---|---|
| *5pm* | Terry and the Pirates | Front Page Feature | Hop Harrigan | Feature Wire |
| *5:15* | Sky King | Tom Hanlon, news | The Adventures of Superman | News |
| *5:30* | Jack Armstrong, the All-American Boy | Harry W. Flannery, news | Captain Midnight | A Date with Judy |
| *5:45* | News | Henry Garred, news | Tom Mix and His Ralston Straightshooters | |
| *6pm* | Songs | Vox Pop | Gabriel Heatter, news | Amos 'n' Andy |
| *6:15* | Music Perferrred | | Real Stories from Real Life | |
| *6:30* | Music | Before Their Time | The Mysterious Traveler | Fibber McGee and Molly |
| *6:45* | | | | |
| *7pm* | Modern Music | The Woman's Forum | Crime Cases of Warden Lawes | The Pepsodent Show, Bob Hope |
| *7:15* | | | Special Investigator | |
| *7:30* | The Bobby Doyle Show | Melodies America Loves | Red Ryder | The Raleigh Cigarette Program, Red Skelton |
| *7:45* | Alvin Wilder, news | | | |
| *8pm* | Lum and Abner | Lowell Thomas, news | The Count of Monte Cristo | The Chesterfield Supper Club |
| *8:15* | Earl Godwin, news | The Jack Smith Show | | Fleetwood Lawton, news |
| *8:30* | Dark Venture | The Mel Blanc Show | The Falcon | At Home With The Berles |
| *8:45* | | Carroll Alcott, news (8:55PM) | | |
| *9pm* | Boston Symphony Orchestra | Big Town | Glenn Hardy, news | Favorite Story |
| *9:15* | | | James Crowley, news | |
| *9:30* | | Tapestries of Life | The Inside of Sports | The Pleasure Parade |
| *9:45* | | | Men of Destiny | Madison 2345, Times Information |
| *10pm* | Sports | The Ten o'Clock Wire | Fulton Lewis Jr., news | The Richfield Reporter |
| *10:15* | News | Bob Elson Interviews | News | Music |
| *10:30* | Elmer Davis, news | Open Hearing | The Peter Potter Show | Inside the News |
| *10:45* | Freddy Martin Orchestra | | | Melody Time |

## EVENING — SPRING, 1947

*Wednesday*

| ABC | CBS | MBS | NBC | |
|---|---|---|---|---|
| Terry and the Pirates | Front Page Feature | Hop Harrigan | Feature Wire | *5pm* |
| Sky King | Tom Hanlon, news | The Adventures of Superman | News | *5:15* |
| Jack Armstrong, the All-American Boy | Harry W. Flannery, news | Captain Midnight | Casa Cugat | *5:30* |
| News | Henry Garred, news | Tom Mix and His Ralston Straightshooters | Elmer Patterson, news | *5:45* |
| Paul Whiteman Orchestra | Songs By Sinatra | Gabriel Heatter, news | Duffy's Tavern | *6pm* |
| | | Real Stories from Real Life | | *6:15* |
| The Court of Mssing Heirs | The Ford Show, Dinah Shore | The American Forum of the Air | The Skippy Hollywood Theater | *6:30* |
| | | | | *6:45* |
| The Lone Ranger | The World of Dance | | The Big Story | *7pm* |
| | | The Vic Damone Show | | *7:15* |
| Movie Drama | Information, Please | The Cisco Kid | Kay Kyser's College of Musical Knowledge | *7:30* |
| The Betty Russell Show | | | | *7:45* |
| Lum and Abner | Lowell Thomas, news | What's the Name of That Song | The Chesterfield Supper Club | *8pm* |
| Feature Page | The Jack Smith Show | | Fleetwood Lawton, news | *8:15* |
| The Beulah Show | Dr. Christian | Johnny Madero, Pier 24 | The Great Gildersleeve | *8:30* |
| | Carroll Alcott, news (8:55PM) | | | *8:45* |
| Philco Radio Time, Bing Crosby | The Jack Carson Show | Glenn Hardy, news | A Day in the Life of Dennis Day | *9pm* |
| | | Mel Ventner, news | | *9:15* |
| The Henry Morgan Show | The Adventures of Ellery Queen | The Inside of Sports | Mr. District Attorney | *9:30* |
| | | Music | | *9:45* |
| Sports | The Ten o'Clock Wire | Fulton Lewis Jr., news | The Richfield Reporter | *10pm* |
| News | Bob Elson Interviews | News | The Barry Wood Show | *10:15* |
| Elmer Davis, news | The Symphonette | The Peter Potter Show | Inside the News | *10:30* |
| Freddy Martin Orchestra | | | Melody Time | *10:45* |

## EVENING — SPRING, 1947

*Thursday*

| | ABC | CBS | MBS | NBC |
|---|---|---|---|---|
| *5pm* | Terry and the Pirates | Front Page Feature | Hop Harrigan | Feature Wire |
| *5:15* | Sky King | Tom Hanlon, news | The Adventures of Superman | News |
| *5:30* | Jack Armstrong, the All-American Boy | Harry W. Flannery, news | Captain Midnight | Casa Cugat |
| *5:45* | News | Henry Garred, news | Tom Mix and His Ralston Straightshooters | Elmer Patterson, news |
| *6pm* | The Studs Terkel Show | The Dick Haymes Show | Gabriel Heatter, news | The Kraft Music Hall, Eddie Foy |
| *6:15* | | | Real Stories from Real Life | |
| *6:30* | Real Story | Casey, Crime Photographer | The Treasure Hour of Song | Grand Marquee |
| *6:45* | America's Town Meeting of the Air | | | |
| *7pm* | | The Radio Reader's Digest | The Family Theater | Abbott and Costello |
| *7:15* | | | | |
| *7:30* | | A Man Called X | Red Ryder | Pabst Blue Ribbon Time, Eddie Cantor |
| *7:45* | Monitor Views | | | |
| *8pm* | Lum and Abner | Lowell Thomas, news | Public Affairs | The Chesterfield Supper Club |
| *8:15* | Feature Page | The Jack Smith Show | | Fleetwood Lawton, news |
| *8:30* | Philo Vance | The FBI in Peace and War | California Melodies | The Aldrich Family |
| *8:45* | | Carroll Alcott, news (8:55PM) | | |
| *9pm* | World Security Workshop | Suspense | Glenn Hardy, news | Maxwell House Coffee Time, Burns and Allen |
| *9:15* | | | James Crowley, news | |
| *9:30* | Retribution | Ford Sterling, news | The Inside of Sports | Noah Webster Says |
| *9:45* | | The Hobby Hour | Arthur Hale, news | |
| *10pm* | Sports | The Ten o'Clock Wire | Fulton Lewis Jr., news | The Richfield Reporter |
| *10:15* | News | Bob Elson Interviews | News | Mayor Bowron, comment |
| *10:30* | Elmer Davis, news | Sweeney and March | The Peter Potter Show | Inside the News |
| *10:45* | Freddy Martin Orchestra | | | Melody Time |

# EVENING — SPRING, 1947

*Friday*

| ABC | CBS | MBS | NBC | |
|---|---|---|---|---|
| Terry and the Pirates | Front Page Feature | Hop Harrigan | Feature Wire | *5pm* |
| Sky King | Tom Hanlon, news | The Adventures of Superman | News | *5:15* |
| Jack Armstrong, the All-American Boy | Harry W. Flannery, news | Captain Midnight | Casa Cugat | *5:30* |
| News | Henry Garred, news | Tom Mix and His Ralston Straightshooters | Elmer Patterson, news | *5:45* |
| Those Sensational Years | The Ginny Simms Show | Gabriel Heatter, news | People Are Funny | *6pm* |
| | | Real Stories from Real Life | | *6:15* |
| The Sheriff | The Jimmy Durante Show | The Crime Club | Waltz Time | *6:30* |
| | | | | *6:45* |
| Madison Square Garden Boxing | It Pays to Be Ignorant | Meet the Press | The Hank McCune Show | *7pm* |
| | | | | *7:15* |
| | My Friend Irma | The Cisco Kid | The Colgate Sports Newsreel, Bill Stern | *7:30* |
| | | | Cabbages and Kings | *7:45* |
| Lightnin' Jim | Lowell Thomas, news | Let George Do It | The Chesterfield Supper Club | *8pm* |
| | The Jack Smith Show | | Fleetwood Lawton, news | *8:15* |
| This is Your FBI | Free for All | The Burl Ives Show | The Alan Young Show | *8:30* |
| | Carroll Alcott, news (8:55PM) | California Caravan | | *8:45* |
| Break the Bank | The Baby Snooks Show | Glenn Hardy, news | The King's Men | *9pm* |
| | | Mel Ventner, news | Latin Serenade | *9:15* |
| Famous Jury Trials | The Adventures of the Thin Man | The Inside of Sports | The Molle' Mystery Theater | *9:30* |
| | | Henry J. Taylor, news | | *9:45* |
| Sports | The Ten o'Clock Wire | Fulton Lewis Jr., news | The Richfield Reporter | *10pm* |
| News | Bob Elson Interviews | News | The Barry Wood Show | *10:15* |
| Elmer Davis, news | The Symphonette | The Peter Potter Show | Inside the News | *10:30* |
| Freddy Martin Orchestra | | | Melody Time | *10:45* |

## EVENING — SPRING, 1947

*Saturday*

| | ABC | CBS | MBS | NBC |
|---|---|---|---|---|
| *5pm* | The Piano Playhouse | Front Page Feature | News | The Wizard of Odds |
| *5:15* | | Sports | The Christian Science Monitor | News |
| *5:30* | Harry Wismer, news | Harry W. Flannery, news | Sports | Madison 2345, Times Information |
| *5:45* | News | Henry Garred, news | Piano Magic | Elmer Patterson, news |
| *6pm* | Youth and the Government | The Bill Goodwin Show | The Mighty Casey | Your Hit Parade |
| *6:15* | | | | |
| *6:30* | Holiday for Music, Curt Massey | The Sportsmen Quartet | Family Doctor | Can You Top This |
| *6:45* | | Saturday Night Serenade | | |
| *7pm* | The Avenger | | The Quiz of Two Cities | The Judy Canova Show |
| *7:15* | | This is Hollywood | | |
| *7:30* | I Deal in Crime | | Red Ryder | Grand Ole Opry |
| *7:45* | | The Ghost That Walks | | |
| *8pm* | The Lone Ranger | The Camel Caravan, Vaughn Monroe | Boston Blackie | Truth or Consequences |
| *8:15* | | | | |
| *8:30* | The Fat Man | The Mayor of the Town | Did Justice Triumph | The Life of Riley |
| *8:45* | | Carroll Alcott, news (8:55PM) | | |
| *9pm* | Gangbusters | The Jean Sablon Show | Glenn Hardy, news | Mystery is My Hobby |
| *9:15* | | The Hollywood Barn Dance | Criminologist | |
| *9:30* | Murder and Mr. Malone | | The Fishing and Hunting Club | Conquest |
| *9:45* | | | | |
| *10pm* | Norman Thomas, comment | The Ten o'Clock Wire | Date Night | News |
| *10:15* | Freddy Martin Orchestra | Music | | Grandpa's Day |
| *10:30* | | | The Peter Potter Show | The Sealtest Village Store, Arden and Haley |
| *10:45* | | Dark Velvet | | |

| DAYTIME — SPRING, 1947 | | | | |
|---|---|---|---|---|
| *Sunday* | | | | |
| | ABC | CBS | MBS | NBC |
| *8am* | Message of Israel | Wings Over Jordan | Dr. Talbot Choir | The Bible Hour |
| *8:15* | | | | The Old Hymnal |
| *8:30* | The Hour of Faith | The Salt Lake Tabernacle Choir | The Voice of Prophecy | The L. A. Times Funnies |
| *8:45* | | | | |
| *9am* | It Happened During the Week | Invitation to Learning | The Pilgrim Hour | The Eternal Light |
| *9:15* | Washington Inside and Out | | | |
| *9:30* | Sunday Strings | As Others See It | The Lutheran Hour | Echoes and Encores |
| *9:45* | Raymond Gram Swing, news | | | |
| *10am* | Music | The People's Platform | Glenn Hardy, news | Sports |
| *10:15* | | | Commander Scott | The Home Town Parade |
| *10:30* | Sammy Kaye's Sunday Serenade | News | Juvenile Jury | The University of Chicago Round Table |
| *10:45* | | Howard K. Smith, news | | |
| *11am* | Music | The Weekly News Review | The Vic Damone Show | The RCA Victor Show |
| *11:15* | | | The Band Concert | |
| *11:30* | National Vespers | Here's to You | | Harvest of Stars |
| *11:45* | | | The Canary Pet Shop | |
| *12pm* | Warriors of Peace | New York Philharmonic Orchestra | Broadway News | The Sheaffer Parade |
| *12:15* | | | Child Psychology | |
| *12:30* | The Vagabonds Quartet | | Carelessness | One Man's Family |
| *12:45* | Samuel Pettengill, news | | | |
| *1pm* | Are These Our Children | | The House of Mystery | The Quiz Kids |
| *1:15* | | | | |
| *1:30* | Wayne King Orchestra | The Hour of Charm | True Detective Mysteries | The Talent Show |

## DAYTIME — SPRING, 1947

*Monday-Friday*

| ABC | CBS | MBS | NBC | |
|---|---|---|---|---|
| The Breakfast Club | The Johnny Murray Show | Cecil Brown, news | Fred Waring Orchestra | *8am* |
| | News | News | | *8:15* |
| | Grand Slam | The Editor's Diary | The Jack Berch Show | *8:30* |
| | Rosemary | Victor Lindlahr, health | Lora Lawton | *8:45* |
| Glamor Manor, Kenny Baker | Kate Smith Speaks | Easy Does It / Notes at 9 | Edward Jorgenson, news | *9am* |
| | Aunt Jenny's True Life Stories | The Coke Club, Morton Downey | Ladies' Day | *9:15* |
| Breakfast at Sardi's | The Romance of Helen Trent | Music | | *9:30* |
| | Our Gal Sunday | | | *9:45* |
| Galen Drake, talk | Big Sister | Glenn Hardy, news | Time for Music | *10am* |
| Between the Bookends | Ma Perkins | Jackie Hill, talk | What You Say | *10:15* |
| My True Story | Young Dr. Malone | The Ben Alexander Show | | *10:30* |
| | The Road of Life | | Joyce Jordan, MD | *10:45* |
| Hymns of All Churches | The Second Mrs. Burton | Talk and Music | Today's Children | *11am* |
| H. R. Baukhage, news | Perry Mason | Smile Time | The Woman in White | *11:15* |
| Club Time / Listening Post | Lone Journey | Queen for a Day | Masquerade | *11:30* |
| The Frank Parker Show | Rose of My Dreams | | The Light of the World | *11:45* |
| News | Bob and Victoria, songs | Broadway News | The Farm Reporter | *12pm* |
| Cliff Edwards, songs | The Sons of the Pioneers | Sing, America Sing | Ma Perkins | *12:15* |
| Edwin C. Hill, news | Knox Manning, news | Louise Masser, news | Pepper Young's Family | *12:30* |
| Dorothy Dix, news | The Story of Myrt and Marge | The Shady Valley Folks | The Right to Happiness | *12:45* |
| Hits and Encores | House Party | Checkboard | Mary Noble, Backstage Wife | *1pm* |
| Studio Tour | | Norma Dixon, talk | Stella Dallas | *1:15* |
| Walter Kiernan, news | The Strange Romance of Evelyn Winters | Nancy Young, talk | Lorenzo Jones | *1:30* |

## DAYTIME — SPRING, 1947

*Sunday*

| | ABC | CBS | MBS | NBC |
|---|---|---|---|---|
| *1:45* | | | | News |
| *2pm* | Darts for Dough | The Prudential Family Hour | The Shadow | NBC Symphony Orchestra |
| *2:15* | | | | |
| *2:30* | Counterspy | The Hoagy Carmichael Show | Quick as a Flash | |
| *2:45* | | William L. Shirer, news | | |
| *3pm* | Deadline Mystery | The Adventures of Ozzie and Harriet | Those Websters | The Catholic Hour |
| *3:15* | | | | |
| *3:30* | The Greatest Story Ever Told | The Hope Chest | Nick Carter, Master Detective | Sincerely Yours |
| *3:45* | | | | The Melody Parade |
| *4pm* | Tales of Willie Piper | Gene Autry's Melody Ranch | I Was a Convict | The Lucky Strike Program, Jack Benny |
| *4:15* | | | | |
| *4:30* | The Hollywood Music Hall | The Western Show | The Northwestern Reviwing Stand | The Phil Harris - Alice Faye Show |
| *4:45* | | | | |

## DAYTIME — SPRING, 1947

*Monday-Friday*

| ABC | CBS | MBS | NBC | |
|---|---|---|---|---|
| Ethel and Albert | The Bill Bryon Trio | | Young Widder Brown | *1:45* |
| What's Doing Ladies | The American School of the Air | Melody Matinee | When a Girl Marries | *2pm* |
| | | | Portia Faces Life | *2:15* |
| Bride and Groom | Meet the Missus | Heart's Desire | Just Plain Bill | *2:30* |
| | | | Front Page Farrell | *2:45* |
| Ladies Be Seated | Eric Sevareid, news | Music | The Road of Life | *3pm* |
| | The Housewive's Protective League | The Johnson Family | Life Can Be Beautiful | *3:15* |
| Howard K. Smith, news | | Adventure Parade | Aunt Mary | *3:30* |
| The Frances Scully Show | The World Today | Fact and Fallacy | Dr. Paul | *3:45* |
| Taylor Grant, news | Money on the Line | Fulton Lewis Jr., news | One Woman's Secret | *4pm* |
| Alvin Wilder, news | Talk / Melody House | Rex Miller, news | News of the World | *4:15* |
| Dick Tracy | Talk / The American Melody Hour / | Erskine Johnson, gossip | Art Baker's Notebook | *4:30* |
| Tennessee Jed | Mr. Keen, Tracer of Lost Persons | News | | *4:45* |

## DAYTIME — SPRING, 1947

*Saturday*

| | ABC | CBS | MBS | NBC |
|---|---|---|---|---|
| *8am* | Sagebrush (7:45AM) | Let's Pretend | Music | Jump-Jump and the Ice Queen |
| *8:15* | | | | The Coffee Concert |
| *8:30* | | The Adventurer's Club | Melodies | Smilin' Ed's Buster Brown Gang |
| *8:45* | | | | |
| *9am* | Texas Jim Robertson, songs | The Armstrong Theater of Today | Music | Young America Speaks |
| *9:15* | Mirandy | | | By Request |
| *9:30* | The American Farmer | Stars Over Hollywood | Flight of the Past | Meet the Author |
| *9:45* | | | | The Kitchen |
| *10am* | Music | Grand Central Station | Glenn Hardy, news | The National Farm and Home Hour |
| *10:15* | | | Songs of Good Cheer | |
| *10:30* | The Bible | County Fair | The Clinic Forum | The Veterans Advisor |
| *10:45* | Tell Me Doctor | | | The Christian Science Monitor |
| *11am* | Our Town Speaks | Mary Lee Taylor, cooking | On the Swing Side | Teen Timers |
| *11:15* | | | | |
| *11:30* | American Radio | Give and Take | This is Jazz | The Baxters |
| *11:45* | Public Affairs | | | The Camp Meetin' Choir |
| *12pm* | News | Fred Robbins' Record Shop | Broadway News | The Farm Reporter |
| *12:15* | Speaking of Songs | | The Kenny Baker Show | The Man on the Farm |
| *12:30* | Sunset Roundup | Cross-Section USA | Louise Massey, songs | |
| *12:45* | | | Music | Easy Listening |
| *1pm* | Horse Racing | Meet the Missus | Horse Racing | Doctors, Then and Now |
| *1:15* | Music | | The Veteran's Voice | |
| *1:30* | The Treasury Band Show | Adventures in Science | The Board of Education | Horse Racing |
| *1:45* | | Of Men and Books | Policing L.A. | |

## DAYTIME — SPRING, 1947

*Saturday*

| | ABC | CBS | MBS | NBC |
|---|---|---|---|---|
| *2pm* | The Saturday Concert | Philadelphia Symphony Orchestra | For Your Approval | News |
| *2:15* | | | | Proudly We Hail |
| *2:30* | | | Open House | Horse Racing |
| *2:45* | | | | The King Cole Trio |
| *3pm* | Junior Junction | The D. Gayle Show | Bands and Bonds | Home is What You Make It |
| *3:15* | | The Los Angeles Story | | |
| *3:30* | The Teenage Advisor | | Jackie Hill, talk | On the Scouting Trail |
| *3:45* | Labor USA | The World Today | | |
| *4pm* | The Year in Business | The Garden Gate | Hawaii Calls | Our Foreign Policy |
| *4:15* | Highland Swing | Music | | |
| *4:30* | The Music Library | Battle of the B's | Repeats of Motion | Curtain Time |
| *4:45* | | | Ken Barton, comment | |

# EVENING — SUMMER, 1947

*Sunday*

| | ABC | CBS | MBS | NBC |
|---|---|---|---|---|
| *5pm* | Detroit Symphony Orchestra | A Man Named Jordan | Under Arrest | The Manhattan Merry-Go-Round |
| *5:15* | | | | |
| *5:30* | | The Texaco Star Theater, Tony Martin | Nick Carter, Master Detective | The American Album of Familiar Music |
| *5:45* | | Ned Calmer, news (5:55PM) | | |
| *6pm* | Views of the News | Take It or Leave It | Exploring the Unknown | Tonight's Story |
| *6:15* | Louella Parsons, gossip | | | |
| *6:30* | Jimmy Fidler, gossip | The Hope Chest | Listen and Care | The Big Break |
| *6:45* | Prelude to Strings | | | |
| *7pm* | The Hour of Music | Crime Doctor | Mystery is My Hobby | Author Meets the Critics |
| *7:15* | | | | |
| *7:30* | | Blondie | Leave It to the Girls | The Standard Symphony Hour |
| *7:45* | | | | |
| *8pm* | Drew Pearson, news | Meet Corliss Archer | Twenty Questions | |
| *8:15* | Don Gardiner, news | | | |
| *8:30* | The Green Hornet | The Couple Next Door | Walter Winchell's Jergens Journal | The Jack Paar Show |
| *8:45* | | | Sheila Graham, gossip | |
| *9pm* | Pat Novak for Hire | The Adventures of Sam Spade | Glenn Hardy, news | Music |
| *9:15* | | | Rex Miller, news | |
| *9:30* | Eastside Serenade | Romance of the Ranchos | The Chicago Theater of the Air | Rogue's Gallery |
| *9:45* | | | | |
| *10pm* | Freddy Martin Orchestra | The Ten o'Clock Wire | | The Richfield Reporter |
| *10:15* | | Meet the Author | | |
| *10:30* | | America Speaks | Quiet, Please | Inside the News |
| *10:45* | | Guest Star | | Melody Time |

## EVENING — SUMMER, 1947

*Monday*

| ABC | CBS | MBS | NBC | |
|---|---|---|---|---|
| Terry and the Pirates | Front Page Feature | Hop Harrigan | Feature Wire | *5pm* |
| Sky King | Tom Hanlon, news | The Melody Theater | News | *5:15* |
| Headline Edition | Harry W. Flannery, news | Adventure Parade | Dr. I. Q., the Mental Banker | *5:30* |
| News | Henry Garred, news | Tom Mix and His Ralston Straightshooters | | *5:45* |
| Those Sensational Years | My Friend Irma | Gabriel Heatter, news | The Carnation Contented Hour | *6pm* |
| | | Real Stories from Real Life | | *6:15* |
| So You Want to Lead a Band | The Bob Hawk Show | Guy Lombardo Orchestra | The First Piano Quartet | *6:30* |
| | | | | *6:45* |
| The Lone Ranger | Lowell Thomas, news | California Melodies | The Chesterfield Supper Club | *7pm* |
| | The Robert Q. Lewis Show | | Fleetwood Lawton, news | *7:15* |
| Treasury Agent | Arthur Godfrey Talent Scouts | The Cisco Kid | Music | *7:30* |
| | | | | *7:45* |
| Lum and Abner | Inner Sanctum Mysteries | Richard Davis | The Bell Telephone Hour | *8pm* |
| News | | | | *8:15* |
| The Clock | Club Fifteen | Scotland Yard's Inspector Burke | The Voice of Firestone | *8:30* |
| | Robert Trout, news | | | *8:45* |
| The Doctors Talk It Over | You Are There | Glenn Hardy, news | Plays By Ear | *9pm* |
| Report to the People | | The Johnson Family | | *9:15* |
| Music | Escape | The Inside of Sports | The Big Story | *9:30* |
| | | Henry J. Taylor, news | | *9:45* |
| Sports | The Ten o'Clock Wire | Fulton Lewis Jr., news | The Richfield Reporter | *10pm* |
| News | Bob Elson Interviews | News | The Barry Wood Show | *10:15* |
| Elmer Davis, news | The Symphonette | The Peter Potter Show | Inside the News | *10:30* |
| Rainbow Rendezvous | | | Melody Time | *10:45* |

## EVENING — SUMMER, 1947

*Tuesday*

| | ABC | CBS | MBS | NBC |
|---|---|---|---|---|
| *5pm* | Terry and the Pirates | Front Page Feature | Hop Harrigan | Feature Wire |
| *5:15* | Sky King | Tom Hanlon, news | The Melody Theater | News |
| *5:30* | Headline Edition | Harry W. Flannery, news | Adventure Parade | A Date with Judy |
| *5:45* | News | Henry Garred, news | Tom Mix and His Ralston Straightshooters | |
| *6pm* | The Vagabonds Quartet | The Women's Forum | Gabriel Heatter, news | The Pleasure Parade |
| *6:15* | Music Preferred | | Real Stories from Real Life | Madison 2345, Times Information |
| *6:30* | The Berkshire Festival | Melodies | Justice | An Evening with Romberg |
| *6:45* | | | | |
| *7pm* | | Lowell Thomas, news | The Crime Cases of Warden Lawes | The Chesterfield Supper Club |
| *7:15* | | The Robert Q. Lewis Show | Pan America | Fleetwood Lawton, news |
| *7:30* | Toby Reed's Hollywood Scrapbook | Mr. and Mrs. North | Red Ryder | At Home With the Berles |
| *7:45* | Alvin Wilder, news | | | |
| *8pm* | Lum and Abner | Big Town | The Count of Monte Cristo | The Hollywood Theater |
| *8:15* | News | | | |
| *8:30* | Dark Venture | Club Fifteen | The Falcon | Fred Waring Orchestra |
| *8:45* | | Robert Trout, news | | |
| *9pm* | Retribution | Larabee | Glenn Hardy, news | The Adventures of Philip Marlowe |
| *9:15* | | | The Johnson Family | |
| *9:30* | Warriors of Peace | Tapestries of Life | The Inside of Sports | Call the Police |
| *9:45* | | | The Wizard of Odds | |
| *10pm* | Sports | The Ten o'Clock Wire | Fulton Lewis Jr., news | The Richfield Reporter |
| *10:15* | News | Bob Elson Interviews | News | Music |
| *10:30* | Elmer Davis, news | Open Hearing | The Peter Potter Show | Inside the News |
| *10:45* | Freddy Martin Orchestra | | | Melody Time |

# EVENING — SUMMER, 1947

*Wednesday*

| ABC | CBS | MBS | NBC | |
|---|---|---|---|---|
| Terry and the Pirates | Front Page Feature | Hop Harrigan | Feature Wire | *5pm* |
| Sky King | Tom Hanlon, news | The Melody Theater | News | *5:15* |
| Headline Edition | Harry W. Flannery, news | Adventure Parade | Casa Cugat | *5:30* |
| News | Henry Garred, news | Tom Mix and His Ralston Straightshooters | Elmer Patterson, news | *5:45* |
| The Beulah Show | Rhapsody in Rhythm | Gabriel Heatter, news | The American Way | *6pm* |
| | | Real Stories from Real Life | | *6:15* |
| The Eddy Albert Show | Dr. Sterling, health | The American Forum of the Air | The Summer Theater | *6:30* |
| | The Hobby Hour | | | *6:45* |
| The Lone Ranger | Lowell Thomas, news | | The Chesterfield Supper Club | *7pm* |
| | The Robert Q. Lewis Show | Scout About Town | Fleetwood Lawton, news | *7:15* |
| Music Preferred | Dr. Christian | The Cisco Kid | Summerfield Bandstand | *7:30* |
| Marilyn King, songs | | | | *7:45* |
| Lum and Abner | The Whistler | What's the Name of That Song | News | *8pm* |
| News | | | I Want It | *8:15* |
| Paul Whiteman Orchestra | Club Fifteen | Johnny Madero, Pier 23 | The Skippy Hollywood Theater | *8:30* |
| | Robert Trout, news | | | *8:45* |
| The Phil Silvers Show | The Saint | Glenn Hardy, news | Hi Jinx | *9pm* |
| | | The Johnson Family | | *9:15* |
| Lights Out | The Marie Wilson Show | The Inside of Sports | Mr. District Attorney | *9:30* |
| | | Land O' the Free | | *9:45* |
| Sports | The Ten o'Clock Wire | Fulton Lewis Jr., news | The Richfield Reporter | *10pm* |
| News | Bob Elson Interviews | News | The Barry Wood Show | *10:15* |
| Elmer Davis, news | The Symphonette | The Peter Potter Show | Inside the News | *10:30* |
| Freddy Martin Orchestra | | | Melody Time | *10:45* |

# EVENING — SUMMER, 1947

*Thursday*

| | ABC | CBS | MBS | NBC |
|---|---|---|---|---|
| *5pm* | Terry and the Pirates | Front Page Feature | Hop Harrigan | Feature Wire |
| *5:15* | Sky King | Tom Hanlon, news | The Melody Theater | News |
| *5:30* | Headline Edition | Harry W. Flannery, news | Adventure Parade | Casa Cugat |
| *5:45* | News | Henry Garred, news | Tom Mix and His Ralston Straightshooters | Elmer Patterson, news |
| *6pm* | Public Affairs | The Radio Reader's Digest | Gabriel Heatter, news | The Wax Museum |
| *6:15* | | | Real Stories from Real Life | |
| *6:30* | Real Story | The Man Called X | Mutual's Block Party | Musical Americana |
| *6:45* | American Tradition | | | |
| *7pm* | Tales of Willie Piper | Lowell Thomas, news | The Family Theater | The Chesterfield Supper Club |
| *7:15* | | The Robert Q. Lewis Show | | Fleetwood Lawton, news |
| *7:30* | Toby Reed's Hollywood Scrapbook | The Masquerade Club | Red Ryder | Music |
| *7:45* | News | | | |
| *8pm* | Lum and Abner | Suspense | The Mysterious Traveler | The Francis Langford Show |
| *8:15* | News | | | |
| *8:30* | America's Town Meeting of the Air | Club Fifteen | The Voyage of the Scarlet Queen | Noah Webster Says |
| *8:45* | | Robert Trout, news | | |
| *9pm* | | Lawyer Tucker | Glenn Hardy, news | The Kraft Music Hall, Nelson Eddy |
| *9:15* | | | The Johnson Family | |
| *9:30* | Mr. President | Casey, Crime Photographer | The Inside of Sports | Grand Marquee |
| *9:45* | | | The Wizard of Odds | |
| *10pm* | Sports | The Ten o'Clock Wire | Fulton Lewis Jr., news | The Richfield Reporter |
| *10:15* | News | Bob Elson Interviews | News | Mayor Bowron, comment |
| *10:30* | Elmer Davis, news | Doorway | The Peter Potter Show | Inside the News |
| *10:45* | Freddy Martin Orchestra | | | Melody Time |

| EVENING — SUMMER, 1947 | | | | |
|---|---|---|---|---|
| *Friday* | | | | |
| ABC | CBS | MBS | NBC | |
| Terry and the Pirates | Front Page Feature | Hop Harrigan | Feature Wire | *5pm* |
| Sky King | Tom Hanlon, news | The Melody Theater | News | *5:15* |
| Headline Edition | Harry W. Flannery, news | Adventure Parade | Casa Cugat | *5:30* |
| News | Henry Garred, news | Tom Mix and His Ralston Straightshooters | Elmer Patterson, news | *5:45* |
| The Music Library | It Pays To Be Ignorant | Gabriel Heatter, news | Paul Owen, songs | *6pm* |
| | | Real Stories from Real Life | Tonight Tunes | *6:15* |
| The Sheriff | Eileen Farrell, songs | Shadows | The Colgate Sports Newsreel, Bill Stern | *6:30* |
| | | | Cabbages and Kings | *6:45* |
| Madison Square Garden Boxing | Lowell Thomas, news | Meet the Press | The Chesterfield Supper Club | *7pm* |
| | The Robert Q. Lewis Show | | Fleetwood Lawton, news | *7:15* |
| | Free for All | The Cisco Kid | American Novels | *7:30* |
| | | | | *7:45* |
| Lightnin' Jim | Fiesta | Let George Do It | The King's Men | *8pm* |
| | | | Latin Serenade | *8:15* |
| This is Your FBI | Club Fifteen | The Burl Ives Show | The Hank McCune Show | *8:30* |
| | Robert Trout, news | Memorable Moments | | *8:45* |
| Break the Bank | Arthur's Place | Glenn Hardy, news | Waltz Time | *9pm* |
| | | The Johnson Family | | *9:15* |
| Famous Jury Trials | Arthur Godfrey Talent Scouts | The Inside of Sports | The Molle' Mystery Theater | *9:30* |
| | | Henry J. Taylor, news | | *9:45* |
| Sports | The Ten o'Clock Wire | Fulton Lewis Jr., news | The Richfield Reporter | *10pm* |
| News | Bob Elson Interviews | News | The Barry Wood Show | *10:15* |
| Elmer Davis, news | The Symphonette | The Peter Potter Show | Inside the News | *10:30* |
| Freddy Martin Orchestra | | | Melody Time | *10:45* |

## EVENING — SUMMER, 1947

*Saturday*

| | ABC | CBS | MBS | NBC |
|---|---|---|---|---|
| *5pm* | Music Miracle | Something Done | News | Sports |
| *5:15* | | Sports | The Christian Science Monitor | News |
| *5:30* | Highland Swing | Harry W. Flannery, news | Public Affairs | Riddles and Rhythm |
| *5:45* | News | Henry Garred, news | Piano Magic | Elmer Patterson, news |
| *6pm* | Youth Meets the Government | Saturday Night Serenade | The Mighty Casey | Saturday Songs |
| *6:15* | | | | |
| *6:30* | Hayloft Hoedown | The Bill Goodwin Show | Family Doctor | Grand Ole Opry |
| *6:45* | | | | |
| *7pm* | The Avenger | Hawk Larabee | The Quiz of Two Cities | The KFI Tavern |
| *7:15* | | | | |
| *7:30* | I Deal in Crime | Sweeney and March | Red Ryder | The Bates Brothers |
| *7:45* | | | | |
| *8pm* | The Lone Ranger | The Robert Q. Lewis Show | Latin Serenade | Your Hit Parade |
| *8:15* | | | | |
| *8:30* | The Fat Man | The Camel Caravan, Vaughn Monroe | Hawaii Calls | Can You Top This |
| *8:45* | | | Ted Irwin, sports | |
| *9pm* | The Adventures of Bill Lance | Winner Take Alll | News | Mystery Without Murder |
| *9:15* | | | Holly House | |
| *9:30* | Murder and Mr. Malone | The Hollywood Barn Dance | The Fishing and Hunting Club | Conquest |
| *9:45* | | | | |
| *10pm* | Music | The Ten o'Clock Wire | The Marty Drake Show | News |
| *10:15* | | Music | Music | Music |
| *10:30* | Freddy Martin Orchestra | | The Peter Potter Show | The Sealtest Village Store, Arden and Haley |
| *10:45* | | | | |

## DAYTIME — SUMMER, 1947

*Sunday*

| | ABC | CBS | MBS | NBC |
|---|---|---|---|---|
| *8am* | Message of Israel | Invitation to Learning | News | The L. A. Times Funnies |
| *8:15* | | | Music | |
| *8:30* | The Hour of Faith | As Others See It | The Voice of Prophecy | The Eternal Light |
| *8:45* | | | | |
| *9am* | It Happened During the Week | The People's Platform | The Pilgrim Hour | For the Family |
| *9:15* | Washington Inside and Out | | | |
| *9:30* | Sunday Strings | News | The Lutheran Hour | Sports |
| *9:45* | | Howard K. Smith, news | | The Home Town Parade |
| *10am* | The American Way | The Weekly News Review | Glenn Hardy, news | The RCA Victor Show |
| *10:15* | | | Commander Scott | |
| *10:30* | Sammy Kaye's Sunday Serenade | Here's to You | The Music Show | Harvest of Stars |
| *10:45* | | | | |
| *11am* | Music Miracles | New York Philharmonic Orchestra | The Band Concert | The Sheaffer Parade |
| *11:15* | | | | |
| *11:30* | National Vespers | | News | One Man's Family |
| *11:45* | | | The Canary Pet Shop | |
| *12pm* | Lassie | | Broadway News | The Quiz Kids |
| *12:15* | Johnny Thompson, songs | | Bobby Norris, songs | |
| *12:30* | Are These Our Children | The Electric Summer Hour | The Crime Club | News |
| *12:45* | | | | Time Out for Music |
| *1pm* | Wayne King Orchestra | The Prudential Family Hour | The House of Mystery | NBC Symphony Orchestra |
| *1:15* | | | | |
| *1:30* | California Caravan | The Jean Sablon Show | True Detective Mysteries | |
| *1:45* | | Chet Huntley, news | | |

## DAYTIME — SUMMER, 1947

*Monday-Friday*

| ABC | CBS | MBS | NBC | |
|---|---|---|---|---|
| The Breakfast Club | The Johnny Murray Show | Cecil Brown, news | Fred Waring Orchestra | *8am* |
| | Aunt Jenny's True Life Stories | News | | *8:15* |
| | The Romance of Helen Trent | The Editor's Diary | The Jack Berch Show | *8:30* |
| | Our Gal Sunday | Merv Griffin, songs | Lora Lawton | *8:45* |
| Welcome Travelers | Big Sister | Kate Smith Speaks | Edward Jorgenson, news | *9am* |
| | Ma Perkins | Victor Lindlahr, health | Ladies' Day | *9:15* |
| Breakfast at Sardi's | Young Dr. Malone | The Bill Gwinn Show | | *9:30* |
| | The Guiding Light | | What You Say | *9:45* |
| Galen Drake, talk | Wendy Warren and the News | Glenn Hardy, news | Today's Children | *10am* |
| Between the Bookends | Perry Mason | Hospitality | The Women in White | *10:15* |
| My True Story | Lone Journey | The Ben Alexander Show | Masquerade | *10:30* |
| | Rose of My Dreams | | The Light of the World | *10:45* |
| Hymns of All Churches | Double or Nothing | Bobby Norris, songs | Life Can Be Beautiful | *11am* |
| H. R. Baukhage, news | | Erskine Johnson, gossip | Ma Perkins | *11:15* |
| Club Time / Listening Post | The Second Mrs. Burton | Queen for a Day | Pepper Young's Family | *11:30* |
| The Frank Parker Show | Grand Slam | | The Right to Happiness | *11:45* |
| News | Rosemary | Broadway News | The Farm Reporter | *12pm* |
| Walter Kiernan, news | Knox Manning, news | Sing America, Sing | Stella Dallas | *12:15* |
| Paul Whiteman's Record Club | The Strange Romance of Evelyn Winters | Louise Masser, news | Lorenzo Jones | *12:30* |
| | The Story of Myrt ahd Marge | Singin' Sam | Young Widder Brown | *12:45* |
| | House Party | The Sons of the Pioneers | When a Girl Marries | *1pm* |
| | | Nancy Young, talk | Portia Faces Life | *1:15* |
| Music | Meet the Missus | Norma Dixon, talk | Just Plain Bill | *1:30* |
| Ethel and Albert | | | Front Page Farrell | *1:45* |

## DAYTIME — SUMMER, 1947

*Sunday*

| | ABC | CBS | MBS | NBC |
|---|---|---|---|---|
| *2pm* | Darts for Dough | The Silver Theater | Those Websters | The Catholic Hour |
| *2:15* | | | | |
| *2:30* | Counterspy | Sound Off | The Abbott Mysteries | News |
| *2:45* | | | | The Melody Parade |
| *3pm* | Deadline Mystery | Gene Autry's Melody Ranch | High Adventure | The Jack Paar Show |
| *3:15* | | | | |
| *3:30* | The Greatest Story Ever Told | Jack of All Trades | The Harlem Hospitality Club | Easy Listening |
| *3:45* | | | | |
| *4pm* | The Candid Microphone | The Private Practice of Dr. Dana | Reunion | AlexTempleton Time |
| *4:15* | | | | |
| *4:30* | The Hollywood Music Hall | The City | The Northwestern Reviewing Stand | Front and Center, Dorothy Lamour |
| *4:45* | | | | |

## DAYTIME — SUMMER, 1947

*Monday-Friday*

| ABC | CBS | MBS | NBC | |
|---|---|---|---|---|
| What's Doing Ladies | Eric Sevareid, news | Heart's Desire | The Road of Life | *2pm* |
| | In My Opinion | | Joyce Jordan, MD | *2:15* |
| Bride and Groom | Talk | Melody Matinee | Aunt Mary | *2:30* |
| | Mr. Information | | Dr. Paul | *2:45* |
| Ladies Be Seated | The Housewives' Protective League | Philip Keyne Gordon, news | One Woman's Secret | *3pm* |
| | | The Johnson Family | News of the World | *3:15* |
| Norwood Smith Sings | Arthur Godfrey Time | Gas Again | Mary Noble, Backstage Wife | *3:30* |
| The Frances Scully Show | | The Quaker City Serenade | Bob and Victoria, songs | *3:45* |
| | Talk and Music / The American Melody Hour | Fulton Lewis Jr., news | Downtown | *4pm* |
| Alvin Wilder, news | | News | Missing Hits | *4:15* |
| Variety Parade | Your Only Young Once | Two-Ton Baker | Art Baker's Notebook | *4:30* |
| | The Todds | Sports | | *4:45* |

| DAYTIME — SUMMER, 1947 | | | | |
|---|---|---|---|---|
| *Saturday* | | | | |
| | ABC | CBS | MBS | NBC |
| *8am* | Al Pearce and His Gang | The Armstrong Theater of Today | Music | Jump-Jump and the Ice Queen |
| *8:15* | | | | Music |
| *8:30* | | Stars Over Hollywood | Play Ball | Smilin' Ed's Buster Brown Gang |
| *8:45* | | | Ted Irwin, sports | |
| *9am* | Texas Jim Robertson, songs | Grand Central Station | Sideshow | Nature Sketches |
| *9:15* | Mirandy | | | The Saturday Chef |
| *9:30* | Wake Up and Smile | County Fair | Veteran Information | The Veterans Advisor |
| *9:45* | Ladies' Day | | Policing L.A. | The Kitchen |
| *10am* | The American Farmer | Give and Take | Glenn Hardy, news | The National Farm and Home Hour |
| *10:15* | | | Two-Ton Baker | |
| *10:30* | The Lincoln Papers | The Adventurer's Club | The Clinic Forum | The Baxters |
| *10:45* | | | | Christian Science Monitor |
| *11am* | Our Town Speaks | Mary Lee Taylor, cooking | This is Jazz | Archie Andrews |
| *11:15* | | | | |
| *11:30* | Roundup Time | Let's Pretend | Sports Roundup | There's Music |
| *11:45* | | | | |
| *12pm* | News | Horse Racing | Broadway News | The Farm Reporter |
| *12:15* | The American Way | Music | The Shady Valley Folks | The Man on the Farm |
| *12:30* | The Treasury Band Show | Columbia's Country Journal | Louise Massey, songs | |
| *12:45* | | | The Veteran's Voice | Easy Listening |
| *1pm* | Sunset Roundup | Cross-Section USA | Sports | News |
| *1:15* | | | | Music |
| *1:30* | Stars in the Afternoon | The Los Angeles Story | | The Three Suns |
| *1:45* | For You | Inventory | | |

## DAYTIME — SUMMER, 1947

*Saturday*

| | ABC | CBS | MBS | NBC |
|---|---|---|---|---|
| *2pm* | The Saturday Concert | The D. Gayle Show | | Edward Tomlinson, news |
| *2:15* | | | | Meet Your Navy |
| *2:30* | | Sports | | Home is What You Make It |
| *2:45* | | The World Today | | |
| *3pm* | Junior Junction | St. Louis Municipal Opera | | Our Foreign Policy |
| *3:15* | | | | |
| *3:30* | Music | Talk | | Curtain Time |
| *3:45* | Labor, USA | Juan Rolando, organ | | |
| *4pm* | The Summer Show | News | | For You |
| *4:15* | Harry Wismer, news | Call Tokyo | | Proudly We Hail |
| *4:30* | Challenge of the Yukon | Oklahoma Roundup | | The Platter Prom |
| *4:45* | | | | The Tea Party |

## EVENING — FALL, 1947

*Sunday*

| | ABC | CBS | MBS | NBC |
|---|---|---|---|---|
| *5pm* | Detroit Symphony Orchestra | The Private Practice of Dr. Dana | A. L. Alexander's Mediation Board | The Charlie McCarthy Show |
| *5:15* | | | | |
| *5:30* | | Jack of All Trades | Jimmy Fidler, gossip | The Fred Allen Show |
| *5:45* | | | The Lamplighter | |
| *6pm* | Walter Winchell's Jergens Journal | Romance of the Ranchos | Meet Me at Parky's | The Manhattan Merry-Go-Round |
| *6:15* | Louella Parsons, gossip | | | |
| *6:30* | The Theater Guild of the Air | The Texaco Star Theater, Tony Martin | The Jim Backus Show | The American Album of Familiar Music |
| *6:45* | | | | |
| *7pm* | | The Adventures of Christopher Wells | A Brighter Tomorrow | Take It or Leave It |
| *7:15* | | | | |
| *7:30* | Jimmy Fidler, gossip | The Hope Chest | The Quiz of Two Cities | The Big Break |
| *7:45* | Don't You Believe It | | | |
| *8pm* | Drew Pearson, news | Crime Doctor | Twenty Questions | Hollywood Star Favorite |
| *8:15* | Don Gardiner, news | News (8:25PM) | | |
| *8:30* | The Green Hornet | Surprise Theater | Walter Winchell's Jergens Journal | The Standard Symphony Hour |
| *8:45* | | | Sheila Graham, gossip | |
| *9pm* | Pat Novak for Hire | The Adventures of Sam Spade | Glenn Hardy, news | |
| *9:15* | | | The Veteran's Voice | |
| *9:30* | Eastside Serenade | Meet Corliss Archer | The Patsy Kelly - Barry Wood Show | The Lucky Strike Program, Jack Benny |
| *9:45* | | | | |
| *10pm* | Freddy Martin Orchestra | The Ten o'Clock Wire | | The Richfield Reporter |
| *10:15* | | Sports | | The Chapel Quartet |
| *10:30* | | Time for Reason | The Edmund Hockeridge Show | Inside the News |
| *10:45* | | | | Melody Time |

# EVENING — FALL, 1947

*Monday*

| ABC | CBS | MBS | NBC | |
|---|---|---|---|---|
| Dick Tracy | Front Page Feature | News | Feature Wire | *5pm* |
| Terry and the Pirates | Tom Hanlon, news | The Adventures of Superman | News | *5:15* |
| Sky King | Harry W. Flannery, news | Captain Midnight | The Voice of Firestone | *5:30* |
| | Henry Garred, news | Tom Mix and His Ralston Straightshooters | | *5:45* |
| Headline Edition | The Lux Radio Theater | Gabriel Heatter, news | The American Way | *6pm* |
| News | | Merv Griffin, songs | | *6:15* |
| On Stage America | | Did Justice Triumph | Dr. I. Q., the Mental Banker | *6:30* |
| | | | | *6:45* |
| The Lone Ranger | My Friend Irma | Callifornia Melodies | The Carnation Contented Hour | *7pm* |
| | | | | *7:15* |
| So You Want to Lead a Band | The Lady Esther Screen Guild Theater | The Cisco Kid | Fred Waring Orchestra | *7:30* |
| | | | | *7:45* |
| Point Sublime | Lowell Thomas, news | Richard Davis | The Chesterfield Supper Club | *8pm* |
| | The Jack Smith Show | | Fleetwood Lawton, news | *8:15* |
| The Opie Cates Show | Arthur Godfrey's Talent Scouts | Charlie Chan | The Cavalcade of America | *8:30* |
| | Carroll Alcott, news (8:55PM) | | | *8:45* |
| You Bet Your Life | Inner Sanctum Mysteries | Glenn Hardy, news | The Bell Telephone Hour | *9pm* |
| | | Mystery of the Week | | *9:15* |
| The Candid Microphone | Club Fifteen | The Inside of Sports | The Big Story | *9:30* |
| | Edward R. Murrow, news | Henry J. Taylor, news | | *9:45* |
| Sports | The Ten o'Clock Wire | Fulton Lewis Jr., news | The Richfield Reporter | *10pm* |
| News | Bob Elson Interviews | News | The Barry Wood Show | *10:15* |
| Elmer Davis, news | The Symphonette | The Peter Potter Show | Inside the News | *10:30* |
| Rainbow Rendezvous | | | Melody Time | *10:45* |

| EVENING — FALL, 1947 | | | | |
|---|---|---|---|---|
| *Tuesday* | | | | |
| | ABC | CBS | MBS | NBC |
| *5pm* | Dick Tracy | Front Page Feature | News | Feature Wire |
| *5:15* | Terry and the Pirates | Tom Hanlon, news | The Adventures of Superman | News |
| *5:30* | Jack Armstrong, the All-American Boy | Harry W. Flannery, news | Captain Midnight | A Date with Judy |
| *5:45* | | Henry Garred, news | Tom Mix and His Ralston Straightshooters | |
| *6pm* | Headline Edition | The Women's Forum | Gabriel Heatter, news | Amos 'n' Andy |
| *6:15* | News | | Johnny Desmond, songs | |
| *6:30* | Boston Symphony Orchestra | Studio One | The Zane Grey Theater | Fibber McGee and Molly |
| *6:45* | | | | |
| *7pm* | | | Scotland Yard's Inspector Burke | The Pepsodent Show, Bob Hope |
| *7:15* | | | | |
| *7:30* | Report to the People | Melodies America Loves | Red Ryder | The Raleigh Cigarette Program, Red Skelton |
| *7:45* | Alvin Wilder, news | | | |
| *8pm* | Youth Asks The Government | Lowell Thomas, news | The Count of Monte Cristo | The Chesterfield Supper Club |
| *8:15* | News | The Jack Smith Show | | Fleetwood Lawton, news |
| *8:30* | World Security Workshop | Mr. and Mrs. North | Official Detective | At Home With The Berles |
| *8:45* | | Carroll Alcott, news (8:55PM) | | |
| *9pm* | America's Town Meeting of the Air | Big Town | Glenn Hardy, news | Favorite Story |
| *9:15* | | | Mystery of the Week | |
| *9:30* | | Club Fifteen | The Inside of Sports | The Pleasure Parade |
| *9:45* | | Edward R. Murrow, news | The Wizard of Odds | Madison 2345, Times Information |
| *10pm* | Sports | The Ten o'Clock Wire | Fulton Lewis Jr., news | The Richfield Reporter |
| *10:15* | News | Bob Elson Interviews | News | Music |
| *10:30* | Elmer Davis, news | Sweeney and March | The Peter Potter Show | Inside the News |
| *10:45* | Freddy Martin Orchestra | | | Melody Time |

## EVENING — FALL, 1947

*Wednesday*

| ABC | CBS | MBS | NBC | |
|---|---|---|---|---|
| Dick Tracy | Front Page Feature | News | Feature Wire | *5pm* |
| Terry and the Pirates | Tom Hanlon, news | The Adventures of Superman | News | *5:15* |
| Sky King | Harry W. Flannery, news | Captain Midnight | Casa Cugat | *5:30* |
| | Henry Garred, news | Tom Mix and His Ralston Straightshooters | Elmer Patterson, news | *5:45* |
| Headline Edition | The Frank Morgan Show | Gabriel Heatter, news | Duffy's Tavern | *6pm* |
| News | | Merv Griffin, songs | | *6:15* |
| Vox Pop | Sports | The American Forum of the Air | The Skippy Hollywood Theater | *6:30* |
| | The Hobby Hour | | | *6:45* |
| The Lone Ranger | The Saint | Mel Ventner, news | Conquest | *7pm* |
| | | Sports | | *7:15* |
| The Mayor of the Town | The Whistler | The Cisco Kid | The Jimmy Durante Show | *7:30* |
| | | | | *7:45* |
| Abbott and Costello | Lowell Thomas, news | What's the Name of That Song | The Chesterfield Supper Club | *8pm* |
| | The Jack Smith Show | | Fleetwood Lawton, news | *8:15* |
| The Jack Paar Show | Dr. Christian | Quiet, Please | The Great Gildersleeve | *8:30* |
| | Carroll Alcott, news (8:55PM) | | | *8:45* |
| Philco Radio Time, Bing Crosby | The Melody Hour | Glenn Hardy, news | A Day in the Life of Dennis Day | *9pm* |
| | | Mystery of the Week | | *9:15* |
| The Henry Morgan Show | Club Fifteen | The Inside of Sports | Mr. District Attorney | *9:30* |
| | Edward R. Murrow, news | Land O' the Free | | *9:45* |
| Sports | The Ten o'Clock Wire | Fulton Lewis Jr., news | The Richfield Reporter | *10pm* |
| News | Bob Elson Interviews | News | The Barry Wood Show | *10:15* |
| Elmer Davis, news | The Symphonette | The Peter Potter Show | Inside the News | *10:30* |
| Freddy Martin Orchestra | | | Melody Time | *10:45* |

# EVENING — FALL, 1947

*Thursday*

| | ABC | CBS | MBS | NBC |
|---|---|---|---|---|
| *5pm* | Dick Tracy | Front Page Feature | News | Feature Wire |
| *5:15* | Terry and the Pirates | Tom Hanlon, news | The Adventures of Superman | News |
| *5:30* | Jack Armstrong, the All-American Boy | Harry W. Flannery, news | Captain Midnight | Casa Cugat |
| *5:45* | | Henry Garred, news | Tom Mix and His Ralston Straightshooters | Elmer Patterson, news |
| *6pm* | Headline Edition | The Dick Haymes Show | Gabriel Heatter, news | The Kraft Music Hall, Al Jolson |
| *6:15* | News | | Johnny Desmond, songs | |
| *6:30* | Darts for Dough | Casey, Crime Photographer | Mutual's Block Party | Ted Lewis Orchestra |
| *6:45* | | | | |
| *7pm* | The Treasury Department | The Radio Reader's Digest | The Family Theater | The Bob Hawk Show |
| *7:15* | News | | | |
| *7:30* | The Clock | The Man Called X | Red Ryder | Pabst Blue Ribbon Time, Eddie Cantor |
| *7:45* | | | | |
| *8pm* | Tales of Willie Piper | Lowell Thomas, news | The Mysterious Traveler | The Chesterfield Supper Club |
| *8:15* | | The Jack Smith Show | | Fleetwood Lawton, news |
| *8:30* | Mr. President | Mr. Keen, Tracer of Lost Persons | The Voyage of the Scarlet Queen | The Aldrich Family |
| *8:45* | | Carroll Alcott, news (8:55PM) | | |
| *9pm* | Challenge of the Yukon | Suspense | Glenn Hardy, news | Maxwell House Coffee Time, Burns and Allen |
| *9:15* | | | Mystery of the Week | |
| *9:30* | Retribution | Club Fifteen | The Inside of Sports | Noah Webster Says |
| *9:45* | | Edward R. Murrow, news | The Wizard of Odds | |
| *10pm* | Sports | The Ten o'Clock Wire | Fulton Lewis Jr., news | The Richfield Reporter |
| *10:15* | News | Bob Elson Interviews | News | Mayor Bowron, comment |
| *10:30* | Elmer Davis, news | Doorway to Life | The Peter Potter Show | Inside the News |
| *10:45* | Freddy Martin Orchestra | | | Melody Time |

## EVENING — FALL, 1947

*Friday*

| ABC | CBS | MBS | NBC | |
|---|---|---|---|---|
| Dick Tracy | Front Page Feature | News | Feature Wire | *5pm* |
| Terry and the Pirates | Tom Hanlon, news | The Adventures of Superman | News | *5:15* |
| Sky King | Harry W. Flannery, news | Captain Midnight | Casa Cugat | *5:30* |
| | Henry Garred, news | Tom Mix and His Ralston Straightshooters | Elmer Patterson, news | *5:45* |
| Headline Edition | Mark Warnow Orchestra | Gabriel Heatter, news | People Are Funny | *6pm* |
| News | | Merv Griffin, songs | | *6:15* |
| The Sheriff | The FBI in Peace and War | Information, Please | Waltz Time | *6:30* |
| | | | | *6:45* |
| Madison Square Garden Boxing | It Pays to Be Ignorant | Meet the Press | The Hank McCune Show | *7pm* |
| | | | | *7:15* |
| | Spotlight Revue | The Cisco Kid | The Colgate Sports Newsreel, Bill Stern | *7:30* |
| | | | Cabbages and Kings | *7:45* |
| The Fat Man | Lowell Thomas, news | Let George Do It | The Chesterfield Supper Club | *8pm* |
| | The Jack Smith Show | | Fleetwood Lawton, news | *8:15* |
| This is Your FBI | The Adventures of the Thin Man | The Burl Ives Show | Can You Top This | *8:30* |
| | Carroll Alcott, news (8:55PM) | Remember When | | *8:45* |
| Break the Bank | The Baby Snooks Show | Glenn Hardy, news | The David Street Show | *9pm* |
| | | Mystery of the Week | The Kenny Baker Show | *9:15* |
| Famous Jury Trials | Club Fifteen | The Inside of Sports | Mystery Theater | *9:30* |
| | Edward R. Murrow, news | Henry J. Taylor, news | | *9:45* |
| Sports | The Ten o'Clock Wire | Fulton Lewis Jr., news | The Richfield Reporter | *10pm* |
| News | Bob Elson Interviews | News | The Barry Wood Show | *10:15* |
| Elmer Davis, news | The Symphonette | The Peter Potter Show | Inside the News | *10:30* |
| Freddy Martin Orchestra | | | Melody Time | *10:45* |

| EVENING — FALL, 1947 | | | | |
|---|---|---|---|---|
| *Saturday* | | | | |
| | ABC | CBS | MBS | NBC |
| *5pm* | The Piano Playhouse | The First Nighter Program | News | Sports |
| *5:15* | | | The Christian Science Monitor | News |
| *5:30* | Harry Wismer, news | Harry W. Flannery, news | Sports | I Want It |
| *5:45* | Sports | Henry Garred, news | Piano Magic | Elmer Patterson, news |
| *6pm* | U. N. Highlights | Leave It to Joan | The Melody Theater | The Bob Mitchell Show |
| *6:15* | | | | |
| *6:30* | Music | The All-Star Western Theater | Family Doctor | The Judy Canova Show |
| *6:45* | | | | |
| *7pm* | Diary of Fate | Saturday Night Serenade | The Harlem Hospitality Club | Kay Kyser's College of Musical Knowledge |
| *7:15* | | | | |
| *7:30* | I Deal in Crime | The Bill Goodwin Show | Leave It to the Girls | Grand Ole Opry |
| *7:45* | | | | |
| *8pm* | The Lone Ranger | Tapestries of Life | Have U Heard | The Life of Riley |
| *8:15* | | | | |
| *8:30* | Exploring the Unknown | Great Life | Hawaii Calls | Truth or Consequences |
| *8:45* | | Carroll Alcott, news (8:55PM) | | |
| *9pm* | Gangbusters | The Hollywood Barn Dance | Glenn Hardy, news | Your Hit Parade |
| *9:15* | | | Talk | |
| *9:30* | Murder and Mr. Malone | The Camel Caravan, Vaughn Monroe | The Fishing and Hunting Club | The Hollywood Music Hour |
| *9:45* | | | | |
| *10pm* | Dark Venture | The Ten o'Clock Wire | Music | News |
| *10:15* | | Sports | | Music |
| *10:30* | Freddy Martin Orchestra | The Abe Burrows Show | The Peter Potter Show | The Sealtest Village Store, Arden and Carson |
| *10:45* | | Dance Orchestra | | |

| DAYTIME — FALL, 1947 | | | | |
|---|---|---|---|---|
| *Sunday* | | | | |
| | ABC | CBS | MBS | NBC |
| *8am* | Message of Israel | News and Views | News | The L. A. Times Funnies |
| *8:15* | | | Policing L. A. | |
| *8:30* | The Hour of Faith | The Salt Lake Tabernacle Choir | The Voice of Prophecy | The Christian Science Monitor |
| *8:45* | | | | Outdoor Reporter |
| *9am* | It Happened During the Week | Invitation to Learning | The Pilgrim Hour | The Eternal Light |
| *9:15* | Washington Inside and Out | | | |
| *9:30* | Feature Page | As Others See It | The Lutheran Hour | Echoes and Encores |
| *9:45* | | | | |
| *10am* | Music | The People's Platform | Glenn Hardy, news | Sports |
| *10:15* | The American Way | | Commander Scott | News |
| *10:30* | Sammy Kaye's Sunday Serenade | News | Morning Melodies | The University of Chicago Round Table |
| *10:45* | | Sound Off | | |
| *11am* | Music Miracles | Meet the Author | The Band Concert | The RCA Victor Show |
| *11:15* | | The University Explorer | | |
| *11:30* | National Vespers | Bob Reid Sings | News | Harvest of Stars |
| *11:45* | | Here's to You | The Canary Pet Shop | |
| *12pm* | Lassie | New York Philharmonic Orchestra | Broadway News | The Sheaffer Parade |
| *12:15* | Samuel Pettingill, news | | Western Serenade | |
| *12:30* | This Week Around the World | | Juvenile Jury | One Man's Family |
| *12:45* | | | | |
| *1pm* | Are These Our Children | | The House of Mystery | The Quiz Kids |
| *1:15* | | | | |
| *1:30* | California Caravan | The Hour of Charm | True Detective Mysteries | News |

## DAYTIME — FALL, 1947

*Monday-Friday*

| ABC | CBS | MBS | NBC | |
|---|---|---|---|---|
| The Breakfast Club | The Johnny Murray Show | Cecil Brown, news | Fred Waring Orchestra | *8am* |
| | News | News | | *8:15* |
| | Grand Slam | The Editor's Diary | The Jack Berch Show | *8:30* |
| | Rosemary | Emily Post, manners | Lora Lawton | *8:45* |
| Welcome Travelers | Wendy Warren and the News | Kate Smith Speaks | Edward Jorgenson, news | *9am* |
| | Aunt Jenny's True Life Stories | Victor Lindlahr, health | Ladies' Day | *9:15* |
| Breakfast at Sardi's | The Romance of Helen Trent | The Johnson Familiy | | *9:30* |
| | Our Gal Sunday | Music | Bob and Victoria, songs | *9:45* |
| Galen Drake, talk | Big Sister | Glenn Hardy, news | All Around | *10am* |
| Between the Bookends | Ma Perkins | Griffin and Gwinn | What You Say | *10:15* |
| My True Story | Young Dr. Malone | The Ben Alexander Show | News | *10:30* |
| | The Guiding Light | | Joyce Jordan, MD | *10:45* |
| The Magazine of the Air | The Second Mrs. Burton | Talk and Music | Today's Children | *11am* |
| H. R. Baukhage, news | Perry Mason | Erskine Johnson, gossip | The Woman in White | *11:15* |
| Club Time / Listening Post / Doorthy Kilgallen, gossip | The Val Delmar Show | Queen for a Day | The Story of Holly Sloan | *11:30* |
| Between the Girls | Rose of My Dreams | | The Light of the World | *11:45* |
| News | Double or Nothing | Broadway News | The Farm Reporter | *12pm* |
| Walter Kiernan, news | | Sing, America Sing | Ma Perkins | *12:15* |
| Paul Whiteman's Record Club | Knox Manning, news | Louise Massey, songs | Pepper Young's Family | *12:30* |
| | News | Singin' Sam, the Barbasol Man | The Right to Happiness | *12:45* |
| | The American School of the Air | Music | Mary Noble, Backstage Wife | *1pm* |
| | | Norma Dixon, talk | Stella Dallas | *1:15* |
| Quizzicale / Music Miracles | The Barbara Wheeler Show | Nancy Young, talk | Lorenzo Jones | *1:30* |

## DAYTIME — FALL, 1947

*Sunday*

| | ABC | CBS | MBS | NBC |
|---|---|---|---|---|
| *1:45* | | | | American Favorites |
| *2pm* | The Adventures of Bill Lance | The Prudential Family Hour | The Shadow | The Ford Theater |
| *2:15* | | | | |
| *2:30* | Counterspy | The Jean Sablon Show | Quick as a Flash | |
| *2:45* | | Chet Huntley, news | | |
| *3pm* | The Patti Page Show | The Adventures of Ozzie and Harriet | Those Websters | The Catholic Hour |
| *3:15* | | | | |
| *3:30* | The Greatest Story Ever Told | The Pause That Refreshes | Nick Carter, Master Detective | News |
| *3:45* | | | | The Melody Parade |
| *4pm* | Rex Maupin Orchestra | Gene Autry's Melody Ranch | California Tales | The Lucky Strike Program, Jack Benny |
| *4:15* | | | | |
| *4:30* | The Hollywood Music Hall | Miss Sherlock | | The Phil Harris - Alice Faye Show |
| *4:45* | | | | |

## DAYTIME — FALL, 1947

*Monday-Friday*

| ABC | CBS | MBS | NBC | |
|---|---|---|---|---|
| Ethel and Albert | | | Young Widder Brown | *1:45* |
| What's Doing Ladies | Winner Take All | Heart's Desire | When a Girl Marries | *2pm* |
| | | | Portia Faces Life | *2:15* |
| Bride and Groom | House Party | The Martin Block Show | Just Plain Bill | *2:30* |
| | | | Front Page Farrell | *2:45* |
| Ladies Be Seated | Meet the Missus | Music | The Road of Life | *3pm* |
| | | | Life Can Be Beautiful | *3:15* |
| Records | Arthur Godfrey Time | Stranger | Aunt Mary | *3:30* |
| The Frances Scully Show | | Gas Again | Dr. Paul | *3:45* |
| | The Strange Romance of Evelyn Winters | Fulton Lewis Jr., news | One Woman's Secret | *4pm* |
| Alvin Wilder, news | Radio Views / George Fisher, gossip | Rex Miller, news | News of the World | *4:15* |
| Variety Parade | News | Hop Harrigan | Art Baker's Notebook | *4:30* |
| | Lum and Abner | Adventure Parade | | *4:45* |

## DAYTIME — FALL, 1947

*Saturday*

| | ABC | CBS | MBS | NBC |
|---|---|---|---|---|
| *8am* | Junior Junction | Let's Pretend | Louise Massey, songs | On the Scouting Trail |
| *8:15* | | | News | |
| *8:30* | | The Adventurer's Club | The Land of the Lost | Smilin' Ed's Buster Brown Gang |
| *8:45* | | | | |
| *9am* | Johnny Thompson, songs | The Armstrong Theater of Today | The Warblers | Jump-Jump and the Ice Queen |
| *9:15* | Mirandy | | | Young America Speaks |
| *9:30* | Tommy Bartlett Time | Stars Over Hollywood | Eskimos | The Saturday Chef |
| *9:45* | | | | The Kitchen |
| *10am* | The American Farmer | Grand Central Station | Glenn Hardy, news | The National Farm and Home Hour |
| *10:15* | | | News | |
| *10:30* | Our Town Speaks | County Fair | Sports | The Gregson Show |
| *10:45* | | | | |
| *11am* | Fascinating Rhythm | Mary Lee Taylor, cooking | | Archie Andrews |
| *11:15* | | | | |
| *11:30* | Sports | Give and Take | | Sports |
| *11:45* | | | | |
| *12pm* | | Sports | | |
| *12:15* | | | | |
| *12:30* | | | | |
| *12:45* | | | | |
| *1pm* | | | | |
| *1:15* | | | | |
| *1:30* | | | News | |
| *1:45* | | | Music | |

## DAYTIME — FALL, 1947

*Saturday*

| | ABC | CBS | MBS | NBC |
|---|---|---|---|---|
| *2pm* | | News and Views | Sports | |
| *2:15* | | | | |
| *2:30* | | Saturday at the Chase | | The Mel Torme Show |
| *2:45* | | | | The King Cole Trio |
| *3pm* | The American Way | The Los Angeles Story | | The Man on the Farm |
| *3:15* | | Dr. Abbott, health | | |
| *3:30* | About Songs | | | NBC Symphony Orchestra |
| *3:45* | Let Freedom Ring | The World Today | | |
| *4pm* | Madhouse Music | Hawk Larabee | | |
| *4:15* | Betty Russell, songs | | | |
| *4:30* | Sunset Roundup | Sports | | Curtain Time |
| *4:45* | | | | Tea Party |

# LISTINGS FOR 1948

## EVENING — WINTER, 1948

*Sunday*

| | ABC | CBS | MBS | NBC |
|---|---|---|---|---|
| *5pm* | Detroit Symphony Orchestra | Suspense (4:30PM) | A. L. Alexander's Mediation Board | The Charlie McCarthy Show |
| *5:15* | | | | |
| *5:30* | | The Private Practice of Dr. Dana | Jimmy Fidler, gossip | The Fred Allen Show |
| *5:45* | | | Newscope | |
| *6pm* | Walter Winchell's Jergens Journal | Romance of the Ranchos | Meet Me at Parky's | The Manhattan Merry-Go-Round |
| *6:15* | Louella Parsons, gossip | | | |
| *6:30* | The Theater Guild of the Air | The Gordon MacRae Show | The Jim Backus Show | The American Album of Familiar Music |
| *6:45* | | | | |
| *7pm* | | The Adventures of Christopher Wells | Behind the Front Page | Take It or Leave It |
| *7:15* | | | | |
| *7:30* | Jimmy Fidler, gossip | Strike It Rich | The Quiz of Two Cities | The Youth Opportunity Program |
| *7:45* | Don't You Believe It | | | |
| *8pm* | Drew Pearson, news | The Man Called X | Twenty Questions | Hollywood Star Favorite |
| *8:15* | Don Gardiner, news | News (8:25PM) | | |
| *8:30* | The Green Hornet | Blondie | Walter Winchell's Jergens Journal | The Standard Symphony Hour |
| *8:45* | | | Sheila Graham, gossip | |
| *9pm* | The G, Norman Show | The Adventures of Sam Spade | Glenn Hardy, news | |
| *9:15* | | | Sleepy People | |
| *9:30* | We CARE | Meet Corliss Archer | The Chicago Theater of the Air | The Lucky Strike Program, Jack Benny |
| *9:45* | | | | |
| *10pm* | Foreign Report | The Ten o'Clock Wire | | The Richfield Reporter |
| *10:15* | Freddy Martin Orchestra | Bob Graham, news | | The Chapel Quartet |
| *10:30* | | Escape | Serenade | Inside the News |
| *10:45* | | | | Melody Time |

# EVENING — WINTER, 1948

*Monday*

| ABC | CBS | MBS | NBC | |
|---|---|---|---|---|
| Happy Theater | Front Page Feature | News | Feature Wire | *5pm* |
| Terry and the Pirates | Sports | The Adventures of Superman | News | *5:15* |
| Sky King | Charles Collingwood, news | Captain Midnight | The Voice of Firestone | *5:30* |
| | Henry Garred, news | Tom Mix and His Ralston Straightshooters | | *5:45* |
| Headline Edition | The Lux Radio Theater | Gabriel Heatter, news | The American Way | *6pm* |
| News | | Merv Griffin, songs | | *6:15* |
| So You Want to Lead a Band | | High Adventure | Dr. I. Q., the Mental Banker | *6:30* |
| | | | | *6:45* |
| The Lone Ranger | My Friend Irma | The Mysterious Traveler | The Carnation Contented Hour | *7pm* |
| | | | | *7:15* |
| On Stage America | The Lady Esther Screen Guild Theater | The Cisco Kid | Fred Waring Orchestra | *7:30* |
| | | | | *7:45* |
| Point Sublime | Lowell Thomas, news | Let George Do It | The Chesterfield Supper Club | *8pm* |
| | The Jack Smith Show | | Fleetwood Lawton, news | *8:15* |
| The Opie Cates Show | Arthur Godfrey's Talent Scouts | Charlie Chan | The Cavalcade of America | *8:30* |
| | Carroll Alcott, news (8:55PM) | | | *8:45* |
| Music | Inner Sanctum Mysteries | Glenn Hardy, news | The Bell Telephone Hour | *9pm* |
| | | The Beulah Show | | *9:15* |
| News | Club Fifteen | The Inside of Sports | The Big Story | *9:30* |
| The Buddy Weed Trio | Edward R. Murrow, news | Henry J. Taylor, news | | *9:45* |
| Sports | The Ten o'Clock Wire | Fulton Lewis Jr., news | The Richfield Reporter | *10pm* |
| News | Bob Elson Interviews | Music | The Barry Wood Show | *10:15* |
| Elmer Davis, news | The Symphonette | The Peter Potter Show | Inside the News | *10:30* |
| Rainbow Rendezvous | | | Melody Time | *10:45* |

## EVENING — WINTER, 1948

*Tuesday*

| | ABC | CBS | MBS | NBC |
|---|---|---|---|---|
| *5pm* | Happy Theater | Front Page Feature | News | Feature Wire |
| *5:15* | Terry and the Pirates | Sports | The Adventures of Superman | News |
| *5:30* | Jack Armstrong, the All-American Boy | Charles Collingwood, news | Captain Midnight | A Date with Judy |
| *5:45* | | Henry Garred, news | Tom Mix and His Ralston Straightshooters | |
| *6pm* | Headline Edition | The Women's Forum | Gabriel Heatter, news | Amos 'n' Andy |
| *6:15* | News | | Merv Griffin, songs | |
| *6:30* | Boston Symphony Orchestra | Studio One | The Reviewing Stand | Fibber McGee and Molly |
| *6:45* | | | | |
| *7pm* | | | The American Forum of the Air | The Pepsodent Show, Bob Hope |
| *7:15* | | | | |
| *7:30* | Report to the People | Melodies America Loves | Red Ryder | The Raleigh Cigarette Program, Red Skelton |
| *7:45* | Alvin Wilder, news | | | |
| *8pm* | The Atwater-Kent Radio Auditions | Lowell Thomas, news | The Count of Monte Cristo | The Chesterfield Supper Club |
| *8:15* | News | The Jack Smith Show | | Fleetwood Lawton, news |
| *8:30* | World Security Workshop | Mr. and Mrs. North | Official Detective | At Home With The Berles |
| *8:45* | | Carroll Alcott, news (8:55PM) | | |
| *9pm* | America's Town Meeting of the Air | Big Town | Glenn Hardy, news | Favorite Story |
| *9:15* | | | The Beulah Show | |
| *9:30* | | Club Fifteen | The Inside of Sports | The Pleasure Parade |
| *9:45* | | Edward R. Murrow, news | Newscope | Madison 2345, Times Information |
| *10pm* | Sports | The Ten o'Clock Wire | Fulton Lewis Jr., news | The Richfield Reporter |
| *10:15* | News | Bob Elson Interviews | Songs | Music |
| *10:30* | Elmer Davis, news | Open Hearing | The Peter Potter Show | Inside the News |
| *10:45* | Freddy Martin Orchestra | | | Melody Time |

## EVENING — WINTER, 1948

*Wednesday*

| ABC | CBS | MBS | NBC | |
|---|---|---|---|---|
| Happy Theater | Front Page Feature | News | Feature Wire | *5pm* |
| Terry and the Pirates | Sports | The Adventures of Superman | News | *5:15* |
| Sky King | Charles Collingwood, news | Captain Midnight | Casa Cugat | *5:30* |
| | Henry Garred, news | Tom Mix and His Ralston Straightshooters | Elmer Patterson, news | *5:45* |
| Headline Edition | The New Border Program | Gabriel Heatter, news | Duffy's Tavern | *6pm* |
| News | | Merv Griffin, songs | | *6:15* |
| Vox Pop | Sweeney and March | The Tex Beneke Review | The Skippy Hollywood Theater | *6:30* |
| | | | | *6:45* |
| The Lone Ranger | The Saint | California Melodies | Conquest | *7pm* |
| | | | | *7:15* |
| The Mayor of the Town | The Whistler | The Cisco Kid | The Jimmy Durante Show | *7:30* |
| | | | | *7:45* |
| Abbott and Costello | Lowell Thomas, news | What's the Name of That Song | The Chesterfield Supper Club | *8pm* |
| | The Jack Smith Show | | Fleetwood Lawton, news | *8:15* |
| You Bet Your Life | Dr. Christian | Quiet, Please | The Great Gildersleeve | *8:30* |
| | Carroll Alcott, news (8:55PM) | | | *8:45* |
| Philco Radio Time, Bing Crosby | You Are There | Glenn Hardy, news | A Day in the LIfe of Dennis Day | *9pm* |
| | | The Beulah Show | | *9:15* |
| The Texaco Star Theater, Tony Martin | Club Fifteen | The Inside of Sports | Mr. District Attorney | *9:30* |
| | Edward R. Murrow, news | Land O' the Free | | *9:45* |
| Sports | The Ten o'Clock Wire | Fulton Lewis Jr., news | The Richfield Reporter | *10pm* |
| News | Bob Elson Interviews | Music | The Barry Wood Show | *10:15* |
| Elmer Davis, news | The Symphonette | The Peter Potter Show | Inside the News | *10:30* |
| Freddy Martin Orchestra | | | Melody Time | *10:45* |

## EVENING — WINTER, 1948

*Thursday*

| | ABC | CBS | MBS | NBC |
|---|---|---|---|---|
| *5pm* | Happy Theater | Front Page Feature | News | Feature Wire |
| *5:15* | Terry and the Pirates | Sports | The Adventures of Superman | News |
| *5:30* | Jack Armstrong, the All-American Boy | Charles Collingwood, news | Captain Midnight | Casa Cugat |
| *5:45* | | Henry Garred, news | Tom Mix and His Ralston Straightshooters | Elmer Patterson, news |
| *6pm* | Headline Edition | The Dick Haymes Show | Gabriel Heatter, news | The Kraft Music Hall, Al Jolson |
| *6:15* | News | | Merv Griffin, songs | |
| *6:30* | The Lee Sweetland Show | Casey, Crime Photographer | R. F. D. America | The Sealtest Village Store, Arden and Carson |
| *6:45* | | | | |
| *7pm* | The Adventures of Ellery Queen | The Radio Reader's Digest | The Family Theater | The Bob Hawk Show |
| *7:15* | | | | |
| *7:30* | The Clock | The First Nighter Program | Red Ryder | Pabst Blue Ribbon Time, Eddie Cantor |
| *7:45* | | | | |
| *8pm* | Tales of Willie Piper | Lowell Thomas, news | The Falcon | The Chesterfield Supper Club |
| *8:15* | | The Jack Smith Show | | Fleetwood Lawton, news |
| *8:30* | The Candid Microphone | Mr. Keen, Tracer of Lost Persons | The Block Party | The Aldrich Family |
| *8:45* | | Carroll Alcott, news (8:55PM) | | |
| *9pm* | Mr. President | The FBI in Peace and War | Glenn Hardy, news | Maxwell House Coffee Time, Burns and Allen |
| *9:15* | | | The Beulah Show | |
| *9:30* | News | Club Fifteen | The Inside of Sports | Noah Webster Says |
| *9:45* | The Lennie Herman Quintet | Edward R. Murrow, news | Newscope | |
| *10pm* | Sports | The Ten o'Clock Wire | Fulton Lewis Jr., news | The Richfield Reporter |
| *10:15* | News | Bob Elson Interviews | Songs | Mayor Bowron, comment |
| *10:30* | Elmer Davis, news | Doorway to Life | The Peter Potter Show | Inside the News |
| *10:45* | Freddy Martin Orchestra | | | Melody Time |

## EVENING — WINTER, 1948

*Friday*

| ABC | CBS | MBS | NBC | |
|---|---|---|---|---|
| Happy Theater | Front Page Feature | News | Feature Wire | *5pm* |
| Terry and the Pirates | Sports | The Adventures of Superman | News | *5:15* |
| Sky King | Charles Collingwood, news | Captain Midnight | Casa Cugat | *5:30* |
| | Henry Garred, news | Tom Mix and His Ralston Straightshooters | Elmer Patterson, news | *5:45* |
| Headline Edition | The Bickersons | Gabriel Heatter, news | People Are Funny | *6pm* |
| News | | Merv Griffin, songs | | *6:15* |
| The Sheriff | The Adventures of Ozzie and Harriet | Information, Please | Waltz Time | *6:30* |
| | | | | *6:45* |
| Madison Square Garden Boxing | It Pays to Be Ignorant | Meet the Press | The Hank McCune Show | *7pm* |
| | | | | *7:15* |
| | Spotlight Revue | The Cisco Kid | The Colgate Sports Newsreel, Bill Stern | *7:30* |
| | | | Cabbages and Kings | *7:45* |
| The Fat Man | Lowell Thomas, news | The Voyage of the Scarlet Queen | The Chesterfield Supper Club | *8pm* |
| | The Jack Smith Show | | Fleetwood Lawton, news | *8:15* |
| This is Your FBI | The Danny Thomas Show | The Burl Ives Show | Can You Top This | *8:30* |
| | Carroll Alcott, news (8:55PM) | Remember When | | *8:45* |
| Break the Bank | The Baby Snooks Show | Glenn Hardy, news | The David Street Show | *9pm* |
| | | The Beulah Show | Music | *9:15* |
| Famous Jury Trials | Club Fifteen | The Inside of Sports | Mystery Theater | *9:30* |
| | Edward R. Murrow, news | Henry J. Taylor, news | | *9:45* |
| Sports | The Ten o'Clock Wire | Fulton Lewis Jr., news | The Richfield Reporter | *10pm* |
| News | Bob Elson Interviews | Music | The Barry Wood Show | *10:15* |
| Elmer Davis, news | The Symphonette | The Peter Potter Show | Inside the News | *10:30* |
| Freddy Martin Orchestra | | | Melody Time | *10:45* |

## EVENING — WINTER, 1948

*Saturday*

| | ABC | CBS | MBS | NBC |
|---|---|---|---|---|
| *5pm* | Music Miracles | News | News | Sports |
| *5:15* | | Sports | The Christian Science Monitor | News |
| *5:30* | Harry Wismer, news | Charles Collingwood, news | True or False | I Want It |
| *5:45* | Sports | Henry Garred, news | Music | Elmer Patterson, news |
| *6pm* | Exploring the Unknown | Leave It to Joan | Stop Me If You've Heard This One | Guy Lombardo Orchstra |
| *6:15* | | | | |
| *6:30* | Music | The All-Star Western Theater | Family Doctor | The Judy Canova Show |
| *6:45* | | | | |
| *7pm* | Diary of Fate | Saturday Night Serenade | The Zane Grey Theater | Kay Kyser's College of Musical Knowledge |
| *7:15* | | | | |
| *7:30* | Red Dolan, Detective | Frankie Carle Orchestra | Leave It to the Girls | Grand Ole Opry |
| *7:45* | | | | |
| *8pm* | The Lone Ranger | Next Door | The Fishing and Hunting Club | The Life of Riley |
| *8:15* | | | | |
| *8:30* | Challenge of the Yukon | Great Life | Hawaii Calls | Truth or Consequences |
| *8:45* | | Carroll Alcott, news (8:55PM) | | |
| *9pm* | Gangbusters | The Abe Burrow Show | Glenn Hardy, news | Your Hit Parade |
| *9:15* | | The Hoagy Carmichael Show | Sports | |
| *9:30* | Murder and Mr. Malone | The Camel Caravan, Vaughn Monroe | Songs | The Hollywood Music Hour |
| *9:45* | | | Newscope | |
| *10pm* | News and Views | The Ten o'Clock Wire | Music | News |
| *10:15* | | Bob Graham, songs | | Stairway to the Stars |
| *10:30* | Freddy Martin Orchestra | Music | The Peter Potter Show | |
| *10:45* | | | | Sweet and Lovely |

## DAYTIME — WINTER, 1948

*Sunday*

| | ABC | CBS | MBS | NBC |
|---|---|---|---|---|
| *8am* | Message of Israel | News and Views | The Young People's Church (7:30AM) | The L. A. Times Funnies |
| *8:15* | | | Policing L. A. | |
| *8:30* | The Hour of Faith | The Salt Lake Tabernacle Choir | The Voice of Prophecy | The Christian Science Monitor |
| *8:45* | | | | Outdoor Reporter |
| *9am* | It Happened During the Week | Invitation to Learning | The Pilgrim Hour | The Eternal Light |
| *9:15* | Washington Inside and Out | | | |
| *9:30* | The Don Otis Show | The People's Platform | The Lutheran Hour | Echoes and Encores |
| *9:45* | | | | |
| *10am* | Music | The Treasury Department | Glenn Hardy, news | Sports |
| *10:15* | News | Adventures in Science | Commander Scott | News |
| *10:30* | The Don Otis Show | News | Morning Melodies | The University of Chicago Round Table |
| *10:45* | | Income Tax | | |
| *11am* | The Atwater-Kent Radio Auditions | Meet the Author | William L. Shirer, news | The RCA Victor Show |
| *11:15* | | The University Explorer | Garden Chats | |
| *11:30* | National Vespers | Joseph C. Harsch, news | News | Harvest of Stars |
| *11:45* | | Bob Reid Sings | The Canary Pet Shop | |
| *12pm* | Lassie | New York Philharmonic Orchestra | Broadway News | The Sheaffer Parade |
| *12:15* | Samuel Pettingill, news | | Singin' Sam, the Barbasol Man | |
| *12:30* | This Week Around the World | | Juvenile Jury | One Man's Family |
| *12:45* | | | | |
| *1pm* | Sound Off | | The House of Mystery | The Quiz Kids |
| *1:15* | | | | |
| *1:30* | The Metropolitan Opera Auditions | Tapestries of Life | True Detective Mysteries | News |

## DAYTIME — WINTER, 1948

*Monday-Friday*

| ABC | CBS | MBS | NBC | |
|---|---|---|---|---|
| The Breakfast Club | The Johnny Murray Show | Cecil Brown, news | Fred Waring Orchestra | *8am* |
| | News | News | | *8:15* |
| | Grand Slam | The Editor's Diary | The Jack Berch Show | *8:30* |
| | Rosemary | News | Lora Lawton | *8:45* |
| Welcome Travelers | Wendy Warren and the News | Kate Smith Speaks | Edward Jorgenson, news | *9am* |
| | Aunt Jenny's True Life Stories | Victor Lindlahr, health | Ladies' Day | *9:15* |
| Breakfast at Sardi's | The Romance of Helen Trent | The Johnson Familiy | | *9:30* |
| | Our Gal Sunday | Music | Charles Collins, news | *9:45* |
| Galen Drake, talk | Big Sister | Glenn Hardy, news | All Around | *10am* |
| Between the Bookends | Ma Perkins | Barbara Quinn, talk | What You Say | *10:15* |
| My True Story | Young Dr. Malone | The Jedge / Morning Matinee | News | *10:30* |
| | The Guiding Light | | Joyce Jordan, MD | *10:45* |
| The Magazine of the Air | The Second Mrs. Burton | Organ Music | Today's Children | *11am* |
| Club Time / Listening Post / Dorothy Kilgallen, gossip | Perry Mason | Erskine Johnson, gossip | The Woman in White | *11:15* |
| H. R. Baukhage, news | The Bob Graham Show | Queen for a Day | The Story of Holly Sloan | *11:30* |
| Between the Girls | Rose of My Dreams | | The Light of the World | *11:45* |
| News | Double or Nothing | Broadway News | The Farm Reporter | *12pm* |
| Walter Kiernan, news | | Sing, America Sing | Ma Perkins | *12:15* |
| Paul Whiteman's Record Club | Knox Manning, news | Louise Massey, songs | Pepper Young's Family | *12:30* |
| | News | Rush Hughes, news | The Right to Happiness | *12:45* |
| | The American School of the Air | Music | Mary Noble, Backstage Wife | *1pm* |
| | | Norma Dixon, talk | Stella Dallas | *1:15* |
| Quizzicale / Music Miracles | The Barbara Wheeler Show | Nancy Young, talk | Lorenzo Jones | *1:30* |

## DAYTIME — WINTER, 1948

*Sunday*

| | ABC | CBS | MBS | NBC |
|---|---|---|---|---|
| *1:45* | | | | American Favorites |
| *2pm* | Treasury Agent | Pueblo Serenade | The Shadow | The Ford Theater |
| *2:15* | | Here's to You | | |
| *2:30* | Counterspy | The Hour of Charm | Quick as a Flash | |
| *2:45* | | | | |
| *3pm* | California Caravan | The Prudential Family Hour | Those Websters | The Catholic Hour |
| *3:15* | | | | |
| *3:30* | The Greatest Story Ever Told | The Pause That Refreshes | Nick Carter, Master Detective | News |
| *3:45* | | | | The Melody Parade |
| *4pm* | Child's World | Gene Autry's Melody Ranch | Sherlock Holmes | The Lucky Strike Program, Jack Benny |
| *4:15* | | | | |
| *4:30* | Sammy Kaye's Sunday Serenade | Suspense | California Tales | The Phil Harris - Alice Faye Show |
| *4:45* | | | | |

# DAYTIME — WINTER, 1948

*Monday-Friday*

| ABC | CBS | MBS | NBC | |
|---|---|---|---|---|
| Ethel and Albert | | | Young Widder Brown | *1:45* |
| What's Doing Ladies | Winner Take All | Heart's Desire | When a Girl Marries | *2pm* |
| | | | Portia Faces Life | *2:15* |
| Bride and Groom | House Party | The Martin Block Show | Just Plain Bill | *2:30* |
| | | | Front Page Farrell | *2:45* |
| Ladies Be Seated | Meet the Missus | Music / The Harlem Hospitality Club / A. L. Alexander's Mediation Board / Racket Smashers | The Road of Life | *3pm* |
| | | | Life Can Be Beautiful | *3:15* |
| Records | Arthur Godfrey Time | Stranger | Aunt Mary | *3:30* |
| The Frances Scully Show | | Serenade | Dr. Paul | *3:45* |
| | Hint Hunt | Fulton Lewis Jr., news | One Woman's Secret | *4pm* |
| Alvin Wilder, news | The Strange Romance of Evelyn Winters | Rex Miller, news | News of the World | *4:15* |
| Variety Parade | News | Adventure Parade | Art Baker's Notebook | *4:30* |
| | Lum and Abner | Sleepy Joe / Raggedy Ann and Andy | | *4:45* |

## DAYTIME — WINTER, 1948

*Saturday*

| | ABC | CBS | MBS | NBC |
|---|---|---|---|---|
| *8am* | The Abbott and Costello Children's Show | Let's Pretend | Louise Massey, songs | Western Music |
| *8:15* | | | News | |
| *8:30* | The Land of the Lost | Escape | The Clinic Forum | Smilin' Ed's Buster Brown Gang |
| *8:45* | | | | |
| *9am* | Collins Calling | The Armstrong Theater of Today | Pan Americana | Jump-Jump and the Ice Queen |
| *9:15* | Mirandy | | Policing L. A. | Young America Speaks |
| *9:30* | Tommy Bartlett Time | Stars Over Hollywood | Music | The Saturday Chef |
| *9:45* | | | | The Kitchen |
| *10am* | The American Farmer | Grand Central Station | Glenn Hardy, news | The National Farm and Home Hour |
| *10:15* | | | The Garden Guide | |
| *10:30* | Our Town Speaks | County Fair | Music | Meet the Meeks |
| *10:45* | | | | |
| *11am* | The Metropolitan Opera | Mary Lee Taylor, cooking | The Penny Parade | Archie Andrews |
| *11:15* | | | | |
| *11:30* | | Give and Take | McAllister Music | The Gregson Show |
| *11:45* | | | | |
| *12pm* | | Meet the Missus | News | The Farm Reporter |
| *12:15* | | | Songs of Good Cheer | The Man on the Farm |
| *12:30* | | Free for All | Louise Massey, songs | |
| *12:45* | | | The Warblers | Here Comes the Band |
| *1pm* | | Treasury Bandstand | Sports Parade | Doctors Today |
| *1:15* | | | | |
| *1:30* | | Saturday at the Chase | Income Tax | Home is What You Make It |
| *1:45* | Tea and Crumpets | | In Your Name | |

## DAYTIME — WINTER, 1948

*Saturday*

| | ABC | CBS | MBS | NBC |
|---|---|---|---|---|
| *2pm* | | Philadelphia Symphony Orchestra | Music | News |
| *2:15* | | | | Youth Sings |
| *2:30* | | | | Music |
| *2:45* | The American Way | | | |
| *3pm* | The Piano Playhouse | Cross-Section USA | The Bob Shannon Show | On the Scouting Trail |
| *3:15* | | | | |
| *3:30* | In the Family | The Los Angeles Story | The Side Show | NBC Symphony Orchestra |
| *3:45* | It's Your Business | The Garden Gate | | |
| *4pm* | Madhouse Music | Hawk Larabee | Mel Allen, sports | |
| *4:15* | Pubilc Affairs | | News | |
| *4:30* | Music | Thirty Seconds to Go | Music | Curtain Time |
| *4:45* | News | | | |

## EVENING — SPRING, 1948

*Sunday*

| | ABC | CBS | MBS | NBC |
|---|---|---|---|---|
| *5pm* | Stop the Music | Suspense (4:30PM) | The Golden Hour (4:30PM) | The Charlie McCarthy Show |
| *5:15* | | | | |
| *5:30* | | The Private Practice of Dr. Dana | Jimmy Fidler, gossip | The Fred Allen Show |
| *5:45* | | | Newscope | |
| *6pm* | Walter Winchell's Jergens Journal | Melodies America Loves | Meet Me at Parky's | The Manhattan Merry-Go-Round |
| *6:15* | Louella Parsons, gossip | | | |
| *6:30* | The Theater Guild of the Air | Shorty Bell | The Jim Backus Show | The American Album of Familiar Music |
| *6:45* | | | | |
| *7pm* | | Escape | Behind the Front Page | Take It or Leave It |
| *7:15* | | | | |
| *7:30* | Jimmy Fidler, gossip | Strike It Rich | The Quiz of Two Cities | The Youth Opportunity Program |
| *7:45* | The News Looks Ahead | | | |
| *8pm* | Drew Pearson, news | The Man Called X | Twenty Questions | The Hollywood Star Preview |
| *8:15* | Don Gardiner, news | News (8:25PM) | | |
| *8:30* | The Green Hornet | Blondie | Walter Winchell's Jergens Journal | The Standard Symphony Hour |
| *8:45* | | | Sheila Graham, gossip | |
| *9pm* | The Unexpected | The Adventures of Sam Spade | Glenn Hardy, news | |
| *9:15* | Music | | Erskine Johnson, gossip | |
| *9:30* | | Romance of the Ranchos | The Chicago Theater of the Air | The Lucky Strike Program, Jack Benny |
| *9:45* | | | | |
| *10pm* | We CARE | The Ten o'Clock Wire | | The Richfield Reporter |
| *10:15* | Freddy Martin Orchestra | The University Explorer | | The Chapel Quartet |
| *10:30* | | You Are There | What Might Have Been | Inside the News |
| *10:45* | | | | Melody Time |

| EVENING — SPRING, 1948 | | | | |
|---|---|---|---|---|
| *Monday* | | | | |
| ABC | CBS | MBS | NBC | |
| Happy Theater | Front Page Feature | Raggedy Ann and Andy | Feature Wire | *5pm* |
| Terry and the Pirates | Sports | The Adventures of Superman | News | *5:15* |
| Sky King | Charles Collingwood, news | Captain Midnight | The Voice of Firestone | *5:30* |
| | Henry Garred, news | Tom Mix and His Ralston Straightshooters | | *5:45* |
| Headline Edition | The Lux Radio Theater | Gabriel Heatter, news | The American Way | *6pm* |
| News | | The Mutual Newsreel | | *6:15* |
| Child's World | | California Melodies | Dr. I. Q., the Mental Banker | *6:30* |
| | | | | *6:45* |
| The Lone Ranger | My Friend Irma | The Mysterious Traveler | The Carnation Contented Hour | *7pm* |
| | | | | *7:15* |
| On Stage America | The Lady Esther Screen Guild Theater | The Cisco Kid | Fred Waring Orchestra | *7:30* |
| | | | | *7:45* |
| Point Sublime | Lowell Thomas, news | Let George Do It | The Chesterfield Supper Club | *8pm* |
| | The Jack Smith Show | | Fleetwood Lawton, news | *8:15* |
| Sound Off | Arthur Godfrey's Talent Scouts | Charlie Chan | The Cavalcade of America | *8:30* |
| | Carroll Alcott, news (8:55 PM) | | | *8:45* |
| News | Inner Sanctum Mysteries | Glenn Hardy, news | The Bell Telephone Hour | *9pm* |
| Earl Godwin, news | | News | | *9:15* |
| So You Want to Lead a Band | The Beulah Show | The Inside of Sports | The Big Story | *9:30* |
| | Conflict | Henry J. Taylor, news | | *9:45* |
| Casa Cugat | The Ten o'Clock Wire | Fulton Lewis Jr., news | The Richfield Reporter | *10pm* |
| News | Bob Elson Interviews | Music Hilites | The Music Shop | *10:15* |
| Elmer Davis, news | The Symphonette | The B. Arlington Show | Inside the News | *10:30* |
| Rainbow Rendezvous | | | Melody Time | *10:45* |

| EVENING — SPRING, 1948 | | | | |
|---|---|---|---|---|
| *Tuesday* | | | | |
| | ABC | CBS | MBS | NBC |
| *5pm* | Happy Theater | Front Page Feature | Sleepy Joe | Feature Wire |
| *5:15* | Terry and the Pirates | Sports | The Adventures of Superman | News |
| *5:30* | Jack Armstrong, the All-American Boy | Charles Collingwood, news | Captain Midnight | A Date with Judy |
| *5:45* | | Henry Garred, news | Tom Mix and His Ralston Straightshooters | |
| *6pm* | Headline Edition | The Women's Forum | Gabriel Heatter, news | Amos 'n' Andy |
| *6:15* | News | | The Mutual Newsreel | |
| *6:30* | Boston Symphony Orchestra | The Adventures of Christopher Wells | Special Agent | Fibber McGee and Molly |
| *6:45* | | | | |
| *7pm* | | Studio One | Quiet, Please | The Pepsodent Show, Bob Hope |
| *7:15* | | | | |
| *7:30* | Report to the People | | Red Ryder | The Raleigh Cigarette Program, Red Skelton |
| *7:45* | Here's Hollywood | | | |
| *8pm* | Washington Date | Lowell Thomas, news | The Count of Monte Cristo | The Chesterfield Supper Club |
| *8:15* | News | The Jack Smith Show | | Fleetwood Lawton, news |
| *8:30* | On Trial | Mr. and Mrs. North | Official Detective | Call for Music |
| *8:45* | | Carroll Alcott, news (8:55PM) | | |
| *9pm* | America's Town Meeting of the Air | Big Town | Glenn Hardy, news | Favorite Story |
| *9:15* | | | News | |
| *9:30* | | The Beulah Show | The Inside of Sports | The Pleasure Parade |
| *9:45* | | The Night Editor | Newscope | Remember That Music |
| *10pm* | Casa Cugat | The Ten o'Clock Wire | Fulton Lewis Jr., news | The Richfield Reporter |
| *10:15* | News | Bob Elson Interviews | Music Hilites | Music |
| *10:30* | Elmer Davis, news | Music | The B. Arlington Show | Inside the News |
| *10:45* | Freddy Martin Orchestra | | | Melody Time |

# EVENING — SPRING, 1948

*Wednesday*

| ABC | CBS | MBS | NBC | |
|---|---|---|---|---|
| Happy Theater | Front Page Feature | Raggedy Ann and Andy | Feature Wire | *5pm* |
| Terry and the Pirates | Sports | The Adventures of Superman | News | *5:15* |
| Sky King | Charles Collingwood, news | Captain Midnight | Casa Cugat | *5:30* |
| | Henry Garred, news | Tom Mix and His Ralston Straightshooters | Elmer Patterson, news | *5:45* |
| Headline Edition | Your Song and Mine | Gabriel Heatter, news | Duffy's Tavern | *6pm* |
| News | | The Mutual Newsreel | | *6:15* |
| Vox Pop | Harvest of Stars | The Tex Beneke Review | The Skippy Hollywood Theater | *6:30* |
| | | | | *6:45* |
| The Lone Ranger | The Saint | The Casebook of Gregory Hood | The Hollywood Bowl Auditions | *7pm* |
| | | | | *7:15* |
| The Mayor of the Town | The Whistler | The Cisco Kid | The Jimmy Durante Show | *7:30* |
| | | | | *7:45* |
| Abbott and Costello | Lowell Thomas, news | What's the Name of That Song | The Chesterfield Supper Club | *8pm* |
| | The Jack Smith Show | | Fleetwood Lawton, news | *8:15* |
| You Bet Your Life | Dr. Christian | Leave It to the Girls | The Great Gildersleeve | *8:30* |
| | Carroll Alcott, news (8:55PM) | | | *8:45* |
| Philco Radio Time, Bing Crosby | Presidential Timber | Glenn Hardy, news | A Day in the Life of Dennis Day | *9pm* |
| | Capitol Cloak Room | News | | *9:15* |
| The Texaco Star Theater, Gordan McRae | The Beulah Show | The Inside of Sports | Mr. District Attorney | *9:30* |
| | Conflict | Land O' the Free | | *9:45* |
| Casa Cugat | The Ten o'Clock Wire | Fulton Lewis Jr., news | The Richfield Reporter | *10pm* |
| News | Bob Elson Interviews | Music Hilites | The Music Shop | *10:15* |
| Elmer Davis, news | The Symphonette | The B. Arlington Show | Inside the News | *10:30* |
| Freddy Martin Orchestra | | | Melody Time | *10:45* |

## EVENING — SPRING, 1948

*Thursday*

| | ABC | CBS | MBS | NBC |
|---|---|---|---|---|
| *5pm* | Happy Theater | Front Page Feature | Sleepy Joe | Feature Wire |
| *5:15* | Terry and the Pirates | Sports | The Adventures of Superman | News |
| *5:30* | Jack Armstrong, the All-American Boy | Charles Collingwood, news | Captain Midnight | Casa Cugat |
| *5:45* | | Henry Garred, news | Tom Mix and His Ralston Straightshooters | Elmer Patterson, news |
| *6pm* | Headline Edition | The Dick Haymes Show | Gabriel Heatter, news | The Kraft Music Hall, Al Jolson |
| *6:15* | News | | The Mutual Newsreel | |
| *6:30* | The Smiths of Hollywood | Casey, Crime Photographer | Roger Kilgore, Public Defender | The Sealtest Village Store, Arden and Carson |
| *6:45* | | | | |
| *7pm* | The Adventures of Ellery Queen | The Radio Reader's Digest | The Family Theater | The Bob Hawk Show |
| *7:15* | | | | |
| *7:30* | The Henry Morgan Show | The First Nighter Program | Red Ryder | Pabst Blue Ribbon Time, Eddie Cantor |
| *7:45* | | | | |
| *8pm* | Tales of Willie Piper | Lowell Thomas, news | The Falcon | The Chesterfield Supper Club |
| *8:15* | | The Jack Smith Show | | Fleetwood Lawton, news |
| *8:30* | The Candid Microphone | Mr. Keen, Tracer of Lost Persons | Music | The Aldrich Family |
| *8:45* | | Carroll Alcott, news (8:55PM) | | |
| *9pm* | Mr. President | The FBI in Peace and War | Glenn Hardy, news | Maxwell House Coffee Time, Burns and Allen |
| *9:15* | | | News | |
| *9:30* | Hits and Encores | The Beulah Show | The Inside of Sports | Noah Webster Says |
| *9:45* | | Conflict | Newscope | |
| *10pm* | Casa Cugat | The Ten o'Clock Wire | Fulton Lewis Jr., news | The Richfield Reporter |
| *10:15* | News | Bob Elson Interviews | Music Hilites | Mayor Bowron, comment |
| *10:30* | Elmer Davis, news | Music | The B. Arlington Show | Inside the News |
| *10:45* | Freddy Martin Orchestra | | | Melody Time |

## EVENING — SPRING, 1948

*Friday*

| ABC | CBS | MBS | NBC | |
|---|---|---|---|---|
| Happy Theater | Front Page Feature | Raggedy Ann and Andy | Feature Wire | *5pm* |
| Terry and the Pirates | Sports | The Adventures of Superman | News | *5:15* |
| Sky King | Charles Collingwood, news | Captain Midnight | Casa Cugat | *5:30* |
| | Henry Garred, news | Tom Mix and His Ralston Straightshooters | Elmer Patterson, news | *5:45* |
| Headline Edition | The Bickersons | Gabriel Heatter, news | People Are Funny | *6pm* |
| News | | The Mutual Newsreel | | *6:15* |
| The Sheriff | The Adventures of Ozzie and Harriet | Information, Please | Waltz Time | *6:30* |
| | | | | *6:45* |
| Madison Square Garden Boxing | Everybody Wins | Meet the Press | The Hank McCune Show | *7pm* |
| | | | | *7:15* |
| | Spotlight Revue | The Cisco Kid | The Colgate Sports Newsreel, Bill Stern | *7:30* |
| | | | Sports | *7:45* |
| The Fat Man | Lowell Thomas, news | The Answer Game | The Chesterfield Supper Club | *8pm* |
| | The Jack Smith Show | | Fleetwood Lawton, news | *8:15* |
| This is Your FBI | The Danny Thomas Show | High Adventure | Can You Top This | *8:30* |
| | Carroll Alcott, news (8:55PM) | | | *8:45* |
| Break the Bank | The Baby Snooks Show | Glenn Hardy, news | Conquest | *9pm* |
| | | News | | *9:15* |
| Famous Jury Trials | The Beulah Show | The Inside of Sports | Mystery Theater | *9:30* |
| | The Night Editor | Your Land | | *9:45* |
| Casa Cugat | The Ten o'Clock Wire | Fulton Lewis Jr., news | The Richfield Reporter | *10pm* |
| News | Bob Elson Interviews | Music Hilites | The Music Shop | *10:15* |
| Elmer Davis, news | The Symphonette | The B. Arlington Show | Inside the News | *10:30* |
| Freddy Martin Orchestra | | | Melody Time | *10:45* |

## EVENING — SPRING, 1948

*Saturday*

| | ABC | CBS | MBS | NBC |
|---|---|---|---|---|
| *5pm* | Music Miracles | News | Take a Number | The Spring Concert |
| *5:15* | | Sports | | |
| *5:30* | Harry Wismer, news | Charles Collingwood, news False | True or Riddles | Rhythm and |
| *5:45* | Sports | Henry Garred, news | | Elmer Patterson, news |
| *6pm* | Melody, Inc. | Leave It to Joan | Stop Me If You've Heard This One | Guy Lombardo Orchstra |
| *6:15* | | | | |
| *6:30* | Music of Manhattan | Padded Cell | Parents vs. Kids | The Judy Canova Show |
| *6:45* | | | | |
| *7pm* | Diary of Fate | Saturday Night Serenade | Talent Hunt | Kay Kyser's College of Musical Knowledge |
| *7:15* | | | | |
| *7:30* | Red Dolan, Detective | It Pays to Be Ignorant | The All-Star Western Theater | Grand Ole Opry |
| *7:45* | | | | |
| *8pm* | The Lone Ranger | Great Life | The Fishing and Hunting Club | The Life of Riley |
| *8:15* | | | | |
| *8:30* | Challenge of the Yukon | Find a Clue | Hawaii Calls | Truth or Consequences |
| *8:45* | | Carroll Alcott, news (8:55PM) | | |
| *9pm* | Gangbusters | The Abe Burrow Show | Glenn Hardy, news | Your Hit Parade |
| *9:15* | | The Hoagy Carmichael Show | Sports | |
| *9:30* | Murder and Mr. Malone | The Camel Caravan, Vaughn Monroe | News | The Hollywood Music Hour |
| *9:45* | | | Newscope | |
| *10pm* | The Atwater-Kent Radio Auditions | The Ten o'Clock Wire | Music | News |
| *10:15* | | Music | | Stairway to the Stars |
| *10:30* | Freddy Martin Orchestra | | | |
| *10:45* | | | Newscope | |

## DAYTIME — SPRING, 1948

*Sunday*

| | ABC | CBS | MBS | NBC |
|---|---|---|---|---|
| *8am* | Message of Israel | Howard K. Smith, news | The Radio Bible Class | The L. A. Times Funnies |
| *8:15* | | As Others See Us | | |
| *8:30* | The Hour of Faith | The Salt Lake Tabernacle Choir | The Voice of Prophecy | The Christian Science Monitor |
| *8:45* | | | | Outdoor Reporter |
| *9am* | It Happened During the Week | Invitation to Learning | The Young People's Church | You in America |
| *9:15* | Washington Inside and Out | | | Music |
| *9:30* | Centennial Year | The People's Platform | The Lutheran Hour | Taylor Made Melodies |
| *9:45* | | | | |
| *10am* | Foreign Reporters | Doorway to Life | Glenn Hardy, news | Sports |
| *10:15* | Editor at Home | | Commander Scott | News |
| *10:30* | Musical Cavalcade | News | Morning Melodies | The University of Chicago Round Table |
| *10:45* | | Income Tax | | |
| *11am* | Music Miracles | Tell It Again | William L. Shirer, news | Olmstead and Company |
| *11:15* | | | News and Views | |
| *11:30* | National Vespers | Joseph C. Harsch, news | | The RCA Victor Show |
| *11:45* | | Where the People Stand | The Canary Pet Shop | |
| *12pm* | Lassie | New York Philharmonic Orchestra | Broadway News | The Sheaffer Parade |
| *12:15* | Samuel Pettingill, news | | Singin' Sam, the Barbasol Man | |
| *12:30* | Sammy Kaye's Sunday Serenade | | Juvenile Jury | One Man's Family |
| *12:45* | | | | |
| *1pm* | Speak Up, America | | The House of Mystery | The Quiz Kids |
| *1:15* | Think | | | |
| *1:30* | The Metropolitan Opera Auditions | Tapestries of LIfe | True Detective Mysteries | News |
| *1:45* | | | | American Favorites |

## DAYTIME — SPRING, 1948

*Monday-Friday*

| ABC | CBS | MBS | NBC | |
|---|---|---|---|---|
| The Breakfast Club | The Johnny Murray Show | Cecil Brown, news | Fred Waring Orchestra | *8am* |
| | News | News | | *8:15* |
| | Grand Slam | The Editor's Diary | The Jack Berch Show | *8:30* |
| | Rosemary | News | Lora Lawton | *8:45* |
| Welcome Travelers | Wendy Warren and the News | Kate Smith Speaks | Ladies' Day | *9am* |
| | Aunt Jenny's True Life Stories | Victor Lindlahr, health | | *9:15* |
| Breakfast at Sardi's | The Romance of Helen Trent | The Johnson Familiy | | *9:30* |
| | Our Gal Sunday | Music | Chuck Collins, news | *9:45* |
| Galen Drake, talk | Big Sister | Glenn Hardy, news | Downtown | *10am* |
| Between the Bookends | Ma Perkins | Merv Griffin, songs | What You Say | *10:15* |
| My True Story | Young Dr. Malone | The Jedge / Morning Matinee | News | *10:30* |
| | The Guiding Light | | Joyce Jordan, MD | *10:45* |
| The Magazine of the Air | The Second Mrs. Burton | The Happy Gang | Today's Children | *11am* |
| Club Time / Listening Post / Dorothy Kilgallen, gossip | Perry Mason | Erskine Johnson, gossip | The Woman in White | *11:15* |
| Casa Cugat | This is Nora Drake | Queen for a Day | The Story of Holly Sloan | *11:30* |
| Between the Girls | Rose of My Dreams | | The Light of the World | *11:45* |
| Sam Hayes, news | Double or Nothing | Broadway News | The Farm Reporter | *12pm* |
| H. R. Baukhage, news | | Sing, America Sing | Ma Perkins | *12:15* |
| Paul Whiteman's Record Club | Knox Manning, news | The Shady Valley Folks | Pepper Young's Family | *12:30* |
| | News | Melody Matinee | The Right to Happiness | *12:45* |
| | The American School of the Air | | Mary Noble, Backstage Wife | *1pm* |
| | | Norma Dixon, talk | Stella Dallas | *1:15* |
| Quizzicale / Music Miracles | The Barbara Wheeler Show | Nancy Young, talk | Lorenzo Jones | *1:30* |
| Ethel and Albert | | | Young Widder Brown | *1:45* |

## DAYTIME — SPRING, 1948

*Sunday*

| | ABC | CBS | MBS | NBC |
|---|---|---|---|---|
| *2pm* | Treasury Agent | Pueblo Serenade | The Shadow | The Ford Theater |
| *2:15* | | Here's to You | | |
| *2:30* | Counterspy | The Hour of Charm | Quick as a Flash | |
| *2:45* | | | | |
| *3pm* | California Caravan | The Prudential Family Hour | Those Websters | The Catholic Hour |
| *3:15* | | | | |
| *3:30* | The Greatest Story Ever Told | The Pause That Refreshes | Nick Carter, Master Detective | News |
| *3:45* | | | | The Melody Parade |
| *4pm* | I Love Adventure | Gene Autry's Melody Ranch | Sherlock Holmes | The Lucky Strike Program, Jack Benny |
| *4:15* | | | | |
| *4:30* | The Clock | Suspense | The Golden Hour | The Phil Harris - Alice Faye Show |
| *4:45* | | | | |

## DAYTIME — SPRING, 1948

*Monday-Friday*

| ABC | CBS | MBS | NBC | |
|---|---|---|---|---|
| Surprise Package | Winner Take All | Heart's Desire | When a Girl Marries | *2pm* |
| | | | Portia Faces Life | *2:15* |
| Bride and Groom | House Party | Hollywood Favorites | Just Plain Bill | *2:30* |
| | | Postal Employee / Two-Ton Baker | Front Page Farrell | *2:45* |
| Ladies Be Seated | Meet the Missus | Music / The Hampton Show / Leave It to the Girls / A. L. Alexander's Mediation Board / Racket Smashers | The Road of Life | *3pm* |
| | | | Life Can Be Beautiful | *3:15* |
| Records | Arthur Godfrey Time | Red Hook 31 | Aunt Mary | *3:30* |
| The Frances Scully Show | | Adventure Parade | This is Nora Drake | *3:45* |
| | Hint Hunt | Fulton Lewis Jr., news | One Woman's Secret | *4pm* |
| Alvin Wilder, news | | Rex Miller, news | News of the World | *4:15* |
| Variety Parade | Club Fifteen | The Passing Parade | Art Baker's Notebook | *4:30* |
| | Edward R. Murrow, news | Frank Hemingway, news | | *4:45* |

## DAYTIME — SPRING, 1948

*Saturday*

| | ABC | CBS | MBS | NBC |
|---|---|---|---|---|
| *8am* | Shoppers Special | Let's Pretend | Music | The Coffee Concert |
| *8:15* | | | News | |
| *8:30* | Collins Calling | Junior Miss | The Clinic Forum | Smilin' Ed's Buster Brown Gang |
| *8:45* | Mirandy | | | |
| *9am* | The Abbott and Costello Children's Show | The Armstrong Theater of Today | The Veteran Wants to Know | Jump-Jump and the Ice Queen |
| *9:15* | | | Policing L. A. | Young America Speaks |
| *9:30* | The Land of the Lost | Stars Over Hollywood | The All-Girl Corps | The Saturday Chef |
| *9:45* | | | | The Kitchen |
| *10am* | The American Farmer | Grand Central Station | Glenn Hardy, news | The National Farm and Home Hour |
| *10:15* | | | The Garden Guide | |
| *10:30* | Hollywood Headlines | County Fair | Music | Meet the Meeks |
| *10:45* | Chemists | | | |
| *11am* | Fascinating Rhythm | Mary Lee Taylor, cooking | Movie Mystery | Archie Andrews |
| *11:15* | | | | |
| *11:30* | The Hitching Post | Give and Take | Teen Timers | The Gregson Show |
| *11:45* | | | | |
| *12pm* | News | Meet the Missus | News | The Farm Reporter |
| *12:15* | The American Way | | In Washington | Here Comes the Band |
| *12:30* | ABC Symphony Orchestra | Free for All | Strings and Voices | Youth Sings |
| *12:45* | | | | |
| *1pm* | | Know Your Radio | Sports Parade | Orchestras of the Nation |
| *1:15* | | The Treasury Department | | |
| *1:30* | Sports Spotlight | Columbia's Country Journal | Music | |
| *1:45* | Sports | | In Your Name | |

## DAYTIME — SPRING, 1948

*Saturday*

| | ABC | CBS | MBS | NBC |
|---|---|---|---|---|
| *2pm* | | Saturday at the Chase | Opinionaire | I Want It |
| *2:15* | | | | |
| *2:30* | The Piano Playhouse | Horse Racing | The Reviewing Stand | Dr. I. Q. Jr. |
| *2:45* | | Music | | |
| *3pm* | Junior Junction | The D. Pryor Show | The Tex Beneke Review | On the Scouting Trail |
| *3:15* | | Horse Racing | | |
| *3:30* | In the Family | | The Side Show | NBC Symphony Orchestra |
| *3:45* | It's Your Business | News | | |
| *4pm* | Songs | Mr. ace & JANE | Mel Allen, sports | |
| *4:15* | Sports | | Frank Hemingway, news | |
| *4:30* | Records | The Los Angeles Story | The B. Harrington Show | Curtain Time |
| *4:45* | News | The Garden Gate | The Christian Science Monitor | |

## EVENING — SUMMER, 1948

*Sunday*

| | ABC | CBS | MBS | NBC |
|---|---|---|---|---|
| *5pm* | Stop the Music | Cabin B-13 | A. L. Alexander's Mediation Board | Robert Shaw Chorale |
| *5:15* | | | | |
| *5:30* | | The Private Practice of Dr. Dana | Jimmy Fidler, gossip | RFD America |
| *5:45* | | | Newscope | |
| *6pm* | Arlene Francis, talk | Winner Take All | Secret Mission | The Manhattan Merry-Go-Round |
| *6:15* | Louella Parsons, gossip | | | |
| *6:30* | Superstition on the Air | Strike It Rich | Music | The American Album of Familiar Music |
| *6:45* | | | | |
| *7pm* | The Comedy Writers Show | Box 13 | Behind the Front Page | Take It or Leave It |
| *7:15* | | | | |
| *7:30* | Jimmy Fidler, gossip | Hollywood Showcase | The Quiz of Two Cities | The Youth Opportunity Program |
| *7:45* | The News Looks Ahead | | | |
| *8pm* | Drew Pearson, news | The Man Called X | Twenty Questions | The Hollywood Star Theater |
| *8:15* | Don Gardiner, news | | | |
| *8:30* | The Green Hornet | Blondie | For Stardom | The Standard Symphony Hour |
| *8:45* | | | Sheila Graham, gossip | |
| *9pm* | The Unexpected | The Adventures of Sam Spade | Glenn Hardy, news | |
| *9:15* | We CARE | | Erskine Johnson, gossip | |
| *9:30* | Rex Maupin's Musicale | Romance of the Ranchos | The Chicago Theater of the Air | Let's Talk Hollywood |
| *9:45* | | | | |
| *10pm* | Freddy Martin Orchestra | The Ten o'Clock Wire | | The Richfield Reporter |
| *10:15* | | The University Explorer | | The Chapel Quartet |
| *10:30* | | Return Engagement | Music | Inside the News |
| *10:45* | | | | Melody Time |

## EVENING — SUMMER, 1948

*Monday*

| ABC | CBS | MBS | NBC | |
|---|---|---|---|---|
| Happy Theater | Front Page Feature | Raggedy Ann and Andy | Feature Wire | *5pm* |
| Fun House | Sports | Chandu, the Magician | News | *5:15* |
| Headline Edition | Charles Collingwood, news | The Adventures of Superman | The Voice of Firestone | *5:30* |
| Elmer Davis, news | Henry Garred, news | Tom Mix and His Ralston Straightshooters | | *5:45* |
| Music | Our Miss Brooks | Gabriel Heatter, news | The American Way | *6pm* |
| News | | The Mutual Newsreel | | *6:15* |
| Child's World | The Amazing Mr. Tutt | California Melodies | Dr. I. Q., the Mental Banker | *6:30* |
| | | | | *6:45* |
| The Lone Ranger | The Camel Caravan, Vaughn Monroe | The Mysterious Traveler | The Carnation Contented Hour | *7pm* |
| | | | | *7:15* |
| Tomorrow's Tops | Jack of All Trades | The Cisco Kid | Fred Waring Orchestra | *7:30* |
| | | | | *7:45* |
| Sound Off | Lowell Thomas, news | Let George Do It | The Chesterfield Supper Club | *8pm* |
| | The Treasury Band Show | | Fleetwood Lawton, news | *8:15* |
| Stars in the Night | Find That Clue | The Casebook of Gregory Hood | Hollywood Open House | *8:30* |
| | | | | *8:45* |
| News | Inner Sanctum Mysteries | Glenn Hardy, news | The Bell Telephone Hour | *9pm* |
| Earl Godwin, news | | News | | *9:15* |
| The Curt Massey Show | The Robert Q. Lewis Show | The Inside of Sports | Appointment with Music | *9:30* |
| | The Night Editor | Your Land and Mine | | *9:45* |
| Casa Cugat | The Ten o'Clock Wire | Fulton Lewis Jr., news | The Richfield Reporter | *10pm* |
| Walter Kiernan, news | Bob Elson Interviews | Music Hilites | The Music Shop | *10:15* |
| Elmer Davis, news | The Symphonette | Public Affairs | Inside the News | *10:30* |
| Rainbow Rendezvous | | | Melody Time | *10:45* |

| EVENING — SUMMER, 1948 | | | | |
|---|---|---|---|---|
| *Tuesday* | | | | |
| | ABC | CBS | MBS | NBC |
| *5pm* | Happy Theater | Front Page Feature | Sleepy Joe | Feature Wire |
| *5:15* | Fun House | Sports | Chandu, the Magician | News |
| *5:30* | Headline Edition | Charles Collingwood, news | The Adventures of Superman | Carmen Cavallero Orchestra |
| *5:45* | Elmer Davis, news | Henry Garred, news | Tom Mix and His Ralston Straightshooters | |
| *6pm* | Animal Court | The Women's Forum | Gabriel Heatter, news | The New Adventures of the Thin Man |
| *6:15* | News | | The Mutual Newsreel | |
| *6:30* | Festival Concert | Hit the Jackpot | Talent Jackpot | Music Styles |
| *6:45* | | | News (6:55PM) | |
| *7pm* | | Studio One | Roger Kildore, Public Defender | Meet Corliss Archer |
| *7:15* | | | | |
| *7:30* | Report to the People | | Red Ryder | An Evening with Romberg |
| *7:45* | Here's Hollywood | | | |
| *8pm* | Youth and the Government | Lowell Thomas, news | The Count of Monte Cristo | The Chesterfield Supper Club |
| *8:15* | News | The Treasury Band Show | | Fleetwood Lawton, news |
| *8:30* | The Piano Playhouse | Mr. and Mrs. North | Official Detective | The Mel Torme Show |
| *8:45* | | | | |
| *9pm* | America's Town Meeting of the Air | Mystery Theater | Glenn Hardy, news | Proudly We Hail |
| *9:15* | | | News | |
| *9:30* | | The Robert Q. Lewis Show | The Inside of Sports | The Pleasure Parade |
| *9:45* | | The Night Editor | Newscope | Remember That Music |
| *10pm* | Casa Cugat | The Ten o'Clock Wire | Fulton Lewis Jr., news | The Richfield Reporter |
| *10:15* | Walter Kiernan, news | Bob Elson Interviews | Music Hilites | I Want It |
| *10:30* | Elmer Davis, news | Music | The B. Arlington Show | Inside the News |
| *10:45* | Freddy Martin Orchestra | | | Melody Time |

| EVENING — SUMMER, 1948 | | | | |
|---|---|---|---|---|
| *Wednesday* | | | | |
| ABC | CBS | MBS | NBC | |
| Happy Theater | Front Page Feature | Raggedy Ann and Andy | Feature Wire | *5pm* |
| Fun House | Sports | Chandu, the Magician | News | *5:15* |
| Headline Edition | Charles Collingwood, news | The Adventures of Superman | Casa Cugat | *5:30* |
| Elmer Davis, news | Henry Garred, news | Tom Mix and His Ralston Straightshooters | Elmer Patterson, news | *5:45* |
| News and Views | County Fair | Gabriel Heatter, news | Hi Jinx | *6pm* |
| | | The Mutual Newsreel | | *6:15* |
| On Stage America | Harvest of Stars | The Lone Wolf | The Skippy Hollywood Theater | *6:30* |
| | | | | *6:45* |
| The Lone Ranger | Free for All | The Falcon | The Hollywood Bowl Auditions | *7pm* |
| | | | | *7:15* |
| Xavier Cugat Orchestra | The Whistler | The Cisco Kid | Vacation Serenade | *7:30* |
| | | | | *7:45* |
| Abbott and Costello | Lowell Thomas, news | What's the Name of That Song | The Chesterfield Supper Club | *8pm* |
| | The Treasury Band Show | | Fleetwood Lawton, news | *8:15* |
| Go for the House | Dr. Christian | Leave It to the Girls | Jack and Cliff | *8:30* |
| | | | | *8:45* |
| The Texaco StarTheater, Gordon MacRae | Capitol Cloak Room | Glenn Hardy, news | Hollywood Open House | *9pm* |
| | | News | | *9:15* |
| On Trial | The Robert Q. Lewis Show | The Inside of Sports | Mr. District Attorney | *9:30* |
| | The Night Editor | Land O' the Free | | *9:45* |
| Casa Cugat | The Ten o'Clock Wire | Fulton Lewis Jr., news | The Richfield Reporter | *10pm* |
| Walter Kiernan, news | Bob Elson Interviews | Music Hilites | The Music Shop | *10:15* |
| Elmer Davis, news | The Symphonette | Music | Inside the News | *10:30* |
| Freddy Martin Orchestra | | | Melody Time | *10:45* |

| EVENING — SUMMER, 1948 | | | | |
|---|---|---|---|---|
| *Thursday* | | | | |
| | ABC | CBS | MBS | NBC |
| *5pm* | Happy Theater | Front Page Feature | Sleepy Joe | Feature Wire |
| *5:15* | Fun House | Sports | Chandu, the Magician | News |
| *5:30* | Headline Edition | Charles Collingwood, news | The Adventures of Superman | Casa Cugat |
| *5:45* | Elmer Davis, news | Henry Garred, news | Tom Mix and His Ralston Straightshooters | Elmer Patterson, news |
| *6pm* | Animal Court | Suspense | Gabriel Heatter, news | The Kraft Music Hall, Nelson Eddy |
| *6:15* | News | | The Mutual Newsreel | |
| *6:30* | The Smiths of Hollywood | Casey, Crime Photographer | Quiet, Please | Ray Noble Orchestra |
| *6:45* | | | | |
| *7pm* | Criminal Casebook | The Hallmark Playhouse | The Family Theater | The Bob Hawk Show |
| *7:15* | | | | |
| *7:30* | The Dick Powell Show | Melodies America Loves | Red Ryder | A Time, A Tune and A Place |
| *7:45* | | | | |
| *8pm* | Mr. President | Lowell Thomas, news | Straight Arrow | The Chesterfield Supper Club |
| *8:15* | | The Treasury Band Show | | Fleetwood Lawton, news |
| *8:30* | Cavalcade of Sports | Mr. Keen, Tracer of Lost Persons | The All-Star Revue | Hollywood Open House |
| *8:45* | | | Remember When | |
| *9pm* | Joe Hasel's Sports Page | Fiesta | Glenn Hardy, news | New Faces of 1948 |
| *9:15* | | | News | |
| *9:30* | The Candid Microphone | The Robert Q. Lewis Show | The Inside of Sports | Noah Webster Says |
| *9:45* | | The Night Editor | Newscope | |
| *10pm* | Casa Cugat | The Ten o'Clock Wire | Fulton Lewis Jr., news | The Richfield Reporter |
| *10:15* | Walter Kiernan, news | Bob Elson Interviews | Music Hilites | Mayor Bowron, comment |
| *10:30* | Elmer Davis, news | Escape | Music | Inside the News |
| *10:45* | Freddy Martin Orchestra | | | Melody Time |

## EVENING — SUMMER, 1948

*Friday*

| ABC | CBS | MBS | NBC | |
|---|---|---|---|---|
| Happy Theater | Front Page Feature | Raggedy Ann and Andy | Feature Wire | *5pm* |
| Fun House | Sports | Chandu, the Magician | News | *5:15* |
| Headline Edition | Charles Collingwood, news | The Adventures of Superman | Casa Cugat | *5:30* |
| Elmer Davis, news | Henry Garred, news | Tom Mix and His Ralston Straightshooters | Elmer Patterson, news | *5:45* |
| News and Views | My Favorite Husband | Gabriel Heatter, news | The NBC University Theater | *6pm* |
| | | The Mutual Newsreel | | *6:15* |
| The Sheriff | Musicomedy | Colonel Stoopnagle | | *6:30* |
| | | | | *6:45* |
| Dance Band Jamboree | Everybody Wins | Meet the Press | The Hank McCune Show | *7pm* |
| | | | | *7:15* |
| | Spotlight Revue | The Cisco Kid | The Colgate Sports Newsreel, Bill Stern | *7:30* |
| | | | Sports | *7:45* |
| The Fat Man | Lowell Thomas, news | The Answer Game | The Chesterfield Supper Club | *8pm* |
| | The Treasury Band Show | | Fleetwood Lawton, news | *8:15* |
| This is Your FBI | A Man Called Jordan | High Adventure | Stairway to the Stars | *8:30* |
| | | | | *8:45* |
| Break the Bank | Mr. ace & JANE | Glenn Hardy, news | Call the Police | *9pm* |
| | | News | | *9:15* |
| Famous Jury Trials | The Robert Q. Lewis Show | The Inside of Sports | Hollywood Open House | *9:30* |
| | The Night Editor | Your Land and Mine | | *9:45* |
| Casa Cugat | The Ten o'Clock Wire | Fulton Lewis Jr., news | The Richfield Reporter | *10pm* |
| Walter Kiernan, news | Bob Elson Interviews | Music Hilites | The Music Shop | *10:15* |
| Elmer Davis, news | The Symphonette | The B. Artlington Show | Inside the News | *10:30* |
| Freddy Martin Orchestra | | | Melody Time | *10:45* |

## EVENING — SUMMER, 1948

*Saturday*

| | ABC | CBS | MBS | NBC |
|---|---|---|---|---|
| *5pm* | Prayer | Front Page Feature | Take a Number | Sports |
| *5:15* | Horse Racing | Sports | | News |
| *5:30* | News | Charles Collingwood, news | True or False | Sports |
| *5:45* | Sports | Henry Garred, news | | Elmer Patterson, news |
| *6pm* | Challenge of the Yukon | Always Albert | Three for the Money | Guy Lombardo Orchstra |
| *6:15* | | | | |
| *6:30* | Music of Manhattan | The Morey Amsterdam Show | | Can You Top This |
| *6:45* | | | | |
| *7pm* | Bulldog Drummond | The Steve Allen Show | Stop Me If You've Heard This One | Grand Ole Opry |
| *7:15* | | | | |
| *7:30* | Red Dolan, Detective | It Pays to Be Ignorant | The All-Star Western Theater | The Radio City Playhouse |
| *7:45* | | | | |
| *8pm* | The Lone Ranger | Saturday Night Serenade | The Fishing and Hunting Club | Dance Orchestra |
| *8:15* | | | | |
| *8:30* | The Amazing Mr. Malone | Sing It Again | Hawaii Calls | |
| *8:45* | | | | |
| *9pm* | Gangbusters | | Glenn Hardy, news | Your Hit Parade |
| *9:15* | | | Sports | |
| *9:30* | What's My Name | Special Investigator | Music | The Hollywood Music Hour |
| *9:45* | | | | |
| *10pm* | News | The Ten o'Clock Wire | The Spooner | News |
| *10:15* | News | Music | Whelan Sings | Music |
| *10:30* | Freddy Martin Orchestra | | Music | Sweet and Lovely |
| *10:45* | | | | |

| DAYTIME — SUMMER, 1948 | | | | |
|---|---|---|---|---|
| *Sunday* | | | | |
| | ABC | CBS | MBS | NBC |
| *8am* | Message of Israel | Howard K. Smith, news | The Radio Bible Class | The L. A. Times Funnies |
| *8:15* | | The Newsmakers | | |
| *8:30* | The Hour of Faith | The Salt Lake Tabernacle Choir | The Voice of Prophecy | The Christian Science Monitor |
| *8:45* | | | | Outdoor Reporter |
| *9am* | It Happened During the Week | Invitation to Learning | The Young People's Church | The Eternal Light |
| *9:15* | Washington Inside and Out | | | |
| *9:30* | Centennial Year | The People's Platform | The Lutheran Hour | Taylor Made Melodies |
| *9:45* | | | | |
| *10am* | Foreign Reporters | Doorway to Life | Glenn Hardy, news | Sports |
| *10:15* | Editor at Home | | Commander Scott | News |
| *10:30* | Musical Cavalcade | News | Bands and Bonds | The University of Chicago Round Table |
| *10:45* | | Behind the Lens | | |
| *11am* | Music Miracles | Tell It Again | William L. Shirer, news | Father Flannagan Program |
| *11:15* | | | The Veteran Wants to Know | |
| *11:30* | National Vespers | Joseph G.. Harsch, news | News | The RCA Victor Show |
| *11:45* | | Where the People Stand | The Canary Pet Shop | |
| *12pm* | This World | Hollywood Bowl Symphony Orchestra | Broadway News | Convention Special |
| *12:15* | Samuel Pettingill, news | | Singin' Sam, the Barbasol Man | |
| *12:30* | The Treasury Band Show | | Life Begins at Eighty | One Man's Family |
| *12:45* | | | | |
| *1pm* | Cal Tinney, news | | The House of Mystery | The Quiz Kids |
| *1:15* | Johnny Thompson, songs | | | |
| *1:30* | Milton Cross Opera Album | Make Mine Music | True Detective Mysteries | News |
| *1:45* | | | | American Favorites |

## DAYTIME — SUMMER, 1948

*Monday-Friday*

| ABC | CBS | MBS | NBC | |
|---|---|---|---|---|
| The Breakfast Club | Wescomes Breakfast | Cecil Brown, news | Fred Waring Orchestra | *8am* |
| | News | News | | *8:15* |
| | Grand Slam | The Editor's Diary | The Jack Berch Show | *8:30* |
| | Rosemary | News | Lora Lawton | *8:45* |
| Welcome Travelers | Wendy Warren and the News | Kate Smith Speaks | Ladies' Day | *9am* |
| | Aunt Jenny's True Life Stories | News | | *9:15* |
| Breakfast at Sardi's | The Romance of Helen Trent | Moods in Music | | *9:30* |
| | Our Gal Sunday | | Chuck Collins, news | *9:45* |
| Galen Drake, talk | Big Sister | Glenn Hardy, news | Downtown | *10am* |
| Between the Bookends | Ma Perkins | Music / Two-Ton Baker | What You Say | *10:15* |
| My True Story | Young Dr. Malone | The Jedge / Morning Matinee | News | *10:30* |
| | The Guiding Light | | Joyce Jordan, MD | *10:45* |
| The Magazine of the Air | The Second Mrs. Burton | Songs | Double or Nothing | *11am* |
| Club Time / Listening Post / Dorothy Kilgallen, gossip | Perry Mason | Tell Your Neighbor | | *11:15* |
| Casa Cugat | This is Nora Drake | Queen for a Day | Today's Children | *11:30* |
| Between the Girls | The Strange Romance of Evelyn Winters | | The Light of the World | *11:45* |
| Sam Hayes, news | In a Nutshell | Broadway News | The Farm Reporter | *12pm* |
| H. R. Baukhage, news | Lynn Cole, talk | Sing, America Sing | Ma Perkins | *12:15* |
| Second Honeymoon | Knox Manning, news | The Shady Valley Folks | Pepper Young's Family | *12:30* |
| | News | Melody Matinee | The Right to Happiness | *12:45* |
| Listen to This | The B. Wheeler Show | | Mary Noble, Backstage Wife | *1pm* |
| | | Norma Dixon, talk | Stella Dallas | *1:15* |
| Quizzicale / Records | Winner Take All | Nancy Young, talk | Lorenzo Jones | *1:30* |
| Ethel and Albert | | | Young Widder Brown | *1:45* |

## DAYTIME — SUMMER, 1948

*Sunday*

| | ABC | CBS | MBS | NBC |
|---|---|---|---|---|
| *2pm* | The Southernaires Quartet | Wagon Tales | Under Arrest | Author Meets the Critics |
| *2:15* | | Here's to You | | |
| *2:30* | Counterspy | Sunday at the Chase | What Makes You Tick | Pickens Party |
| *2:45* | | | | |
| *3pm* | California Caravan | The Prudential Family Hour | Those Websters | The Catholic Hour |
| *3:15* | | | | |
| *3:30* | The Hope of Peace | The Pause That Refreshes | Nick Carter, Master Detective | News |
| *3:45* | Music | | | The Melody Parade |
| *4pm* | Personal Autograph | Gene Autry's Melody Ranch | Mystery Playhouse | Let's Talk Hollywood |
| *4:15* | | | | |
| *4:30* | Johnny Fletcher | Dr. Standish, Medical Examiner | Lucky Partner | The Summer Theater |
| *4:45* | | | | |

## DAYTIME — SUMMER, 1948

*Monday-Friday*

| ABC | CBS | MBS | NBC | |
|---|---|---|---|---|
| Surprise Package | Your Stand In | Heart's Desire | When a Girl Marries | *2pm* |
| | | | Portia Faces Life | *2:15* |
| Bride and Groom | House Party | Hollywood Favorites | Just Plain Bill | *2:30* |
| | | Red Hook 31 | Front Page Farrell | *2:45* |
| Ladies Be Seated | Meet the Missus | Music / Always a Woman / Leave It to the Girls / A. L. Alexander's Mediation Board | The Road of Life | *3pm* |
| | | | Life Can Be Beautiful | *3:15* |
| Norwood Smith Sings | Arthur Godfrey Time | The Johnson Family | Aunt Mary | *3:30* |
| The Frances Scully Show | | Adventure Parade | This is Nora Drake | *3:45* |
| | Hint Hunt | News | One Woman's Secret | *4pm* |
| Alvin Wilder, news | | Frank Hemingway, news | News of the World | *4:15* |
| Records | The Wayne Show | The Passing Parade | Art Baker's Notebook | *4:30* |
| | Edward R. Murrow, news | Rex Miller, news | | *4:45* |

## DAYTIME — SUMMER, 1948

*Saturday*

| | ABC | CBS | MBS | NBC |
|---|---|---|---|---|
| *8am* | Shoppers Special | Let's Pretend | The Treasury Department | The Coffee Concert |
| *8:15* | | | Policing L. A. | |
| *8:30* | | Junior Miss | The Clinic Forum | Smilin' Ed's Buster Brown Gang |
| *8:45* | Mirandy | | | |
| *9am* | The Abbott and Costello Children's Show | The Armstrong Theater of Today | Time for Melody | Jump-Jump and the Ice Queen |
| *9:15* | | | | Storyland |
| *9:30* | News | Stars Over Hollywood | The All-Girl Corps | The Kitchen |
| *9:45* | The B. Weed Show | | | The Saturday Chef |
| *10am* | The American Farmer | Grand Central Station | Glenn Hardy, news | The National Farm and Home Hour |
| *10:15* | | | The Garden Guide | |
| *10:30* | Hollywood Headlines | County Fair | The Pacific Music Festival | Meet the Meeks |
| *10:45* | Chemists | | | |
| *11am* | Fascinating Rhythm | Mary Lee Taylor, cooking | Movie Matinee | Archie Andrews |
| *11:15* | | | | |
| *11:30* | The Hitching Post | Give and Take | The Teen Timers Club | The Veterans Advisor |
| *11:45* | | | | |
| *12pm* | News | Meet the Missus | News | The Farm Reporter |
| *12:15* | The American Way | | In Washington | Here Comes the Band |
| *12:30* | ABC Symphony Orchestra | Fun to Be Young | Sports Parade | Easy Listening |
| *12:45* | | | | |
| *1pm* | | Know Your Radio | News | Living 1948 |
| *1:15* | | Guest Star | Horse Racing | |
| *1:30* | Sports | Columbia's Country Journal | Public Affairs | Musiciana |
| *1:45* | Race of the Day | | In Your Name | |

## DAYTIME — SUMMER, 1948

*Saturday*

| | ABC | CBS | MBS | NBC |
|---|---|---|---|---|
| *2pm* | The Summer Concert | Make Way for Youth | Opinionaire | News |
| *2:15* | | | | Lassie |
| *2:30* | The Piano Playhouse | Music | The Northwestern Reviewing Stand | Dr. I. Q. Jr. |
| *2:45* | | | | |
| *3pm* | Junior Junction | Cross-Section USA | The Tex Beneke Review | Nature Sketch |
| *3:15* | | | | The Art of Living |
| *3:30* | Melodies to Remember | News | Special Agent | NBC Symphony Orchestra |
| *3:45* | It's Your Business | At the Hollywood Bowl | | |
| *4pm* | Songs | St. Louis Municipal Opera | Mel Allen, sports | |
| *4:15* | Sports | | Frank Hemingway, news | |
| *4:30* | Records | The Los Angeles Story | Songs | Curtain Time |
| *4:45* | News | The Todds | The Christian Science Monitor | |

## EVENING — FALL, 1948

*Sunday*

| | ABC | CBS | MBS | NBC |
|---|---|---|---|---|
| *5pm* | Go for the House | Gene Autry's Melody Ranch | Sherlock Holmes | The Lucky Strike Program, Jack Benny |
| *5:15* | | | | |
| *5:30* | The Curt Massey Show | Amos 'n' Andy | News | The Phil Harris - Alice Faye Show |
| *5:45* | | | The Cavalcade of Stars | |
| *6pm* | Stop the Music | My Favorite Husband | A. L. Alexander's Mediation Board | The Charlie McCarthy Show |
| *6:15* | | | | |
| *6:30* | | Find That Clue | The Quiz of Two Cities | The Fred Allen Show |
| *6:45* | | | | |
| *7pm* | Walter Winchell's Jourgan's Journal | The Electric Theater | Behind the Front Page | The Manhattan Merry-Go-Round |
| *7:15* | Louella Parsons, gossip | | | |
| *7:30* | The Theater Guild on the Air | Our Miss Brooks | Jimmy Fidler, gossip | The American Album of Familiar Music |
| *7:45* | | | Views of the News | |
| *8pm* | | Lum and Abner | Twenty Questions | Take It or Leave It |
| *8:15* | | | | |
| *8:30* | Jimmy Fidler, gossip | Strike It Rich | Walter Winchell's Jourgan's Journal | The Youth Opportunity Program |
| *8:45* | News | | Stars in the Spotlight | |
| *9pm* | Drew Pearson, news | The Adventures of Sam Spade | Glenn Hardy, news | The Adventures of Ozzie and Harriet |
| *9:15* | Don Gardiner, news | | Admiral Zacharias, comment | |
| *9:30* | Tex Williams Orchestra | The Whistler | It's a Living | The Standard Symphony Hour |
| *9:45* | | | | |
| *10pm* | The Richfield Reporter | Box 13 | Music | |
| *10:15* | Washington News | | | |
| *10:30* | Stars Behind the Mike | The Symphonette | The Chicago Theater of the Air | The Lucky Strike Program, Jack Benny |
| *10:45* | Here's Hollywood | | | |

## EVENING — FALL, 1948

*Monday*

| ABC | CBS | MBS | NBC | |
|---|---|---|---|---|
| Challenge of the Yukon | Front Page Feature | Fulton Lewis, Jr., news | One Woman's Secret | *5pm* |
| | Sports | Chandu, the Magician | News | *5:15* |
| Jack Armstrong, the All-American Boy | Club Fifteen | Captain Midnight | Murray Talks | *5:30* |
| | Edward R. Murrow, news | Tom Mix and His Ralston Straightshooters | Feature Wire | *5:45* |
| Animal Court | Charles Collingwood, news | The Falcon | The Night Reporter | *6pm* |
| The Democratic Record Show | Henry Garred, news | | Downbeat | *6:15* |
| Child's World | Arthur Godfrey's Talent Scouts | The Hampton Show | The Voice of Firestone | *6:30* |
| | | | | *6:45* |
| The Lone Ranger | The Lux Radio Theater | Gabriel Heatter, news | The American Way | *7pm* |
| | | The Mutual Newsreel | | *7:15* |
| Starr Time | | The Cisco Kid | Dr. I. Q., the Mental Banker | *7:30* |
| | | Bill Henry, news (7:55PM) | | *7:45* |
| The Railroad Hour | My Friend Irma | Let George Do It | The Carnation Contented Hour | *8pm* |
| | | | | *8:15* |
| | The Bob Hawk Show | The Casebook of Gregory Hood | Henry Wallace, comment | *8:30* |
| The Newspaper Forum | | | Here's Harmony | *8:45* |
| News | Lowell Thomas, news | Glenn Hardy, news | The Chesterfield Supper Club | *9pm* |
| Earl Godwin, news | The Jack Smith Show | Fleetwoood Lawton, news | World News | *9:15* |
| Johnny Fletcher | Inner Sanctum Mysteries | The Inside of Sports | The Cavalcade of America | *9:30* |
| | | Your Land and Mine | | *9:45* |
| The Richfield Reporter | The Ten o'Clock Wire | Fulton Lewis Jr., news | The Bell Telephone Hour | *10pm* |
| Music | The Beulah Show | Public Affairs | | *10:15* |
| Hawthorne House | The Night Editor | Music | The Big Story | *10:30* |
| | Sports | In Your Name | | *10:45* |

## EVENING — FALL, 1948

*Tuesday*

| | ABC | CBS | MBS | NBC |
|---|---|---|---|---|
| *5pm* | The Green Hornet | Front Page Feature | Fulton Lewis Jr., news | One Woman's Secret |
| *5:15* | | Sports | Chandu, the Magician | News |
| *5:30* | Sky King | Club Fifteen | Captain Midnight | Murray Talks |
| *5:45* | | Edward R. Murrow, news | Tom Mix and His Ralston Straightshooters | Feature Wire |
| *6pm* | Animal Court | Charles Collingwood, news | The Mysterious Traveler | The Night Reporter |
| *6:15* | Elmer Davis, news | Henry Garred, news | | Remember That Music |
| *6:30* | Relaxin' Time | Mr. and Mrs. North | Sounds in the Night | A Date with Judy |
| *6:45* | | | | |
| *7pm* | Youth and the Government | The Women's Forum | Gabriel Heatter, news | The Bob Hope Show |
| *7:15* | | | The Mutual Newsreel | |
| *7:30* | Report to the People | Melodies America Loves | Red Ryder | Fibber McGee and Molly |
| *7:45* | The Chamber Music Society of Lower Basin Street | | Bill Henry, news (7:55PM) | |
| *8pm* | The Newspaper Forum | Hit the Jackpot | The Count of Monte Cristo | Favorite Story |
| *8:15* | | | | |
| *8:30* | America's Town Meeting of the Air | Life with Luigi | Official Detective | People Are Funny |
| *8:45* | | | | |
| *9pm* | | Lowell Thomas, news | Glenn Hardy, news | The Chesterfield Supper Club |
| *9:15* | | The Jack Smith Show | Fleetwood Lawton, news | World News |
| *9:30* | | Mystery Theater | The Inside of Sports | The Mel Torme Show |
| *9:45* | Special Event | | Public Affars | |
| *10pm* | The Richfield Reporter | The Ten o'Clock Wire | Fulton Lewis Jr., news | Big Town |
| *10:15* | Music | The Beulah Show | Music Hilites | |
| *10:30* | Hawthorne House | The Night Editor | Music | The Pleasure Parade |
| *10:45* | | Sports | | Melody Time |

## EVENING — FALL, 1948

*Wednesday*

| ABC | CBS | MBS | NBC | |
|---|---|---|---|---|
| Challenge of the Yukon | Front Page Feature | Fulton Lewis Jr., news | One Woman's Secret | *5pm* |
| | Sports | Chandu, the Magician | News | *5:15* |
| Jack Armstrong, the All-American Boy | Club Fifteen | Captain Midnight | Murray Talks | *5:30* |
| | Edward R. Murrow, news | Tom Mix and His Ralston Straightshooters | Feature Wire | *5:45* |
| Animal Court | Charles Collingwood, news | Can You Top This | The Night Reporter | *6pm* |
| The Democratic Record Show | Henry Garred, news | | Mayor Bowron, comment | *6:15* |
| Meredith Willson Orchestra | Dr. Christian | The Lone Wolf | Music | *6:30* |
| | | | Elmer Patterson, news | *6:45* |
| The Lone Ranger | Your Song and Mine | Gabriel Heatter, news | Duffy's Tavern | *7pm* |
| | | The Mutual Newsreel | | *7:15* |
| Ted Mack's Original Amateur Hour | Harvest of Stars | The Cisco Kid | The Skippy Hollywood Theater | *7:30* |
| | | Bill Henry, news (7:55PM) | | *7:45* |
| | The Music Hall | What's the Name of That Song | The Hollywood Bowl Auditions | *8pm* |
| | | | | *8:15* |
| You Bet Your Life | Free for All | The Hollywood Story | Curtain Time | *8:30* |
| | | | | *8:45* |
| Philco Radio Time, Bing Crosby | Lowell Thomas, news | Glenn Hardy, news | The Chesterfield Supper Club | *9pm* |
| | The Jack Smith Show | Fleetwood Lawton, news | World News | *9:15* |
| The Texaco Star Theater, Milton Berle | Citizen's Commision | The Inside of Sports | The Great Gildersleeve | *9:30* |
| | | Your Land and Mine | | *9:45* |
| The Richfield Reporter | The Ten o'Clock Wire | Fulton Lewis Jr., news | Blondie | *10pm* |
| Music | The Beulah Show | Music Hilites | | *10:15* |
| Hawthorne House | The Night Editor | Music | Mr. District Attorney | *10:30* |
| | Sports | Organ Recital | | *10:45* |

## EVENING — FALL, 1948

*Thursday*

| | ABC | CBS | MBS | NBC |
|---|---|---|---|---|
| *5pm* | The Green Hornet | Front Page Feature | Fulton Lewis Jr., news | One Woman's Secret |
| *5:15* | | Sports | Chandu, the Magician | News |
| *5:30* | Sky King | Club Fifteen | Captain Midnight | Murray Talks |
| *5:45* | | Edward R. Murrow, news | Tom Mix and His Ralston Straightshooters | Feature Wire |
| *6pm* | Animal Court | Charles Collingwood, news | The Family Theater | News |
| *6:15* | Elmer Davis, news | Herny Garred, news | | Here's Harmony |
| *6:30* | Henry Wallace, comment | The FBI in Peace and War | The Better Half | Music |
| *6:45* | Personal Autograph | | | Elmer Patterson, news |
| *7pm* | Mr. President | Suspense | Gabriel Heatter, news | The Kraft Music Hall, Al Jolson |
| *7:15* | | | The Mutual Newsreel | |
| *7:30* | Abbott and Costello | Casey, Crime Photorgrapher | Red Ryder | The Sealtest Variety Theater, Dorothy Lamour |
| *7:45* | | | Bill Henry, news (7:55PM) | |
| *8pm* | Final Edition | The Hallmark Playhouse | Straight Arrow | The Camel Screen Guild Players |
| *8:15* | | | | |
| *8:30* | The Dick Powell Show | The First Nighter Program | The All-Star Revue | Fred Waring Orchestra |
| *8:45* | | | | |
| *9pm* | Public Affairs | Lowell Thomas, news | Glenn Hardy, news | The Chesterfield Supper Club |
| *9:15* | Music | The Jack Smith Show | Fleetwood Lawton, news | World News |
| *9:30* | Songs of 1948 | Mr. Keen, Tracer of Lost Persons | The Inside of Sports | The Aldrich Family |
| *9:45* | Public Affairs | | Newscope | |
| *10pm* | The Richfield Reporter | The Ten o'Clock Wire | Fulton Lewis Jr., news | Maxwell House Coffee Time, Burns and Allen |
| *10:15* | Walter Kiernan, news | The Beulah Show | Music Hilites | |
| *10:30* | Hawthorne House | The Night Editor | Music | Noah Webster Says |
| *10:45* | | Sports | Organ Recital | |

| EVENING — FALL, 1948 | | | | |
|---|---|---|---|---|
| *Friday* | | | | |
| ABC | CBS | MBS | NBC | |
| Challenge of the Yukon | Front Page Feature | Fulton Lewis Jr., news | One Woman's Secret | *5pm* |
| | Sports | Chandu, the Magician | News | *5:15* |
| Jack Armstrong, the All-American Boy | Club Fifteen | Captain Midnight | Murray Talks | *5:30* |
| | Edward R. Murrow, news | Tom Mix and His Ralston Straightshooters | Feature Wire | *5:45* |
| Animal Court | Charles Collingwood, news | Roger Kilgore, Public Defender | News | *6pm* |
| The Democratic Record Show | Henry Garred, news | | Public Affairs | *6:15* |
| Famous Jury Trials | Mr. ace & JANE | Touchdown Tips | Music | *6:30* |
| | | Remember When | Elmer Patterson, news | *6:45* |
| Break the Bank | The Ford Theater | Gabriel Heatter, news | Pabst Blue Ribbon Town, Eddie Cantor | *7pm* |
| | | The Mutual Newsreel | | *7:15* |
| The Sheriff | | The Cisco Kid | The Raleigh Cigarette Program, Red Skelton | *7:30* |
| | | Bill Henry, news (7:55PM) | | *7:45* |
| Madison Square Garden Boxing | Everybody Wins | Great Scenes from Great Plays | The Life of Riley | *8pm* |
| | | | | *8:15* |
| Sports and Swing | Spotlight Revue | Leave It to the Girls | The Colgate Sports Newsreel, Bill Stern | *8:30* |
| | | | Sports | *8:45* |
| The Fat Man | Lowell Thomas, news | Glenn Hardy, news | The Chesterfield Supper Club | *9pm* |
| | The Jack Smith Show | Fleetwood Lawton, news | World News | *9:15* |
| This is Your FBI | The Jack Carson Show | The Inside of Sports | The Jimmy Durante Show | *9:30* |
| | | Your Land and Mine | | *9:45* |
| The Richfield Reporter | The Ten o'Clock Wire | Fulton Lewis Jr., news | Hollywood Open House | *10pm* |
| Walter Kiernan, news | The Beulah Show | Music Hilites | | *10:15* |
| Hawthorne House | The Night Editor | Music | Melody Time | *10:30* |
| | Sports | | Public Affairs | *10:45* |

## EVENING — FALL, 1948

*Saturday*

| | ABC | CBS | MBS | NBC |
|---|---|---|---|---|
| *5pm* | Speaking of Songs | Front Page Feature | Take a Number | NBC Symphony Orchestra (4:30PM) |
| *5:15* | Here's Hollywood | Sports | | |
| *5:30* | News | The Adventures of Philip Marlowe | True or False | Archie Andrews |
| *5:45* | Football Scores | | | |
| *6pm* | Music | Charles Collingwood, news | News | News |
| *6:15* | | Henry Garred, news | Sports | Downbeat |
| *6:30* | Mr. President | The Symphonette | Opinionaire | Sports |
| *6:45* | | | | Elmer Patterson, news |
| *7pm* | Bulldog Drummond | The Morey Amsterdam Show | Meet the Press | Guy Lombardo Orchestra |
| *7:15* | | | | |
| *7:30* | What's My Name | It Pays to Be Ignorant | The All-Star Western Theater | The Judy Canova Show |
| *7:45* | | | | |
| *8pm* | The Lone Ranger | Sing It Again | The Fishing and Hunting Club | A Day in the Life of Dennis Day |
| *8:15* | | | | |
| *8:30* | Whiz Quiz | | Meet the Boss | Grand Ole Opry |
| *8:45* | | | | |
| *9pm* | Gangbusters | The Camel Caravan, Vaughn Monroe | Glenn Hardy, news | The Pet Milk Show, Vic Damone |
| *9:15* | | | Sports | |
| *9:30* | The Amazing Mr. Malone | Special Investigator | Life Begins at Eighty | Truth or Consequences |
| *9:45* | | | | |
| *10pm* | News | The Ten o'Clock Wire | The Lanny Ross Show | Your Hit Parade |
| *10:15* | Sports | Music | Whelan Sings | |
| *10:30* | Hawthorne House | The National Military Ball | Music | The Hollywood Star Theater |
| *10:45* | | | | |

## DAYTIME — FALL, 1948

*Sunday*

| | ABC | CBS | MBS | NBC |
|---|---|---|---|---|
| *8am* | Message of Israel | The CBS Church of the Air | The Radio Bible Class | The L. A. Times Funnies |
| *8:15* | | | | |
| *8:30* | The Southernaires Quartet | | The Voice of Prophecy | The Christian Science Monitor |
| *8:45* | | | | Outdoor Reporter |
| *9am* | It Happened During the Week | Howard K. Smith, news | The Young People's Church | The National Radio Pulpit |
| *9:15* | Music | The University Explorer | | |
| *9:30* | The Hour of Faith | The Salt Lake Tabernacle Choir | The Week in Washington | Parent-Youth Forum |
| *9:45* | | | Random Notes | |
| *10am* | Texas Jim Robertson, songs | Invitation to Learning | Glenn Hardy, news | The Eternal Light |
| *10:15* | U. N. Reporter | | Commander Scott | |
| *10:30* | Centennial Year | The People's Platform | The Lutheran Hour | Melodies |
| *10:45* | | | | |
| *11am* | Music Miracles | Joseph C. Harsch, news | News and Views | Herbert J. Mann, sports |
| *11:15* | | Where the People Stand | | News |
| *11:30* | National Vespers | News | Henry Wallace, comment | The University of Chicago Round Table |
| *11:45* | | Behind the Lens | The Canary Pet Shop | |
| *12pm* | This Week Around the World | Festival of Song | Broadway News | The American Legion |
| *12:15* | | | Music | |
| *12:30* | The Piano Playhouse | You Are There | News | The NBC University Theater |
| *12:45* | | | The Veteran Wants to Know | |
| *1pm* | This World | New York Philharmonic Orchestra | The Air Force Band | |
| *1:15* | The Future of America | | | |
| *1:30* | The Treasury Band Show | | Juvenile Jury | One Man's Family |

## DAYTIME — FALL, 1948

*Monday-Friday*

| ABC | CBS | MBS | NBC | |
|---|---|---|---|---|
| The Breakfast Club | Songs | Cecil Brown, news | Fred Waring Orchestra | *8am* |
| | News | News | | *8:15* |
| | Music for You | The Editor's Diary | Inside the News | *8:30* |
| | | Breakfast Time | Sam Hayes, news | *8:45* |
| Welcome Travelers | Your Stand In | The Jedge | Art Baker's Notebook | *9am* |
| | | Victor Lindlahr, health | | *9:15* |
| Kay Kyser's College of Musical Knowledge | Grand Slam | Moods in Music | The Jack Berch Show | *9:30* |
| What Makes You Tick | Rosemary | | Lora Lawton | *9:45* |
| Between the Bookends | Wendy Warren and the News | Glenn Hardy, news | Ladies' Day | *10am* |
| Galen Drake, talk | Aunt Jenny's True Life Stories | The Gospel Singer | | *10:15* |
| My True Story | The Romance of Helen Trent | Kate Smith Speaks | | *10:30* |
| | Our Gal Sunday | Kate Smith Sings | Missing Hits | *10:45* |
| The Magazine of the Air | Big Sister | Ladies First | All Around Town | *11am* |
| Club Time / Listening Post / Dorothy Kilgallen, gossip | Ma Perkins | | Chuck Collins, news | *11:15* |
| Casa Cugat | Young Dr. Malone | Queen for a Day | What You Say | *11:30* |
| Quizzicale | The Guiding Light | | The Brighter Day | *11:45* |
| Sam Hayes, news | The Second Mrs. Burton | Broadway News | The Farm Reporter | *12pm* |
| H. R. Baukhage, news | Perry Mason | Sing, America Sing | The Road of Life | *12:15* |
| One for the Books | This is Nora Drake | Songs | Today's Children | *12:30* |
| | The Strange Romance of Evelyn Winters | Melody Matinee | The Light of the World | *12:45* |
| Breakfast in Hollywood | Knox Manning, news | Lynn at Hollywood | Life Can Be Beautiful | *1pm* |
| | For Living / George Fisher, gossip | Norma Dixon, talk | Ma Perkins | *1:15* |
| Galen Drake, talk | The B. Wheeler Show | Nancy Young, talk | Pepper Young's Family | *1:30* |

## DAYTIME — FALL, 1948

*Sunday*

| | ABC | CBS | MBS | NBC |
|---|---|---|---|---|
| *1:45* | | | | |
| *2pm* | Songs | | The House of Mystery | The Quiz Kids |
| *2:15* | Editor at Home | | | |
| *2:30* | Milton Cross Opera Album | Skyway to the Stars | True Detective Mysteries | News |
| *2:45* | | | | American Favorites |
| *3pm* | Quiet, Please | Crooks Cruise | The Shadow | Pickens Party |
| *3:15* | | News | | |
| *3:30* | Counterspy | Jack of All Trades | Quick as a Flash | The RCA Victor Show |
| *3:45* | | | | |
| *4pm* | California Caravan | The Prudential Family Hour of Stars | The Roy Rogers Show | The Catholic Hour |
| *4:15* | | | | |
| *4:30* | The Greatest Story Ever Told | The Pause that Refreshes | Nick Carter, Master Detective | News |
| *4:45* | | | | The Melody Parade |

## DAYTIME — FALL, 1948

*Monday-Friday*

| ABC | CBS | MBS | NBC | |
|---|---|---|---|---|
| Ethel and Albert | | | The Right to Happiness | *1:45* |
| Surprise Package | Party Line | Heart's Desire | Mary Noble, Backstage Wife | *2pm* |
| | | | Stella Dallas | *2:15* |
| Bride and Groom | Meet the Missus | Luncheon at Sardis | Lorenzo Jones | *2:30* |
| | | | Young Widder Brown | *2:45* |
| Ladies Be Seated | Hint Hunt | Happy Gang | When a Girl Marries | *3pm* |
| | | | Portia Faces Life | *3:15* |
| Norwood Smith Sings | House Party | Adventure Parade | Just Plain Bill | *3:30* |
| The Frances Scully Show | | The Adventures of Superman | Front Page Farrell | *3:45* |
| The George Fenneman Show | Arthur Godfrey Time | The Mailbag | Double or Nothing | *4pm* |
| | | Frank Hemingway, news | | *4:15* |
| | | The Passing Parade | Aunt Mary | *4:30* |
| Happy Theater | | Rex Miller, news | This is Nora Drake | *4:45* |

# DAYTIME — FALL, 1948

*Saturday*

| | ABC | CBS | MBS | NBC |
|---|---|---|---|---|
| *8am* | Shoppers Special | Songs | The Treasury Department | The Coffee Concert |
| *8:15* | | News | Policing L. A. | |
| *8:30* | | Tell It Again | The Clinic Forum | Inside the News |
| *8:45* | Mirandy | | | Sam Hayes, news |
| *9am* | The Abbott and Costello Children's Show | Let's Pretend | Strings and Voices | Meet the Meek |
| *9:15* | | | | |
| *9:30* | News | Junior Miss | TheTeen Club | Smilin' Ed's Buster Brown Gang |
| *9:45* | The American Way | | | |
| *10am* | | The Armstrong Theater of Today | Glenn Hardy, news | Jump Jump and the Ice Queen |
| *10:15* | Chemists | | The Garden Guide | Young America Speaks |
| *10:30* | The American Farmer | Grand Central Station | The Alll-Girl Corps | The Kitchen |
| *10:45* | | | | The Saturday Chef |
| *11am* | Shore Party | County Fair | Mountain Hayride | The National Farm and Home Hour |
| *11:15* | | | | |
| *11:30* | The B. George Show | Give and Take | | News |
| *11:45* | | | Songs | European Reporter |
| *12pm* | Fascinating Rhythm | Mary Lee Taylor, cooking | News | The Farm Reporter |
| *12:15* | | | Musical Matinee | The Man on the Farm |
| *12:30* | Tunes of the Year | Meet the Missus | | |
| *12:45* | Sports | | | Sports |
| *1pm* | | Fun to Be Young | | |
| *1:15* | | | | |
| *1:30* | | Sports | Saturday Dance | |
| *1:45* | | | | |

## DAYTIME — FALL, 1948

*Saturday*

| | ABC | CBS | MBS | NBC |
|---|---|---|---|---|
| *2pm* | | | | |
| *2:15* | | | Sports | |
| *2:30* | | | | |
| *2:45* | | | | |
| *3pm* | | | | |
| *3:15* | | | | |
| *3:30* | Melodies to Remember | Before Their Time | | Mr. and Mrs. U. N. |
| *3:45* | Let Freedom Ring | | | Lassie |
| *4pm* | Junior Junction | Tomorrow Calls | | News |
| *4:15* | | | | Religion in the News |
| *4:30* | Records | The Los Angeles Story | | NBC Symphony Orchestra |
| *4:45* | News | J. A. Ford, comment | | |

# LISTINGS FOR 1949

## EVENING — WINTER, 1949

*Sunday*

| | ABC | CBS | MBS | NBC |
|---|---|---|---|---|
| *5pm* | Stop the Music | Life with Luigi | A. L. Alexander's Mediation Board | The Fred Allen Show |
| *5:15* | | | | |
| *5:30* | | News | Secret Mission | The NBC Theater |
| *5:45* | | George Fisher, gossip | | |
| *6pm* | Walter Winchell, gossip | The Electric Theater | Under Arrest | The Manhattan Merry-Go-Round |
| *6:15* | Louella Parsons, gossip | | | |
| *6:30* | The Theater Guild of the Air | Our Miss Brooks | Jimmy Fidler, gossip | The American Album of Familiar Music |
| *6:45* | | | News | |
| *7pm* | | Lum and Abner | The Mayor of the Town | Take It or Leave It |
| *7:15* | | | | |
| *7:30* | Jimmy Fidler, gossip | It Pays to Be Ignorant | Can You Top This | The Youth Opportunity Program |
| *7:45* | The News Looks Ahead | | | |
| *8pm* | Drew Pearson, news | Rocky Jordan | Twenty Questions | The Adventures of Ozzie and Harriet |
| *8:15* | Don Gardiner, news | | | |
| *8:30* | Walter Winchell, gossip | The Whistler | Walter Winchell, gossip | The Standard Symphony Hour |
| *8:45* | Washington News | | Louella Parsons, gossip | |
| *9pm* | Music | The Adventures of Sam Spade | Glenn Hardy, news | |
| *9:15* | | | Music Hilites | |
| *9:30* | The Amazing Mr. Malone | The Lucky Strike Program, Jack Benny | The Chicago Theater of the Air | Surprise Service |
| *9:45* | | | | |
| *10pm* | The Richfield Reporter | The Ten o'Clock Wire | | Sam Hayes, news |
| *10:15* | News | The University Explorer | | Mayor Bowron, comment |
| *10:30* | Stars Behind the Mike | Music | Music | Inside the News |
| *10:45* | We CARE | | | Melody Time |

| EVENING — WINTER, 1949 | | | | |
|---|---|---|---|---|
| *Monday* | | | | |
| ABC | CBS | MBS | NBC | |
| Challenge of the Yukon | Front Page Feature | The Adventures of Superman | Feature Wire | *5pm* |
| | Sports | Chandu, the Magician | News | *5:15* |
| Sky King | Charles Collingwood, news | Captain Midnight | The Voice of Firestone | *5:30* |
| | Henry Garred, news | Tom Mix and His Ralston Straightshooters | | *5:45* |
| Headline Edition | The Lux Radio Theater | Gabriel Heatter, news | The American Way | *6pm* |
| Animal Court | | The Mutual Newsreel | | *6:15* |
| Child's World | | The Fishing and Hunting Club | Dr. I. Q., the Mental Banker | *6:30* |
| | | Bill Henry, news (6:55PM) | | *6:45* |
| The Lone Ranger | My Friend Irma | The American Forum of the Air | The Carnation Contented Hour | *7pm* |
| | | | | *7:15* |
| The Kay Starr Show | The Bob Hawk Show | The Cisco Kid | Spelling Bee | *7:30* |
| | | | | *7:45* |
| The Railroad Hour | Lowell Thomas, news | Let George Do It | The Chesterfield Supper Club | *8pm* |
| | The Jack Smith Show | | World News | *8:15* |
| | Arthur Godfrey's Talent Scouts | Sherlock Holmes | The Cavalcade of America | *8:30* |
| News | | | | *8:45* |
| Public Affairs | Inner Sanctum Mysteries | Glenn Hardy, news | The Bell Telephone Hour | *9pm* |
| | | Fleetwood Lawton, news | | *9:15* |
| Famous Jury Trials | The Beulah Show | The Inside of Sports | The Big Story | *9:30* |
| | The Night Editor | Fulton Lewis Jr., news | | *9:45* |
| The Richfield Reporter | The Ten o'Clock Wire | Music | Sam Hayes, news | *10pm* |
| Music | Bob Elson Interviews | The Music Box | Sports | *10:15* |
| One for the Books | The Symphonette | The Veteran Wants to Know | Inside the News | *10:30* |
| | | Land of the Free | Melody Time | *10:45* |

## EVENING — WINTER, 1949

*Tuesday*

| | ABC | CBS | MBS | NBC |
|---|---|---|---|---|
| *5pm* | The Green Hornet | Front Page Feature | The Adventures of Superman | Feature Wire |
| *5:15* | | Sports | Chandu, the Magician | News |
| *5:30* | Jack Armstrong, the All-American Boy | Charles Collingwood, news | Captain Midnight | The Alan Young Show |
| *5:45* | | Henry Garred, news | Tom Mix and His Ralston Straightshooters | |
| *6pm* | Headline Edition | The Women's Forum | Gabriel Heatter, news | The Bob Hope Show |
| *6:15* | Animal Court | | The Mutual Newsreel | |
| *6:30* | Marriage for Milliions | The Morey Amsterdam Show | The Air Force Hour | Fibber McGee and Molly |
| *6:45* | News | | Bill Henry, news (6:55PM) | |
| *7pm* | Counterspy | Hit the Jackpot | The Falcon | Favorite Story |
| *7:15* | | | | |
| *7:30* | Report to the People | Melodies America Loves | Red Ryder | People Are Funny |
| *7:45* | Detroit Symphony Orchestra | | | |
| *8pm* | | Lowell Thomas, news | The Count of Monte Cristo | The Chesterfield Supper Club |
| *8:15* | | The Jack Smith Show | | World News |
| *8:30* | America's Town Meeting of the Air | Mr. and Mrs. North | The New Adventures of the Thin Man | This is Your Life |
| *8:45* | | | | |
| *9pm* | | Mystery Theater | Glenn Hardy, news | Big Town |
| *9:15* | | | Fleetwood Lawton, news | |
| *9:30* | Twin Views of the News | The Beulah Show | The Inside of Sports | The Damon Runyon Theater |
| *9:45* | Here's Hollywood | The Night Editor | Fulton Lewis Jr., news | |
| *10pm* | The Richfield Reporter | The Ten o'Clock Wire | Music | Sam Hayes, news |
| *10:15* | Music | Bob Elson Interviews | The Music Box | Sports |
| *10:30* | One for the Books | Baton and Score | Music | Inside the News |
| *10:45* | | | | Melody Time |

## EVENING — WINTER, 1949

*Wednesday*

| ABC | CBS | MBS | NBC | |
|---|---|---|---|---|
| Challenge of the Yulkon | Front Page Feature | The Adventures of Superman | Feature Wire | *5pm* |
| | Sports | Chandu, the Magician | News | *5:15* |
| Sky King | Charles Collingwood, news | Captain Midnight | Casa Cugat | *5:30* |
| | Henry Garred, news | Tom Mix and His Ralston Straightshooters | Elmer Patterson, news | *5:45* |
| Headline Edition | County Fair | Gabriel Heatter, news | Duffy's Tavern | *6pm* |
| Animal Court | | The Mutual Newsreel | | *6:15* |
| Meredith Willson Orchestra | Harvest of Stars | The Family Theater | The Skippy Hollywood Theater | *6:30* |
| | | Bill Henry, news (6:55PM) | | *6:45* |
| The Lone Ranger | The Music Hall | The Comedy Playhouse | The Hollywood Bowl Auditions | *7pm* |
| | | | | *7:15* |
| Ted Mack's Original Amateur Hour | Free for All | The Cisco Kid | Curtain Time | *7:30* |
| | | | | *7:45* |
| | Lowell Thomas, news | What's the Name of That Song | The Chesterfield Supper Club | *8pm* |
| | The Jack Smith Show | | World News | *8:15* |
| You Bet Your Life | Dr. Christian | High Adventure | The Great Gildersleeve | *8:30* |
| | | | | *8:45* |
| Philco Radio Time, Bing Crosby | Capitol Cloak Room | Glenn Hardy, news | Blondie | *9pm* |
| | | Fleetwood Lawton, news | | *9:15* |
| The Texaco Star Theater, Milton Berle | The Beulah Show | The Inside of Sports | Mr. District Attorney | *9:30* |
| | The Night Editor | Fulton Lewis Jr., news | | *9:45* |
| The Richfield Reporter | The Ten o'Clock Wire | Music | Sam Hayes, news | *10pm* |
| Music | Bob Elson Interviews | The Music Box | Sports | *10:15* |
| One for the Books | The Symphonette | Music | Inside the News | *10:30* |
| | | | Melody Time | *10:45* |

## EVENING — WINTER, 1949

*Thursday*

| | ABC | CBS | MBS | NBC |
|---|---|---|---|---|
| *5pm* | The Green Hornet | Front Page Feature | The Adventures of Superman | Feature Wire |
| *5:15* | | Sports | Chandu, the Magician | News |
| *5:30* | Jack Armstrong, the All-American Boy | Charles Collingwood, news | Captain Midnight | Casa Cugat |
| *5:45* | | Henry Garred, news | Tom Mix and His Ralston Straightshooters | Elmer Patterson, news |
| *6pm* | Headline Edition | Suspense | Gabriel Heatter, news | The Kraft Music Hall, Al Jolson |
| *6:15* | Animal Court | | The Mutual Newsreel | |
| *6:30* | The Jo Stafford Show | Casey, Crime Photographer | Music Hilites | The Sealtest Variety Theater, Dorothy Lamour |
| *6:45* | | | Remember When | |
| *7pm* | Counterspy | The Hallmark Playhouse | | The Camel Screen Guild Players |
| *7:15* | | | | |
| *7:30* | Abbott and Costello | The First Nighter Program | Red Ryder | Fred Waring Orchestra |
| *7:45* | | | | |
| *8pm* | Theater USA | Lowell Thomas, news | Straight Arrow | The Chesterfield Supper Club |
| *8:15* | | The Jack Smith Show | | World News |
| *8:30* | Press Conference | Mr. Keen, Tracer of Lost Persons | The Mysterious Traveler | The Aldrich Family |
| *8:45* | | | | |
| *9pm* | Mr. President | The FBI in Peace and War | Glenn Hardy, news | Maxwell House Coffee Time, Burns and Allen |
| *9:15* | | | Fleetwood Lawton, news | |
| *9:30* | The New Adventures of Michael Shayne | The Beulah Show | The Inside of Sports | Noah Webster Says |
| *9:45* | | The Night Editor | Fulton Lewis Jr., news | |
| *10pm* | The Richfield Reporter | The Ten o'Clock Wire | Music | Sam Hayes, news |
| *10:15* | Music | Bob Elson Interviews | The Music Box | Hollywood Music |
| *10:30* | One for the Books | Baton and Score | Music | Inside the News |
| *10:45* | | | | Melody Time |

## EVENING — WINTER, 1949

*Friday*

| ABC | CBS | MBS | NBC | |
|---|---|---|---|---|
| Challenge of the Yukon | Front Page Feature | The Adventures of Superman | Feature Wire | *5pm* |
| | Sports | Chandu, the Magician | News | *5:15* |
| Sky King | Charles Collingwood, news | Captain Midnight | Casa Cugat | *5:30* |
| | Henry Garred, news | Tom Mix and His Ralston Straightshooters | Elmer Patterson, news | *5:45* |
| Headline Edition | The Ford Theater | Gabriel Heatter, news | Pabst Blue Ribbon Town, Eddie Cantor | *6pm* |
| Animal Court | | The Mutual Newsreel | | *6:15* |
| The Sheriff | | Music Hilites | The Raleigh Cigarette Program, Red Skelton | *6:30* |
| | | Bill Henry, news (6:55PM) | | *6:45* |
| Madison Square Garden Boxing | The Phillip Morris Playhouse | Great Scenes from Great Plays | The Life of Riley | *7pm* |
| | | | | *7:15* |
| | The Pause That Refreshes | The Cisco Kid | The Colgate Sports Newsreel, Bill Stern | *7:30* |
| | | | Sports | *7:45* |
| The Fat Man | Lowell Thomas, news | The Casebook of Gregory Hood | The Chesterfield Supper Club | *8pm* |
| | The Jack Smith Show | | World News | *8:15* |
| This is Your FBI | The Jack Carson Show | Yours for a Song | The Jimmy Durante Show | *8:30* |
| | | | | *8:45* |
| Break the Bank | My Favorite Husband | Glenn Hardy, news | The All-Star Western Theater | *9pm* |
| | | Fleetwood Lawton, news | | *9:15* |
| Bulldog Drummond | The Beulah Show | The Inside of Sports | Remember Music | *9:30* |
| | The Night Editor | Fulton Lewis Jr., news | Public Affairs | *9:45* |
| The Richfield Reporter | The Ten o'Clock Wire | Music | Sam Hayes, news | *10pm* |
| Music | Bob Elson Interviews | The Music Box | Sports | *10:15* |
| One for the Books | The Symphonette | Music | Inside the News | *10:30* |
| | | | Melody Time | *10:45* |

## EVENING — WINTER, 1949

*Saturday*

| | ABC | CBS | MBS | NBC |
|---|---|---|---|---|
| *5pm* | It's Your Business | Gene Autry's Melody Ranch | Hawaii Calls | Orchestras of the Nation (4:30PM) |
| *5:15* | Special Event | | | |
| *5:30* | Harry Wismer, news | Charles Collingwood, news | True or False | Sports |
| *5:45* | Sports | Henry Garred, news | | Elmer Patterson, news |
| *6pm* | Little Herman | Winner Take All | Meet the Press | News |
| *6:15* | | | | Science Edition |
| *6:30* | On Trial | Tales of Fatima | Lombardoland USA | The Judy Canova Show |
| *6:45* | | | | |
| *7pm* | The Curt Massey Show | Sing It Again | Take a Number | A Day in the Life of Dennis Day |
| *7:15* | | | | |
| *7:30* | The All-Star Show | | The George O'Hanlon Show | Grand Ole Opry |
| *7:45* | | | | |
| *8pm* | The Lone Ranger | The Camel Caravan, Vaughn Monroe | Life Begins at Eighty | The Pet Milk Show, Vic Damone |
| *8:15* | | | | |
| *8:30* | Hawthorne's Adventures | Gangbusters | The Western Hit Revue | Truth or Consequences |
| *8:45* | | | | |
| *9pm* | Our Job is Manhattan | Box 13 | Glenn Hardy, news | Your Hit Parade |
| *9:15* | | | Music Hilites | |
| *9:30* | Tex Williams Orchestra | The Adventures of Phillip Marlowe | | The Hollywood Star Theater |
| *9:45* | | | | |
| *10pm* | News | The Ten o'Clock Wire | Monica Sings | News |
| *10:15* | Sports | You Can Live With the Atom | Music | Supervisor Ray Darby, comment |
| *10:30* | Music | Music | | Music |
| *10:45* | | | | |

## DAYTIME — WINTER, 1949

*Sunday*

| | ABC | CBS | MBS | NBC |
|---|---|---|---|---|
| *8am* | Message of Israel | Howard K. Smith, news | The Religious Hour | The L. A. Times Funnies |
| *8:15* | | The Farm Journal | | |
| *8:30* | The Hour of Faith | The Salt Lake Tabernacle Choir | The Voice of Prophecy | The Christian Science Monitor |
| *8:45* | | | | Outdoor Reporter |
| *9am* | It Happened During the Week | Invitation to Learning | The Radio Bible Class | Parent-Youth Forum |
| *9:15* | Centennial Year | | | |
| *9:30* | The Piano Playhouse | The People's Platform | The Lutheran Hour | The Eternal Light |
| *9:45* | | | | |
| *10am* | American Almanac | Joseph C. Harsch, news | Glenn Hardy, news | Herbert J. Mann, sports |
| *10:15* | News | Where the People Stand | Commander Scott | News |
| *10:30* | National Vespers | News | Random Notebook | The University of Chicago Round Table |
| *10:45* | | The Frank Parker Show | Songs By Great Singers | |
| *11am* | Music Miracles | The Festival of Music | William L. Shirer, news | The First Piano Quartet |
| *11:15* | | | John B. Kennedy, news | |
| *11:30* | News | You Are There | Favorites | The NBC UniversityTheater |
| *11:45* | Musical Cavalcade | | The Canary Pet Shop | |
| *12pm* | Editor at Home | New York Philharmonic Orchestra | Broadway News | |
| *12:15* | The Honeydreamers | | Western Music | |
| *12:30* | The Treasury Band Shoiw | | Juvenile Jury | One Man's Family |
| *12:45* | | | | |
| *1pm* | Open House | | The House of Mystery | The Quiz Kids |
| *1:15* | | | | |

## DAYTIME — WINTER, 1949

*Monday-Friday*

| ABC | CBS | MBS | NBC | |
|---|---|---|---|---|
| The Breakfast Club | Songs | Cecil Brown, news | Fred Waring Orchestra | *8am* |
| | News | Victor Lindlahr, health | | *8:15* |
| | Grand Slam | The Editor's Diary | The Jack Berch Show | *8:30* |
| | Rosemary | Breakfast Time | Lora Lawton | *8:45* |
| Welcome Travelers | Wendy Warren and the News | Kate Smith Speaks | Ladies' Day | *9am* |
| | Aunt Jenny's True Life Stories | Kate Smith Sings | | *9:15* |
| Kay Kyser's College of Musical Knowledge | The Romance of Helen Trent | Moods in Music | | *9:30* |
| | Our Gal Sunday | | All Around Town | *9:45* |
| Between the Bookends | Big Sister | Glenn Hardy, news | | *10am* |
| Galen Drake, talk | Ma Perkins | The Gospel Singer | Are You Listening | *10:15* |
| My True Story | Young Dr. Malone | The Bill Slater Show | News | *10:30* |
| | The Guiding Light | | Life Can Be Beautiful | *10:45* |
| The Magazine of the Air | The Second Mrs. Burton | Ladies First | Double or Nothing | *11am* |
| Club Time / Eleanor and Anna Roosevelt, talk / Dorothy Kilgallen, gossip | Perry Mason | | | *11:15* |
| Casa Cugat | This is Nora Drake | Queen for a Day | Today's Children | *11:30* |
| One for the Books | What Makes You Tick | | The Light of the World | *11:45* |
| Sam Hayes, news | The Gordon Mason Show | Broadway News | The Farm Reporter | *12pm* |
| Norwood Smith Sings | | Sing, America Sing | Ma Perkins | *12:15* |
| Art Baker's Notebook | Your Lucky Strike | Melody Matinee | Pepper Young's Family | *12:30* |
| | | | The Right to Happiness | *12:45* |
| Breakfast in Hollywood | Knox Manning, news | Lynn at Hollywood | Mary Noble, Backstage Wife | *1pm* |
| | News | Norma Dixon, talk | Stella Dallas | *1:15* |

| DAYTIME — WINTER, 1949 | | | | |
|---|---|---|---|---|
| *Sunday* | | | | |
| | ABC | CBS | MBS | NBC |
| *1:30* | The Metropolitan Opera Auditions | Skyway to the Stars | True Detective Mysteries | The Melody Parade |
| *1:45* | | | | American Favorites |
| *2pm* | This Week Around the World | The Festival of Song | The Shadow | Songs on Sunday |
| *2:15* | | | | Tropicana |
| *2:30* | Quiet, Please | Strike It Rich | Quick as a Flash | The RCA Victor Show |
| *2:45* | | | | |
| *3pm* | California Caravan | The Prudential Family Hour of Stars | The Roy Rogers Show | The Catholic Hour |
| *3:15* | | | | |
| *3:30* | The Greatest Story Ever Told | The Longines Symphonette | Nick Carter, Master Detective | Close Harmony |
| *3:45* | | | | News |
| *4pm* | Go for the House | The Lucky Strike Program, Jack Benny | The Air Force Hour | The Youth Opportunity Program |
| *4:15* | | | | |
| *4:30* | This Changing World | Amos 'n' Andy | The Northwestern Reviewing Stand | The Phil Harris - Alice Faye Show |
| *4:45* | | | | |

## DAYTIME — WINTER, 1949

*Monday-Friday*

| ABC | CBS | MBS | NBC | |
|---|---|---|---|---|
| Jane Jordan, home economics | Call for Help | Nancy Young, talk | Lorenzo Jones | *1:30* |
| Ethel and Albert | | | Young Widder Brown | *1:45* |
| Surprise Package | Hint Hunt | The Hope Chest | When a Girl Marries | *2pm* |
| | | | Portia Faces Life | *2:15* |
| Bride and Groom | Meet the Missus | Movie Matinee | Just Plain Bill | *2:30* |
| | | | Front Page Farrell | *2:45* |
| Ladies Be Seated | Arthur Godfrey Time | The Happy Gang | The Road of Life | *3pm* |
| | | | The Brighter Day | *3:15* |
| House Party | | Adventure Parade | Aunt Mary | *3:30* |
| | | The Mailbag | Dr. Paul | *3:45* |
| The Frances Scully Show | Alka Seltzer Time, Herb Shriner | Fulton Lewis Jr., news | One Woman's Secret | *4pm* |
| | George Fisher, gossip | Frank Hemingway, news | Murray Talks | *4:15* |
| At Home With the Kirkwoods | Club Fifteen | The Passing Parade | Burritt and Wheeler, talk | *4:30* |
| Happy Theater | Edward R. Murrow, news | Rex Miller, news | | *4:45* |

| DAYTIME — WINTER, 1949 | | | | |
|---|---|---|---|---|
| *Saturday* | | | | |
| | ABC | CBS | MBS | NBC |
| *8am* | News | Let's Pretend | News | News |
| *8:15* | The American Way | | Policing L. A. | Outdoor Reporter |
| *8:30* | Headline Edition | Junior Miss | The Clinic Forum | Smilin' Ed's Buster Brown Gang |
| *8:45* | Mirandy | | | |
| *9am* | The Abbott and Costello Children's Show | The Armstrong Theater of Today | Songs | Jump-Jump and the Ice Queen |
| *9:15* | | | | Young America Speaks |
| *9:30* | Shore Party | Grand Central Station | Music | Music |
| *9:45* | | | Organ Recital | The Saturday Chef |
| *10am* | The American Farmer | Stars Over Hollywood | Glenn Hardy, news | The National Farm and Home Hour |
| *10:15* | | | The Garden Guide | |
| *10:30* | The American Way | Give and Take | Music | Mary Lee Taylor, cooking |
| *10:45* | Chemists | | | |
| *11am* | The Metropolitan Opera | The Handy Man | | RFD America |
| *11:15* | | Get More Out of Life | | |
| *11:30* | | Meet the Missus | The All-Girl Corps | News |
| *11:45* | | | | Report on Europe |
| *12pm* | | Mother Knows Best | News | The Farm Reporter |
| *12:15* | | | Music | The Man on the Farm |
| *12:30* | | Junior Stand In | Sports Parade | |
| *12:45* | | | | Are You Listening |
| *1pm* | | Fun to Be Young | Wings Over Jordan | |
| *1:15* | | | | |
| *1:30* | | Call for Help | College Choir | |
| *1:45* | | | | |

## DAYTIME — WINTER, 1949

*Saturday*

| | ABC | CBS | MBS | NBC |
|---|---|---|---|---|
| *2pm* | | Tell It Again | Take a Number | Lassie |
| *2:15* | Tea and Crumpets | | | Wormwood Forest |
| *2:30* | | Cross-Section USA | Income Tax | Dr. I. Q. Jr. |
| *2:45* | | | Music | |
| *3pm* | Junior Junction | Columbia's Country Journal | | On the Scouting Trail |
| *3:15* | | | | |
| *3:30* | Luncheon | The Los Angeles Story | The Shady Valley Folks | NBC Symphony Orchestra |
| *3:45* | | The Los Angeles County | | |
| *4pm* | Pubilc Affairs | Romance | Mel Allen, sports | |
| *4:15* | Sports | | Frank Hemingway, news | |
| *4:30* | Madhouse Music | Behind the Lens | Tea Dasant | Orchestras of the Nation |
| *4:45* | In the Family | Sports | | |

| EVENING — SPRING, 1949 | | | | |
|---|---|---|---|---|
| *Sunday* | | | | |
| | ABC | CBS | MBS | NBC |
| *5pm* | Stop the Music | News | A. L. Alexander's Mediation Board | The Fred Allen Show |
| *5:15* | | George Fisher, gossip | | |
| *5:30* | | Life with Luigi | The Triumphant Hour | The Henry Morgan Show |
| *5:45* | | | | |
| *6pm* | Walter Winchell, gossip | The Electric Theater | Under Arrest | The NBC Theater |
| *6:15* | Louella Parsons, gossip | | | |
| *6:30* | The Theater Guild of the Air | Our Miss Brooks | Jimmy Fidler, gossip | The American Album of Familiar Music |
| *6:45* | | | The Kenny Baker Show | |
| *7pm* | | Lum and Abner | The Mayor of the Town | Take It or Leave It |
| *7:15* | | | | |
| *7:30* | Jimmy Fidler, gossip | It Pays to Be Ignorant | Can You Top This | The Youth Opportunity Program |
| *7:45* | Through the Looking Glass | | | |
| *8pm* | Drew Pearson, news | Rocky Jordan | Twenty Questions | The Martin and Lewis Show |
| *8:15* | Don Gardiner, news | | | |
| *8:30* | Walter Winchell, gossip | The Whistler | Walter Winchell, gossip | The Standard Symphony Hour |
| *8:45* | Jimmy Roosevelt, comment | | Louella Parsons, gossip | |
| *9pm* | The Tobe Reed Show | The Adventures of Sam Spade | Glenn Hardy, news | |
| *9:15* | Music | | News | |
| *9:30* | Pat Novak for Hire | The Lucky Strike Program, Jack Benny | The Chicago Theater of the Air | The Musical Playhouse |
| *9:45* | | | | |
| *10pm* | The Richfield Reporter | The Ten o'Clock Wire | | Sam Hayes, news |
| *10:15* | Drew Pearson, news | The University Explorer | | Mary A. Mercer, news |
| *10:30* | News | Yours Truly, Johnny Dollar | Music | Inside the News |
| *10:45* | Music | | | Melody Time |

## EVENING — SPRING, 1949

*Monday*

| ABC | CBS | MBS | NBC | |
|---|---|---|---|---|
| Challenge of the Yukon | Front Page Feature | The Adventures of Superman | Feature Wire | *5pm* |
| | Sports | | News | *5:15* |
| Sky King | Charles Collingwood, news | Captain Midnight | The Voice of Firestone | *5:30* |
| | Henry Garred, news | Tom Mix and His Ralston Straightshooters | | *5:45* |
| Headline Edition | The Lux Radio Theater | Gabriel Heatter, news | The American Way | *6pm* |
| Sports | | The Mutual Newsreel | | *6:15* |
| Child's World | | The Fishing and Hunting Club | Dr. I. Q., the Mental Banker | *6:30* |
| Music | | Bill Henry, news (6:55PM) | | *6:45* |
| The Lone Ranger | My Friend Irma | The American Forum of the Air | The Carnation Contented Hour | *7pm* |
| | | | | *7:15* |
| Take a Chorus | The Bob Hawk Show | The Cisco Kid | Spelling Bee | *7:30* |
| | | | | *7:45* |
| The Railroad Hour | Lowell Thomas, news | Let George Do It | The Chesterfield Supper Club | *8pm* |
| | The Jack Smith Show | | World News | *8:15* |
| | Arthur Godfrey's Talent Scouts | Sherlock Holmes | The Cavalcade of America | *8:30* |
| Your Land and Mine | | | | *8:45* |
| News and Views | Inner Sanctum Mysteries | Glenn Hardy, news | The Bell Telephone Hour | *9pm* |
| | | Fleetwood Lawton, news | | *9:15* |
| Famous Jury Trials | The Beulah Show | The Inside of Sports | The Big Story | *9:30* |
| | The Night Editor | Fulton Lewis Jr., news | | *9:45* |
| The Richfield Reporter | The Ten o'Clock Wire | Music | Sam Hayes, news | *10pm* |
| Music | Bob Elson Interviews | | Sports | *10:15* |
| One for the Books | The Symphonette | | Inside the News | *10:30* |
| | | | Melody Time | *10:45* |

## EVENING — SPRING, 1949

*Tuesday*

| | ABC | CBS | MBS | NBC |
|---|---|---|---|---|
| *5pm* | The Green Hornet | Front Page Feature | Straight Arrow | Feature Wire |
| *5:15* | | Sports | | News |
| *5:30* | Jack Armstrong, the All-American Boy | Charles Collingwood, news | Captain Midnight | The Alan Young Show |
| *5:45* | | Henry Garred, news | Tom Mix and His Ralston Straightshooters | |
| *6pm* | Headline Edition | The Women's Forum | Gabriel Heatter, news | The Bob Hope Show |
| *6:15* | Sports | | The Mutual Newsreel | |
| *6:30* | Talent Tour | Melodies America Loves | The Air Force Hour | Fibber McGee and Molly |
| *6:45* | | | Bill Henry, news (6:55PM) | |
| *7pm* | Counterspy | Hit the Jackpot | The Casebook of Gregory Hood | The Hollywood Theater |
| *7:15* | | | | |
| *7:30* | Report to the People | Pass the Buck | Red Ryder | People Are Funny |
| *7:45* | Rex Maupin Entertains | | | |
| *8pm* | | Lowell Thomas, news | The Count of Monte Cristo | The Chesterfield Supper Club |
| *8:15* | | The Jack Smith Show | | World News |
| *8:30* | America's Town Meeting of the Air | Mr. and Mrs. North | Official Detective | This is Your Life |
| *8:45* | | | | |
| *9pm* | | Mystery Theater | Glenn Hardy, news | Big Town |
| *9:15* | | | Fleetwood Lawton, news | |
| *9:30* | Twin Views of the News | The Beulah Show | The Inside of Sports | The Damon Runyon Theater |
| *9:45* | Here's Hollywood | The Night Editor | Fulton Lewis Jr., news | |
| *10pm* | The Richfield Reporter | The Ten o'Clock Wire | Music | Sam Hayes, news |
| *10:15* | Music | Bob Elson Interviews | Olympic Fights | Sports |
| *10:30* | One for the Books | Baton and Score | | Inside the News |
| *10:45* | | | | Melody Time |

## EVENING — SPRING, 1949

*Wednesday*

| ABC | CBS | MBS | NBC | |
|---|---|---|---|---|
| Challenge of the Yulkon | Front Page Feature | The Adventures of Superman | Feature Wire | *5pm* |
| | Sports | | News | *5:15* |
| Sky King | Charles Collingwood, news | Captain Midnight | Casa Cugat | *5:30* |
| | Henry Garred, news | Tom Mix and His Ralston Straightshooters | Elmer Patterson, news | *5:45* |
| Headline Edition | County Fair | Gabriel Heatter, news | Duffy's Tavern | *6pm* |
| Sports | | The Mutual Newsreel | | *6:15* |
| The Kenny Baker Show | The Time of Her Life | The Family Theater | Musical Americana | *6:30* |
| | | Bill Henry, news (6:55PM) | | *6:45* |
| The Lone Ranger | The Music Hall | The Comedy Playhouse | The Hollywood Bowl Auditions | *7pm* |
| | | | | *7:15* |
| Ted Mack's Original Amateur Hour | Beat the Clock | The Cisco Kid | Curtain Time | *7:30* |
| | | | | *7:45* |
| | Lowell Thomas, news | What's the Name of That Song | The Chesterfield Supper Club | *8pm* |
| | The Jack Smith Show | | World News | *8:15* |
| You Bet Your Life | Dr. Christian | Scattergood Baines | The Great Gildersleeve | *8:30* |
| | | | | *8:45* |
| Philco Radio Time, Bing Crosby | Capitol Cloak Room | Glenn Hardy, news | Blondie | *9pm* |
| | | Fleetwood Lawton, news | | *9:15* |
| The Texaco StarTheater, Milton Berle | The Beulah Show | The Inside of Sports | Mr. District Attorney | *9:30* |
| | The Night Editor | Fulton Lewis Jr., news | | *9:45* |
| The Richfield Reporter | The Ten o'Clock Wire | Music | Sam Hayes, news | *10pm* |
| Music | Bob Elson Interviews | | Sports | *10:15* |
| One for the Books | The Symphonette | | Inside the News | *10:30* |
| | | | Melody Time | *10:45* |

## EVENING — SPRING, 1949

*Thursday*

| | ABC | CBS | MBS | NBC |
|---|---|---|---|---|
| *5pm* | The Green Hornet | Front Page Feature | Straight Arrow | Feature Wire |
| *5:15* | | Sports | | News |
| *5:30* | Jack Armstrong, the All-American Boy | Charles Collingwood, news | Captain Midnight | Casa Cugat |
| *5:45* | | Henry Garred, news | Tom Mix and His Ralston Straightshooters | Elmer Patterson, news |
| *6pm* | Headline Edition | Suspense | Gabriel Heatter, news | The Kraft Music Hall, Al Jolson |
| *6:15* | Sports | | The Mutual Newsreel | |
| *6:30* | The Jo Stafford Show | Casey, Crime Photographer | Remember When | The Sealtest Variety Theater, Dorothy Lamour |
| *6:45* | | | Music | |
| *7pm* | Counterspy | The Hallmark Playhouse | The Falcon | The Camel Screen Guild Players |
| *7:15* | | | | |
| *7:30* | Abbott and Costello | The First Nighter Program | Red Ryder | Fred Waring Orchestra |
| *7:45* | | | | |
| *8pm* | Press Conference | Lowell Thomas, news | Chandu, the Magician | The Chesterfield Supper Club |
| *8:15* | | The Jack Smith Show | | World News |
| *8:30* | Theater USA | Mr. Keen, Tracer of Lost Persons | The Mysterious Traveler | The Aldrich Family |
| *8:45* | | | | |
| *9pm* | Mr. President | The FBI in Peace and War | Glenn Hardy, news | Maxwell House Coffee Time, Burns and Allen |
| *9:15* | | | Fleetwood Lawton, news | |
| *9:30* | Go for the House | The Beulah Show | The Inside of Sports | Noah Webster Says |
| *9:45* | | The Night Editor | Fulton Lewis Jr., news | |
| *10pm* | The Richfield Reporter | The Ten o'Clock Wire | Music | Sam Hayes, news |
| *10:15* | Music | Bob Elson Interviews | | Hollywood Music |
| *10:30* | One for the Books | Baton and Score | | Inside the News |
| *10:45* | | | | Melody Time |

## EVENING — SPRING, 1949

*Firday*

| ABC | CBS | MBS | NBC | |
|---|---|---|---|---|
| Challenge of the Yukon | Front Page Feature | The Adventures of Superman | Feature Wire | *5pm* |
| | Sports | | News | *5:15* |
| Sky King | Charles Collingwood, news | Captain Midnight | Casa Cugat | *5:30* |
| | Henry Garred, news | Tom Mix and His Ralston Straightshooters | Elmer Patterson, news | *5:45* |
| Headline Edition | The Ford Theater | Gabriel Heatter, news | Pabst Blue Ribbon Town, Eddie Cantor | *6pm* |
| Sports | | The Mutual Newsreel | | *6:15* |
| The Sheriff | | The Garden Guide | The Raleigh Cigarette Program, Red Skelton | *6:30* |
| | | Hit Tunes | | *6:45* |
| Madison Square Garden Boxing | The Phillip Morris Playhouse | This is Paris, Maurice Chevalier | The Life of Riley | *7pm* |
| | | | | *7:15* |
| | Box 13 | The Cisco Kid | The Colgate Sports Newsreel, Bill Stern | *7:30* |
| | | | Mayor Bowron, comment | *7:45* |
| The Fat Man | Lowell Thomas, news | Straight Arrow | The Chesterfield Supper Club | *8pm* |
| | The Jack Smith Show | | World News | *8:15* |
| This is Your FBI | The Jack Carson Show | Yours for a Song | The Jimmy Durante Show | *8:30* |
| | | | | *8:45* |
| Break the Bank | My Favorite Husband | Glenn Hardy, news | Music of Hollywood | *9pm* |
| | | Fleetwood Lawton, news | | *9:15* |
| Bulldog Drummond | The Beulah Show | The Inside of Sports | Remember Music | *9:30* |
| | The Night Editor | Fulton Lewis Jr., news | | *9:45* |
| The Richfield Reporter | The Ten o'Clock Wire | Music | Sam Hayes, news | *10pm* |
| Music | Bob Elson Interviews | | Sports | *10:15* |
| One for the Books | The Symphonette | | Inside the News | *10:30* |
| | | | Melody Time | *10:45* |

| EVENING — SPRING, 1949 | | | | |
|---|---|---|---|---|
| *Saturday* | | | | |
| | ABC | CBS | MBS | NBC |
| *5pm* | Let Freedom Ring | Gene Autry's Melody Ranch | Hawaii Calls | Orchestras of the Nation (4:30PM) |
| *5:15* | Special Event | | | |
| *5:30* | Harry Wismer, news | Charles Collingwood, news | True or False | Sports |
| *5:45* | Sports | Henry Garred, news | | Elmer Patterson, news |
| *6pm* | Little Herman | The Adventures of Phillip Marlowe | Meet the Press | News |
| *6:15* | | | | Science Edition |
| *6:30* | On Trial | Tales of Fatima | Lombardoland USA | The Judy Canova Show |
| *6:45* | | | | |
| *7pm* | The Curt Massey Show | Sing It Again | Take a Number | A Day in the LIfe of Dennis Day |
| *7:15* | | | | |
| *7:30* | Hayloft Hoedown | | Plantation Jubilee | Grand Ole Opry |
| *7:45* | | | | |
| *8pm* | The Lone Ranger | The Camel Caravan, Vaughn Monroe | Life Begins at Eighty | The Pet Milk Show, Vic Damone |
| *8:15* | | | | |
| *8:30* | Good Health to All | Gangbusters | The Western Hit Revue | Truth or Consequences |
| *8:45* | | | | |
| *9pm* | Personal Autograph | Spotlight Revue | Glenn Hardy, news | Your Hit Parade |
| *9:15* | | | Sports | |
| *9:30* | Tex Williams, songs | Escape | Experience Speaks | The Hollywood Star Theater |
| *9:45* | | | | |
| *10pm* | News | The Ten o'Clock Wire | Monica Sings | News |
| *10:15* | Sports | The National Miltary Ball | Policing L. A. | Supervisor Ray Darby, comment |
| *10:30* | Music | Music | Music | Music |
| *10:45* | | | | |

## DAYTIME — SPRING, 1949

*Sunday*

| | ABC | CBS | MBS | NBC |
|---|---|---|---|---|
| *8am* | Message of Israel | Howard K. Smith, news | The Religious Hour | The L. A. Times Funnies |
| *8:15* | | The Farm Journal | | |
| *8:30* | The Hour of Faith | The Salt Lake Tabernacle Choir | The Voice of Prophecy | The Christian Science Monitor |
| *8:45* | | | | Outdoor Reporter |
| *9am* | It Happened During the Week | Invitation to Learning | The Radio Bible Class | Parent-Youth Forum |
| *9:15* | Centennial Year | | | |
| *9:30* | The Piano Playhouse | The People's Platform | The Lutheran Hour | The Eternal Light |
| *9:45* | | | | |
| *10am* | American Almanac | Charles Collingwood, news | Glenn Hardy, news | Herbert J. Mann, sports |
| *10:15* | Commander Scott | Where the People Stand | News | News |
| *10:30* | National Vespers | News | Random Notebook | The University of Chicago Round Table |
| *10:45* | | The Frank Parker Show | The Music Box | |
| *11am* | Music Miracles | The Longines Symphonette | The Quiz Club | America United |
| *11:15* | | | John B. Kennedy, news | |
| *11:30* | Good Music | You Are There | Favorites | The NBC University E723Theater |
| *11:45* | Cavalcade of Music | | The Canary Pet Shop | |
| *12pm* | Editor at Home | New York Philharmonic Orchestra | Broadway News | |
| *12:15* | Foreign Reporters | | Music | |
| *12:30* | Speaking of Songs | | Juvenile Jury | One Man's Family |
| *12:45* | | | | |
| *1pm* | Music Today | | The House of Mystery | The Quiz Kids |
| *1:15* | | | | |
| *1:30* | Milton Cross Opera Album | Skyway to the Stars | True Detective Mysteries | The Melody Parade |

## DAYTIME — SPRING, 1949

*Monday-Friday*

| ABC | CBS | MBS | NBC | |
|---|---|---|---|---|
| The Breakfast Club | Songs | Cecil Brown, news | Fred Waring Orchestra | *8am* |
| | News | Victor Lindlahr, health | | *8:15* |
| | Grand Slam | The Editor's Diary | The Jack Berch Show | *8:30* |
| | Rosemary | The Quiz Club | Lora Lawton | *8:45* |
| Welcome Travelers | Wendy Warren and the News | Kate Smith Speaks | Ladies' Day | *9am* |
| | Aunt Jenny's True Life Stories | Kate Smith Sings | | *9:15* |
| Kay Kyser's College of Musical Knowledge | The Romance of Helen Trent | Moods in Music | | *9:30* |
| | Our Gal Sunday | | All Around Town | *9:45* |
| Between the Bookends | Big Sister | Glenn Hardy, news | | *10am* |
| Galen Drake, talk | Ma Perkins | The Gospel Singer | Are You Listening | *10:15* |
| My True Story | Young Dr. Malone | The Bill Slater Show | News | *10:30* |
| | The Guiding Light | | Life Can Be Beautiful | *10:45* |
| The Magazine of the Air | The Second Mrs. Burton | Ladies First | Double or Nothing | *11am* |
| Club Time / Get More Out of Life / Dorothy Kilgallen, gossip | Perry Mason | | | *11:15* |
| Casa Cugat | This is Nora Drake | Queen for a Day | Today's Children | *11:30* |
| One for the Books | What Makes You Tick | | The Light of the World | *11:45* |
| Sam Hayes, news | The Gordon Mason Show | Broadway News | The Farm Reporter | *12pm* |
| News | | Musicale | Ma Perkins | *12:15* |
| Art Baker's Notebook | Knox Manning, news | Sing, America Sing | Pepper Young's Family | *12:30* |
| | Songs / E. H. Wileman, news | Melody Matinee | The Right to Happiness | *12:45* |
| Modern Romances | Call for Help | Lynn at Hollywood | Mary Noble, Backstage Wife | *1pm* |
| | | Norma Dixon, talk | Stella Dallas | *1:15* |
| Ethel and Albert | Winner Take All | Nancy Young, talk | Lorenzo Jones | *1:30* |

# DAYTIME — SPRING, 1949

*Sunday*

| | ABC | CBS | MBS | NBC |
|---|---|---|---|---|
| *1:45* | | | | Songs on Sunday |
| *2pm* | Music for Today | The Longines Choraliers | The Shadow | Music of America |
| *2:15* | | | | |
| *2:30* | Quiet, Please | Broadway is My Beat | Quick as a Flash | Harvest of Stars |
| *2:45* | | | | |
| *3pm* | California Caravan | The Prudential Family Hour of Stars | The Roy Rogers Show | The Catholic Hour |
| *3:15* | | | | |
| *3:30* | The Greatest Story Ever Told | The Adventures of Ozzie and Harriet | Nick Carter, Master Detective | California Senators |
| *3:45* | | | | News |
| *4pm* | Sunday With You | The Lucky Strike Program, Jack Benny | The Band Concert | Pickens Party |
| *4:15* | | | | |
| *4:30* | This Changing World | Amos 'n' Andy | The Northwestern Reviewing Stand | The Phil Harris - Alice Faye Show |
| *4:45* | Songs | | | |

## DAYTIME — SPRING, 1949

*Monday-Friday*

| ABC | CBS | MBS | NBC | |
|---|---|---|---|---|
| Eleanor and Anna Roosevelt, talk | George Fisher, gossip | | Young Widder Brown | *1:45* |
| Surprise Package | Hint Hunt | Music | When a Girl Marries | *2pm* |
| | | | Portia Faces Life | *2:15* |
| Bride and Groom | Meet the Missus | Anniversary Club | Just Plain Bill | *2:30* |
| | | | Front Page Farrell | *2:45* |
| Talk Your Way Out of It / Ladies Be Seated | Arthur Godfrey Time | The Happy Gang | The Road of Life | *3pm* |
| | | | The Brighter Day | *3:15* |
| House Party | | Music | Aunt Mary | *3:30* |
| | | The Mailbag | We Love and Learn | *3:45* |
| Party Time | Alka Seltzer Time, Herb Shriner | Fulton Lewis Jr., news | One Woman's Secret | *4pm* |
| The Frances Scully Show | Your Stand In | Frank Hemingway, news | Murray Talks | *4:15* |
| | Club Fifteen | The Passing Parade | Burritt and Wheeler, talk | *4:30* |
| Happy Theater | Edward R. Murrow, news | Rex Miller, news | | *4:45* |

## DAYTIME — SPRING, 1949

*Saturday*

| | ABC | CBS | MBS | NBC |
|---|---|---|---|---|
| *8am* | Shoppers Special | Let's Pretend | The Treasury Department | Meet the Meeks |
| *8:15* | | | Veterans for Wars | |
| *8:30* | What's My Name | Junior Miss | The School Show | Smilin' Ed's Buster Brown Gang |
| *8:45* | | | Land of the Free | |
| *9am* | The Girl Corps | The Armstrong Theater of Today | Flying Feet | Jump-Jump and the Ice Queen |
| *9:15* | | | | Young America Speaks |
| *9:30* | Mirandy | Grand Central Station | Mountain Hayride | Piano Music |
| *9:45* | Saturday Circus | | | Home Town |
| *10am* | The US Navy Band | Stars Over Hollywood | Glenn Hardy, news | The National Farm and Home Hour |
| *10:15* | | | Organ Recital | |
| *10:30* | Big 'n' Little | Give and Take | Music | Mary Lee Taylor, cooking |
| *10:45* | | | | |
| *11am* | Ira Cook, talk | The Handy Man | | RFD America |
| *11:15* | | Get More Out of Life | | |
| *11:30* | | Meet the Missus | The Coast Guard Band | News |
| *11:45* | | | | Report on Europe |
| *12pm* | | Mother Knows Best | News | The Farm Reporter |
| *12:15* | | | Time to Shine | The Platter Society |
| *12:30* | | Free for All | Sports Parade | |
| *12:45* | | | | Are You Listening |
| *1pm* | Beach Party | Fun to Be Young | Songs | |
| *1:15* | | | Horse Racing | |
| *1:30* | | Junior Stand In | | |
| *1:45* | | | | |

## DAYTIME — SPRING, 1949

*Saturday*

| | ABC | CBS | MBS | NBC |
|---|---|---|---|---|
| *2pm* | | Call for Help | Take a Number | Lassie |
| *2:15* | | | | Wormwood Forest |
| *2:30* | | Saturday at the Chase | Music | A' Cappella Choir |
| *2:45* | | | | |
| *3pm* | Junior Junction | Columbia's Country Journal | Wings Over Jordan | On the Scouting Trail |
| *3:15* | | | | |
| *3:30* | The American Farmer | The Garden Gate | Extra Time | NBC Symphony Orchestra |
| *3:45* | | J. A. Ford, comment | The Windy City | |
| *4pm* | Chemists | Cross-Section USA | Mel Allen, sports | |
| *4:15* | Bible Message | | Frank Hemingway, news | |
| *4:30* | Madhouse Music | The Los Angeles Story | Sports | Orchestras of the Nation |
| *4:45* | In the Family | Sports | Smoke Rings | |

## EVENING — SUMMER, 1949

*Sunday*

| | ABC | CBS | MBS | NBC |
|---|---|---|---|---|
| *5pm* | Think Fast | Rocky Jordan | A. L. Alexander's Mediation Board | Adventures in Music |
| *5:15* | | | | |
| *5:30* | Yesterday on Broadway | News | Can You Top This | NBC Symphony Orchestra |
| *5:45* | Cavalcade of Music | George Fisher, gossip | | |
| *6pm* | Walter Winchell, gossip | Earn Your Vacation | Charmer and the Dell | |
| *6:15* | Louella Parsons, gossip | | | |
| *6:30* | Go for the House | Our Miss Brooks | Sheila Graham, gossip | The American Album of Familiar Music |
| *6:45* | | | Twin Views of the News | |
| *7pm* | Jimmy Fidler, gossip | Life with Luigi | Murder By Experts | Take It or Leave It |
| *7:15* | Between the Bookends | | | |
| *7:30* | Music | The Green Lama | True or False | The Youth Opportunity Program |
| *7:45* | Sketches from Life | | | |
| *8pm* | Drew Pearson, news | The Adventures of Phillip Marlowe | Twenty Questions | The Four Star Playhouse |
| *8:15* | Don Gardiner, news | | | |
| *8:30* | Walter Winchell, gossip | The Whistler | Walter Winchell, gossip | The Standard Symphony Hour |
| *8:45* | Jimmy Roosevelt, comment | | The Kenny Baker Show | |
| *9pm* | Music | The Adventures of Sam Spade | Glenn Hardy, news | |
| *9:15* | | | Twin Views of the News | |
| *9:30* | Two Billion Strong | Your Hit Parade on Parade | Music | Richard Diamond, Private Detective |
| *9:45* | | | | |
| *10pm* | The Richfield Reporter | The Ten o'Clock Wire | The John J. Anthony Program | Sam Hayes, news |
| *10:15* | News | The Night Editor | | Mary A. Mercer, news |
| *10:30* | We CARE | Music | | Inside the News |
| *10:45* | Music | | | Melody Time |

# EVENING — SUMMER, 1949

*Monday*

| ABC | CBS | MBS | NBC | |
|---|---|---|---|---|
| The Green Hornet | Front Page Feature | Ted Drake, Guardian of the Big Top | Feature Wire | *5pm* |
| | Sports | | News | *5:15* |
| Johnny Lujack of Notre Dame | Charles Collingwood, news | The Adventures of Champion | News and Views | *5:30* |
| | Henry Garred, news | Tom Mix and His Ralston Straightshooters | | *5:45* |
| Headline Edition | Leave It to Joan | Gabriel Heatter, news | The American Way | *6pm* |
| Sports | | The Mutual Newsreel | | *6:15* |
| Music | Breakfast with Burrows | The Affairs of Peter Salem | Pickens Party | *6:30* |
| With Song | | Bill Henry, news (6:55PM) | | *6:45* |
| The Lone Ranger | The Straw Hat Concert | The American Forum of the Air | The Carnation Contented Hour | *7pm* |
| | | | | *7:15* |
| Hits and Encores | Chicagoans Orchestra | The Cisco Kid | Spelling Bee | *7:30* |
| | | | | *7:45* |
| The Railroad Hour | Lowell Thomas, news | Let George Do It | The Chesterfield Supper Club | *8pm* |
| | Music | | World News | *8:15* |
| Ella Mae Time | Young Love | The Saint | One Man's Family | *8:30* |
| Your Land and Mine | | | | *8:45* |
| News and Views | Inner Sanctum Mysteries | Glenn Hardy, news | The Bell Telephone Hour | *9pm* |
| | | Sammy Kaye's Showroom | | *9:15* |
| On Trial | Spin to Win | The Inside of Sports | The Big Story | *9:30* |
| | Club Fifteen | Fulton Lewis Jr., news | | *9:45* |
| The Richfield Reporter | The Ten o'Clock Wire | Music | Sam Hayes, news | *10pm* |
| Music | Bob Elson Interviews | | Sports | *10:15* |
| News | Music | | Inside the News | *10:30* |
| One for the Books | | | Melody Time | *10:45* |

## EVENING — SUMMER, 1949

*Tuesday*

| | ABC | CBS | MBS | NBC |
|---|---|---|---|---|
| *5pm* | Challenge of the Yukon | Front Page Feature | Bobby Benson | Feature Wire |
| *5:15* | | Sports | | News |
| *5:30* | Sky King | Charles Collingwood, news | The Adventures of Champion | Me and James |
| *5:45* | | Henry Garred, news | The Tom Mix Ralston Straightshooters | |
| *6pm* | Headline Edition | The Women's Forum | Gabriel Heatter, news | The Martin and Lewis Show |
| *6:15* | Sports | | The Mutual Newsreel | |
| *6:30* | Report by the People | It Pays to Be Ignorant | Official Detective | The King's Men |
| *6:45* | Music | | Bill Henry, news (6:55PM) | |
| *7pm* | Counterspy | Hit the Jackpot | The Casebook of Gregory Hood | The Hollywood Theater |
| *7:15* | | | | |
| *7:30* | Little Herman | Melodies America Loves | Red Ryder | A Life in Your Hands |
| *7:45* | | | | |
| *8pm* | Rex Maupin Entertains | Lowell Thomas, news | The Count of Monte Cristo | The Chesterfield Supper Club |
| *8:15* | | Music | | World News |
| *8:30* | America's Town Meeting of the Air | Mr. and Mrs. North | John Steele, Adventurer | Hogan's Daughter |
| *8:45* | | | | |
| *9pm* | | Mystery Theater | Glenn Hardy, news | Big Town |
| *9:15* | | | Remember When | |
| *9:30* | Twin Views of the News | Spin to Win | The Inside of Sports | The Damon Runyon Theater |
| *9:45* | Here's Hollywood | Club Fifteen | Fulton Lewis Jr., news | |
| *10pm* | The Richfield Reporter | The Ten o'Clock Wire | Music | Sam Hayes, news |
| *10:15* | Music | Bob Elson Interviews | | Sports |
| *10:30* | News | Music | | Inside the News |
| *10:45* | One for the Books | | | Melody Time |

## EVENING — SUMMER, 1949

*Wednesday*

| ABC | CBS | MBS | NBC | |
|---|---|---|---|---|
| Challenge of the Yukon | Front Page Feature | Ted Drake, Guardian of the Big Top | Feature Wire | *5pm* |
| | Sports | | News | *5:15* |
| Johnny Lujak cof Notre Dame | Charles Collingwood, news | The Adventures of Champion | Casa Cugat | *5:30* |
| | Henry Garred, news | The Tom Mix Ralston Straightshooters | Elmer Patterson, news | *5:45* |
| Headline Edition | The Lewison Stadium Concerts | Gabriel Heatter, news | Chicken Every Sunday | *6pm* |
| Sports | | The Mutual Newsreel | | *6:15* |
| Stars in the Night | | International Airport | Musical Americana | *6:30* |
| | | Bill Henry, news (6:55PM) | | *6:45* |
| The Lone Ranger | | The Comedy Playhouse | The Musical Playhouse | *7pm* |
| | | | | *7:15* |
| Ted Mack's Original Amateur Hour | The Music Hall | The Cisco Kid | Curtain Time | *7:30* |
| | | | | *7:45* |
| | Lowell Thomas, news | What's the Name of That Song | The Chesterfield Supper Club | *8pm* |
| | Music | | World News | *8:15* |
| Lawrence Welk High Life Revue | Dr. Christian | The Family Theater | Archie Andrews | *8:30* |
| | | | | *8:45* |
| Fishing Time | Capitol Cloak Room | Glenn Hardy, news | The Henry Morgan Show | *9pm* |
| | | Sammy Kaye's Showroom | | *9:15* |
| Time for Music | Spin to Win | The Inside of Sports | Mr. District Attorney | *9:30* |
| | Club Fifteen | Fulton Lewis Jr., news | | *9:45* |
| The Richfield Reporter | The Ten o'Clock Wire | Music | Sam Hayes, news | *10pm* |
| Music | Bob Elson Interviews | | Sports | *10:15* |
| News | Music | | Inside the News | *10:30* |
| One for the Books | | | Melody Time | *10:45* |

## EVENING — SUMMER, 1949

*Thursday*

| | ABC | CBS | MBS | NBC |
|---|---|---|---|---|
| *5pm* | Fun House | Front Page Feature | Bobby Benson | Feature Wire |
| *5:15* | | Sports | | News |
| *5:30* | Sky King | Charles Collingwood, news | The Adventures of Champion | Casa Cugat |
| *5:45* | | Henry Garred, news | The Tom Mix Ralston Straightshooters | Elmer Patterson, news |
| *6pm* | Headline Edition | Suspense | Gabriel Heatter, news | The Kraft Music Hall, Nelson Eddy |
| *6:15* | Sports | | The Mutual Newsreel | |
| *6:30* | Name the Movie | Casey, Crime Photographer | Music | Run, Man Run |
| *6:45* | | | Bill Henry, news (6:55PM) | |
| *7pm* | Counterspy | The First Nighter Program | The Falcon | Fred Waring Orchestra |
| *7:15* | | | | |
| *7:30* | Press Conference | Chicagoans Orchestra | Red Ryder | Melodies |
| *7:45* | | | | |
| *8pm* | Heinie and His Band | Lowell Thomas, news | Hopalong Cassidy | The Chesterfield Supper Club |
| *8:15* | | Music | | World News |
| *8:30* | Moon Mist | Mr. Keen, Tracer of Lost Persons | The Fishing and Hunting Club | My Silent Partner |
| *8:45* | | | | |
| *9pm* | Play It Again | Broadway is My Beat | Glenn Hardy, news | Eight by Request |
| *9:15* | | | The Garden Guide | |
| *9:30* | Personal Autograph | Spin to Win | The Inside of Sports | Noah Webster Says |
| *9:45* | | Club Fifteen | Fulton Lewis Jr., news | |
| *10pm* | The Richfield Reporter | The Ten o'Clock Wire | Music | Sam Hayes, news |
| *10:15* | Music | Bob Elson Interviews | | Sports |
| *10:30* | News | Music | | Inside the News |
| *10:45* | One for the Books | | | Melody Time |

## EVENING — SUMMER, 1949

*Friday*

| ABC | CBS | MBS | NBC | |
|---|---|---|---|---|
| The Green Hornet | Front Page Feature | Ted Drake, Guardian of the Big Top | Feature Wire | *5pm* |
| | Sports | | News | *5:15* |
| Johnny Lujack of Notre Dame | Charles Collingwood, news | The Adventures of Champion | Casa Cugat | *5:30* |
| | Henry Garred, news | The Tom Mix Ralston Straightshooters | Elmer Patterson, news | *5:45* |
| Headline Edition | The Ford Theater | Gabriel Heatter, news | The Screen Director's Playhouse | *6pm* |
| Sports | | The Mutual Newsreel | | *6:15* |
| The Sheriff | | Show Tunes | Music of Hollywood | *6:30* |
| | | Bill Henry, news (6:55PM) | | *6:45* |
| Music | The Phillip Morris Playhouse | This is Paris, Maurice Chevalier | Dr. I. Q., the Mental Banker | *7pm* |
| | | | | *7:15* |
| The Eye | Xavier Cugat Orchestra | The Cisco Kid | The Colgate Sports Newsreel, Bill Stern | *7:30* |
| | | | Mayor Bowron, comment | *7:45* |
| The Fat Man | Lowell Thomas, news | Straight Arrow | The Chesterfield Supper Club | *8pm* |
| | Music | | World News | *8:15* |
| This is Your FBI | Summer in St. Louis | The Mysterious Traveler | A Tree Grows in Brooklyn | *8:30* |
| | | | | *8:45* |
| Break the Bank | | Glenn Hardy, news | Dragnet | *9pm* |
| | | Sammy Kaye's Showroom | | *9:15* |
| Mr. President | Spin to Win | The Inside of Sports | Remember Music | *9:30* |
| | Club Fifteen | Fulton Lewis Jr., news | Pro and Con | *9:45* |
| The Richfield Reporter | The Ten o'Clock Wire | Music | Sam Hayes, news | *10pm* |
| Music | Bob Elson Interviews | | Sports | *10:15* |
| News | Music | | Inside the News | *10:30* |
| One for the Books | | | Melody Time | *10:45* |

## EVENING — SUMMER, 1949

*Saturday*

| | ABC | CBS | MBS | NBC |
|---|---|---|---|---|
| *5pm* | It's Your Business | Sports | Hawaii Calls | Saturday Special (2:00PM) |
| *5:15* | Special Event | Music | | |
| *5:30* | Rendezvous with Music | Charles Collingwood, news | Sing for Your Supper | Sports |
| *5:45* | Sports | Henry Garred, news | | Elmer Patterson, news |
| *6pm* | Musical Etchings | The Bob Hope Show | Meet the Press | News |
| *6:15* | | | | Public Affairs |
| *6:30* | The Three Suns | Tales of Fatima | Lombardoland USA | Dangerous Assignment |
| *6:45* | Bert Andrews, news | | | |
| *7pm* | Dance Orchestra | Sing It Again | Take a Number | My Good Wife |
| *7:15* | | | | |
| *7:30* | | | Meet Your Match | Grand Ole Opry |
| *7:45* | | | | |
| *8pm* | The Lone Ranger | The Camel Caravan, Vaughn Monroe | Life Begins at Eighty | The Pet Milk Show, Vic Damone |
| *8:15* | | | | |
| *8:30* | The Treasury Band Show | Gene Autry's Melody Ranch | Music | Music |
| *8:45* | | | | |
| *9pm* | Buzz Adlam's Playroom | Gangbusters | Glenn Hardy, news | Your Hit Parade |
| *9:15* | | | Sports | |
| *9:30* | Madhouse Music | Music | Plantation Jubilee | Proudly We Hail |
| *9:45* | | | | |
| *10pm* | News | The Ten o'Clock Wire | Monica Sings | News |
| *10:15* | The Retail Clerks' Union | What Would I Say | Policing L. A. | Supervisor Ray Darby, comment |
| *10:30* | Music | Music | The Chicago Theater of the Air | Tex Williams Orchestra |
| *10:45* | | | | Melody Time |

## DAYTIME — SUMMER, 1949

*Sunday*

| | ABC | CBS | MBS | NBC |
|---|---|---|---|---|
| *8am* | The Old Fashioned Revival Hour | The Farm Journal | The Religious Hour | The L. A. Times Funnies |
| *8:15* | | Howard K. Smith, news | | |
| *8:30* | | The Salt Lake Tabernacle Choir | The Voice of Prophecy | The Christian Science Monitor |
| *8:45* | | | | Outdoor Reporter |
| *9am* | The Southernaires Quartet | Invitation to Learning | The Radio Bible Class | Parent-Youth Forum |
| *9:15* | | | | |
| *9:30* | The Voice of Prophecy | The People's Platform | The Lutheran Hour | The Eternal Light |
| *9:45* | | | | |
| *10am* | News | News | Glenn Hardy, news | Herbert J. Mann, sports |
| *10:15* | Commander Scott | Where the People Stand | News | News |
| *10:30* | National Vespers | Charles Collingwood, news | Random Notebook | The University of Chicago Round Table |
| *10:45* | | The Frank Parker Show | Organ Recital | |
| *11am* | Melodies | The Longines Choraliers | Music | America United |
| *11:15* | Just Good Music | | | |
| *11:30* | The Piano Playhouse | Melodies | Favorites | The NBC UniversityTheater |
| *11:45* | | | The Canary Pet Shop | |
| *12pm* | News | CBS Symphony Orchestra | Broadway News | |
| *12:15* | Foreign Reporters | | Bill Cunningham, news | |
| *12:30* | The Hour of Faith | | Mystery Hall | Boston Symphony Orchestra |
| *12:45* | | | | |
| *1pm* | Milton Cross Opera Album | | The House of Mystery | |
| *1:15* | | | | |

| DAYTIME — SUMMER, 1949 | | | | |
|---|---|---|---|---|
| *Monday-Friday* | | | | |
| ABC | CBS | MBS | NBC | |
| The Breakfast Club | News | Cecil Brown, news | Honeymoon in New York | *8am* |
| | News | The Editor's Diary | | *8:15* |
| | Grand Slam | News | The Jack Berch Show | *8:30* |
| | Rosemary | Tom, Dick, and Harry, songs | To Boys and Girls | *8:45* |
| Ira Cook, talk | Wendy Warren and the News | Kate Smith Speaks | Ladies' Day | *9am* |
| | Aunt Jenny's True Life Stories | Kate Smith Sings | | *9:15* |
| Kay Kyser's College of Musical Knowledge | The Romance of Helen Trent | Moods in Music | | *9:30* |
| | Our Gal Sunday | | All Around Town | *9:45* |
| Between the Bookends | Big Sister | Glenn Hardy, news | | *10am* |
| Thomas Dewey, comment | Ma Perkins | The Gospel Singer | Are You Listening | *10:15* |
| My True Story | Young Dr. Malone | The Bill Slater Show | News | *10:30* |
| | The Guiding Light | | Life Can Be Beautiful | *10:45* |
| The Magazine of the Air | The Second Mrs. Burton | Ladies First | Double or Nothing | *11am* |
| Club Time / Get More Out of Life / Dorothy Kilgallen, gossip | Perry Mason | | | *11:15* |
| H. R. Baukhage, news | This is Nora Drake | Queen for a Day | Today's Children | *11:30* |
| Lend Me Your Books | What Makes You Tick | | The Light of the World | *11:45* |
| Sam Hayes, news | The Knox Manning Show | Broadway News | The Farm Reporter | *12pm* |
| Norwood Smith Sings | | Stu Wilson, news | Ma Perkins | *12:15* |
| Art Baker's Notebook | Knox Manning, news | Sing, America Sing | Pepper Young's Family | *12:30* |
| | The Harry Babbitt Show | Melody Matinee | The Right to Happiness | *12:45* |
| Modern Romances | Call for Help | Lynn at Hollywood | Mary Noble, Backstage Wife | *1pm* |
| | | Music | Stella Dallas | *1:15* |

| DAYTIME — SUMMER, 1949 | | | | |
|---|---|---|---|---|
| *Sunday* | | | | |
| | ABC | CBS | MBS | NBC |
| *1:30* | Message of Israel | Art Mooney Orchestra | True Detective Mysteries | Who Said That |
| *1:45* | | | | |
| *2pm* | This Changing World | Music for You | Under Arrest | The Catholic Hour |
| *2:15* | The Song Salesman | | | |
| *2:30* | This Week Around the World | The Longines Symphonette | Mr. Fix-It | Hollywood Calling |
| *2:45* | | | Jimmy Powers, sports | |
| *3pm* | California Caravan | The Prudential Family Hour of Stars | The Roy Rogers Show | |
| *3:15* | | | | |
| *3:30* | Hollywood Byline | Yours Truly, Johnny Dollar | Nick Carter, Master Detective | News |
| *3:45* | Fantasy in Melody | | | Salute to the Treasury |
| *4pm* | Stop the Music | Your Hit Parade on Parade | Scattergood Baines | Voices and Events |
| *4:15* | | | | |
| *4:30* | | Call the Police | The Northwestern Reviewing Stand | Guy Lombardo Orchestra |
| *4:45* | | | | |

## DAYTIME — SUMMER, 1949

*Monday-Friday*

| ABC | CBS | MBS | NBC | |
|---|---|---|---|---|
| Easy Aces | Winner Take All | Nancy Young, talk | Lorenzo Jones | *1:30* |
| Eleanor and Anna Roosevelt, talk | Beat the Clock | | Young Widder Brown | *1:45* |
| Surprise Package | | Against the Storm | When a Girl Marries | *2pm* |
| | Meet the Missus | | Portia Faces Life | *2:15* |
| Bride and Groom | | Music | Just Plain Bill | *2:30* |
| | Arthur Godfrey Time | | Front Page Farrell | *2:45* |
| Ladies Be Seated | | Temp Tones | Welcome Travelers | *3pm* |
| | | The Todds | | *3:15* |
| Add a Line | | Music | Aunt Mary | *3:30* |
| | | | We Love and Learn | *3:45* |
| Play It Again | Curt Massey, songs | Fulton Lewis Jr., news | One Woman's Secret | *4pm* |
| The Frances Scully Show | Your Stand In | Frank Hemingway, news | Murray Talks | *4:15* |
| | George Fisher, gossip | The Passing Parade | Burritt and Wheeler, talk | *4:30* |
| Happy Theater | Larry Lesueur, news | Rex Miller, news | | *4:45* |

## DAYTIME — SUMMER, 1949

*Saturday*

| | ABC | CBS | MBS | NBC |
|---|---|---|---|---|
| *8am* | Get Together | Let's Pretend | The Treasury Department | Honeymoon in New York |
| *8:15* | | | The Navy Show | |
| *8:30* | Modern Romances | Junior Miss | News | Smilin' Ed's Buster Brown Gang |
| *8:45* | | | Land of the Free | |
| *9am* | The Girl Corps | The Armstrong Theater of Today | Flying Feet | Jump-Jump and the Ice Queen |
| *9:15* | | | | Radio Playmates |
| *9:30* | What's My Name | Grand Central Station | Social Security Report | Piano Recital |
| *9:45* | | | Extra Time | Home Town |
| *10am* | Mirandy | Stars Over Hollywood | Glenn Hardy, news | The National Farm and Home Hour |
| *10:15* | The American Way | | Moon Beams | |
| *10:30* | Fun Fair | Give and Take | | Mary Lee Taylor, cooking |
| *10:45* | | | | |
| *11am* | Ira Cook, talk | County Fair | | RFD America |
| *11:15* | | | | |
| *11:30* | | Meet the Missus | | News |
| *11:45* | | | | Report on Europe |
| *12pm* | | Mother Knows Best | News | The Farm Reporter |
| *12:15* | | | Horse Racing | Multiple Schlerosis |
| *12:30* | | Call for Help | Military Salute | Summer Listening |
| *12:45* | | | | Are You Listening |
| *1pm* | Beach Party | Fun to Be Young | College Choir | |
| *1:15* | | | | |
| *1:30* | | Saturday at the Chase | Utah Festival of Music | |
| *1:45* | | | | |

## DAYTIME — SUMMER, 1949

*Saturday*

| | ABC | CBS | MBS | NBC |
|---|---|---|---|---|
| *2pm* | | The Treasury Band Show | Modern Music | Saturday Special |
| *2:15* | | | | |
| *2:30* | | Music | | |
| *2:45* | | | Feminine Fare | |
| *3pm* | | News | Songs | |
| *3:15* | | CBS Farm News | | |
| *3:30* | The American Farmer | At the Hollywood Bowl | Sports Parade | |
| *3:45* | | J. A. Ford, comment | | |
| *4pm* | Junior Junction | Music | Mel Allen, sports | |
| *4:15* | | | Frank Hemingway, news | |
| *4:30* | Harry James Orchestra | The Los Angeles Story | Smoke Rings | |
| *4:45* | As We See It | Sports | | |

# EVENING — FALL, 1949

*Sunday*

| | ABC | CBS | MBS | NBC |
|---|---|---|---|---|
| *5pm* | Stop the Music | The Charlie McCarhty Show | A. L. Alexander's Mediation Board | The Adventures of Sam Spade |
| *5:15* | | | | |
| *5:30* | | Rocky Jordan | Can You Top This | The Theater Guild of the Air |
| *5:45* | | | | |
| *6pm* | Walter Winchell, gossip | Meet Corliss Archer | Secret Mission | |
| *6:15* | Louella Parsons, gossip | | | |
| *6:30* | Chance of a Lifetime | The Youth Opportunity Program | Sheilah Graham, gossip | The American Album of Familiar Music |
| *6:45* | | | The National Guard | |
| *7pm* | Jimmy Fidler, gossip | The Carnation Contented Hour | Take a Number | Take It or Leave It |
| *7:15* | Between the Bookends | | | |
| *7:30* | Music | The Whistler | The Roy Rogers Show | The Pet Milk Show |
| *7:45* | | | | |
| *8pm* | Drew Pearson, news | Our Miss Brooks | Twenty Questions | The Radio City Playhouse |
| *8:15* | Don Gardiner, news | | | |
| *8:30* | Walter Winchell, gossip | The Charlie McCarthy Show | Walter Winchell, gossip | The Standard Symphony Hour |
| *8:45* | Hits and Encores | | Louella Parsons, gossip | |
| *9pm* | Box 13 | The Red Skelton Show | Glenn Hardy, news | |
| *9:15* | | | The Kenny Baker Show | |
| *9:30* | The Green Hornet | The Lucky Strike Program, Jack Benny | The Chicago Theater of the Air | Music |
| *9:45* | | | | |
| *10pm* | The Richfield Reporter | The Ten o'Clock Wire | | Sam Hayes, news |
| *10:15* | The Retail Clerk's Union | The Night Editor | | Mayor Bowron, comment |
| *10:30* | Stand By | J. A. Ford, comment | Music | Inside the News |
| *10:45* | Music | Guest Star | | Mr. Fix-It |

## EVENING — FALL, 1949

*Monday*

| ABC | CBS | MBS | NBC | |
|---|---|---|---|---|
| Challenge of the Yukon | Front Page Feature | Bobby Benson | Feature Wire | *5pm* |
| | Sports | | News | *5:15* |
| Sky King | Charles Collingwood, news | Tom Mix and His Ralston Straightshooters | The Voice of Firestone | *5:30* |
| | Henry Garred, news | | | *5:45* |
| Headline Edition | The Lux Radio Theater | Gabriel Heatter, news | The American Way | *6pm* |
| Elmer Davis, news | | The Mutual Newsreel | | *6:15* |
| KateSmith Calls | | Tello-Test Quiz | The Martin and Lewis Show | *6:30* |
| | | The Answer Man | | *6:45* |
| The Lone Ranger | My Friend Irma | Murder By Experts | The Henry Morgan Show | *7pm* |
| | | | | *7:15* |
| Share the Wealth | The Bob Hawk Show | The Cisco Kid | The Ethel Merman Show | *7:30* |
| | | | | *7:45* |
| Kate Smith Calls | Lowell Thomas, news | Let George Do It | Light Up Time, Frank Sinatra | *8pm* |
| | The Jack Smith Show | | World News | *8:15* |
| | Arthur Godfrey's Talent Scouts | The Saint | The Railroad Hour | *8:30* |
| Your Land and Mine | | | | *8:45* |
| News | Inner Sanctum Mysteries | Glenn Hardy, news | The Bell Telephone Hour | *9pm* |
| Kate Smith Calls | | Sammy Kaye's Showroom | | *9:15* |
| The Green Hornet | The Beulah Show | Piano Recital | Music | *9:30* |
| | Club Fifteen | | | *9:45* |
| The Richfield Reporter | The Ten o'Clock Wire | I Love a Mystery | Sam Hayes, news | *10pm* |
| Melodies | Bob Elson Interviews | Fulton Lewis Jr., news | The Johnny Murray Show | *10:15* |
| Science of the Mind | The Symphonette | News | Inside the News | *10:30* |
| One for the Books | | Music | Melody Time | *10:45* |

## EVENING — FALL, 1949

*Tuesday*

| | ABC | CBS | MBS | NBC |
|---|---|---|---|---|
| *5pm* | The Green Hornet | Front Page Feature | Straight Arrow | Feature Wire |
| *5:15* | | Sports | | News |
| *5:30* | Jack Armstrong, the All-American Boy | Charles Collingwood, news | Captain Midnight | Me and James |
| *5:45* | | Henry Garred, news | | |
| *6pm* | Headline Edition | The Women's Forum | Gabriel Heatter, news | The Bob Hope Show |
| *6:15* | Elmer Davis, news | | The Mutual Newsreel | |
| *6:30* | Report to the People | Life with Luigi | TelloTest Quiz | Fibber McGee and Molly |
| *6:45* | Music By Bovero | | The Answer Man | |
| *7pm* | Counterspy | Hit the Jackpot | Secret Mission | The Hollywood Theater |
| *7:15* | | | | |
| *7:30* | Solo Soliloquey | Melodies America Loves | Red Ryder | People Are Funny |
| *7:45* | | | | |
| *8pm* | Music | Lowell Thomas, news | The Count of Monte Cristo | Light Up Time, Frank Sinatra |
| *8:15* | | The Jack Smith Show | | World News |
| *8:30* | America's Town Meeting of the Air | Mr. and Mrs. North | Mystery is My Hobby | The Cavalcade of America |
| *8:45* | | | | |
| *9pm* | | Mystery Theater | Glenn Hardy, news | Big Town |
| *9:15* | | | Sammy Kaye's Showroom | |
| *9:30* | Twin Views of the News | The Beulah Show | Official Detective | The Damon Runyon Theater |
| *9:45* | We CARE | Club Fifteen | | |
| *10pm* | The Richfield Reporter | The Ten o'Clock Wire | I Love a Mystery | Sam Hayes, news |
| *10:15* | The Cavalcade of Music | Bob Elson Interviews | Fulton Lewis Jr., news | The Johnny Murray Show |
| *10:30* | Science of the Mind | The Community Chest | News | Inside the News |
| *10:45* | One for the Books | | Music | Melody Time |

## EVENING — FALL, 1949

*Wednesday*

| ABC | CBS | MBS | NBC | |
|---|---|---|---|---|
| Challenge of the Yulkon | Front Page Feature | Bobby Benson | Feature Wire | *5pm* |
| | Sports | | News | *5:15* |
| Sky King | Charles Collingwood, news | Tom Mix and His Ralston Straightshooters | Casa Cugat | *5:30* |
| | Henry Garred, news | | Elmer Patterson, news | *5:45* |
| Headline Edition | You Bet Your Life | Gabriel Heatter, news | This is Your Life | *6pm* |
| Elmer Davis, news | | The Mutual Newsreel | | *6:15* |
| Author Meets the Critics | The Bing Crosby Chesterfield Show | Tello-Test Quiz | The Screen Director's Playhouse | *6:30* |
| | | The Answer Man | | *6:45* |
| The Lone Ranger | Burns and Allen | John Steele, Adventurer | The Big Story | *7pm* |
| | | | | *7:15* |
| The Amazing Mr. Malone | The Hollywood Music Hall | The Cisco Kid | Curtain Time | *7:30* |
| | | | | *7:45* |
| Sherlock Holmes | Lowell Thomas, news | What's the Name of That Song | Light Up Time, Frank Sinatra | *8pm* |
| | The Jack Smith Show | | World News | *8:15* |
| Starring Boris Karloff | Dr. Christian | The Family Theater | The Great Gildersleeve | *8:30* |
| | | | | *8:45* |
| The Croupier | Jeff Regan, Investigator | Glenn Hardy, news | Break the Bank | *9pm* |
| | | Sammy Kaye's Showroom | | *9:15* |
| Lawrence Welk High Life Revue | The Beulah Show | International Airport | Mr. District Attorney | *9:30* |
| | Club Fifteen | | | *9:45* |
| The Richfield Reporter | The Ten o'Clock Wire | I Love a Mystery | Sam Hayes, news | *10pm* |
| Melodies | Bob Elson Interviews | Fulton Lewis Jr., news | The Johnny Murray Show | *10:15* |
| Science of the Mind | The Symphonette | News | Inside the News | *10:30* |
| One for the Books | | Music | Melody Time | *10:45* |

## EVENING — FALL, 1949

*Thursday*

| | ABC | CBS | MBS | NBC |
|---|---|---|---|---|
| *5pm* | The Green Hornet | Man on the Street | Straight Arrow | Feature Wire |
| *5:15* | | Sports | | News |
| *5:30* | Jack Armstrong, the All-American Boy | Charles Collingwood, news | Captain Midnight | Casa Cugat |
| *5:45* | | Henry Garred, news | | Elmer Patterson, news |
| *6pm* | Headline Edition | Suspense | Gabriel Heatter, news | The Camel Screen Guild Players |
| *6:15* | Elmer Davis, news | | The Mutual Newsreel | |
| *6:30* | Family Closeup | Casey, Crime Photographer | Tello-Test Quiz | Duffy's Tavern |
| *6:45* | | | The Answer Man | |
| *7pm* | Counterspy | The Hallmark Playhouse | The Falcon | The Chesterfield Supper Club |
| *7:15* | | | | |
| *7:30* | A Date with Judy | The First Nighter Program | Red Ryder | Dragnet |
| *7:45* | | | | |
| *8pm* | Ted Mack's Original Amateur Hour | Lowell Thomas, news | Hopalong Cassidy | Light Up Time, Frank Sinatra |
| *8:15* | | The Jack Smith Show | | World News |
| *8:30* | | Mr. Keen, Tracer of Lost Persons | The Fishing and Hunting Club | The Aldrich Family |
| *8:45* | | | | |
| *9pm* | Name the Movie | The FBI in Peace and War | Glenn Hardy, news | Father Knows Best |
| *9:15* | Robert Montgomery Speaking | | Sammy Kaye's Showroom | |
| *9:30* | Blondie | The Beulah Show | The Affairs of Peter Salem | Public Affairs |
| *9:45* | | Club Fifteen | | |
| *10pm* | The Richfield Reporter | The Ten o'Clock Wire | I Love a Mystery | Sam Hayes, news |
| *10:15* | The Cavalcade of Music | Bob Elson Interviews | Fulton Lewis Jr., news | The Johnny Murray Show |
| *10:30* | Science of the Mind | Music | News | Inside the News |
| *10:45* | One for the Books | | Music | Melody Time |

# EVENING — FALL, 1949

*Friday*

| ABC | CBS | MBS | NBC | |
|---|---|---|---|---|
| Challenge of the Yukon | Man on the Street | Bobby Benson | Feature Wire | *5pm* |
| | Sports | | News | *5:15* |
| Sky King | Charles Collingwood, news | Tom Mix and His Ralston Straightshooters | Casa Cugat | *5:30* |
| | Henry Garred, news | | Elmer Patterson, news | *5:45* |
| Headline Edition | Leave It to Joan | Gabriel Heatter, news | The Life of Riley | *6pm* |
| Elmer Davis, news | | The Mutual Newsreel | | *6:15* |
| Hits and Encores | Breakfast with Burrows | Tello-Test Quiz | The Jimmy Durante Show | *6:30* |
| | | The Answer Man | | *6:45* |
| Madison Square Garden Boxing | Young Love | Meet the Press | Dr. I. Q., the Mental Banker | *7pm* |
| | | | | *7:15* |
| | Chicagoans Orchestra | The Cisco Kid | The Colgate Sports Newsreel, Bill Stern | *7:30* |
| | | | Here Comes Harmon | *7:45* |
| The Fat Man | Lowell Thomas, news | Straight Arrow | Light Up Time, Frank Sinatra | *8pm* |
| | The Jack Smith Show | | World News | *8:15* |
| This is Your FBI | The Goldbergs | Secret Mission | Candy Matson, YUkon 2-8209 | *8:30* |
| | | | | *8:45* |
| The Adventures of Ozzie and Harriet | My Favorite Husband | Glenn Hardy, news | Richard Diamond, Private Detective | *9pm* |
| | | Sammy Kaye's Showroom | | *9:15* |
| Mr. President | The Beulah Show | Music | The Adventures of Frank Race | *9:30* |
| | Club Fifteen | | | *9:45* |
| The Richfield Reporter | The Ten o'Clock Wire | I Love a Mystery | Sam Hayes, news | *10pm* |
| Melodies | Bob Elson Interviews | Fulton Lewis Jr., news | The Johnny Murray Show | *10:15* |
| Science of the Mind | The Symphonette | News | Inside the News | *10:30* |
| One for the Books | | Music | Melody Time | *10:45* |

# EVENING — FALL, 1949

*Saturday*

| | ABC | CBS | MBS | NBC |
|---|---|---|---|---|
| *5pm* | It's Your Business | Musical Scoreboard | Sports | NBC Symphony Orchestra (4:30PM) |
| *5:15* | Special Event | Man on the Street | Music | |
| *5:30* | The Harmonaires | Chet Huntley, news | Meet Your Match | Sunday Preview |
| *5:45* | The Fifth Quarter | Henry Garred, news | | Elmer Patterson, news |
| *6pm* | Someone You Know | The Adventures of Phillip Marlowe | Quick as a Flash | Proudly We Hail |
| *6:15* | | | | |
| *6:30* | Music | Escape | Hawaii Calls | A Day in the Life of Dennis Day |
| *6:45* | Bert Andrews, news | | | |
| *7pm* | Hollywood Byline | Sing It Again | The Comedy Playhouse | The Judy Canova Show |
| *7:15* | | | | |
| *7:30* | Chandu, the Magician | | | Grand Ole Opry |
| *7:45* | | | | |
| *8pm* | The Lone Ranger | The Camel Caravan, Vaughn Monroe | Music | Truth or Consequences |
| *8:15* | | | | |
| *8:30* | The Casebook of Gregory Hood | Gene Autry's Melody Ranch | Lombardoland USA | Public Affairs |
| *8:45* | | | | |
| *9pm* | Time for Music | Gangbusters | Glenn Hardy, news | Your Hit Parade |
| *9:15* | | | Sports | |
| *9:30* | Madhouse Music | Your Truly, Johnny Dollar | The Treasury Band Show | The Hollywood Star Theater |
| *9:45* | | | | |
| *10pm* | News | The Ten o'Clock Wire | Monica Sings | News |
| *10:15* | Citizen's Committee No. 2 | The Los Angeles Story | Policing L. A. | Supervisor Ray Darby, comment |
| *10:30* | Music | Capitol Cloak Room | Music | Tex Williams Orchestra |
| *10:45* | | | | Melody Time |

# DAYTIME — FALL, 1949

*Sunday*

| | ABC | CBS | MBS | NBC |
|---|---|---|---|---|
| *8am* | The Old Fashioned Revival Hour | The Farm Journal | The Religious Hour | The L. A. Times Funnies |
| *8:15* | | Howard K. Smith, news | | |
| *8:30* | | The Salt Lake Tabernacle Choir | The Voice of Prophecy | America Speaks |
| *8:45* | | | | Outdoor Reporter |
| *9am* | The Southernaires Quartet | Invitation to Learning | The Radio Bible Class | Parent-Youth Forum |
| *9:15* | | | | |
| *9:30* | Message of Israel | The People's Platform | The Lutheran Hour | The Eternal Light |
| *9:45* | | | | |
| *10am* | News | Charles Collingwood, news | Glenn Hardy, news | Herbert J. Mann, sports |
| *10:15* | Commander Scott | Get More Out of Life | Organ Recital | News |
| *10:30* | National Vespers | Where the People Stand | | The University of Chicago Round Table |
| *10:45* | | The Frank Parker Show | Songs | |
| *11am* | Victor Lindlahr, health | The Longines Choraliers | Elder Michaux Congregation | The NBC University Theater |
| *11:15* | Frank and Ernest, songs | | | |
| *11:30* | Foreign Reporters | Syncopation Piece | David Ross Orchestra | |
| *11:45* | Melodies | | The Canary Pet Shop | |
| *12pm* | The Hour of Faith | New York Philharmonic Orchestra | Broadway News | One Man's Family |
| *12:15* | | | Bill Cunningham, news | |
| *12:30* | The Baptist Hour | | Juvenile Jury | The Quiz Kids |
| *12:45* | | | | |
| *1pm* | This Week Around the World | | The House of Mystery | News |
| *1:15* | | | | Home Town |
| *1:30* | The Voice of Prophecy | Sunday at the Chase | Martin Kane, Private Detective | Voices and Events |
| *1:45* | | | | |

| DAYTIME — FALL, 1949 | | | | |
|---|---|---|---|---|
| *Monday-Friday* | | | | |
| ABC | CBS | MBS | NBC | |
| The Breakfast Club | News | Cecil Brown, news | Coffee Time | *8am* |
| | News | News | Marriage for Two | *8:15* |
| | Grand Slam | The Editor's Diary | The Jack Berch Show | *8:30* |
| | Rosemary | Music | Two Boys and Girls | *8:45* |
| House Party | Wendy Warren and the News | Kate Smith Speaks | Ladies' Day | *9am* |
| | Aunt Jenny's True Life Stories | The Quiz Club | | *9:15* |
| Ira Cook, talk | The Romance of Helen Trent | Women are Wonderful | | *9:30* |
| | Our Gal Sunday | | All Around Town | *9:45* |
| | Big Sister | Glenn Hardy, news | | *10am* |
| Galen Drake, talk | Ma Perkins | The Gospel Singer | Are You Listening | *10:15* |
| My True Story | Young Dr. Malone | Ladies Fair | Lora Lawton | *10:30* |
| | The Guiding Light | | Life Can Be Beautiful | *10:45* |
| The Magazine of the Air | The Second Mrs. Burton | Ladies First | Double or Nothing | *11am* |
| Victor Lindlahr, health | Perry Mason | | | *11:15* |
| Modern Romances | This is Nora Drake | Queen for a Day | Today's Children | *11:30* |
| | The Brighter Day | | The Light of the World | *11:45* |
| Sam Hayes, news | News and Talk | Broadway News | The Farm Reporter | *12pm* |
| Norwood Smith Sings | | Stu Wilson, news | The Road of Life | *12:15* |
| The Frances Scully Show | | Dick Haymes, songs | Pepper Young's Family | *12:30* |
| Double Feature | The Harry Babbitt Show | Melody Matinee | The Right to Happiness | *12:45* |
| Pick a Date | Call for Help | Lynn at Hollywood | Mary Noble, Backstage Wife | *1pm* |
| | | Norma Dixon, talk | Stella Dallas | *1:15* |
| Easy Aces | George Fisher, gossip | Nancy Young, talk | Lorenzo Jones | *1:30* |
| H. R. Baukage, news | The Garry Moore Show | | Young Widder Brown | *1:45* |

## DAYTIME — FALL, 1949

*Sunday*

| | ABC | CBS | MBS | NBC |
|---|---|---|---|---|
| *2pm* | The Piano Playhouse | Music for You | The Shadow | |
| *2:15* | | | | |
| *2:30* | The Greatest Story Ever Told | The Longines Symphonette | True Detective Mysteries | Harvest of Stars |
| *2:45* | | | | |
| *3pm* | The Lutheran Hour | The Prudential Family Hour of Stars | California Caravan | The Catholic Hour |
| *3:15* | | | | |
| *3:30* | This Thing Called Life | Boston Blackie | Nick Carter, Master Detective | Hollywood Calling |
| *3:45* | | | | |
| *4pm* | Voices That Live | The Lucky Strike Program, Jack Benny | Scattergood Baines | |
| *4:15* | | | | |
| *4:30* | This Changing World | Amos 'n' Andy | Deems Taylor Concert | The Phil Harris - Alice Faye Show |
| *4:45* | Betty Clark Sings | | Music | |

## DAYTIME — FALL, 1949

*Monday-Friday*

| ABC | CBS | MBS | NBC | |
|---|---|---|---|---|
| Surprise Package | | Against the Storm | When a Girl Marries | *2pm* |
| | Meet the Missus | | Portia Faces Life | *2:15* |
| Bride and Groom | | Public Affairs | Just Plain Bill | *2:30* |
| | Arthur Godfrey Time | | Front Page Farrell | *2:45* |
| At Home With The Kirkwoods / Talk Your Way Out of It | | Hoedown Party | Welcome Travelers | *3pm* |
| | | | | *3:15* |
| Ladies Be Seated | | Music | Aunt Mary | *3:30* |
| | | | We Love and Learn | *3:45* |
| Art Baker's Notebook | Curt Massey, songs | Fulton Lewis Jr., news | One Woman's Secret | *4pm* |
| | Your Stand In | Frank Hemingway, news | Dr. Paul | *4:15* |
| Play It Again | Inside the Doctor's Office | Behind the Story | Burritt and Wheeler, talk | *4:30* |
| Happy Theater | Edward R. Murrow, news | Rex Miller, news | | *4:45* |

## DAYTIME — FALL, 1949

*Saturday*

| | ABC | CBS | MBS | NBC |
|---|---|---|---|---|
| *8am* | Shoppers Special | Let's Pretend | The Treasury Department | Fred Waring Orchestra |
| *8:15* | | | News | |
| *8:30* | The Roger Dann Show | Junior Miss | The Haven of Rest | Smilin' Ed's Buster Brown Gang |
| *8:45* | | | | |
| *9am* | The Girl Corps | The Armstrong Theater of Today | Flying Feet | Mary Lee Taylor, cooking |
| *9:15* | | | | |
| *9:30* | Mirandy | Grand Central Station | Extra Time | On the Scouting Trail |
| *9:45* | The American Way | | | |
| *10am* | Ira Cook, talk | Stars Over Hollywood | Glenn Hardy, news | The National Farm and Home Hour |
| *10:15* | | | Music | |
| *10:30* | | Give and Take | The Coast Guard Band | Lassie |
| *10:45* | Sports | | | Jump Jump and the Ice Queen |
| *11am* | | County Fair | | Sports |
| *11:15* | | | | |
| *11:30* | | Meet the Missus | The Air Force Hour | |
| *11:45* | | | | |
| *12pm* | | Mother Knows Best | News | |
| *12:15* | | | John Flynn, news | |
| *12:30* | | Family Party | The Man on the Farm | |
| *12:45* | | | | |
| *1pm* | | Fun to Be Young | | |
| *1:15* | | | | |
| *1:30* | Peter Plotter's Platter Party | Sports | Bands for Bonds | |
| *1:45* | | | Music | Saturday Special |

## DAYTIME — FALL, 1949

*Saturday*

| | ABC | CBS | MBS | NBC |
|---|---|---|---|---|
| *2pm* | | | College Salute | |
| *2:15* | | | Sports | |
| *2:30* | | | | |
| *2:45* | | | | |
| *3pm* | Junior Junction | | | |
| *3:15* | | | | |
| *3:30* | The American Farmer | | | |
| *3:45* | | | | |
| *4pm* | | | | |
| *4:15* | Sports | | | |
| *4:30* | Church and the Nation | | | NBC Symphony Orchestra |
| *4:45* | As We See It | | Frank Hemingway, news | |

# LISTINGS FOR 1950

## EVENING — WINTER, 1950

*Sunday*

| | ABC | CBS | MBS | NBC |
|---|---|---|---|---|
| *5pm* | Stop the Music | The Charlie McCarhty Show | A. L. Alexander's Mediation Board | The Adventures of Sam Spade |
| *5:15* | | | | |
| *5:30* | | Rocky Jordan | The Enchanted Hour | The Theater Guild of the Air |
| *5:45* | | | | |
| *6pm* | Walter Winchell, gossip | Meet Corliss Archer | News | |
| *6:15* | Louella Parsons, gossip | | Rebuttal | |
| *6:30* | Chance of a Lifetime | The Youth Opportunity Program | Music | The American Album of Familiar Music |
| *6:45* | | | The National Guard | |
| *7pm* | Jimmy Fidler, gossip | The Carnation Contented Hour | Take a Number | Take It or Leave It |
| *7:15* | M Day, 1950 | | | |
| *7:30* | The Amazing Mr. Malone | The Whistler | The Roy Rogers Show | The Pet Milk Show |
| *7:45* | | | | |
| *8pm* | Drew Pearson, news | Our Miss Brooks | Twenty Questions | News |
| *8:15* | Don Gardiner, news | | | Ideas Unlimited |
| *8:30* | Walter Winchell, gossip | The Charlie McCarthy Show | Walter Winchell, gossip | The Standard Symphony Hour |
| *8:45* | Louella Parsons, gossip | | Thereby Hangs a Tale | |
| *9pm* | Think Fast | The Red Skelton Show | Glenn Hardy, news | |
| *9:15* | | | Music | |
| *9:30* | Box 13 | The Lucky Strike Program, Jack Benny | The Chicago Theater of the Air | Science Editor |
| *9:45* | | | | Pescha Kagan, songs |
| *10pm* | The Richfield Reporter | The Ten o'Clock Wire | | Sam Hayes, news |
| *10:15* | The Retail Clerk's Union | The Night Editor | | Mayor Bowron, comment |
| *10:30* | Career Theater | Music | Music | Melody Time |
| *10:45* | | | | Mr. Fix-It |

## EVENING — WINTER, 1950

*Monday*

| ABC | CBS | MBS | NBC | |
|---|---|---|---|---|
| Challenge of the Yukon | Disc Jockey, USA | Bobby Benson | Feature Wire | *5pm* |
| | Sports | | News | *5:15* |
| Sky King | Charles Collingwood, news | Tom Mix and His Ralston Straightshooters | The Voice of Firestone | *5:30* |
| | Henry Garred, news | | | *5:45* |
| Edwin C. Hill, news | The Lux Radio Theater | Gabriel Heatter, news | The American Way | *6pm* |
| Elmer Davis, news | | The Mutual Newsreel | | *6:15* |
| Modern Romances | | Tello-Test Quiz | Candy Matson, YUkon 2-8209 | *6:30* |
| | | The Answer Man | | *6:45* |
| The Lone Ranger | My Friend Irma | Murder By Experts | The Martin and Lewis Show | *7pm* |
| | | | | *7:15* |
| For the Record | The Bob Hawk Show | The Cisco Kid | Maisie | *7:30* |
| | | | | *7:45* |
| Kate Smith Calls | Lowell Thomas, news | Let George Do It | Light Up Time, Frank Sinatra | *8pm* |
| | The Jack Smith Show | | World News | *8:15* |
| Henry J. Taylor, news | Arthur Godfrey's Talent Scouts | The Saint | The Railroad Hour | *8:30* |
| The Bud Weed Trio | | | | *8:45* |
| Ethel and Albert | Inner Sanctum Mysteries | Glenn Hardy, news | The Bell Telephone Hour | *9pm* |
| | | Fulton Lewis Jr., news | | *9:15* |
| Chandu, the Magician | The Beulah Show | Music | Music | *9:30* |
| | Club Fifteen | | | *9:45* |
| The Richfield Reporter | The Ten o'Clock Wire | I Love a Mystery | Sam Hayes, news | *10pm* |
| Between the Bookends | Bob Elson Interviews | News and Views | The Johnny Murray Show | *10:15* |
| Science of the Mind | The Symphonette | | Melody Time | *10:30* |
| One for the Books | | Music | News | *10:45* |

| EVENING — WINTER, 1950 | | | | |
|---|---|---|---|---|
| *Tuesday* | | | | |
| | ABC | CBS | MBS | NBC |
| *5pm* | The Green Hornet | Disc Jockey, USA | Straight Arrow | Feature Wire |
| *5:15* | | Sports | | News |
| *5:30* | Jack Armstrong, the All-American Boy | Charles Collingwood, news | Captain Midnight | The Baby Snooks Show |
| *5:45* | | Henry Garred, news | | |
| *6pm* | Edwin C. Hill, news | Life with Luigi | Gabriel Heatter, news | The Bob Hope Show |
| *6:15* | Elmer Davis, news | | The Mutual Newsreel | |
| *6:30* | Modern Romances | Escape | Tello-Test Quiz | Fibber McGee and Molly |
| *6:45* | | | The Answer Man | |
| *7pm* | Counterspy | Pursuit | The Mysterious Traveler | Big Town |
| *7:15* | | | | |
| *7:30* | William Tusher in Hollywood | Yours Truly, Johnny Dollar | Red Ryder | People Are Funny |
| *7:45* | Report to the People | | | |
| *8pm* | Time for Defense | Lowell Thomas, news | The Count of Monte Cristo | Light Up Time, Frank Sinatra |
| *8:15* | | The Jack Smith Show | | World News |
| *8:30* | Gentlemen of the Press | Mr. and Mrs. North | Mystery is My Hobby | The Cavalcade of America |
| *8:45* | | | | |
| *9pm* | America's Town Meeting of the Air | Mystery Theater | Glenn Hardy, news | The Hardy Family |
| *9:15* | | | Fulton Lewis Jr., news | |
| *9:30* | Twin Views of the News | The Beulah Show | Official Detective | The Tex Wiliams Show |
| *9:45* | We CARE | Club Fifteen | | |
| *10pm* | The Richfield Reporter | The Ten o'Clock Wire | I Love a Mystery | Sam Hayes, news |
| *10:15* | Between the Bookends | Bob Elson Interviews | News and Views | The Johnny Murray Show |
| *10:30* | Science of the Mind | Command Theater | | Melody Time |
| *10:45* | One for the Books | | Music | |

## EVENING — WINTER, 1950

*Wednesday*

| ABC | CBS | MBS | NBC | |
|---|---|---|---|---|
| Challenge of the Yulkon | Disc Jockey, USA | Bobby Benson | Feature Wire | *5pm* |
| | Sports | | News | *5:15* |
| Sky King | Charles Collingwood, news | Tom Mix and His Ralston Straightshooters | Casa Cugat | *5:30* |
| | Henry Garred, news | | Elmer Patterson, news | *5:45* |
| Edwin C. Hill, news | You Bet Your Life | Gabriel Heatter, news | This is Your Life | *6pm* |
| Elmer Davis, news | | The Mutual Newsreel | | *6:15* |
| Modern Romances | The Bing Crosby Chesterfield Show | Tello-Test Quiz | Dial Dave Garroway | *6:30* |
| | | The Answer Man | | *6:45* |
| The Lone Ranger | Burns and Allen | John Steele, Adventurer | The Big Story | *7pm* |
| | | | | *7:15* |
| Dr. I. Q., the Mental Banker | The Hollywood Music Hall | The Cisco Kid | Curtain Time | *7:30* |
| | | | | *7:45* |
| Sherlock Holmes | Lowell Thomas, news | What's the Name of That Song | Light Up Time, Frank Sinatra | *8pm* |
| | The Jack Smith Show | | World News | *8:15* |
| The Casebook of Gregory Hood | Dr. Christian | The Family Theater | The Great Gildersleeve | *8:30* |
| | | | | *8:45* |
| Public Affairs | Jeff Regan, Investigator | Glenn Hardy, news | Break the Bank | *9pm* |
| | | Fulton Lewis Jr., news | | *9:15* |
| Lawrence Welk High Life Revue | The Beulah Show | International Airport | Mr. District Attorney | *9:30* |
| | Club Fifteen | | | *9:45* |
| The Richfield Reporter | The Ten o'Clock Wire | I Love a Mystery | Sam Hayes, news | *10pm* |
| Between the Bookends | Bob Elson Interviews | News and Views | The Johnny Murray Show | *10:15* |
| Science of the Mind | The Symphonette | | Melody Time | *10:30* |
| One for the Books | | Music | | *10:45* |

## EVENING — WINTER, 1950

*Thursday*

| | ABC | CBS | MBS | NBC |
|---|---|---|---|---|
| *5pm* | The Green Hornet | Disc Jockey, USA | Straight Arrow | Feature Wire |
| *5:15* | | Sports | | News |
| *5:30* | Jack Armstrong, the All-American Boy | Charles Collingwood, news | Captain Midnight | Casa Cugat |
| *5:45* | | Henry Garred, news | | Elmer Patterson, news |
| *6pm* | Edwin C. Hill, news | Suspense | Gabriel Heatter, news | The Camel Screen Guild Players |
| *6:15* | Elmer Davis, news | | The Mutual Newsreel | |
| *6:30* | Modern Romances | Casey, Crime Photographer | Tello-Test Quiz | Duffy's Tavern |
| *6:45* | | | The Answer Man | |
| *7pm* | Counterspy | The Hallmark Playhouse | The Falcon | The Chesterfield Supper Club |
| *7:15* | | | | |
| *7:30* | A Date with Judy | The Skippy Hollywood Theater | Red Ryder | Dragnet |
| *7:45* | | | | |
| *8pm* | Ted Mack's Original Amateur Hour | Lowell Thomas, news | Hopalong Cassidy | Light Up Time, Frank Sinatra |
| *8:15* | | The Jack Smith Show | | World News |
| *8:30* | | Mr. Keen, Tracer of Lost Persons | Sports for All | The Aldrich Family |
| *8:45* | Robert Montgomery Speaking | | | |
| *9pm* | Author Meets the Critics | The FBI in Peace and War | Glenn Hardy, news | Father Knows Best |
| *9:15* | | | Fulton Lewis Jr., news | |
| *9:30* | Blondie | The Beulah Show | The Affairs of Peter Salem | The Tex Williams Show |
| *9:45* | | Club Fifteen | | |
| *10pm* | The Richfield Reporter | The Ten o'Clock Wire | I Love a Mystery | Sam Hayes, news |
| *10:15* | Between the Bookends | Bob Elson Interviews | News and Views | The Johnny Murray Show |
| *10:30* | Science of the Mind | Command Theater | | Melody Time |
| *10:45* | One for the Books | | Music | |

# EVENING — WINTER, 1950

*Friday*

| ABC | CBS | MBS | NBC | |
|---|---|---|---|---|
| Challenge of the Yukon | Disc Jockey, USA | Bobby Benson | Feature Wire | *5pm* |
| | Sports | | News | *5:15* |
| Sky King | Charles Collingwood, news | Tom Mix and His Ralston Straightshooters | Casa Cugat | *5:30* |
| | Henry Garred, news | | Elmer Patterson, news | *5:45* |
| Edwin C. Hill, news | Leave It to Joan | Gabriel Heatter, news | The Screen Director's Playhouse | *6pm* |
| Elmer Davis, news | | The Mutual Newsreel | | *6:15* |
| Hits and Encores | Lum and Abner | Tello-Test Quiz | The Jimmy Durante Show | *6:30* |
| | | The Answer Man | | *6:45* |
| Madison Square Garden Boxing | The Show Goes On | Meet the Press | The Life of Riley | *7pm* |
| | | | | *7:15* |
| | The Women's Forum | The Cisco Kid | The Colgate Sports Newsreel, Bill Stern | *7:30* |
| | | | Senators Report | *7:45* |
| The Fat Man | Lowell Thomas, news | Straight Arrow | Light Up Time, Frank Sinatra | *8pm* |
| | The Jack Smith Show | | World News | *8:15* |
| This is Your FBI | The Goldbergs | Meet Your Match | The Halls of Ivy | *8:30* |
| | | | | *8:45* |
| The Adventures of Ozzie and Harriet | My Favorite Husband | Glenn Hardy, news | Crime Does Not Pay | *9pm* |
| | | Fulton Lewis Jr., news | | *9:15* |
| Mr. President | The Beulah Show | Music | Richard Diamond, Private Detective | *9:30* |
| | Club Fifteen | | | *9:45* |
| The Richfield Reporter | The Ten o'Clock Wire | I Love a Mystery | Sam Hayes, news | *10pm* |
| Between the Bookends | Bob Elson Interviews | News and Views | The Johnny Murray Show | *10:15* |
| Science of the Mind | The Symphonette | | Melody Time | *10:30* |
| One for the Books | | Music | | *10:45* |

## EVENING — WINTER, 1950

*Saturday*

| | ABC | CBS | MBS | NBC |
|---|---|---|---|---|
| *5pm* | Robert H. Nathan, news | Disc Jockey, USA | Personalities | Pioneers of Music (4:30PM) |
| *5:15* | Special Event | Sports | | |
| *5:30* | Harry Wismer, sports | Chet Huntley, news | Meet Your Match | Sunday Preview |
| *5:45* | Income Tax | Henry Garred, news | | Elmer Patterson, news |
| *6pm* | The Navy Hour | The Adventures of Phillip Marlowe | The Army and Air Force Show | Proudly We Hail |
| *6:15* | | | | |
| *6:30* | Modern Romances | Broadway is My Beat | Hawaii Calls | A Day in the Life of Dennis Day |
| *6:45* | | | | |
| *7pm* | Hollywood Byline | Sing It Again | The Comedy Playhouse | The Judy Canova Show |
| *7:15* | | | | |
| *7:30* | Through the Listening Glass | | This is Europe | Grand Ole Opry |
| *7:45* | | | | |
| *8pm* | The Lone Ranger | The Camel Caravan, Vaughn Monroe | Music | Truth or Consequences |
| *8:15* | | | | |
| *8:30* | The Adventures of Superman | Gene Autry's Melody Ranch | Lombardoland USA | The Hollywood StarTheater |
| *8:45* | | | | |
| *9pm* | Bob Crosby's Night Shift | Gangbusters | Glenn Hardy, news | Your Hit Parade |
| *9:15* | | | Sports | |
| *9:30* | | Music | True or False | The Story of Dr. Kildare |
| *9:45* | | | | |
| *10pm* | News | The Ten o'Clock Wire | Monica Sings | News |
| *10:15* | Sports | J. A. Ford, comment | Policing L. A. | Supervisor Ray Darby, comment |
| *10:30* | Music | Capitol Cloak Room | Music | Living 1950 |
| *10:45* | | | | |

## DAYTIME — WINTER, 1950

*Sunday*

| | ABC | CBS | MBS | NBC |
|---|---|---|---|---|
| *8am* | The Old Fashoined Revival Hour | The Farm Journal | The Religious Hour (7:00AM) | The L. A. Times Funnies |
| *8:15* | | Howard K. Smith, news | | |
| *8:30* | | The Salt Lake Tabernacle Choir | The Voice of Prophecy | The Christian Science Monitor |
| *8:45* | | | | Hometown Happenings |
| *9am* | The Southernaires Quartet | Invitation to Learning | The Radio Bible Class | Parent-Youth Forum |
| *9:15* | | | | |
| *9:30* | Message of Israel | The People's Platform | The Lutheran Hour | The Eternal Light |
| *9:45* | | | | |
| *10am* | News | Charles Collingwood, news | Glenn Hardy, news | Herbert J. Mann, sports |
| *10:15* | Commander Scott | Get More Out of Life | Songs of Comfort | News |
| *10:30* | National Vespers | Where the People Stand | News | The University of Chicago Round Table |
| *10:45* | | The University Explorer | Bill Lang, news | |
| *11am* | Foreign Reporters | Melodies | The Happiness Hour | The NBC Theater |
| *11:15* | Frank and Ernest, songs | California Holiday | | |
| *11:30* | Yesterday on Broadway | Galen Drake, talk | The House of Hymns | |
| *11:45* | Through the Listening Glass | Ted Steele, talk | The Canary Pet Shop | |
| *12pm* | The Hour of Faith | New York Philharmonic Orchestra | Broadway News | One Man's Family |
| *12:15* | | | Bill Cunningham, news | |
| *12:30* | Milton Cross Opera Album | | Juvenile Jury | The Quiz Kids |
| *12:45* | | | | |
| *1pm* | This Week Around the World | | Mr. Feathers | The NBC Theater |
| *1:15* | | | | |
| *1:30* | The Voice of Prophecy | Sunday at the Chase | Martin Kane, Private Detective | |

| DAYTIME — WINTER, 1950 | | | | |
|---|---|---|---|---|
| *Monday-Friday* | | | | |
| ABC | CBS | MBS | NBC | |
| The Breakfast Club | News | Cecil Brown, news | Coffee Time | *8am* |
| | News | News | Marriage for Two | *8:15* |
| | Grand Slam | Music | The Jack Berch Show | *8:30* |
| | Rosemary | | Meyers Goes to the Market | *8:45* |
| Ladies Be Seated | Wendy Warren and the News | Kate Smith Speaks | Ladies' Day | *9am* |
| | Aunt Jenny's True Life Stories | News | | *9:15* |
| Quick as a Flash | The Romance of Helen Trent | Women are Wonderful | | *9:30* |
| | Our Gal Sunday | | All Around Town | *9:45* |
| Ira Cook, talk | Big Sister | Glenn Hardy, news | | *10am* |
| | Ma Perkins | The Gospel Singer | Are You Listening | *10:15* |
| My True Story | Young Dr. Malone | Ladies Fair | News | *10:30* |
| | The Guiding Light | | Life Can Be Beautiful | *10:45* |
| The Magazine of the Air | The Second Mrs. Burton | Ladies First | Double or Nothing | *11am* |
| Victor Lindlahr, health | Perry Mason | | | *11:15* |
| Ira Cook, talk | This is Nora Drake | Queen for a Day | Today's Children | *11:30* |
| | The Brighter Day | | The Light of the World | *11:45* |
| Sam Hayes, news | News and Talk | Broadway News | The Farm Reporter | *12pm* |
| Norwood Smith Sings | | Stu Wilson, news | The Road of Life | *12:15* |
| Ira Cook, talk | House Party | Melody Matinee | Pepper Young's Family | *12:30* |
| | | | The Right to Happiness | *12:45* |
| The Frances Scully Show | Nona from Nowhere | Lynn at Hollywood | Mary Noble, Backstage Wife | *1pm* |
| | The Harry Babbitt Show | Norma Dixon, talk | Stella Dallas | *1:15* |
| Easy Aces | George Fisher, gossip | Nancy Young, talk | Lorenzo Jones | *1:30* |

## DAYTIME — WINTER, 1950

*Sunday*

| | ABC | CBS | MBS | NBC |
|---|---|---|---|---|
| *1:45* | | | | |
| *2pm* | The Piano Playhouse | Earn Your Vacation | The Shadow | The Musical Playhouse |
| *2:15* | | | | |
| *2:30* | The Greatest Story Ever Told | Treasury Bandstand | True Detective Mysteries | Harvest of Stars |
| *2:45* | | The Melody Parade | | |
| *3pm* | The Lutheran Hour | The Prudential Family Hour of Stars | California Caravan | The Catholic Hour |
| *3:15* | | | | |
| *3:30* | Music with the Hormel Girls | Boston Blackie | Nick Carter, Master Detective | The Henry Morgan Show |
| *3:45* | | | | |
| *4pm* | This Thing Called Life | The Lucky Strike Program, Jack Benny | The Falcon | Hollywood Calling |
| *4:15* | | | | |
| *4:30* | This Changing World | Amos 'n' Andy | Deems Taylor Concert | The Phil Harris - Alice Faye Show |
| *4:45* | Between the Bookends | | | |

## DAYTIME — WINTER, 1950

*Monday-Friday*

| ABC | CBS | MBS | NBC | |
|---|---|---|---|---|
| H. R. Baukage, news | The Garry Moore Show | | Young Widder Brown | *1:45* |
| Surprise Package | | Club 930 | When a Girl Marries | *2pm* |
| | The Steve Allen Show | | Portia Faces Life | *2:15* |
| Bride and Groom | | | Just Plain Bill | *2:30* |
| | Arthur Godfrey Time | | Front Page Farrell | *2:45* |
| Pick a Date | | | Welcome Travelers | *3pm* |
| | | | | *3:15* |
| Hannibal Cobb | | | Aunt Mary | *3:30* |
| | | | We Love and Learn | *3:45* |
| Art Baker's Notebook | Curt Massey, songs | Fulton Lewis Jr., news | One Woman's Secret | *4pm* |
| Looking at Records | Your Stand In | Frank Hemingway, news | Dr. Paul | *4:15* |
| Play It Again | Inside the Doctor's Office | Behind the Story | Burritt and Wheeler, talk | *4:30* |
| Happy Theater | Edward R. Murrow, news | Rex Miller, news | | *4:45* |

| DAYTIME — WINTER, 1950 | | | | |
|---|---|---|---|---|
| *Saturday* | | | | |
| | ABC | CBS | MBS | NBC |
| *8am* | Conversation with Casey | Let's Pretend | Guest Star | Fred Waring Orchestra |
| *8:15* | | | News | |
| *8:30* | The Roger Dann Show | Junior Miss | The Haven of Rest | Smilin' Ed's Buster Brown Gang |
| *8:45* | Mirandy | | | |
| *9am* | Ira Cook, talk | The Armstrong Theater of Today | Flying Feet | Mary Lee Taylor, cooking |
| *9:15* | | | | |
| *9:30* | | Grand Central Station | The Quiz Club | On the Scouting Trail |
| *9:45* | | | Extra Time | |
| *10am* | | Stars Over Hollywood | Newspaper of the Air | Star King |
| *10:15* | | | John Flynn, news | Jerry Marlowe, songs |
| *10:30* | | Give and Take | Symphonies of Youth | Voices Down the Wind |
| *10:45* | | | | |
| *11am* | The Metropolitan Opera | County Fair | | Lassie |
| *11:15* | | | | Here Comes the Band |
| *11:30* | | Meet the Missus | The Air Force Hour | The National Farm and Home Hour |
| *11:45* | | | | |
| *12pm* | | Get More Out of Life | News | The Farm Reporter |
| *12:15* | | The Handy Man | The Internal Revenue | Saturday Special |
| *12:30* | | Family Party | The Man on the Farm | |
| *12:45* | | | | |
| *1pm* | | Meet the Missus | | |
| *1:15* | | | | |
| *1:30* | | News and Views | Sports Parade | |
| *1:45* | | | | |

| DAYTIME — WINTER, 1950 | | | | |
|---|---|---|---|---|
| *Saturday* | | | | |
| | ABC | CBS | MBS | NBC |
| *2pm* | The Jacques Fray Show | | Club 930 | |
| *2:15* | | | | |
| *2:30* | Tea and Crumpets | Cross-Section USA | | |
| *2:45* | | The Garden Gate | | Closeups |
| *3pm* | Junior Junction | George Bandcroft, news | | Young America Speaks |
| *3:15* | | Lake Success | | |
| *3:30* | The American Farmer | Sports | | NBC Symphony Orchestra |
| *3:45* | | Larry Lesueur, news | | |
| *4pm* | Flying Feet | Disc Jockey, USA | Top Tunes with Trendler | |
| *4:15* | | | Frank Hemingway, news | |
| *4:30* | Bible Messages | | Bandstand USA | Pioneers of Music |
| *4:45* | It's Your Bust | | | |

## EVENING — SPRING, 1950

*Sunday*

| | ABC | CBS | MBS | NBC |
|---|---|---|---|---|
| *5pm* | Stop the Music | The Charlie McCarthy Show | A. L. Alexander's Mediation Board | The Adventures of Sam Spade |
| *5:15* | | | | |
| *5:30* | | Rocky Jordan | The Enchanted Hour | The Theater Guild of the Air |
| *5:45* | | | | |
| *6pm* | Walter Winchell, gossip | Meet Corliss Archer | News | |
| *6:15* | Louella Parsons, gossip | | Music | |
| *6:30* | Chance of a Lifetime | The Youth Opportunity Program | Sheilah Graham, gossip | The American Album of Familiar Music |
| *6:45* | | | The Kenny Baker Show | |
| *7pm* | Jimmy Fidler, gossip | The Carnation Contented Hour | Manchester Boddy, news | Take It or Leave It |
| *7:15* | Get More Out of Life | | Bands for Bonds | |
| *7:30* | The Amazing Mr. Malone | The Whistler | Two-Thousand Plus | The Pet Milk Show |
| *7:45* | | | | |
| *8pm* | Drew Pearson, news | Our Miss Brooks | Twenty Questions | Living 1950 |
| *8:15* | Don Gardiner, news | | | |
| *8:30* | Walter Winchell, gossip | The Charlie McCarthy Show | Can You Top This | The Standard Symphony Hour |
| *8:45* | Louella Parsons, gossip | | | |
| *9pm* | Think Fast | The Red Skelton Show | Glenn Hardy, news | |
| *9:15* | | | Supervisor Ray Darby, comment | |
| *9:30* | Box 13 | The Lucky Strike Program, Jack Benny | The Chicago Theater of the Air | Science Editor |
| *9:45* | | | | New Horizons |
| *10pm* | The Richfield Reporter | The Ten o'Clock Wire | | Sam Hayes, news |
| *10:15* | The Retail Clerk's Union | The Night Editor | | Mayor Bowron, comment |
| *10:30* | Career Theater | Freddy Martin Orchestra | College Choir | The American Forum of the Air |
| *10:45* | | | | |

## EVENING — SPRING, 1950

*Monday*

| ABC | CBS | MBS | NBC | |
|---|---|---|---|---|
| Challenge of the Yukon | Larry LeSueur, news | Mark Trail | Feature Wire | *5pm* |
| | Sports | | News | *5:15* |
| Sky King | Charles Collingwood, news | Tom Mix and His Ralston Straightshooters | The Voice of Firestone | *5:30* |
| | Edward R. Murrow, news | | | *5:45* |
| Edwin C. Hill, news | The Lux Radio Theater | Gabriel Heatter, news | The American Way | *6pm* |
| Main Street to Malibu | | The Mutual Newsreel | | *6:15* |
| Modern Romances | | Tello-Test Quiz | Proudly We Hail | *6:30* |
| | | The Answer Man | | *6:45* |
| The Lone Ranger | My Friend Irma | Murder By Experts | Nighbeat | *7pm* |
| | | | | *7:15* |
| Music By Ralph Norman | The Bob Hawk Show | The Cisco Kid | Maisie | *7:30* |
| | | | | *7:45* |
| Strictly from Dixie | Lowell Thomas, news | Let George Do It | Light Up Time, Frank Sinatra | *8pm* |
| | The Jack Smith Show | | World News | *8:15* |
| Henry J. Taylor, news | Arthur Godfrey's Talent Scouts | The Saint | The Railroad Hour | *8:30* |
| Jackie Robinson, sports | | | | *8:45* |
| Ethel and Albert | Inner Sanctum Mysteries | Glenn Hardy, news | The Bell Telephone Hour | *9pm* |
| | | Fulton Lewis Jr., news | | *9:15* |
| Chandu, the Magician | The Beulah Show | Welburn Mayock, comment | Music | *9:30* |
| | Club Fifteen | Music | | *9:45* |
| The Richfield Reporter | The Ten o'Clock Wire | I Love a Mystery | Sam Hayes, news | *10pm* |
| Sports | Bob Elson Interviews | Frank Edwards, news | The Johnny Murray Show | *10:15* |
| Science of the Mind | The Symphonette | Lonesome Gal | The Dave Rose Show | *10:30* |
| One for the Books | | | | *10:45* |

## EVENING — SPRING, 1950

*Tuesday*

| | ABC | CBS | MBS | NBC |
|---|---|---|---|---|
| *5pm* | The Green Hornet | Larry LeSueur, news | Straight Arrow | Feature Wire |
| *5:15* | | Sports | | News |
| *5:30* | Sky King | Charles Collingwood, news | Bobby Benson | The Baby Snooks Show |
| *5:45* | | Edward R. Murrow, news | | |
| *6pm* | Edwin C. Hill, news | Life with Luigi | Gabriel Heatter, news | The Bob Hope Show |
| *6:15* | Main Street to Malibu | | The Mutual Newsreel | |
| *6:30* | Modern Romances | Yours Truly, Johnny Dollar | Tello-Test Quiz | Fibber McGee and Molly |
| *6:45* | | | The Answer Man | |
| *7pm* | Counterspy | The Adventures of Phillip Marlowe | The Mysterious Traveler | Big Town |
| *7:15* | | | | |
| *7:30* | Public Affairs | Pursuit | Red Ryder | People Are Funny |
| *7:45* | Report to the People | | | |
| *8pm* | Time for Defense | Lowell Thomas, news | The Count of Monte Cristo | Light Up Time, Frank Sinatra |
| *8:15* | | The Jack Smith Show | | World News |
| *8:30* | Gentlemen of the Press | Mr. and Mrs. North | Mystery is My Hobby | The Cavalcade of America |
| *8:45* | | | | |
| *9pm* | America's Town Meeting of the Air | Mystery Theater | Glenn Hardy, news | The Hardy Family |
| *9:15* | | | Fulton Lewis Jr., news | |
| *9:30* | Twin Views of the News | The Beulah Show | Official Detective | Tex Williams Orchestra |
| *9:45* | William Tusher in Hollywood | Club Fifteen | | |
| *10pm* | The Richfield Reporter | The Ten o'Clock Wire | I Love a Mystery | Sam Hayes, news |
| *10:15* | Sports | Bob Elson Interviews | Frank Edwards, news | The Johnny Murray Show |
| *10:30* | Science of the Mind | Command Theater | Lonesome Gal | Freddy Martin Orchestra |
| *10:45* | One for the Books | | | |

| EVENING — SPRING, 1950 | | | | |
|---|---|---|---|---|
| *Wednesday* | | | | |
| ABC | CBS | MBS | NBC | |
| Challenge of the Yulkon | Larry LeSueur, news | Mark Trail | Feature Wire | *5pm* |
| | Sports | | News | *5:15* |
| Jack Armstrong, the All-American Boy | Charles Collingwood, news | Tom Mix and His Ralston Straightshooters | Casa Cugat | *5:30* |
| | Edward R. Murrow, news | | Elmer Patterson, news | *5:45* |
| Edwin C. Hill, news | You Bet Your Life | Gabriel Heatter, news | This is Your Life | *6pm* |
| Main Street to Malibu | | The Mutual Newsreel | | *6:15* |
| Modern Romances | The Bing Crosby Chesterfield Show | Tello-Test Quiz | Dangerous Assignment | *6:30* |
| | | The Answer Man | | *6:45* |
| The Lone Ranger | Burns and Allen | John Steele, Adventurer | The Big Story | *7pm* |
| | | | | *7:15* |
| Dr. I. Q., the Mental Banker | The Hollywood Music Hall | The Cisco Kid | Richard Diamond, Private Detective | *7:30* |
| | | | | *7:45* |
| Sherlock Holmes | Lowell Thomas, news | What's the Name of That Song | Light Up Time, Frank Sinatra | *8pm* |
| | The Jack Smith Show | | World News | *8:15* |
| The Casebook of Gregory Hood | Dr. Christian | The Family Theater | The Great Gildersleeve | *8:30* |
| | | | | *8:45* |
| Buzz Adlam's Playroom | Jeff Regan, Investigator | Glenn Hardy, news | Break the Bank | *9pm* |
| | | Fulton Lewis Jr., news | | *9:15* |
| Lawrence Welk High Life Revue | The Beulah Show | International Airport | Mr. District Attorney | *9:30* |
| | Club Fifteen | | | *9:45* |
| The Richfield Reporter | The Ten o'Clock Wire | I Love a Mystery | Sam Hayes, news | *10pm* |
| Sports | Bob Elson Interviews | Frank Edwards, news | The Johnny Murray Show | *10:15* |
| Science of the Mind | The Symphonette | Lonesome Gal | Build a Dream House | *10:30* |
| One for the Books | | | | *10:45* |

## EVENING — SPRING, 1950

*Thursday*

| | ABC | CBS | MBS | NBC |
|---|---|---|---|---|
| *5pm* | The Green Hornet | Larry LeSueur, news | Straight Arrow | Feature Wire |
| *5:15* | | Sports | | News |
| *5:30* | Sky King | Charles Collingwood, news | Bobby Benson | Casa Cugat |
| *5:45* | | Edward R. Murrow, news | | Elmer Patterson, news |
| *6pm* | Edwin C. Hill, news | Suspense | Gabriel Heatter, news | The Camel Screen Guild Players |
| *6:15* | Elmer Davis, news | | The Mutual Newsreel | |
| *6:30* | Modern Romances | Casey, Crime Photographer | Tello-Test Quiz | Duffy's Tavern |
| *6:45* | | | The Answer Man | |
| *7pm* | Counterspy | The Hallmark Playhouse | Crime Fighters | The Chesterfield Supper Club |
| *7:15* | | | | |
| *7:30* | A Date with Judy | The Skippy Hollywood Theater | Red Ryder | Dragnet |
| *7:45* | | | | |
| *8pm* | Ted Mack's Original Amateur Hour | Lowell Thomas, news | The Clyde Beatty Show | Light Up Time, Frank Sinatra |
| *8:15* | | The Jack Smith Show | | World News |
| *8:30* | | Mr. Keen, Tracer of Lost Persons | Sports for All | The Aldrich Family |
| *8:45* | Robert Montgomery Speaking | | | |
| *9pm* | Public Affairs | The FBI in Peace and War | Glenn Hardy, news | Father Knows Best |
| *9:15* | | | Fulton Lewis Jr., news | |
| *9:30* | Blondie | The Beulah Show | The Affairs of Peter Salem | The Tex Williams Show |
| *9:45* | | Club Fifteen | | |
| *10pm* | The Richfield Reporter | The Ten o'Clock Wire | I Love a Mystery | Sam Hayes, news |
| *10:15* | Between the Bookends | Bob Elson Interviews | Frank Edwards, news | The Johnny Murray Show |
| *10:30* | Science of the Mind | Command Theater | Lonesome Gal | Tommy Dorsey Orchestra |
| *10:45* | Pietro Pontrelli Orchestra | | | |

## EVENING — SPRING, 1950

*Friday*

| ABC | CBS | MBS | NBC | |
|---|---|---|---|---|
| Challenge of the Yukon | Larry LeSueur, news | Mark Trail | Feature Wire | *5pm* |
| | Sports | | News | *5:15* |
| Jack Armstrong, the All-American Boy | Charles Collingwood, news | Tom Mix and His Ralston Straightshooters | Casa Cugat | *5:30* |
| | Edward R. Murrow, news | | Elmer Patterson, news | *5:45* |
| Edwin C. Hill, news | Manchester Boddy, news | Gabriel Heatter, news | The Screen Director's Playhouse | *6pm* |
| Elmer Davis, news | Treasury Bandstand | The Mutual Newsreel | | *6:15* |
| Meet the Sportsmen | Lum and Abner | Tello-Test Quiz | The Jimmy Durante Show | *6:30* |
| Hits and Encores | | The Answer Man | | *6:45* |
| Madison Square Garden Boxing | James Roosevelt, comment | Meet the Press | The Life of Riley | *7pm* |
| | Music You Know | | | *7:15* |
| | The Women's Forum | The Cisco Kid | The Colgate Sports Newsreel, Bill Stern | *7:30* |
| | | | Senators Report | *7:45* |
| The Fat Man | Lowell Thomas, news | Proudly We Hail | Light Up Time, Frank Sinatra | *8pm* |
| | The Jack Smith Show | | World News | *8:15* |
| This is Your FBI | Escape | True or False | The Halls of Ivy | *8:30* |
| | | | | *8:45* |
| The Adventures of Ozzie and Harriet | Broadway is My Beat | Glenn Hardy, news | Crime Does Not Pay | *9pm* |
| | | Fulton Lewis Jr., news | | *9:15* |
| Mr. President | The Beulah Show | Music | High Adventure | *9:30* |
| | Club Fifteen | | | *9:45* |
| The Richfield Reporter | The Ten o'Clock Wire | I Love a Mystery | Sam Hayes, news | *10pm* |
| Between the Bookends | Bob Elson Interviews | Frank Edwards, news | The Johnny Murray Show | *10:15* |
| Science of the Mind | The Symphonette | Lonesome Gal | Benny Goodman Orchestra | *10:30* |
| Pietro Pontrelli Orchestra | | | | *10:45* |

# EVENING — SPRING, 1950

*Saturday*

| | ABC | CBS | MBS | NBC |
|---|---|---|---|---|
| *5pm* | As We See It | Horse Racing | The Reviewing Stand | Pioneers of Music (4:30PM) |
| *5:15* | Special Event | | | |
| *5:30* | Harry Wismer, sports | Chet Huntley, news | Radie Harris, interview | Confidential Closeups |
| *5:45* | Chuy Reyes Orchestra | Henry Garred, news | Headlines in the News | Elmer Patterson, news |
| *6pm* | Scout Stars | Earn Your Vacation | The Army and Air Force Show | The Joe DiMaggio Show |
| *6:15* | For the Record | | | |
| *6:30* | Modern Romances | The Goldbergs | Hawaii Calls | A Day in the Life of Dennis Day |
| *6:45* | | | | |
| *7pm* | Hollywood Byline | Sing It Again | Mr. Feathers | The Judy Canova Show |
| *7:15* | | | | |
| *7:30* | Through the Listening Glass | | Salute to Reservists | Grand Ole Opry |
| *7:45* | | | | |
| *8pm* | The Lone Ranger | The Camel Caravan, Vaughn Monroe | Music | Truth or Consequences |
| *8:15* | | | | |
| *8:30* | Dixieland Jambake | Gene Autry's Melody Ranch | Lombardoland USA | Dimension X |
| *8:45* | | | | |
| *9pm* | The Rayburn and Finch Show | Gangbusters | Newspaper of the Air | Your Hit Parade |
| *9:15* | | | Sports | |
| *9:30* | | Arthur Godfrey's Digest | True or False | The Story of Dr. Kildare |
| *9:45* | | | | |
| *10pm* | News | The Ten o'Clock Wire | Monica Sings | News |
| *10:15* | Sports | Chicagoans Orchestra | Music | Supervisor Ray Darby, comment |
| *10:30* | Public Affairs | Capitol Cloak Room | Public Affairs | The Recovery Story |
| *10:45* | Pietro Pontrelli Orchestra | | | |

## DAYTIME — SPRING, 1950

*Sunday*

| | ABC | CBS | MBS | NBC |
|---|---|---|---|---|
| *8am* | The Old Fashioned Revival Hour | The Farm Journal | The Religious Hour | The L. A. Times Funnies |
| *8:15* | | Howard K. Smith, news | | |
| *8:30* | | The Salt Lake Tabernacle Choir | The Voice of Prophecy | The Christian Science Monitor |
| *8:45* | | | | Hometown Happenings |
| *9am* | The Southernaires Quartet | Invitation to Learning | The Radio Bible Class | Parent-Youth Forum |
| *9:15* | | | | |
| *9:30* | Message of Israel | The People's Platform | The Lutheran Hour | The Eternal Light |
| *9:45* | | | | |
| *10am* | News | Melodies | Glenn Hardy, news | Herbert J. Mann, sports |
| *10:15* | Commander Scott | Get More Out of Life | Songs of Comfort | News |
| *10:30* | National Vespers | The Record Parade | News | The University of Chicago Round Table |
| *10:45* | | | Headlines in Chemistry | |
| *11am* | Foreign Reporters | The Longines Choraliers | The Happiness Hour | The NBC Theater |
| *11:15* | Frank and Ernest, songs | | | |
| *11:30* | Yesterday on Broadway | Romance of the Highways | The Gospel Singer | |
| *11:45* | | The University Explorer | The Canary Pet Shop | |
| *12pm* | The Hour of Faith | New York Philharmonic Orchestra | Broadway News | One Man's Family |
| *12:15* | | | Bill Cunningham, news | |
| *12:30* | The Baptist Hour | | Juvenile Jury | The Quiz Kids |
| *12:45* | | | | |
| *1pm* | This Week Around the World | | Hopalong Cassidy | The NBC Theater |
| *1:15* | | | | |
| *1:30* | The Voice of Prophecy | The Longines Symphonette | Martin Kane, Private Detective | |

## DAYTIME — SPRING, 1950

*Monday-Friday*

| ABC | CBS | MBS | NBC | |
|---|---|---|---|---|
| The Breakfast Club | Top of the Morning | Cecil Brown, news | Guess a Tune | *8am* |
| | News | News | Coffee Time | *8:15* |
| | Grand Slam | Bible Institute | The Jack Berch Show | *8:30* |
| | Rosemary | | Meyers Goes to the Market | *8:45* |
| Ladies Be Seated | Wendy Warren and the News | Kate Smith Speaks | Ladies' Day | *9am* |
| | Aunt Jenny's True Life Stories | The Garden Guide | | *9:15* |
| Quick as a Flash | The Romance of Helen Trent | Women are Wonderful | | *9:30* |
| | Our Gal Sunday | | All Around Town | *9:45* |
| Surprise Package | Big Sister | Glenn Hardy, news | | *10am* |
| | Ma Perkins | Harvey Harding, songs | Are You Listening | *10:15* |
| My True Story | Young Dr. Malone | Nancy Young, talk | News | *10:30* |
| | The Guiding Light | | Life Can Be Beautiful | *10:45* |
| The Magazine of the Air | The Second Mrs. Burton | Ladies First | Double or Nothing | *11am* |
| Victor Lindlahr, health | Perry Mason | | | *11:15* |
| Ira Cook, talk | This is Nora Drake | Queen for a Day | Today's Children | *11:30* |
| | The Brighter Day | | The Light of the World | *11:45* |
| Sam Hayes, news | News and Talk | Broadway News | The Farm Reporter | *12pm* |
| Norwood Smith Sings | | Guess a Tune | The Road of Life | *12:15* |
| The Frances Scully Show | House Party | Melody Matinee | Pepper Young's Family | *12:30* |
| Double Feature | | | The Right to Happiness | *12:45* |
| Ira Cook, talk | Nona from Nowhere | Lynn at Hollywood | Mary Noble, Backstage Wife | *1pm* |
| | George Fisher, gossip | Norma Dixon, talk | Stella Dallas | *1:15* |
| Easy Aces | Disc Jockey, USA | | Lorenzo Jones | *1:30* |

## DAYTIME — SPRING, 1950

*Sunday*

| | ABC | CBS | MBS | NBC |
|---|---|---|---|---|
| *1:45* | | | | |
| *2pm* | The Piano Playhouse | Public Affairs | The Shadow | Voices and Events |
| *2:15* | | | | |
| *2:30* | The Greatest Story Ever Told | News | True Detective Mysteries | Harvest of Stars |
| *2:45* | | The Melody Parade | | |
| *3pm* | The Lutheran Hour | My Favorite Husband | The Roy Rogers Show | The Catholic Hour |
| *3:15* | | | | |
| *3:30* | Music with the Hormel Girls | Boston Blackie | Nick Carter, Master Detective | The Henry Morgan Show |
| *3:45* | | | | |
| *4pm* | Dr. Holmes, health | The Lucky Strike Program, Jack Benny | California Caravan | The Adventures of Christopher London |
| *4:15* | | | | |
| *4:30* | Sammy Kaye's Sunday Serenade | Amos 'n' Andy | The Falcon | The Phil Harris - Alice Faye Show |
| *4:45* | | | | |

## DAYTIME — SPRING, 1950

*Monday-Friday*

| ABC | CBS | MBS | NBC | |
|---|---|---|---|---|
| H. R. Baukage, news | | | Young Widder Brown | *1:45* |
| Hannibal Cobb | The Steve Allen Show | Club 930 | When a Girl Marries | *2pm* |
| | | | Portia Faces Life | *2:15* |
| Bride and Groom | This is Bing Crosby | | Just Plain Bill | *2:30* |
| | Arthur Godfrey Time | | Front Page Farrell | *2:45* |
| Pick a Date | | | Welcome Travelers | *3pm* |
| | | | | *3:15* |
| Leyden with Song | | | Aunt Mary | *3:30* |
| | | | We Love and Learn | *3:45* |
| Art Baker's Notebook | Curt Massey, songs | Fulton Lewis Jr., news | One Woman's Secret | *4pm* |
| Play It Again | Strike It Rich | Frank Hemingway, news | Dr. Paul | *4:15* |
| | | Behind the Story | Burritt and Wheeler, talk | *4:30* |
| Happy Theater | The Harry Babbitt Show | Rex Miller, news | | *4:45* |

## DAYTIME — SPRING, 1950

*Saturday*

| | ABC | CBS | MBS | NBC |
|---|---|---|---|---|
| *8am* | No School Today (7:45AM) | Let's Pretend | Guest Star | Fred Waring Orchestra |
| *8:15* | | | News | |
| *8:30* | | Junior Miss | The Haven of Rest | Smilin' Ed's Buster Brown Gang |
| *8:45* | Mirandy | | | |
| *9am* | Ira Cook, talk | The Armstrong Theater of Today | Flying Feet | Mary Lee Taylor, cooking |
| *9:15* | | | | |
| *9:30* | | Grand Central Station | The Veteran Wants to Know | On the Scouting Trail |
| *9:45* | | | Extra Time | |
| *10am* | | Stars Over Hollywood | Newspaper of the Air | Young America Speaks |
| *10:15* | | | The Gospel Singer | |
| *10:30* | | Give and Take | The Valley Barn Dance | Archie Andrews |
| *10:45* | | | | |
| *11am* | | Family Parade | | Lassie |
| *11:15* | | | | Broadway Correspondent |
| *11:30* | | Fun to Be Young | The Air Force Hour | The National Farm and Home Hour |
| *11:45* | | | | |
| *12pm* | News | Get More Out of Life | News | The Farm Reporter |
| *12:15* | Music | | Music to Remember | Saturday Special |
| *12:30* | | Meet the Missus | The Man on the Farm | |
| *12:45* | | | | |
| *1pm* | Horse Racing | The Housewive's Protective League | Dunn on Discs | The Music City Show |
| *1:15* | Old, New, Borrowed and Blue | | | |
| *1:30* | The Treasury Band Show | News | Sports Parade | Saturday Special |
| *1:45* | | Chicagoans Orchestra | | |

## DAYTIME — SPRING, 1950

*Saturday*

| | ABC | CBS | MBS | NBC |
|---|---|---|---|---|
| *2pm* | At Home With Music | Treasury Bandstand | Club 930 | |
| *2:15* | | | | |
| *2:30* | Tea and Crumpets | Cross-Section USA | | |
| *2:45* | | The Garden Gate | | |
| *3pm* | Junior Junction | This is Los Angeles | | |
| *3:15* | | | | Henry Wallace, comment |
| *3:30* | The American Farmer | Lake Success | | The NBC Spring Concert |
| *3:45* | | Larry Lesueur, news | | |
| *4pm* | Flying Feet | Disc Jockey, USA | John Flynn, news | |
| *4:15* | | | News and Views | |
| *4:30* | News | | | Pioneers of Music |
| *4:45* | This is Our Town | | | |

# EVENING — SUMMER, 1950

*Sunday*

| | ABC | CBS | MBS | NBC |
|---|---|---|---|---|
| *5pm* | Stop the Music | The Pause That Refreshes | The World at Mid-Century | The Adventures of Sam Spade |
| *5:15* | | | | |
| *5:30* | | Rocky Jordan | The Enchanted Hour | NBC Symphony Orchestra |
| *5:45* | | | | |
| *6pm* | Music | Rate Your Mate | News | |
| *6:15* | Louella Parsons, gossip | | Take a Number | |
| *6:30* | Crossroads | The Youth Opportunity Program | | My Mother's Husband |
| *6:45* | | | Bands for Bonds | |
| *7pm* | Jimmy Fidler, gossip | The Carnation Contented Hour | Public Affairs | Take It or Leave It |
| *7:15* | For the Record | | | |
| *7:30* | The Amazing Mr. Malone | The Whistler | | The Pet Milk Show |
| *7:45* | | | | |
| *8pm* | Tristram Coffin, news | The Steve Allen Show | Twenty Questions | Pescha Kegan, piano |
| *8:15* | Don Gardiner, news | | | News |
| *8:30* | Walter Winchell, gossip | Jeff Regan, Investigator | The Hollywood Opera House | The Standard Symphony Hour |
| *8:45* | Louella Parsons, gossip | | | |
| *9pm* | Think Fast | Much About Doolittle | Glenn Hardy, news | |
| *9:15* | | | Music | |
| *9:30* | Box 13 | Guy Lombardo Orchestra | The Chicago Theater of the Air | Show Time |
| *9:45* | | | | Trouble is My Business |
| *10pm* | Robert Garred, news | The Ten o'Clock Wire | | The Richfield Reporter |
| *10:15* | The Retail Clerk's Union | Top of the Week | | Mayor Bowron, comment |
| *10:30* | Career Theater | Catalina Orchestra | The Arthur Van Show | The American Forum of the Air |
| *10:45* | | | | |

## EVENING — SUMMER, 1950

*Monday*

| ABC | CBS | MBS | NBC | |
|---|---|---|---|---|
| News | Larry Lesueur, news | Records | Feature Wire | *5pm* |
| Happy Theater | Sports | | Ted Meyers, news | *5:15* |
| The Adventures of Superman | Chet Huntley, news | Bobby Benson | The Voice of Firestone | *5:30* |
| | Frank Goss, news | | | *5:45* |
| Edwin C. Hill, news | Too Many Cooks | Gabriel Heatter, news | The American Way | *6pm* |
| Main Street to Malibu | | The Mutual Newsreel | | *6:15* |
| Hannibal Cobb | Granby's Green Acres | The Answer Man | Proudly We Hail | *6:30* |
| | | Sam Hayes, news | | *6:45* |
| The Lone Ranger | Leave It to Joan | Murder By Experts | Cloak and Dagger | *7pm* |
| | | | | *7:15* |
| This is My Song | Tommy Dorsey Orchestra | The Cisco Kid | Maisie | *7:30* |
| | | | | *7:45* |
| Solo and Siloquey | Eric Sevareid, news | Let George Do It | One Man's Family | *8pm* |
| | Stepping Out | | World News | *8:15* |
| Henry J. Taylor, news | Broadway is My Beat | Under Arrest | The Railroad Hour | *8:30* |
| Jackie Robinson, sports | | | | *8:45* |
| Ethel and Albert | The Hollywood Star Playhouse | Glenn Hardy, news | The Bell Telephone Hour | *9pm* |
| | | Fulton Lewis Jr., news | | *9:15* |
| Chandu, the Magician | The Garry Moore Show | Crime Fighters | Nightbeat | *9:30* |
| | | | | *9:45* |
| Robert Garred, news | The Ten o'Clock Wire | I Love a Mystery | The Richfield Reporter | *10pm* |
| Sports | Bob Elson Interviews | Frank Edwards, news | The Johnny Murray Show | *10:15* |
| Science of the Mind | The Symphonette | Lonesome Gal | Virgil Pinkley, news | *10:30* |
| One for the Books | | | The Dave Rose Show | *10:45* |

## EVENING — SUMMER, 1950

*Tuesday*

| | ABC | CBS | MBS | NBC |
|---|---|---|---|---|
| *5pm* | News | Larry Lesueur, news | Records | Feature Wire |
| *5:15* | Happy Theater | Sports | | Ted Meyers, news |
| *5:30* | Space Patrol | Chet Huntley, news | Bobby Benson | Starlight Concert |
| *5:45* | | Frank Goss, news | | |
| *6pm* | Edwin C. Hill, news | Romance | Gabriel Heatter, news | The Penny Singleton Show |
| *6:15* | Main Street to Malibu | | The Mutual Newsreel | |
| *6:30* | Hannibal Cobb | The Candid Microphone | The Answer Man | Presenting Charles Boyer |
| *6:45* | | | Sam Hayes, news | |
| *7pm* | Counterspy | There's Music in the Air | The Mysterious Traveler | Big Town |
| *7:15* | | | | |
| *7:30* | Paul Whiteman Presents | | Bobby Benson | A Life in Your Hands |
| *7:45* | | | | |
| *8pm* | Time for Defense | Eric Sevareid, news | The Count of Monte Cristo | One Man's Family |
| *8:15* | | Stepping Out | | World News |
| *8:30* | Gentlemen of the Press | Satan's Waiting | Mystery is My Hobby | Who Said That |
| *8:45* | | | | |
| *9pm* | America's Town Meeting of the Air | Mystery Theater | Glenn Hardy, news | The Hardy Family |
| *9:15* | | | Fulton Lewis Jr., news | |
| *9:30* | Edwin D. Canham, news | The Garry Moore Show | Official Detective | Joy Forever |
| *9:45* | Report to the People | | | |
| *10pm* | Robert Garred, news | The Ten o'Clock Wire | I Love a Mystery | The Richfield Reporter |
| *10:15* | Sports | Bob Elson Interviews | Frank Edwards, news | The Johnny Murray Show |
| *10:30* | Science of the Mind | Command Theater | Lonesome Gal | Virgil Pinkley, news |
| *10:45* | One for the Books | | | Freddy Martin Orchestra |

## EVENING — SUMMER, 1950

*Wednesday*

| ABC | CBS | MBS | NBC | |
|---|---|---|---|---|
| News | Larry Lesueur, news | Records | Feature Wire | *5pm* |
| Happy Theater | Sports | | Ted Meyers, news | *5:15* |
| The Adventures of Superman | Chet Huntley, news | Roundtable Discussions | Casa Cugat | *5:30* |
| | Frank Goss, news | | Elmer Patterson, news | *5:45* |
| Edwin C. Hill, news | It Pays to Be Ignorant | Gabriel Heatter, news | Dangerous Assignment | *6pm* |
| Main Street to Malibu | | The Mutual Newsreel | | *6:15* |
| Hannibal Cobb | The ABC's of Music, Robert Q. Lewis | The Answer Man | Cloak and Dagger | *6:30* |
| | | Sam Hayes, news | | *6:45* |
| The Lone Ranger | The Adventures of Phillip Marlowe | John Steele, Adventurer | The Big Story | *7pm* |
| | | | | *7:15* |
| Dr. I. Q., the Mental Banker | The Hollywood Music Hall | The Cisco Kid | Richard Diamond, Private Detective | *7:30* |
| | | | | *7:45* |
| Detour | Eric Sevareid, news | What's the Name of That Song | One Man's Family | *8pm* |
| | Stepping Out | | World News | *8:15* |
| Through the Listening Glass | Dr. Christian | The Family Theater | The Falcon | *8:30* |
| | | | | *8:45* |
| The Cliche' Club | Mr. Chameleon | Glenn Hardy, news | Break the Bank | *9pm* |
| | | Fulton Lewis Jr., news | | *9:15* |
| Lawrence Welk High Life Revue | The Garry Moore Show | Music | Mr. District Attorney | *9:30* |
| | | | | *9:45* |
| Robert Garred, news | The Ten o'Clock Wire | I Love a Mystery | The Richfield Reporter | *10pm* |
| Sports | Let's Go Places | Frank Edwards, news | The Johnny Murray Show | *10:15* |
| Science of the Mind | The Symphonette | Lonesome Gal | Virgil Pinkley, news | *10:30* |
| One for the Books | | | Kay Kyser Orchestra | *10:45* |

## EVENING — SUMMER, 1950

*Thursday*

| | ABC | CBS | MBS | NBC |
|---|---|---|---|---|
| *5pm* | News | Larry Lesueur, news | Crowell's Nest | Feature Wire |
| *5:15* | Happy Theater | Sports | | Ted Meyers, news |
| *5:30* | Space Patrol | Chet Huntley, news | Bobby Benson | Casa Cugat |
| *5:45* | | Frank Goss, news | | Elmer Patterson, news |
| *6pm* | Edwin C. Hill, news | Somebody Knows | Gabriel Heatter, news | The Cass Daley Show |
| *6:15* | Main Street to Malibu | | The Mutual Newsreel | |
| *6:30* | Hannibal Cobb | Casey, Crime Photographer | The Answer Man | Duffy's Tavern |
| *6:45* | | | Sam Hayes, news | |
| *7pm* | Counterspy | Yours Truly, Johnny Dollar | Murder at Midnight | Dragnet |
| *7:15* | | | | |
| *7:30* | The Casebook of Gregory Hood | The Skippy Hollywood Theater | Bobby Benson | Sara's Private Caper |
| *7:45* | | | | |
| *8pm* | Ted Mack's Original Amateur Hour | Eric Sevareid, news | The Clyde Beatty Show | One Man's Family |
| *8:15* | | Stepping Out | | World News |
| *8:30* | | Mr. Keen, Tracer of Lost Persons | The Hidden Truth | The Quick and the Dead |
| *8:45* | The World's Best Seller | | | |
| *9pm* | Author Meets the Critics | Lineup | Glenn Hardy, news | Advance Release |
| *9:15* | | | Fulton Lewis Jr., news | |
| *9:30* | Inner Sanctum Mysteries | The Garry Moore Show | International Airport | Hobby Lobby |
| *9:45* | | | | |
| *10pm* | Robert Garred, news | The Ten o'Clock Wire | I Love a Mystery | The Richfield Reporter |
| *10:15* | Sports | Let's Go Places | Frank Edwards, news | The Johnny Murray Show |
| *10:30* | Science of the Mind | Command Theater | Lonesome Gal | Virgil Pinkley, news |
| *10:45* | One for the Books | | | Tommy Dorsey Orchestra |

# EVENING — SUMMER, 1950

*Friday*

| ABC | CBS | MBS | NBC | |
|---|---|---|---|---|
| News | Larry Lesueur, news | Crowell's Nest | Feature Wire | *5pm* |
| Happy Theater | Sports | | Ted Meyers, news | *5:15* |
| The Green Hornet | Chet Huntley, news | Bobby Benson | Casa Cugat | *5:30* |
| | Frank Goss, news | | Elmer Patterson, news | *5:45* |
| Edwin C. Hill, news | Songs for Sale | Gabriel Heatter, news | World Affairs | *6pm* |
| Main Street to Malibu | | The Mutual Newsreel | | *6:15* |
| Hits and Encores | | The Answer Man | Confidentally Yours | *6:30* |
| | | Sam Hayes, news | | *6:45* |
| The Treasury Band Show | Escape | Meet the Press | Wanted | *7pm* |
| | | | | *7:15* |
| Music | The Women's Forum | The Cisco Kid | The Colgate Sports Newsreel, Bill Stern | *7:30* |
| | | | Senators Report | *7:45* |
| The Fat Man | Eric Sevareid, news | Proudly We Hail | One Man's Family | *8pm* |
| | Stepping Out | | World News | *8:15* |
| This is Your FBI | Cloud Nine | True or False | Dimension X | *8:30* |
| | | | | *8:45* |
| The Adventures of the Thin Man | Up for Parole | Glenn Hardy, news | Crime Does Not Pay | *9pm* |
| | | Fulton Lewis Jr., news | | *9:15* |
| Mr. President | The Garry Moore Show | Comedy of Errors | High Adventure | *9:30* |
| | | | | *9:45* |
| Robert Garred, news | The Ten o'Clock Wire | I Love a Mystery | The Richfield Reporter | *10pm* |
| Sports | Bob Elson Interviews | Frank Edwards, news | The Johnny Murray Show | *10:15* |
| Science of the Mind | The Symphonette | Lonesome Gal | Virgil Pinkley, news | *10:30* |
| One for the Books | | | Les Paul Orchestra | *10:45* |

## EVENING — SUMMER, 1950

*Saturday*

| | ABC | CBS | MBS | NBC |
|---|---|---|---|---|
| *5pm* | The Navy Hour | Horse Racing (4:45PM) | The Northwestern Reviewing Stand | The Saturday Concert (4:30PM) |
| *5:15* | | Sports | | |
| *5:30* | Harry Wismer, sports | Chet Huntley, news | Radie Harris, interview | Bob Considine, news |
| *5:45* | Club Time | Frank Goss, news | Science Reporter | Elmer Patterson, news |
| *6pm* | The Dell Trio | Rate Your Mate | The Army and Air Force Show | The Joe DiMaggio Show |
| *6:15* | For the Record | | | |
| *6:30* | Hannibal Cobb | The Goldbergs | Hawaii Calls | Saturday Dance Date |
| *6:45* | | | | |
| *7pm* | Hollywood Byline | Sing It Again | Mr. Feathers | The Chamber Music Society of Lower Basin Street |
| *7:15* | | | | |
| *7:30* | Buzz Adlam's Playroom | | Salute to Reservists | Grand Ole Opry |
| *7:45* | | | | |
| *8pm* | The Lone Ranger | The Camel Caravan, Vaughn Monroe | News | Tales of the Texas Rangers |
| *8:15* | | | Music | |
| *8:30* | Dixieland Jambake | Pursuit | Lombardoland USA | Stars and Starters |
| *8:45* | | | | |
| *9pm* | The Norman Brokenshire Show | Gangbusters | Newspaper of the Air | Your Hit Parade |
| *9:15* | | | Hoosier Hot Shots | |
| *9:30* | Music By Bovero | Arthur Godfrey's Digest | | The Story of Dr. Kildare |
| *9:45* | | | Music | |
| *10pm* | News | The Ten o'Clock Wire | Monica Sings | The Night Reporter |
| *10:15* | Sports | Catalina Orchestra | Music | Supervisor Ray Darby, comment |
| *10:30* | Music | Capitol Cloak Room | The Arthur Van Show | Riverside Rancho |
| *10:45* | | | | |

| DAYTIME — SUMMER, 1950 | | | | |
|---|---|---|---|---|
| *Sunday* | | | | |
| | ABC | CBS | MBS | NBC |
| *8am* | News | The Farm Journal | Music (7:00AM) | The L. A. Times Funnies |
| *8:15* | Morning Song | Howard K. Smith, news | | |
| *8:30* | Let There Be Music | The Salt Lake Tabernacle Choir | The Voice of Prophecy | The Christian Science Monitor |
| *8:45* | | | | Hometown Happenings |
| *9am* | Negro College Choirs | Invitation to Learning | The Radio Bible Class | Parent-Youth Forum |
| *9:15* | | | | |
| *9:30* | Message of Israel | The People's Platform | The Lutheran Hour | The Eternal Light |
| *9:45* | | | | |
| *10am* | Music of Today | News | Glenn Hardy, news | Herbert J. Mann, sports |
| *10:15* | This World of Ours | Get More Out of Life | Organ Moods | News |
| *10:30* | National Vespers | Starlight Operetta | | The University of Chicago Round Table |
| *10:45* | | | | |
| *11am* | Foreign Reporters | Sunday on Broadway | The Happiness Hour | The NBC Theater |
| *11:15* | Frank and Ernest, songs | Where the People Stand | | |
| *11:30* | Yesterday on Broadway | Romance of the Highways | The Gospel Singer | |
| *11:45* | | The University Explorer | Report from Washington | |
| *12pm* | The Hour of Faith | Invitation to Music | Broadway News | The Truitts |
| *12:15* | | | Bill Cunningham, news | |
| *12:30* | This Week Around the World | | Hashknife Hartley and Sleepy Stevens | The Quiz Kids |
| *12:45* | | | | |
| *1pm* | The Old Fashioned Revival Hour | | Hopalong Cassidy | The NBC Theater |
| *1:15* | | | | |
| *1:30* | | Music for You | Martin Kane, Private Detective | |
| *1:45* | | Treasury Bandstand | | |

## DAYTIME — SUMMER, 1950

*Monday-Friday*

| ABC | CBS | MBS | NBC | |
|---|---|---|---|---|
| The Breakfast Club | Top of the Morning | Cecil Brown, news | The Bell Ringer | *8am* |
| | News | Little Jack Little, songs | Coffee Time | *8:15* |
| | Grand Slam | Bible Institute | The Jack Berch Show | *8:30* |
| | Rosemary | | Meyers Goes to the Market | *8:45* |
| Ladies Be Seated | Wendy Warren and the News | Kate Smith Speaks | Ladies' Day | *9am* |
| | Aunt Jenny's True Life Stories | The Garden Guide | | *9:15* |
| Quick as a Flash | The Romance of Helen Trent | Women are Wonderful | | *9:30* |
| | Our Gal Sunday | | All Around Town | *9:45* |
| Surprise Package | Big Sister | Glenn Hardy, news | | *10am* |
| | Ma Perkins | Tello-Test Quiz | Are You Listening | *10:15* |
| My True Story | Young Dr. Malone | Nancy Young, talk | Report from the Pentagon | *10:30* |
| | The Guiding Light | | Life Can Be Beautiful | *10:45* |
| The Magazine of the Air | The Second Mrs. Burton | Ladies Fair | Double or Nothing | *11am* |
| John B. Kennedy, news | Perry Mason | | | *11:15* |
| Ira Cook, talk | This is Nora Drake | Queen for a Day | Live Like a Millionaire | *11:30* |
| | The Brighter Day | | | *11:45* |
| Hank Weaver, news | News and Talk | Broadway News | The Farm Reporter | *12pm* |
| H. R. Baukhage, news | | Pix-O | The Road of Life | *12:15* |
| The Frances Scully Show | Open House | Norma Dixon, talk | Pepper Young's Family | *12:30* |
| Double Feature | | Sports | The Right to Happiness | *12:45* |
| Ira Cook, talk | Nona from Nowhere | | Mary Noble, Backstage Wife | *1pm* |
| | Hilltop House | | Stella Dallas | *1:15* |
| Easy Aces | Disc Jockey, USA | | Lorenzo Jones | *1:30* |
| Between the Bookends | | | Young Widder Brown | *1:45* |

## DAYTIME — SUMMER, 1950

*Sunday*

| | ABC | CBS | MBS | NBC |
|---|---|---|---|---|
| *2pm* | The Voice of Prophecy | American Rhapsody | The Shadow | The Big Guy |
| *2:15* | | | | |
| *2:30* | The Piano Playhouse | News | True Detective Mysteries | Harvest of Stars |
| *2:45* | | The Melody Parade | | |
| *3pm* | The Lutheran Hour | Earn Your Vacation | The Singing Marshall | The Catholic Hour |
| *3:15* | | | | |
| *3:30* | Sammy Kaye's Sunday Serenade | Boston Blackie | Nick Carter, Master Detective | Tex Williams Orchestra |
| *3:45* | | | | |
| *4pm* | This Thing Called Life | Guy Lombardo Orchestra | California Caravan | $1000 Reward |
| *4:15* | | | | |
| *4:30* | Music with the Hormel Girls | Hit the Jackpot | The Affairs of PeterSalem | The Saint |
| *4:45* | | | | |

## DAYTIME — SUMMER, 1950

*Monday-Friday*

| ABC | CBS | MBS | NBC | |
|---|---|---|---|---|
| Chance of a Lifetime | George Fisher, gossip | | When a Girl Marries | *2pm* |
| | TakeIt Easy Time | | Portia Faces Life | *2:15* |
| Bride and Groom | This is Bing Crosby | | Just Plain Bill | *2:30* |
| | Arthur Godfrey Time | | Front Page Farrell | *2:45* |
| Today in Hollywood | | | Welcome Travelers | *3pm* |
| Leyden with Song | | Baker's Dozen | | *3:15* |
| | | | Aunt Mary | *3:30* |
| | | Lynn at Hollywood | We Love and Learn | *3:45* |
| Art Baker's Notebook | Curt Massey, songs | Fulton Lewis Jr., news | One Woman's Secret | *4pm* |
| Play It Again | Strike It Rich | Frank Hemingway, news | Dr. Paul | *4:15* |
| | | Behind the Story | Burritt and Wheeler, talk | *4:30* |
| Elmer Davis, news | The Harry Babbitt Show | Sam Hayes, news | | *4:45* |

# DAYTIME — SUMMER, 1950

*Saturday*

| | ABC | CBS | MBS | NBC |
|---|---|---|---|---|
| *8am* | No School Today (7:45AM) | Let's Pretend | Femme Fair | Mind Your Manners |
| *8:15* | | | News | |
| *8:30* | | Junior Miss | The Haven of Rest | Archie Andrews |
| *8:45* | Mirandy | | | |
| *9am* | Ira Cook, talk | The Armstrong Theater of Today | Flying Feet | News |
| *9:15* | | | | Public Affairs |
| *9:30* | | Grand Central Station | Bands for Bonds | Luncheon with Lopez |
| *9:45* | | | Guest Star | |
| *10am* | | Stars Over Hollywood | Newspaper of the Air | Are You from Dixie |
| *10:15* | | | The Gospel Singer | |
| *10:30* | | Give and Take | The Battle Creek Choir | |
| *10:45* | | | | |
| *11am* | | Family Parade | Sports | Mary Lee Taylor, cooking |
| *11:15* | | | | |
| *11:30* | | Fun to Be Young | | The National Farm and Home Hour |
| *11:45* | | | | |
| *12pm* | News | Music with the Girls | | The Farm Reporter |
| *12:15* | Records | | | Saturday Special |
| *12:30* | | Meet the Missus | | |
| *12:45* | | | | |
| *1pm* | The Treasury Band Show | The Housewive's Protective League | | |
| *1:15* | | | | |
| *1:30* | Old, New, Borrowed and Blue | | Sid Fuller, sports | |
| *1:45* | | At the Hollywood Bowl | Baker's Dozen | |

## DAYTIME — SUMMER, 1950

*Saturday*

| | ABC | CBS | MBS | NBC |
|---|---|---|---|---|
| *2pm* | Tea and Crumpets | Roy Stevens Orchestra | | |
| *2:15* | | | | |
| *2:30* | A Man and His Music | Make Way for Youth | | Sportscast |
| *2:45* | | | | |
| *3pm* | Junior Junction | This is Los Angeles | | The Music City Show |
| *3:15* | | | | |
| *3:30* | The American Farmer | Sports | | Living 1950 |
| *3:45* | | Larry Lesueur, news | Land of the Free | |
| *4pm* | Flying Feet | Disc Jockey, USA | John Flynn, news | Voices and Events |
| *4:15* | | | Frank Hemingway, news | |
| *4:30* | Talking It Over | | Bandstand USA | The Saturday Concert |
| *4:45* | As We See It | | | |

## EVENING — FALL, 1950

*Sunday*

| | ABC | CBS | MBS | NBC |
|---|---|---|---|---|
| *5pm* | Stop the Music | The Charlie McCarhty Show | Bobby Benson | Tales of the Texas Rangers |
| *5:15* | | | | |
| *5:30* | | News Desk | Music | The Theater Guild of the Air |
| *5:45* | | | | |
| *6pm* | Walter Winchell, gossip | Meet Corliss Archer | News | |
| *6:15* | Louella Parsons, gossip | | The Mutual Newsreel | |
| *6:30* | Crossroads | The Youth Opportunity Program | Gabriel Heatter, news | The American Album of Familiar Music |
| *6:45* | | | Major George Elliott, comment | |
| *7pm* | The Botany Song Shop, Ginny Simms | The Carnation Contented Hour | Two-Thousand Plus | The $64 Question |
| *7:15* | William Tusher in Hollywood | | | |
| *7:30* | The Cliche' Club | The Whistler | Take a Number | Meet Me in St. Louis |
| *7:45* | | | | |
| *8pm* | Drew Pearson, news | Our Miss Brooks | Twenty Questions | Noah Webster Says |
| *8:15* | Don Gardiner, news | | | |
| *8:30* | Walter Winchell, gossip | The Charlie McCarthy Show | The Count of Monte Cristo | The Standard Symphony Hour |
| *8:45* | Louella Parsons, gossip | | | |
| *9pm* | The Richard Wallace Show | The Red Skelton Show | Glenn Hardy, news | |
| *9:15* | | | Henry Brandon, comment | |
| *9:30* | The Piano Playhouse | The Lucky Strike Program, Jack Benny | The Chicago Theater of the Air | Robert L. Gump, news |
| *9:45* | | | | Trouble is My Business |
| *10pm* | George Sokolsky, news | The Ten o'Clock Wire | | The Richfield Reporter |
| *10:15* | The Retail Clerk's Union | Top of the Week | | City Reports |
| *10:30* | Career Theater | Make-Believe Town | The Arthur Van Show | The American Forum of the Air |
| *10:45* | | | | |

## EVENING — FALL, 1950

*Monday*

| ABC | CBS | MBS | NBC | |
|---|---|---|---|---|
| News | Edward R. Murrow, news | Mark Trail | Feature Wire | *5pm* |
| Happy Theater | Tom Harmon, sports | | Ted Meyers, news | *5:15* |
| Space Patrol | Chet Huntley, news | Challenge of the Yukon | The Voice of Firestone | *5:30* |
| Falstaff's Fables (5:55 PM) | Frank Goss, news | | | *5:45* |
| Edwin C. Hill, news | The Lux Radio Theater | Gabriel Heatter, news | The American Way | *6pm* |
| Main Street to Malibu | | The Mutual Newsreel | | *6:15* |
| Waitin' for Wakely | | The Answer Man | Maisie | *6:30* |
| | | Sam Hayes, news | | *6:45* |
| The Lone Ranger | My Friend Irma | War Front, Home Front | NBC Symphony Orchestra | *7pm* |
| | | | | *7:15* |
| United or Not | The Bob Hawk Show | The Cisco Kid | | *7:30* |
| | | | | *7:45* |
| H. G. Douglas, comment | Lowell Thomas, news | Let George Do It | One Man's Family | *8pm* |
| The N. Y. Herald Tribune Forum | The Jack Smith Show | | World News | *8:15* |
| Henry J. Taylor, news | Arthur Godfrey's Talent Scouts | Under Arrest | The Railroad Hour | *8:30* |
| Richard Nixon, comment | | | | *8:45* |
| Mr. President | The Hollywood Star Playhouse | Glenn Hardy, news | The Bell Telephone Hour | *9pm* |
| | | Fulton Lewis Jr., news | | *9:15* |
| Inner Sanctum Mysteries | The Beulah Show | Music for Monday | Werner Janssen Orchestra | *9:30* |
| | Club Fifteen | | | *9:45* |
| Robert Garred, news | The Ten o'Clock Wire | I Love a Mystery | The Richfield Reporter | *10pm* |
| Science of the Mind | Bob Elson Interviews | Frank Edwards, news | H. V. Kaltenborn, news | *10:15* |
| The Symphonette | Starlight Salute | Lonesome Gal | Virgil Pinkley, news | *10:30* |
| | | | The Dave Rose Show | *10:45* |

## EVENING — FALL, 1950

*Tuesday*

| | ABC | CBS | MBS | NBC |
|---|---|---|---|---|
| *5pm* | News | Edward R. Murrow, news | Straight Arrow | Feature Wire |
| *5:15* | Happy Theater | Tom Harmon, sports | | Ted Meyers, news |
| *5:30* | The Adventures of Superman | Chet Huntley, news | Sky King | The Baby Snooks Show |
| *5:45* | Falstaff's Fables (5:55PM) | Frank Goss, news | Dollars and Sense (5:55PM) | |
| *6pm* | Edwin C. Hill, news | Life with Luigi | Gabriel Heatter, news | The Hardy Family |
| *6:15* | Main Street to Malibu | | The Mutual Newsreel | |
| *6:30* | Waitin' for Wakely | Truth or Consequences | The Answer Man | Fibber McGee and Molly |
| *6:45* | | | Sam Hayes, news | |
| *7pm* | Armstrong of the SBI | The Hollywood Music Hall | The Mysterious Traveler | Big Town |
| *7:15* | | | | |
| *7:30* | Governor Warren, comment | Capitol Cloak Room | Red Ryder | People Are Funny |
| *7:45* | Report to the People | | | |
| *8pm* | On Trial | Lowell Thomas, news | Song of Liberty | One Man's Family |
| *8:15* | | The Jack Smith Show | | World News |
| *8:30* | Time for Defense | Mr. and Mrs. North | The Affairs of Peter Salem | The Cavalcade of America |
| *8:45* | | | | |
| *9pm* | America's Town Meeting of the Air | Mystery Theater | Glenn Hardy, news | The Bob Hope Show |
| *9:15* | | | Fulton Lewis Jr., news | |
| *9:30* | Twin Views of the News | The Beulah Show | Official Detective | Music America Loves |
| *9:45* | Pat Brown, comment | Club Fifteen | Five Minute Final (9:55PM) | |
| *10pm* | Robert Garred, news | The Ten o'Clock Wire | I Love a Mystery | The Richfield Reporter |
| *10:15* | Science of the Mind | Bob Elson Interviews | Frank Edwards, news | The Johnny Murray Show |
| *10:30* | The Symphonette | Starlight Salute | Lonesome Gal | Virgil Pinkley, news |
| *10:45* | | | | Freddy Martin Orchestra |

## EVENING — FALL, 1950

*Wednesday*

| ABC | CBS | MBS | NBC | |
|---|---|---|---|---|
| News | Edward R. Murrow, news | Mark Trail | Feature Wire | *5pm* |
| Happy Theater | Tom Harmon, sports | | Ted Meyers, news | *5:15* |
| Blackhawk | Chet Huntley, news | Challenge of the Yukon | Casa Cugat | *5:30* |
| Falstaff's Fables (5:55PM) | Frank Goss, news | | Elmer Patterson, news | *5:45* |
| Edwin C. Hill, news | Honest Harold | Gabriel Heatter, news | Proudly We Hail | *6pm* |
| Main Street to Malibu | | The Mutual Newsreel | | *6:15* |
| Waitin' for Wakely | The Bing Crosby Chesterfield Show | The Answer Man | The Halls of Ivy | *6:30* |
| | | Sam Hayes, news | | *6:45* |
| The Lone Ranger | The Wednesday Night Fights | John Steele, Adventurer | The Big Story | *7pm* |
| | | | | *7:15* |
| Dr. I. Q., the Mental Banker | Music | The Cisco Kid | Richard Diamond, Private Detective | *7:30* |
| | | | | *7:45* |
| Detour | Lowell Thomas, news | What's the Name of That Song | One Man's Family | *8pm* |
| | The Jack Smith Show | | World News | *8:15* |
| Through the Listening Glass | Dr. Christian | The Family Theater | The Great Gildersleeve | *8:30* |
| | | | | *8:45* |
| American Agent | Mr. Chameleon | Glenn Hardy, news | You Bet Your Life | *9pm* |
| | | Fulton Lewis Jr., news | | *9:15* |
| Lawrence Welk High Life Revue | The Beulah Show | Music | Mr. District Attorney | *9:30* |
| | Club Fifteen | Five Minute Final (9:55PM) | | *9:45* |
| Robert Garred, news | The Ten o'Clock Wire | I Love a Mystery | The Richfield Reporter | *10pm* |
| Science of the Mind | Bob Elson Interviews | Frank Edwards, news | H. V. Kaltenborn, news | *10:15* |
| The Symphonette | Starlight Salute | Lonesome Gal | Virgil Pinkley, news | *10:30* |
| | | | Kay Kyser Orchestra | *10:45* |

| EVENING — FALL, 1950 | | | | |
|---|---|---|---|---|
| *Thursday* | | | | |
| | ABC | CBS | MBS | NBC |
| *5pm* | News | Edward R. Murrow, news | Straight Arrow | Feature Wire |
| *5:15* | Happy Theater | Tom Harmon, sports | | Ted Meyers, news |
| *5:30* | The Adventures of Superman | Chet Huntley, news | Sky King | Casa Cugat |
| *5:45* | Falstaff's Fables (5:55PM) | Frank Goss, news | Dollars and Sense (5:55PM) | Elmer Patterson, news |
| *6pm* | Edwin C. Hill, news | Suspense | Gabriel Heatter, news | Dragnet |
| *6:15* | Main Street to Malibu | | The Mutual Newsreel | |
| *6:30* | Waitin' for Wakely | Casey, Crime Photographer | The Answer Man | Music from Hollywood |
| *6:45* | | | Sam Hayes, news | |
| *7pm* | The Screen Guild Theater | The Hallmark Playhouse | Murder By Experts | Top Secret |
| *7:15* | | | | |
| *7:30* | | The Choraliers | Red Ryder | Presenting Charles Boyer |
| *7:45* | | | | |
| *8pm* | Ted Mack's Original Amateur Hour | Lowell Thomas, news | The Clyde Beatty Show | One Man's Family |
| *8:15* | | The Jack Smith Show | | World News |
| *8:30* | | Mr. Keen, Tracer of Lost Persons | Reporter's Roundup | The Aldrich Family |
| *8:45* | Robert Montgomery Speaking | | | |
| *9pm* | World's Best Seller | The FBI in Peace and War | Glenn Hardy, news | Father Knows Best |
| *9:15* | This is California | | Fulton Lewis Jr., news | |
| *9:30* | Hollywood Byline | The Beulah Show | The Rod and Gun Club | Musical Americana |
| *9:45* | | Club Fifteen | Five Minute Final (9:55PM) | |
| *10pm* | Robert Garred, news | The Ten o'Clock Wire | I Love a Mystery | The Richfield Reporter |
| *10:15* | Science of the Mind | Bob Elson Interviews | Frank Edwards, news | The Johnny Murray Show |
| *10:30* | The Symphonette | Starlight Salute | Lonesome Gal | Virgil Pinkley, news |
| *10:45* | | | | Tommy Dorsey Orchestra |

## EVENING — FALL, 1950

*Friday*

| ABC | CBS | MBS | NBC | |
|---|---|---|---|---|
| News | Edward R. Murrow, news | Mark Trail | Feature Wire | *5pm* |
| Happy Theater | Tom Harmon, sports | | Ted Meyers, news | *5:15* |
| Space Patrol | Chet Huntley, news | Challenge of the Yukon | Casa Cugat | *5:30* |
| Falstaff's Fables (5:55 PM) | Frank Goss, news | | Elmer Patterson, news | *5:45* |
| Edwin C. Hill, news | Songs for Sale | Gabriel Heatter, news | Nightbeat | *6pm* |
| Main Street to Malibu | | The Mutual Newsreel | | *6:15* |
| Hits and Encores | | The Answer Man | Counterspy | *6:30* |
| | | Sam Hayes, news | | *6:45* |
| Madison Square Garden Boxing | One Nation Indivisible | The Hidden Truth | The Life of Riley | *7pm* |
| | | | | *7:15* |
| | The Women's Forum | The Cisco Kid | The Colgate Sports Newsreel, Bill Stern | *7:30* |
| | | | Governor Warren, comment | *7:45* |
| The Fat Man | Lowell Thomas, news | Tomorrow's Football | One Man's Family | *8pm* |
| | The Jack Smith Show | John Flynn, news | World News | *8:15* |
| This is Your FBI | Broadway is My Beat | True or False | The New Adventures of Nero Wolfe | *8:30* |
| | | | | *8:45* |
| The Adventures of Ozzie and Harriet | Escape | Glenn Hardy, news | The Man Called X | *9pm* |
| | | Fulton Lewis Jr., news | | *9:15* |
| Armstrong of the SBI | The Beulah Show | Comedy of Errors | Crime Does Not Pay | *9:30* |
| | Club Fifteen | Five Minute Final (9:55PM) | | *9:45* |
| Robert Garred, news | The Ten o'Clock Wire | I Love a Mystery | The Richfield Reporter | *10pm* |
| Science of the Mind | Bob Elson Interviews | Frank Edwards, news | H. V. Kaltenborn, news | *10:15* |
| The Symphonette | Starlight Salute | Lonesome Gal | Virgil Pinkley, news | *10:30* |
| | | | Benny Goodman Orchestra | *10:45* |

## EVENING — FALL, 1950

*Saturday*

| | ABC | CBS | MBS | NBC |
|---|---|---|---|---|
| *5pm* | The Navy Hour | Musical Scoreboard | Frank Hemingway, news | The Saturday Concert (4:45PM) |
| *5:15* | | Tom Harmon, sports | Dollars and Sense | |
| *5:30* | Harry Wismer, sports | Chet Huntley, news | Sports | |
| *5:45* | Club Time | Frank Goss, news | Sam Hayes, news | Elmer Patterson, news |
| *6pm* | Buzz Adlam's Playroom | Yours Truly, Johnny Dollar | The Army and Air Force Show | Hallelujah Time |
| *6:15* | | | | |
| *6:30* | Waitin' for Wakely | My Favorite Husband | Hawaii Calls | A Day in the Life of Dennis Day |
| *6:45* | | | | |
| *7pm* | Merry-Go-Round, Jimmy Blaine | Sing It Again | Know Your Schools | The Judy Canova Show |
| *7:15* | | | | |
| *7:30* | Can You Top This | | The Ben Pollack Show | Grand Ole Opry |
| *7:45* | | | | |
| *8pm* | The Lone Ranger | The Camel Caravan, Vaughn Monroe | Salute to the Reservists | US Navy Recruiting |
| *8:15* | | | | Bob Considine, news |
| *8:30* | The American Barndance | Gene Autry's Melody Ranch | Lombardoland USA | Hedda Hopper's Hollywood |
| *8:45* | | | | |
| *9pm* | What Makes You Tick | Hopalong Cassidy | Newspaper of the Air | Your Hit Parade |
| *9:15* | | | Dance Orchestra | |
| *9:30* | Shoot the Moon | Gangbusters | Buddy Manero, songs | The Story of Dr. Kildare |
| *9:45* | | | News | |
| *10pm* | Robert Garred, news | The Ten o'Clock Wire | Monica Sings | The Night Reporter |
| *10:15* | News | George Fisher, gossip | Dance Orchestra | Supervisor Ray Darby, comment |
| *10:30* | Scouting the Stars | Starlight Salute | The Arthur Van Show | The Cass Daley Show |
| *10:45* | Pietro Pontrelli Orchestra | | | |

## DAYTIME — FALL, 1950

*Sunday*

| | ABC | CBS | MBS | NBC |
|---|---|---|---|---|
| *8am* | The Band Box Revue (7:30AM) | The Salt Lake Tabernacle Choir | The Religious Hour | Grandpa Reads the Funnies |
| *8:15* | | | | |
| *8:30* | Flying Feet | Invitation to Learning | Music | The Christian Science Monitor |
| *8:45* | | | | Hometown Happenings |
| *9am* | Sunday with Bill Davidson | The People's Platform | The Radio Bible Class | Parent-Youth Forum |
| *9:15* | | | | |
| *9:30* | | Howard K. Smith, news | The Voice of Prophecy | The Eternal Light |
| *9:45* | | Charles Collingwood, news | | |
| *10am* | | Invitation to Music | Glenn Hardy, news | Herbert J. Mann, sports |
| *10:15* | | | Organ Moods | Crime is Your Problem |
| *10:30* | | | The Lutheran Hour | The University of Chicago Round Table |
| *10:45* | | | | |
| *11am* | National Vespers | | Frank and Ernest, songs | The Catholic Hour |
| *11:15* | | | Science Reporter | |
| *11:30* | Reel Music | The Longine Symphonette | The Gospel Singer | Voices and Events |
| *11:45* | | | The Canary Pet Shop | |
| *12pm* | The Hour of Faith | News | Broadway News | The NBC University Theater |
| *12:15* | | Romance of the Highways | Bill Cunningham, news | |
| *12:30* | Music with the Hormel Girls | The University Explorer | Hashknife Hartley and Sleepy Stevens | The Quiz Kids |
| *12:45* | | The Melody Parade | | |
| *1pm* | The Old Fashioned Revival Hour | Earn Your Vacation | The Singing Marshall | The NBC Theater |
| *1:15* | | | | |
| *1:30* | | Arthur Godfrey's Digest | Martin Kane, Private Detective | |
| *1:45* | | | | |

## DAYTIME — FALL, 1950

*Monday-Friday*

| ABC | CBS | MBS | NBC | |
|---|---|---|---|---|
| The Breakfast Club | Top of the Morning | Cecil Brown, news | Break the Bank | *8am* |
| | News | News | | *8:15* |
| | Grand Slam | Bible Institute | The Jack Berch Show | *8:30* |
| | Rosemary | | Meyers Goes to the Market | *8:45* |
| Johnny Olsen's Luncheon Club | Wendy Warren and the News | Kate Smith Speaks | Ladies' Day | *9am* |
| | Aunt Jenny's True Life Stories | The Gospel Singer | | *9:15* |
| Quick as a Flash | The Romance of Helen Trent | Women are Wonderful | | *9:30* |
| | Our Gal Sunday | | All Around Town | *9:45* |
| Victor Lindlahr, health | Big Sister | Glenn Hardy, news | | *10am* |
| Yesterday on Broadway | Ma Perkins | Tello-Test Quiz | Are You Listening | *10:15* |
| My True Story | Young Dr. Malone | Nancy Young, talk | Wendell Noble, news | *10:30* |
| | The Guiding Light | | Life Can Be Beautiful | *10:45* |
| The Magazine of the Air | The Second Mrs. Burton | Ladies Fair | Double or Nothing | *11am* |
| Easy Aces | Perry Mason | | | *11:15* |
| John B. Kennedy, news | This is Nora Drake | Queen for a Day | Live Like a Millionaire | *11:30* |
| Ira Cook, talk | The Brighter Day | | | *11:45* |
| Hank Weaver, gossip | News | Broadway News | The Farm Reporter | *12pm* |
| H. R. Baukage, news | George Fisher, gossip | Cedric Foster, news | The Road of Life | *12:15* |
| Modern Romances | House Party | Norma Dixon, talk | Pepper Young's Family | *12:30* |
| | | The Dave Rose Show | The Right to Happiness | *12:45* |
| Ira Cook, talk | Nona from Nowhere | The Jack Kirkwood Show | Mary Noble, Backstage Wife | *1pm* |
| | Hilltop House | | Stella Dallas | *1:15* |
| | The Housewive's Protective League | Chucklewagon | Lorenzo Jones | *1:30* |
| The Frances Scully Show | | Music | Young Widder Brown | *1:45* |

## DAYTIME — FALL, 1950

*Sunday*

| | ABC | CBS | MBS | NBC |
|---|---|---|---|---|
| *2pm* | The Voice of Prophecy | Syncopation Piece | The Shadow | The Falcon |
| *2:15* | | | | |
| *2:30* | The Greatest Story Ever Told | Music for You | True Detective Mysteries | Charlie Wild, Private Detective |
| *2:45* | | | | |
| *3pm* | The Lutheran Hour | American Rhapsody | The Roy Rogers Show | Speak My Language |
| *3:15* | | | | |
| *3:30* | Sammy Kaye's Sunday Serenade | Memo from Molly | Nick Carter, Master Detective | Tex Williams Orchestra |
| *3:45* | | | | |
| *4pm* | This Thing Called Life | The Lucky Strike Program, Jack Benny | California Caravan | $1000 Reward |
| *4:15* | | | | |
| *4:30* | This Week Around the World | Amos 'n' Andy | The Affairs of Peter Salem | The Phil Harris - Alice Faye Show |
| *4:45* | | | | |

## DAYTIME — FALL, 1950

*Monday-Friday*

| ABC | CBS | MBS | NBC | |
|---|---|---|---|---|
| Surprise Package | Disc Jockey, USA | | When a Girl Marries | *2pm* |
| | | Club 930 | Portia Faces Life | *2:15* |
| Chance of a Lifetime | | | Just Plain Bill | *2:30* |
| | Freddy Martin Orchestra | | Front Page Farrell | *2:45* |
| Today in Hollywood | Arthur Godfrey Time | | Welcome Travelers | *3pm* |
| Peace of Mind | | | | *3:15* |
| The Rudy Vallee Show | | | Aunt Mary | *3:30* |
| | | Lynn at Hollywood | We Love and Learn | *3:45* |
| Art Baker's Notebook | Curt Massey, songs | Fulton Lewis Jr., news | One Woman's Secret | *4pm* |
| | Strike It Rich | Frank Hemingway, news | Dr. Paul | *4:15* |
| Play It Again | | Behind the Story | Burritt and Wheeler, talk | *4:30* |
| Elmer Davis, news | The Harry Babbitt Show | Sam Hayes, news | | *4:45* |

## DAYTIME — FALL, 1950

*Saturday*

| | ABC | CBS | MBS | NBC |
|---|---|---|---|---|
| *8am* | No School Today (7:45AM) | Let's Pretend | Your New Social Security | Archie Andrews |
| *8:15* | | | News | |
| *8:30* | | Junior Miss | The Haven of Rest | Smilin' Ed's Buster Brown Gang |
| *8:45* | Mirandy | | | |
| *9am* | Ira Cook, talk | The Armstrong Theater of Today | Flying Feet | On the Scouting Trail |
| *9:15* | | | | |
| *9:30* | | Grand Central Station | Music | The Young of America |
| *9:45* | | | | |
| *10am* | | Stars Over Hollywood | Newspaper of the Air | Are You from Dixie |
| *10:15* | | | Music | |
| *10:30* | | Give and Take | College Choir | |
| *10:45* | | | | |
| *11am* | | The Carnation Family Party | The Air Force Hour | Mary Lee Taylor, cooking |
| *11:15* | Sports | | | |
| *11:30* | | Music with the Hormel Girls | | The National Farm and Home Hour |
| *11:45* | | | | |
| *12pm* | | The Coke Club, Morton Downey | News | The Farm Reporter |
| *12:15* | | | Music | Quick, What's the Answer |
| *12:30* | | Sports | The Man on the Farm | |
| *12:45* | | | | |
| *1pm* | | | | |
| *1:15* | | | | |
| *1:30* | | | Club 930 | |
| *1:45* | Ira Cook, talk | | | Sports |

# DAYTIME — FALL, 1950

*Saturday*

| | ABC | CBS | MBS | NBC |
|---|---|---|---|---|
| *2pm* | | | | |
| *2:15* | | | Sports | |
| *2:30* | | Meet the Missus | | |
| *2:45* | | | | |
| *3pm* | Junior Junction | The Housewive's Protective League | | |
| *3:15* | | | | |
| *3:30* | The American Farmer | Sports | | |
| *3:45* | | News | | |
| *4pm* | Flying Feet | This is Los Angeles | | |
| *4:15* | | | | |
| *4:30* | It's Your Business | Disc Jockey, USA | | |
| *4:45* | Robert Nathan, news | | Music | The Saturday Concert |

# LISTINGS FOR 1951

## EVENING — WINTER, 1951

*Sunday*

| | ABC | CBS | MBS | NBC |
|---|---|---|---|---|
| *5pm* | Stop the Music | The Charlie McCarhty Show | The Singing Marshall | Hedda Hopper's Hollywood |
| *5:15* | | | | |
| *5:30* | | Chet Huntley, news | The Voices of America | The Theater Guild of the Air |
| *5:45* | | Tom Harmon, sports | | |
| *6pm* | Walter Winchell, gossip | Meet Corliss Archer | News | |
| *6:15* | Louella Parsons, gossip | | The Mutual Newsreel | |
| *6:30* | The American Album of Familiar Music | The Youth Opportunity Program | Gabriel Heatter, news | Music with the Hormel Girls |
| *6:45* | | | Get More Out of LIfe | |
| *7pm* | The Botany Song Shop, Ginny Simms | The Carnation Contented Hour | Comedy of Errors | The $64 Question |
| *7:15* | Paul Harvey, news | | | |
| *7:30* | The Ted Mack Family Hour | The Whistler | Take a Number | Voices and Events |
| *7:45* | | | | |
| *8pm* | Drew Pearson, news | Our Miss Brooks | Twenty Questions | Melody Time |
| *8:15* | Don Gardiner, news | | | |
| *8:30* | Walter Winchell, gossip | The Charlie McCarthy Show | The Count of Monte Cristo | The Standard Symphony Hour |
| *8:45* | Radie Harris, gossip | | | |
| *9pm* | Mystery File | The Red Skelton Show | Glenn Hardy, news | |
| *9:15* | | | Washington Reports | |
| *9:30* | Sammy Kaye's Sunday Serenade | The Lucky Strike Program, Jack Benny | The Chicago Theater of the Air | Robert L. Gump, news |
| *9:45* | | | | Trouble is My Business |
| *10pm* | William Tusher in Holllywood | The Ten o'Clock Wire | | The Richfield Reporter |
| *10:15* | The Retail Clerk's Union | Top of the Week | | Mayor Bowron, comment |
| *10:30* | Career Theater | Your Tropical Trip | The Arthur Van Show | The Saint |
| *10:45* | | | | |

## EVENING — WINTER, 1951

*Monday*

| ABC | CBS | MBS | NBC | |
|---|---|---|---|---|
| News | Edward R. Murrow, news | Mark Trail | Feature Wire | *5pm* |
| Elmer Davis, news | Tom Harmon, sports | | Ted Meyers, news | *5:15* |
| Lou Crosby Orchestra | Chet Huntley, news | Clyde Beatty Adventures | The Voice of Firestone | *5:30* |
| | Frank Goss, news | Victor Borge, piano (5:55PM) | | *5:45* |
| Edwin C. Hill, news | The Lux Radio Theater | Gabriel Heatter, news | The American Way | *6pm* |
| Main Street to Malibu | | The Mutual Newsreel | | *6:15* |
| Boston Blackie | | The Answer Man | The Dick Haymes Show | *6:30* |
| | | Sam Hayes, news | | *6:45* |
| The Lone Ranger | My Friend Irma | War Front, Home Front | NBC Symphony Orchestra | *7pm* |
| | | | | *7:15* |
| Inner Sanctum Mysteries | The Bob Hawk Show | The Cisco Kid | | *7:30* |
| | | | | *7:45* |
| Ralph Flanagan Orchestra | Lowell Thomas, news | Let George Do It | One Man's Family | *8pm* |
| | The Jack Smith Show | | World News | *8:15* |
| Henry J. Taylor, news | Arthur Godfrey's Talent Scouts | Under Arrest | The Railroad Hour | *8:30* |
| World News | | | | *8:45* |
| The Richard Wallace Show | The Hollywood Star Playhouse | Glenn Hardy, news | The Bell Telephone Hour | *9pm* |
| | | Fulton Lewis Jr., news | | *9:15* |
| The Piano Playhouse | The Beulah Show | Crime Fighters | Boston Pops Orchestra | *9:30* |
| | Club Fifteen | Five Minute Final (9:55PM) | | *9:45* |
| Robert Garred, news | The Ten o'Clock Wire | I Love a Mystery | The Richfield Reporter | *10pm* |
| Science of the Mind | Bob Elson Interviews | Frank Edwards, news | Virgil Pinkley, news | *10:15* |
| One for the Books | Starlight Salute | Lonesome Gal | The Johnny Murray Show | *10:30* |
| | | | Sports | *10:45* |

# EVENING — WINTER, 1951

*Tuesday*

| | ABC | CBS | MBS | NBC |
|---|---|---|---|---|
| *5pm* | News | Edward R. Murrow, news | Straight Arrow | Feature Wire |
| *5:15* | Elmer Davis, news | Tom Harmon, sports | | Ted Meyers, news |
| *5:30* | Lou Crosby Orchestra | Chet Huntley, news | Sky King | The Baby Snooks Show |
| *5:45* | | Frank Goss, news | Bobby Benson (5:55PM) | |
| *6pm* | Edwin C. Hill, news | Life with Luigi | Gabriel Heatter, news | The Hardy Family |
| *6:15* | Main Street to Malibu | | The Mutual Newsreel | |
| *6:30* | Philo Vance | Truth or Consequences | The Answer Man | Fibber McGee and Molly |
| *6:45* | | | Sam Hayes, news | |
| *7pm* | Armstrong of the SBI | The Hollywood Music Hall | The Mysterious Traveler | Big Town |
| *7:15* | | | | |
| *7:30* | Can You Top This | Charlie Wild, Private Detective | Red Ryder | People Are Funny |
| *7:45* | | | | |
| *8pm* | I Fly Anything | Lowell Thomas, news | Song of Liberty | One Man's Family |
| *8:15* | | The Jack Smith Show | | World News |
| *8:30* | The Metropolitan Opera Auditions | Mr. and Mrs. North | Two-Thousand Plus | The Cavalcade of America |
| *8:45* | | | | |
| *9pm* | America's Town Meeting of the Air | Mystery Theater | Glenn Hardy, news | The Bob Hope Show |
| *9:15* | | | Fulton Lewis Jr., news | |
| *9:30* | Twin Views of the News | The Beulah Show | Official Detective | Information, Please |
| *9:45* | Edwin Canham, news | Club Fifteen | Five Minute Final (9:55PM) | |
| *10pm* | Robert Garred, news | The Ten o'Clock Wire | I Love a Mystery | The Richfield Reporter |
| *10:15* | Science of the Mind | Bob Elson Interviews | Frank Edwards, news | Virgil Pinkley, news |
| *10:30* | One for the Books | Starlight Salute | Lonesome Gal | The Johnny Murray Show |
| *10:45* | | | | How to Build Your Dream House |

## EVENING — WINTER, 1951

*Wednesday*

| ABC | CBS | MBS | NBC | |
|---|---|---|---|---|
| News | Edward R. Murrow, news | Mark Trail | Feature Wire | *5pm* |
| Elmer Davis, news | Tom Harmon, sports | | Ted Meyers, news | *5:15* |
| Lou Crosby Orchestra | Chet Huntley, news | Clyde Beatty Adventures | Casa Cugat | *5:30* |
| | Frank Goss, news | Victor Borge, piano (5:55PM) | Elmer Patterson, news | *5:45* |
| Edwin C. Hill, news | Honest Harold | Gabriel Heatter, news | Tales of the Texas Rangers | *6pm* |
| Main Street to Malibu | | The Mutual Newsreel | | *6:15* |
| Boston Blackie | The Bing Crosby Chesterfield Show | The Answer Man | The Halls of Ivy | *6:30* |
| | | Sam Hayes, news | | *6:45* |
| The Lone Ranger | The Wednesday Night Fights | John Steele, Adventurer | The Big Story | *7pm* |
| | | | | *7:15* |
| American Agent | Music | The Cisco Kid | The NBC University Theater | *7:30* |
| | | | | *7:45* |
| The Fat Man | Lowell Thomas, news | What's the Name of That Song | One Man's Family | *8pm* |
| | The Jack Smith Show | | World News | *8:15* |
| Rogue's Gallery | Dr. Christian | The Family Theater | The Great Gildersleeve | *8:30* |
| | | | | *8:45* |
| Mr. President | Mr. Chameleon | Glenn Hardy, news | You Bet Your Life | *9pm* |
| | | Fulton Lewis Jr., news | | *9:15* |
| Lawrence Welk High Life Revue | The Beulah Show | International Airport | Mr. District Attorney | *9:30* |
| | Club Fifteen | Five Minute Final (9:55PM) | | *9:45* |
| Robert Garred, news | The Ten o'Clock Wire | I Love a Mystery | The Richfield Reporter | *10pm* |
| Science of the Mind | Bob Elson Interviews | Frank Edwards, news | Virgil Pinkley, news | *10:15* |
| One for the Books | Starlight Salute | Lonesome Gal | The Johnny Murray Show | *10:30* |
| | | | Sports | *10:45* |

## EVENING — WINTER, 1951

*Thursday*

| | ABC | CBS | MBS | NBC |
|---|---|---|---|---|
| *5pm* | News | Edward R. Murrow, news | Straight Arrow | Feature Wire |
| *5:15* | Elmer Davis, news | Tom Harmon, sports | | Ted Meyers, news |
| *5:30* | Lou Crosby Orchestra | Chet Huntley, news | Sky King | Casa Cugat |
| *5:45* | | Frank Goss, news | Bobby Benson (5:55PM) | Elmer Patterson, news |
| *6pm* | Edwin C. Hill, news | Suspense | Gabriel Heatter, news | Dragnet |
| *6:15* | Main Street to Malibu | | The Mutual Newsreel | |
| *6:30* | Philo Vance | The Hallmark Playhouse | The Answer Man | Melody Time |
| *6:45* | | | Sam Hayes, news | |
| *7pm* | The Screen Guild Theater | The Lineup | Murder By Experts | The Screen Director's Playhouse |
| *7:15* | | | | |
| *7:30* | | The Choraliers | Hashknife Hartley and Sleepy Stevens | |
| *7:45* | | | | |
| *8pm* | Ted Mack's Original Amateur Hour | Lowell Thomas, news | Tarzan | One Man's Family |
| *8:15* | | The Jack Smith Show | | World News |
| *8:30* | | Mr. Keen, Tracer of Lost Persons | Reporter's Roundup | The Aldrich Family |
| *8:45* | Robert Montgomery Speaking | | | |
| *9pm* | Time for Defense | The FBI in Peace and War | Glenn Hardy, news | Father Knows Best |
| *9:15* | | | Fulton Lewis Jr., news | |
| *9:30* | Author Meets the Critics | The Beulah Show | The Rod and Gun Club | Counterspy |
| *9:45* | | Club Fifteen | Five Minute Final (9:55PM) | |
| *10pm* | Robert Garred, news | The Ten o'Clock Wire | I Love a Mystery | The Richfield Reporter |
| *10:15* | Science of the Mind | Bob Elson Interviews | Frank Edwards, news | Virgil Pinkley, news |
| *10:30* | One for the Books | Starlight Salute | Lonesome Gal | The Johnny Murray Show |
| *10:45* | | | | Sports |

## EVENING — WINTER, 1951

*Friday*

| ABC | CBS | MBS | NBC | |
|---|---|---|---|---|
| News | Edward R. Murrow, news | Mark Trail | Feature Wire | *5pm* |
| Elmer Davis, news | Tom Harmon, sports | | Ted Meyers, news | *5:15* |
| Lou Crosby Orchestra | Chet Huntley, news | Clyde Beatty Adventures | Casa Cugat | *5:30* |
| | Frank Goss, news | Victor Borge, piano (5:55PM) | Elmer Patterson, news | *5:45* |
| Edwin C. Hill, news | Capitol Cloak Room | Gabriel Heatter, news | Melody Time | *6pm* |
| Main Street to Malibu | | The Mutual Newsreel | | *6:15* |
| Boston Blackie | Quiet Town | The Answer Man | Duffy's Tavern | *6:30* |
| | | Sam Hayes, news | | *6:45* |
| Madison Square Garden Boxing | Command Theater | The Hidden Truth | The Life of Riley | *7pm* |
| | | | | *7:15* |
| | The Women's Forum | The Cisco Kid | The Colgate Sports Newsreel, Bill Stern | *7:30* |
| | | | Your Income Tax | *7:45* |
| Richard Diamond, Private Detective | Lowell Thomas, news | Bobby Benson | One Man's Family | *8pm* |
| | The Jack Smith Show | | World News | *8:15* |
| This is Your FBI | Hear It Now | True or False | The New Adventures of Nero Wolfe | *8:30* |
| | | | | *8:45* |
| The Adventures of Ozzie and Harriet | | Glenn Hardy, news | The NBC Theater | *9pm* |
| | | Fulton Lewis Jr., news | | *9:15* |
| Armstrong of the SBI | The Beulah Show | The Army and Air Force Show | | *9:30* |
| | Club Fifteen | Five Minute Final (9:55PM) | | *9:45* |
| Robert Garred, news | The Ten o'Clock Wire | I Love a Mystery | The Richfield Reporter | *10pm* |
| Science of the Mind | Bob Elson Interviews | Frank Edwards, news | Virgil Pinkley, news | *10:15* |
| One for the Books | Starlight Salute | Lonesome Gal | The Johnny Murray Show | *10:30* |
| | | | Sports | *10:45* |

## EVENING — WINTER, 1951

*Saturday*

| | ABC | CBS | MBS | NBC |
|---|---|---|---|---|
| *5pm* | The Navy Hour | Radio Reporter's Scratchpad | Salute to the Reservists | Harmony and Home (2:00PM) |
| *5:15* | | Tom Harmon, sports | | |
| *5:30* | Harry Wismer, sports | Chet Huntley, news | Sports Scoreboard | Mr. and Mrs. Blandings |
| *5:45* | News | Frank Goss, news | Twin Views of the News | |
| *6pm* | Buzz Adlam's Playroom | Yours Truly, Johnny Dollar | Hawaii Calls | Hallelujah Time |
| *6:15* | | | | |
| *6:30* | Report to the People | My Favorite Husband | Top Tunes with Tendler | A Day in the Life of Dennis Day |
| *6:45* | Bert Andrews, news | | | |
| *7pm* | Merry-Go-Round, Jimmy Blaine | Sing It Again | Know Your Schools | The Judy Canova Show |
| *7:15* | | | | |
| *7:30* | Jay Stewart's Fun Fair | | Bobby Benson | Grand Ole Opry |
| *7:45* | | | | |
| *8pm* | The Lone Ranger | The Camel Caravan, Vaughn Monroe | Dude Ranch Roundup | Dangerous Assignment |
| *8:15* | | | | |
| *8:30* | Shoot the Moon | Gene Autry's Melody Ranch | Lombardoland USA | The Man Called X |
| *8:45* | | | | |
| *9pm* | What Makes You Tick | Hopalong Cassidy | Newspaper of the Air | Your Hit Parade |
| *9:15* | | | Music | |
| *9:30* | Music | Gangbusters | The Eddie Howard Show | Crime Does Not Pay |
| *9:45* | | | | |
| *10pm* | Robert Garred, news | The Ten o'Clock Wire | Monica Sings | The Night Reporter |
| *10:15* | Income Tax | Get More Out of Life | Music | Supervisor Ray Darby, comment |
| *10:30* | Scouting the Stars | Starlight Salute | News and Views | Spade Cooley Orchestra |
| *10:45* | Pietro Pontrelli Orchestra | | | |

## DAYTIME — WINTER, 1951

*Sunday*

| | ABC | CBS | MBS | NBC |
|---|---|---|---|---|
| *8am* | The Sunday School Hour | The Salt Lake Tabernacle Choir | The Happiness Hour (7:30AM) | Grandpa Reads the Funnies |
| *8:15* | | | | |
| *8:30* | Flying Feet | Invitation to Learning | The Northwestern Reviewing Stand | The Christian Science Monitor |
| *8:45* | | | | Hometown Happenings |
| *9am* | Sunday with Bill Davidson | The People's Platform | The Radio Bible Class | Parent-Youth Forum |
| *9:15* | | | | |
| *9:30* | | Howard K. Smith, news | The Voice of Prophecy | The Eternal Light |
| *9:45* | | Get More Out of Life | | |
| *10am* | | New York Philharmonic Orchestra | Glenn Hardy, news | Herbert J. Mann, sports |
| *10:15* | | | War Review | Mr. Fixit |
| *10:30* | | | The Lutheran Hour | The University of Chicago Round Table |
| *10:45* | | | | |
| *11am* | | | Frank and Ernest, songs | The Catholic Hour |
| *11:15* | | | Science Reporter | |
| *11:30* | National Vespers | The Longine Symphonette | The Gospel Singer | Mancini Moods |
| *11:45* | | | The Canary Pet Shop | Edwin C. Hill, news |
| *12pm* | Christian in Action | News | Broadway News | The American Forum of the Air |
| *12:15* | | Romance of the Highways | Bill Cunningham, news | |
| *12:30* | Message of Israel | Get More Out of Life | Juvenile Jury | The Quiz Kids |
| *12:45* | | The Melody Parade | | |
| *1pm* | The Old Fashioned Revival Hour | Dollar a Minute | The Hollywood Open House | Public Affairs |
| *1:15* | | | | Songs for Sunday |
| *1:30* | | Arthur Godfrey's Digest | Martin Kane, Private Detective | The Story of Dr. Kildare |
| *1:45* | | | | |

## DAYTIME — WINTER, 1951

*Monday-Friday*

| ABC | CBS | MBS | NBC | |
|---|---|---|---|---|
| The Breakfast Club | Top of the Morning | Cecil Brown, news | Break the Bank | *8am* |
| | News | News | | *8:15* |
| | Grand Slam | Bible Institute | The Jack Berch Show | *8:30* |
| | Rosemary | | Meyers Goes to the Market | *8:45* |
| Johnny Olsen's Luncheon Club | Wendy Warren and the News | Kate Smith Speaks | Newsroom | *9am* |
| | Aunt Jenny's True Life Stories | The Gospel Singer | Dial Dave Garroway | *9:15* |
| Quick as a Flash | The Romance of Helen Trent | Nancy Young, talk | Ladies' Day | *9:30* |
| | Our Gal Sunday | | | *9:45* |
| Victor Lindlahr, health | Big Sister | Glenn Hardy, news | All Around Town | *10am* |
| Yesterday on Broadway | Ma Perkins | Tello-Test Quiz | | *10:15* |
| My True Story | Young Dr. Malone | In the Morgan Manner | Wendell Noble, news | *10:30* |
| | The Guiding Light | Dick Haymes, songs | Life Can Be Beautiful | *10:45* |
| The Magazine of the Air | The Second Mrs. Burton | Ladies Fair | Double or Nothing | *11am* |
| Easy Aces | Perry Mason | | | *11:15* |
| John B. Kennedy, news | This is Nora Drake | Queen for a Day | Live Like a Millionaire | *11:30* |
| H. R. Baukage, news | The Brighter Day | | | *11:45* |
| Hank Weaver, gossip | News | Broadway News | The Farm Reporter | *12pm* |
| Play It Again | Hilltop House | The Bell Ringer | The Road of Life | *12:15* |
| Modern Romances | House Party | Norma Dixon, talk | Pepper Young's Family | *12:30* |
| | | Cedric Foster, news | The Right to Happiness | *12:45* |
| Ira Cook, talk | Let's Go Places | The Jack Kirkwood Show | Mary Noble, Backstage Wife | *1pm* |
| | Jack Owens, news | | Stella Dallas | *1:15* |
| | The Housewive's Protective League | Double or Nothing | Lorenzo Jones | *1:30* |
| | | | Young Widder Brown | *1:45* |

## DAYTIME — WINTER, 1951

*Sunday*

| | ABC | CBS | MBS | NBC |
|---|---|---|---|---|
| *2pm* | The Voice of Prophecy | Meet Frank Sinatra | The Shadow | The Falcon |
| *2:15* | | | | |
| *2:30* | The Greatest Story Ever Told | The University Explorer | True Detective Mysteries | Maisie |
| *2:45* | | Eric Sevareid, news | | |
| *3pm* | The Lutheran Hour | American Rhapsody | The Roy Rogers Show | The Big Show |
| *3:15* | | | | |
| *3:30* | The Hour of Decision | Memo from Molly | Nick Carter, Master Detective | |
| *3:45* | | | | |
| *4pm* | This Thing Called Life | The Lucky Strike Program, Jack Benny | California Caravan | |
| *4:15* | | | | |
| *4:30* | This Week Around the World | Amos 'n' Andy | The Affairs of Peter Salem | The Phil Harris - Alice Faye Show |
| *4:45* | | | | |

## DAYTIME — WINTER, 1951

*Monday-Friday*

| ABC | CBS | MBS | NBC | |
|---|---|---|---|---|
| Surprise Package | Paul Masterson, talk | News | When a Girl Marries | *2pm* |
| | | Luncheon with Lopez | Portia Faces Life | *2:15* |
| Chance of a Lifetime | | Women are Wonderful | Just Plain Bill | *2:30* |
| Today in Hollywood (2:55PM) | George Fisher, gossip | | Front Page Farrell | *2:45* |
| The Rudy ValleeShow | Arthur Godfrey Time | Club 930 | Welcome Travelers | *3pm* |
| | | | | *3:15* |
| The Frances Scully Show | | | Aunt Mary | *3:30* |
| Peace of Mind | | Lynn at Hollywood | We Love and Learn | *3:45* |
| Between the Bookends | Curt Massey, songs | Fulton Lewis Jr., news | One Woman's Secret | *4pm* |
| Talk Back with Happy Felton | Strike It Rich | Frank Hemingway, news | Dr. Paul | *4:15* |
| Happy Theater | | Behind the Story | Burritt and Wheeler, talk | *4:30* |
| Headline Edition | The Harry Babbitt Show | Sam Hayes, news | | *4:45* |

| DAYTIME — WINTER, 1951 | | | | |
|---|---|---|---|---|
| *Saturday* | | | | |
| | ABC | CBS | MBS | NBC |
| *8am* | No School Today (7:45AM) | Let's Pretend | Leslie Nichols, songs | Archie Andrews |
| *8:15* | | | News | |
| *8:30* | | The Somerset Maughm Theater | The Haven of Rest | Smilin' Ed's Buster Brown Gang |
| *8:45* | Mirandy | | | |
| *9am* | No School Today | The Armstrong Theater of Today | Flying Feet | Young America Speaks |
| *9:15* | | | | |
| *9:30* | | Grand Central Station | Your Income Tax | The US Marine Band |
| *9:45* | | Cedric Adams, news (9:55AM) | Extra Time | |
| *10am* | Ira Cook, talk | Stars Over Hollywood | Newspaper of the Air | Pickens Party |
| *10:15* | | | Land of the Free | Home Town |
| *10:30* | | Give and Take | Helen Hall, songs | Parent-Youth Forum |
| *10:45* | | | Bands for Bonds | |
| *11am* | The Metropolitan Opera | The Carnation Family Party | Symphonies for Youth | Mary Lee Taylor, cooking |
| *11:15* | | | | |
| *11:30* | | Music with the Hormel Girls | | The National Farm and Home Hour |
| *11:45* | | | | |
| *12pm* | | The Coke Club, Morton Downey | News | The Farm Reporter |
| *12:15* | | | Music | Quick, What's the Answer |
| *12:30* | | Meet the Missus | The Man on the Farm | |
| *12:45* | | | | |
| *1pm* | | Fun to Be Young | | |
| *1:15* | | | | Are You from Dixie |
| *1:30* | | Galen Drake, talk | To the Races | |
| *1:45* | | News | Music | |

## DAYTIME — WINTER, 1951

*Saturday*

| | ABC | CBS | MBS | NBC |
|---|---|---|---|---|
| *2pm* | | The Housewive's Protective League | The Air Force Hour | Harmony and Home |
| *2:15* | | | | |
| *2:30* | Tea and Crumpets | Cross-Section USA | Georgia Crackers | |
| *2:45* | Fascinating Rhythm | | | |
| *3pm* | Junior Junction | CBS Farm News | Dunn on Discs | |
| *3:15* | | Income Tax | | |
| *3:30* | Space Patrol | This is Los Angeles | Sports Parade | |
| *3:45* | | | | |
| *4pm* | The American Farmer | Paul Masterson, talk | John Flynn, news | |
| *4:15* | | | Frank Hemingway, news | |
| *4:30* | Robert Nathan, news | | Bandstand USA | |
| *4:45* | It's Your Business | | | |

# EVENING — SPRING, 1951

*Sunday*

| | ABC | CBS | MBS | NBC |
|---|---|---|---|---|
| *5pm* | Stop the Music | The Charlie McCarhty Show | California Caravan | Hedda Hopper's Hollywood |
| *5:15* | | | | |
| *5:30* | | Dick Joy, news | The Affairs of Peter Salem | The Theater Guild of the Air |
| *5:45* | | Tom Harmon, sports | | |
| *6pm* | Walter Winchell, gossip | Meet Corliss Archer | News | |
| *6:15* | Louella Parsons, gossip | | Bands for Bonds | |
| *6:30* | The American Album of Familiar Music | The Youth Opportunity Program | Gabriel Heatter, news | Music with the Hormel Girls |
| *6:45* | | | Major George Elliott, comment | |
| *7pm* | Paul Harvey, news | The Carnation Contented Hour | Take a Number | The $64 Question |
| *7:15* | Gloria Parker, songs | | | |
| *7:30* | The Ted Mack Family Hour | The Whistler | Comedy of Errors | Voices and Events |
| *7:45* | | | | |
| *8pm* | Drew Pearson, news | Our Miss Brooks | Twenty Questions | Serenade in Blue |
| *8:15* | Don Gardiner, news | | | |
| *8:30* | Walter Winchell, gossip | The Charlie McCarthy Show | The Count of Monte Cristo | The Standard Symphony Hour |
| *8:45* | William Tusher in Hollywood | | | |
| *9pm* | Q. E. D. | The Red Skelton Show | Glenn Hardy, news | |
| *9:15* | | | Report from the Pentagon | |
| *9:30* | Sammy Kaye's Sunday Serenade | The Lucky Strike Program, Jack Benny | The Chicago Theater of the Air | Senator's Report |
| *9:45* | | | | Trouble is My Business |
| *10pm* | News | The Ten o'Clock Wire | | The Richfield Reporter |
| *10:15* | Sports | Top of the Week | | Mayor Bowron, comment |
| *10:30* | Career Theater | The Lineup | The Arthur Van Show | The Saint |
| *10:45* | | | | |

## EVENING — SPRING, 1951

*Monday*

| ABC | CBS | MBS | NBC | |
|---|---|---|---|---|
| News | Edward R. Murrow, news | Mark Trail | Feature Wire | *5pm* |
| Elmer Davis, news | Tom Harmon, sports | | Ted Meyers, news | *5:15* |
| Chet Huntley, news | Griffin Bancroft, news | Clyde Beatty Adventures | The Voice of Firestone | *5:30* |
| Robert Garred, news | Frank Goss, news | Victor Borge, piano (5:55PM) | | *5:45* |
| Main Street to Malibu | The Lux Radio Theater | Gabriel Heatter, news | The American Way | *6pm* |
| Hannibal Cobb | | The Mutual Newsreel | | *6:15* |
| Boston Blackie | | The Answer Man | Candy Matson, YUkon 2-8209 | *6:30* |
| | | Sam Hayes, news | | *6:45* |
| The Lone Ranger | My Friend Irma | War Front, Home Front | NBC Symphony Orchestra | *7pm* |
| | | | | *7:15* |
| Inner Sanctum Mysteries | The Bob Hawk Show | The Cisco Kid | | *7:30* |
| | | | | *7:45* |
| Ralph Flanagan Orchestra | Lowell Thomas, news | Let George Do It | One Man's Family | *8pm* |
| | The Jack Smith Show | | World News | *8:15* |
| Henry J. Taylor, news | Arthur Godfrey's Talent Scouts | Under Arrest | The Railroad Hour | *8:30* |
| World News | | | | *8:45* |
| The Richard Wallace Show | The Hollywood Star Playhouse | Glenn Hardy, news | The Bell Telephone Hour | *9pm* |
| | | Fulton Lewis Jr., news | | *9:15* |
| The Piano Playhouse | The Beulah Show | Crime Fighters | The Dave Rose Show | *9:30* |
| | Club Fifteen | Five Minute Final (9:55PM) | | *9:45* |
| News | The Ten o'Clock Wire | I Love a Mystery | The Richfield Reporter | *10pm* |
| Science of the Mind | Bob Elson Interviews | Frank Edwards, news | Virgil Pinkley, news | *10:15* |
| Dream Harbor | Starlight Salute | Lonesome Gal | The Johnny Murray Show | *10:30* |
| The New Yorkers | | | Sports | *10:45* |

## EVENING — SPRING, 1951

*Tuesday*

| | ABC | CBS | MBS | NBC |
|---|---|---|---|---|
| *5pm* | News | Edward R. Murrow, news | Straight Arrow | Feature Wire |
| *5:15* | Elmer Davis, news | Tom Harmon, sports | | Ted Meyers, news |
| *5:30* | Chet Huntley, news | Griffin Bancroft, news | Sky King | The Baby Snooks Show |
| *5:45* | Robert Garred, news | Frank Goss, news | Bobby Benson (5:55PM) | |
| *6pm* | Main Street to Malibu | Life with Luigi | Gabriel Heatter, news | The Hardy Family |
| *6:15* | Hannibal Cobb | | The Mutual Newsreel | |
| *6:30* | Philo Vance | Truth or Consequences | The Answer Man | Fibber McGee and Molly |
| *6:45* | | | Sam Hayes, news | |
| *7pm* | Armstrong of the SBI | The Hollywood Music Hall | The Mysterious Traveler | Big Town |
| *7:15* | | | | |
| *7:30* | Can You Top This | Charlie Wild, Private Detective | Challenge of the Yukon | People Are Funny |
| *7:45* | | | | |
| *8pm* | I Fly Anything | Lowell Thomas, news | Song of Liberty | One Man's Family |
| *8:15* | | The Jack Smith Show | | World News |
| *8:30* | Time for Defense | Mr. and Mrs. North | Two-Thousand Plus | The Cavalcade of America |
| *8:45* | | | | |
| *9pm* | America's Town Meeting of the Air | Mystery Theater | Glenn Hardy, news | The Bob Hope Show |
| *9:15* | | | Fulton Lewis Jr., news | |
| *9:30* | | The Beulah Show | Official Detective | Information, Please |
| *9:45* | Twin Views of the News | Club Fifteen | News (9:55PM) | |
| *10pm* | News | The Ten o'Clock Wire | I Love a Mystery | The Richfield Reporter |
| *10:15* | Science of the Mind | Bob Elson Interviews | Frank Edwards, news | Virgil Pinkley, news |
| *10:30* | Dream Harbor | Starlight Salute | Lonesome Gal | The Johnny Murray Show |
| *10:45* | The New Yorkers | | | Sports |

## EVENING — SPRING, 1951

*Wednesday*

| ABC | CBS | MBS | NBC | |
|---|---|---|---|---|
| News | Edward R. Murrow, news | Mark Trail | Feature Wire | *5pm* |
| Elmer Davis, news | Tom Harmon, sports | | Ted Meyers, news | *5:15* |
| Chet Huntley, news | Griffin Bancroft, news | Clyde Beatty Adventures | Casa Cugat | *5:30* |
| Robert Garred, news | Frank Goss, news | Victor Borge, piano (5:55PM) | Elmer Patterson, news | *5:45* |
| Main Street to Malibu | Honest Harold | Gabriel Heatter, news | Tales of the Texas Rangers | *6pm* |
| Hannibal Cobb | | The Mutual Newsreel | | *6:15* |
| Boston Blackie | The Bing Crosby Chesterfield Show | The Answer Man | The Halls of Ivy | *6:30* |
| | | Sam Hayes, news | | *6:45* |
| The Lone Ranger | The Wednesday Night Fights | John Steele, Adventurer | The Big Story | *7pm* |
| | | | | *7:15* |
| American Agent | Music | The Cisco Kid | This is Our Town | *7:30* |
| | | | | *7:45* |
| The Fat Man | Lowell Thomas, news | What's the Name of That Song | One Man's Family | *8pm* |
| | The Jack Smith Show | | World News | *8:15* |
| Rogue's Gallery | Dr. Christian | Murder By Experts | The Great Gildersleeve | *8:30* |
| | | | | *8:45* |
| Mr. President | Mr. Chameleon | Glenn Hardy, news | You Bet Your Life | *9pm* |
| | | Fulton Lewis Jr., news | | *9:15* |
| Lawrence Welk Orchestra | The Beulah Show | International Airport | Mr. District Attorney | *9:30* |
| | Club Fifteen | Five Minute Final (9:55PM) | | *9:45* |
| News | The Ten o'Clock Wire | I Love a Mystery | The Richfield Reporter | *10pm* |
| Science of the Mind | Bob Elson Interviews | Frank Edwards, news | Virgil Pinkley, news | *10:15* |
| Dream Harbor | Starlight Salute | Lonesome Gal | The Johnny Murray Show | *10:30* |
| The New Yorkers | | | Sports | *10:45* |

| EVENING — SPRING, 1951 | | | | |
|---|---|---|---|---|
| *Thursday* | | | | |
| | ABC | CBS | MBS | NBC |
| *5pm* | News | Edward R. Murrow, news | Straight Arrow | Feature Wire |
| *5:15* | Elmer Davis, news | Tom Harmon, sports | | Ted Meyers, news |
| *5:30* | Chet Huntley, news | Griffin Bancroft, news | Sky King | Casa Cugat |
| *5:45* | Robert Garred, news | Frank Goss, news | Bobby Benson (5:55PM) | Elmer Patterson, news |
| *6pm* | Main Street to Malibu | Suspense | Gabriel Heatter, news | Dragnet |
| *6:15* | Hannibal Cobb | | The Mutual Newsreel | |
| *6:30* | Philo Vance | The Hallmark Playhouse | The Answer Man | Bold Venture |
| *6:45* | | | Sam Hayes, news | |
| *7pm* | The Screen Guild Theater | The Phillip Morris Playhouse | Murder By Experts | The Screen Director's Playhouse |
| *7:15* | | | | |
| *7:30* | | The Choraliers | Challenge of the Yukon | |
| *7:45* | | | | |
| *8pm* | Ted Mack's Original Amateur Hour | Lowell Thomas, news | Tarzan | One Man's Family |
| *8:15* | | The Jack Smith Show | | World News |
| *8:30* | | Mr. Keen, Tracer of Lost Persons | Reporter's Roundup | The Aldrich Family |
| *8:45* | Robert Montgomery Speaking | | | |
| *9pm* | Newstand Theater | The FBI in Peace and War | Glenn Hardy, news | Father Knows Best |
| *9:15* | | | Fulton Lewis Jr., news | |
| *9:30* | Author Meets the Critics | The Beulah Show | The Rod and Gun Club | Melody Time |
| *9:45* | | Club Fifteen | News (9:55PM) | |
| *10pm* | News | The Ten o'Clock Wire | I Love a Mystery | The Richfield Reporter |
| *10:15* | Science of the Mind | Bob Elson Interviews | Frank Edwards, news | Virgil Pinkley, news |
| *10:30* | Dream Harbor | Starlight Salute | Lonesome Gal | The Johnny Murray Show |
| *10:45* | The New Yorkers | | | Sports |

| EVENING — SPRING, 1951 | | | | |
|---|---|---|---|---|
| *Friday* | | | | |
| ABC | CBS | MBS | NBC | |
| News | Edward R. Murrow, news | Mark Trail | Feature Wire | *5pm* |
| Elmer Davis, news | Tom Harmon, sports | | Ted Meyers, news | *5:15* |
| Chet Huntley, news | Griffin Bancroft, news | Clyde Beatty Adventures | Casa Cugat | *5:30* |
| Robert Garred, news | Frank Goss, news | Victor Borge, piano (5:55PM) | Elmer Patterson, news | *5:45* |
| Main Street to Malibu | Capitol Cloak Room | Gabriel Heatter, news | The Magnificent Montague | *6pm* |
| Hannibal Cobb | | The Mutual Newsreel | | *6:15* |
| Boston Blackie | Quiet Town | The Answer Man | Duffy's Tavern | *6:30* |
| | | Sam Hayes, news | | *6:45* |
| Madison Square Garden Boxing | Command Theater | The Hidden Truth | The Life of Riley | *7pm* |
| | | | | *7:15* |
| | The Women's Forum | The Cisco Kid | The Colgate Sports Newsreel, Bill Stern | *7:30* |
| | | | Science Reporter | *7:45* |
| Richard Diamond, Private Detective | Lowell Thomas, news | Magazine Theater | One Man's Family | *8pm* |
| | The Jack Smith Show | | World News | *8:15* |
| This is Your FBI | Hear It Now | True or False | Lyn Murray Orchestra | *8:30* |
| | | | | *8:45* |
| The Adventures of Ozzie and Harriet | | Glenn Hardy, news | The NBC Theater | *9pm* |
| | | Fulton Lewis Jr., news | | *9:15* |
| Armstrong of the SBI | The Beulah Show | The Army and Air Force Show | | *9:30* |
| | Club Fifteen | Five Minute Final (9:55PM) | | *9:45* |
| News | The Ten o'Clock Wire | I Love a Mystery | The Richfield Reporter | *10pm* |
| Science of the Mind | Bob Elson Interviews | Frank Edwards, news | Virgil Pinkley, news | *10:15* |
| Lawrence Welk Orchestra | Starlight Salute | Lonesome Gal | The Johnny Murray Show | *10:30* |
| | | | Sports | *10:45* |

# EVENING — SPRING, 1951

*Saturday*

| | ABC | CBS | MBS | NBC |
|---|---|---|---|---|
| *5pm* | As We See It | Radio Reporter's Scratchpad | The Singing Marshall | Mr. and Mrs. Blandings |
| *5:15* | Talking It Over | Tom Harmon, sports | | |
| *5:30* | Chet Huntley, news | Griffin Bancroft, news | Bobby Benson | Song Festival |
| *5:45* | News | Frank Goss, news | | Elmer Patterson, news |
| *6pm* | The Navy Hour | Hopalong Cassidy | Hawaii Calls | Maisie |
| *6:15* | | | | |
| *6:30* | Science Reporter | Litte Night Music | Top Tunes with Tendler | A Day in the Life of Dennis Day |
| *6:45* | Report to the People | | | |
| *7pm* | World Opinion | Sing It Again | Know Your Schools | The Judy Canova Show |
| *7:15* | | | | |
| *7:30* | Shoot the Moon | | Salute to the Reservists | Grand Ole Opry |
| *7:45* | | | | |
| *8pm* | The Lone Ranger | The Camel Caravan, Vaughn Monroe | Dude Ranch Roundup | Dangerous Assignment |
| *8:15* | | | | |
| *8:30* | The Sheriff | Gene Autry's Melody Ranch | Lombardoland USA | The Man Called X |
| *8:45* | | | | |
| *9pm* | Dance Party | Gangbusters | Newspaper of the Air | Your Hit Parade |
| *9:15* | | | Mr. Mystery | |
| *9:30* | | Broadway is My Beat | Firehouse Five + Two | Crime Does Not Pay |
| *9:45* | | | | |
| *10pm* | News | The Ten o'Clock Wire | Monica Sings | The Night Reporter |
| *10:15* | Science Editor | George Fisher, gossip | Music | Supervisor Ray Darby, comment |
| *10:30* | Lawrence Welk Orchestra | Starlight Salute | The Arthur Van Show | Charlene Hawkes Orchestra |
| *10:45* | | | | |

## DAYTIME — SPRING, 1951

*Sunday*

| | ABC | CBS | MBS | NBC |
|---|---|---|---|---|
| *8am* | News | The Salt Lake Tabernacle Choir | The Religious Hour | Grandpa Reads the Funnies |
| *8:15* | Morning Song | | | |
| *8:30* | Flying Feet | Invitation to Learning | The Northwestern Reviewing Stand | The U. N. is My Beat |
| *8:45* | | | | Hometown Happenings |
| *9am* | The Sunday School Hour | The People's Platform | The Radio Bible Class | The Garden Show |
| *9:15* | | | | The Christian Science Monitor |
| *9:30* | Sunday with Bill Davidson | The Garden Gate | The Voice of Prophecy | The Eternal Light |
| *9:45* | | Howard K. Smith, news | | |
| *10am* | | New York Philharmonic Orchestra | Glenn Hardy, news | Herbert J. Mann, sports |
| *10:15* | | | Real Estate | Action for Survival |
| *10:30* | | | The Lutheran Hour | The University of Chicago Round Table |
| *10:45* | | | | |
| *11am* | | | Frank and Ernest, songs | The Catholic Hour |
| *11:15* | | | Dink Templeton, news | |
| *11:30* | National Vespers | The Longine Symphonette | The Voice of Freedom | Bob Considine, sports |
| *11:45* | | | The Canary Pet Shop | TheWorld of Books |
| *12pm* | Christian in Action | News | Broadway News | The American Forum of the Air |
| *12:15* | | Romance of the Highways | Bill Cunningham, news | |
| *12:30* | Message of Israel | The University Explorer | Hashknifre Hartley and Sleepy Stevens | David Lawrence, news |
| *12:45* | | Callifornia Holiday | | John Cameron Swayze, news |
| *1pm* | The Old Fashioned Revival Hour | Dollar a Minute | Wild Bill Hickock | The Falcon |
| *1:15* | | | | |
| *1:30* | | Newsroom | Martin Kane, Private Detective | The Story of Dr. Kildare |
| *1:45* | | | | |

## DAYTIME — SPRING, 1951

*Monday-Friday*

| ABC | CBS | MBS | NBC | |
|---|---|---|---|---|
| The Breakfast Club | The Ralph Story Show | Cecil Brown, news | Break the Bank | *8am* |
| | News | News | | *8:15* |
| | Grand Slam | Bible Institute | The Jack Berch Show | *8:30* |
| | Rosemary | | Dial Dave Garroway | *8:45* |
| Johnny Olsen's Luncheon Club | Wendy Warren and the News | Kate Smith Speaks | Newsroom | *9am* |
| | Aunt Jenny's True Life Stories | The Gospel Singer | Meyers Goes to the Market | *9:15* |
| Quick as a Flash | The Romance of Helen Trent | Nancy Young, talk | Ladies' Day | *9:30* |
| | Our Gal Sunday | | | *9:45* |
| Victor Lindlahr, health | Big Sister | Glenn Hardy, news | All Around Town | *10am* |
| Yesterday on Broadway | Ma Perkins | Tello-Test Quiz | | *10:15* |
| My True Story | Young Dr. Malone | In the Morgan Manner | News | *10:30* |
| | The Guiding Light | Dick Haymes, songs | Life Can Be Beautiful | *10:45* |
| The Magazine of the Air | The Second Mrs. Burton | Ladies Fair | Double or Nothing | *11am* |
| Easy Aces | Perry Mason | | | *11:15* |
| Sweeney and March | This is Nora Drake | Queen for a Day | Live Like a Millionaire | *11:30* |
| Paul Harvey, news | The Brighter Day | | | *11:45* |
| Hank Weaver, gossip | News | Broadway News | The Farm Reporter | *12pm* |
| Altar Bound | Wendell Noble, news | Cedric Foster, news | The Road of Life | *12:15* |
| Modern Romances | House Party | Norma Dixon, talk | Pepper Young's Family | *12:30* |
| Peace of Mind | | Carmen Cavallero Orchestra | The Right to Happiness | *12:45* |
| Ira Cook, talk | Hilltop House | The Jack Kirkwood Show | Mary Noble, Backstage Wife | *1pm* |
| | King's Row | | Stella Dallas | *1:15* |
| | The Housewive's Protective League | Double or Nothing | Lorenzo Jones | *1:30* |
| | | | Young Widder Brown | *1:45* |

## DAYTIME — SPRING, 1951

*Sunday*

| | ABC | CBS | MBS | NBC |
|---|---|---|---|---|
| *2pm* | The Voice of Prophecy | Meet Frank Sinatra | The Shadow | The Phil Regan Show |
| *2:15* | | | | |
| *2:30* | The Greatest Story Ever Told | | True Detective Mysteries | Behind the Headlines |
| *2:45* | | Ed Miller, news | | The Paul Coates Show |
| *3pm* | The Hour of Decision | American Rhapsody | The Roy Rogers Show | The Big Show |
| *3:15* | | | | |
| *3:30* | Sunday Notebook | Memo from Molly | Nick Carter, Master Detective | |
| *3:45* | | | | |
| *4pm* | This Thing Called Life | The Lucky Strike Program, Jack Benny | Harmony House | |
| *4:15* | | | | |
| *4:30* | The Layman's Hour | Amos 'n' Andy | | The Phil Harris - Alice Faye Show |
| *4:45* | | | | |

## DAYTIME — SPRING, 1951

*Monday-Friday*

| ABC | CBS | MBS | NBC | |
|---|---|---|---|---|
| Mary Margaret McBride, talk | Paul Masterson, talk | News | When a Girl Marries | *2pm* |
| | | Luncheon with Lopez | Portia Faces Life | *2:15* |
| Variety Fare | Jack Owens, news | Women are Wonderful | Just Plain Bill | *2:30* |
| | George Fisher, gossip | | Front Page Farrell | *2:45* |
| The Rudy Vallee Show | Arthur Godfrey Time | Club 930 | Welcome Travelers | *3pm* |
| | | | | *3:15* |
| The Frances Scully Show | | | Aunt Mary | *3:30* |
| | | Lynn at Hollywood | The Woman in My House | *3:45* |
| Surprise Package | Curt Massey, songs | Fulton Lewis Jr., news | One Woman's Secret | *4pm* |
| | Strike It Rich | Frank Hemingway, news | Dr. Paul | *4:15* |
| Happy Theater | | Behind the Story | Burritt and Wheeler, talk | *4:30* |
| Headline Edition | The Harry Babbitt Show | Sam Hayes, news | | *4:45* |

| DAYTIME — SPRING, 1951 | | | | |
|---|---|---|---|---|
| *Saturday* | | | | |
| | ABC | CBS | MBS | NBC |
| *8am* | No School Today (7:45AM) | Let's Pretend | Cecil Brown, news | Archie Andrews |
| *8:15* | | | News | |
| *8:30* | | The Somerset Maughm Theater | The Haven of Rest | Smilin' Ed's Buster Brown Gang |
| *8:45* | Mirandy | | | |
| *9am* | Ira Cook's Beach Party | The Armstrong Theater of Today | Flying Feet | Young America Speaks |
| *9:15* | | | | |
| *9:30* | | Grand Central Station | Here's to Veterans | The US Marine Band |
| *9:45* | | Cedric Adams, news (9:55AM) | Extra Time | |
| *10am* | | Stars Over Hollywood | Newspaper of the Air | Boston Symphony Orchestra |
| *10:15* | | | Land of the Free | |
| *10:30* | | Alias Jane Doe | Your Science Reporter | Parent-Youth Forum |
| *10:45* | | | Guest Star | |
| *11am* | | Music with the Hormel Girls | Dunn on Discs | Mary Lee Taylor, cooking |
| *11:15* | | | | |
| *11:30* | Music from Canada | Meet the Missus | | The National Farm and Home Hour |
| *11:45* | | | | |
| *12pm* | Pan-American Union Concert | The Coke Club, Morton Downey | News | The Farm Reporter |
| *12:15* | | | Caribbean Crossroads | Quick, What's the Answer |
| *12:30* | Exhibit A | Fun to Be Young | The Man on the Farm | |
| *12:45* | | | | |
| *1pm* | Horse Racing | Yours Truly, Johnny Dollar | Sports Parade | |
| *1:15* | News | | | Are You from Dixie |
| *1:30* | American Jazz | Galen Drake, talk | Jack Ross Campus | |
| *1:45* | | America's Last Frontier | | |

## DAYTIME — SPRING, 1951

*Saturday*

| | ABC | CBS | MBS | NBC |
|---|---|---|---|---|
| *2pm* | Music | The Phil Norman Show | The Air Force Hour | |
| *2:15* | | | | Harmony and Home |
| *2:30* | Vacationland, USA | This is Living | Georgia Crackers | |
| *2:45* | Bible Messages | | | |
| *3pm* | Junior Junction | Cross-Section USA | Bands for Bonds | |
| *3:15* | | | | |
| *3:30* | Harry Wismer, sports | This is Los Angeles | The US Marine Band | |
| *3:45* | Bill Watson, news | | | |
| *4pm* | The American Farmer | CBS Farm News | John Flynn, news | |
| *4:15* | | Paul Masterson, talk | Frank Hemingway, news | |
| *4:30* | Space Patrol | | Al Helfer, news | |
| *4:45* | | | Twin Views of the News | |

# EVENING — SUMMER, 1951

*Sunday*

| | ABC | CBS | MBS | NBC |
|---|---|---|---|---|
| *5pm* | Stop the Music | The Mario Lanza Show | The Northwestern Reviewing Stand | The New Theater (4:30PM) |
| *5:15* | | | | |
| *5:30* | | Dick Joy, news | The Enchanted Hour | NBC Summer Symphony |
| *5:45* | | Tom Harmon, sports | | |
| *6pm* | Walter Winchell, gossip | Broadway is My Beat | News | |
| *6:15* | Louella Parsons, gossip | | Bands for Bonds | |
| *6:30* | The Law and You | The Carnation Contented Hour | Gabriel Heatter, news | Music with the Hormel Girls |
| *6:45* | Dr. Gino's Musicale | | Major George Elliott, comment | |
| *7pm* | Paul Harvey, news | The Adventures of Phillip Marlower | Take a Number | The $64 Question |
| *7:15* | William Tusher in Hollywood | | | |
| *7:30* | The Ted Mack Family Hour | The Whistler | Comedy of Errors | The American Forum of the Air |
| *7:45* | | | | |
| *8pm* | Drew Pearson, news | The Youth Opportunity Program | Twenty Questions | This is Our Town |
| *8:15* | Don Gardiner, news | | | |
| *8:30* | Walter Winchell, gossip | O'Hara | Top Tunes with Tendler | The Standard Symphony Hour |
| *8:45* | Chet Huntley, news | | | |
| *9pm* | Q. E. D. | Mr. Aladdin | Glenn Hardy, news | |
| *9:15* | | | Report from the Pentagon | |
| *9:30* | This Week Around the World | Guy Lombardo Orchestra | The Chicago Theater of the Air | Senator's Report |
| *9:45* | | | | Trouble is My Business |
| *10pm* | News | The Ten o'Clock Wire | | The Richfield Reporter |
| *10:15* | George Sokolsky, news | Elmo Roper, news | | Mayor Bowron, comment |
| *10:30* | Career Theater | Music from Avalon | The Arthur Van Show | Short Story |
| *10:45* | | | | |

# EVENING — SUMMER, 1951

*Monday*

| ABC | CBS | MBS | NBC | |
|---|---|---|---|---|
| News | Don Hollenbeck, news | Mert's Record Adventure | Feature Wire | *5pm* |
| Erwin Howard, news | Tom Harmon, sports | | Ted Meyers, news | *5:15* |
| Chet Huntley, news | The World Today | The Singing Marshall | The Voice of Firestone | *5:30* |
| Robert Garred, news | Frank Goss, news | Mel Allen's Popsicle Clubhouse (5:55PM) | | *5:45* |
| Main Street to Malibu | Theater of Romance | Gabriel Heatter, news | America's Music | *6pm* |
| Elmer Davis, news | | The Mutual Newsreel | | *6:15* |
| Boston Blackie | Meet Millie | The Answer Man | The American Way | *6:30* |
| | | Sam Hayes, news | | *6:45* |
| The Lone Ranger | The Straw Hat Concert | Bobby Benson | Boston Pops Orchestra | *7pm* |
| | | | | *7:15* |
| The Man from Homicide | Dance Orchestra | The Cisco Kid | | *7:30* |
| | | | | *7:45* |
| Dance Orchestra | Lowell Thomas, news | Let George Do It | One Man's Family | *8pm* |
| | Dance Orchestra | | World News | *8:15* |
| Henry J. Taylor, news | Arthur Godfrey's Talent Scouts | Under Arrest | The Railroad Hour | *8:30* |
| World News | | | | *8:45* |
| Buzz Adlam's Playhouse | The Hollywood Star Playhouse | Glenn Hardy, news | The Bell Telephone Hour | *9pm* |
| | | Robert Hurleigh, news | | *9:15* |
| The Navy Hour | Robert Q. Lewis's Waxworks | War Front, Home Front | Ray Bloch Orchestra | *9:30* |
| | | Five Minute Final (9:55PM) | | *9:45* |
| News | The Ten o'Clock Wire | I Love a Mystery | The Richfield Reporter | *10pm* |
| Science of the Mind | Tom Harmon, sports | Frank Edwards, news | Michael Hinn, news | *10:15* |
| Sports | The Phil Norman Show | Lonesome Gal | The Passing Parade | *10:30* |
| Dream Harbor | | | At Home With Lionel Barrymore | *10:45* |

## EVENING — SUMMER, 1951

*Tuesday*

| | ABC | CBS | MBS | NBC |
|---|---|---|---|---|
| *5pm* | News | Don Hollenbeck, news | Challenge of the Yukon | Feature Wire |
| *5:15* | Erwin Howard, news | Tom Harmon, sports | | Ted Meyers, news |
| *5:30* | Chet Huntley, news | The World Today | Bobby Benson | The Record Album Review |
| *5:45* | Robert Garred, news | Frank Goss, news | | Elmer Patterson, news |
| *6pm* | Main Street to Malibu | Pursuit | Gabriel Heatter, news | The Hardy Family |
| *6:15* | Elmer Davis, news | | The Mutual Newsreel | |
| *6:30* | Philo Vance | The Bickersons | The Answer Man | The Jack Pearl Show |
| *6:45* | | | Sam Hayes, news | |
| *7pm* | Mr. Mercury | The Hollywood Music Hall | John Steele, Adventure | Big Town |
| *7:15* | | | | |
| *7:30* | Chance of a Lifetime | Dance Orchestra | The Count of Monte Cristo | Summer Time Serenade |
| *7:45* | | | | |
| *8pm* | I Fly Anything | Lowell Thomas, news | Song of Liberty | One Man's Family |
| *8:15* | | Dance Orchestra | | World News |
| *8:30* | Time for Defense | Mr. and Mrs. North | Two-Thousand Plus | American Portraits |
| *8:45* | | | | |
| *9pm* | America's Town Meeting of the Air | Operation Underground | Glenn Hardy, news | Nightbeat |
| *9:15* | | | Robert Hurleigh, news | |
| *9:30* | | Robert Q. Lewis's Waxworks | Official Detective | KFI Calling |
| *9:45* | Twin Views of the News | | Five Minute Final (9:55PM) | |
| *10pm* | News | The Ten o'Clock Wire | I Love a Mystery | The Richfield Reporter |
| *10:15* | Science of the Mind | Tom Harmon, sports | Frank Edwards, news | Michael Hinn, news |
| *10:30* | Sports | The Phil Norman Show | Lonesome Gal | The Passing Parade |
| *10:45* | Dream Harbor | | | At Home With Lionel Barrymore |

# EVENING — SUMMER, 1951

*Wednesday*

| ABC | CBS | MBS | NBC | |
|---|---|---|---|---|
| News | Don Hollenbeck, news | Mert's Record Adventure | Feature Wire | *5pm* |
| Erwin Howard, news | Tom Harmon, sports | | Ted Meyers, news | *5:15* |
| Chet Huntley, news | The World Today | The Singing Marshall | Casa Cugat | *5:30* |
| Robert Garred, news | Frank Goss, news | Mel Allen's Popsicle Clubhouse (5:55PM) | Elmer Patterson, news | *5:45* |
| Main Street to Malibu | Escape | Gabriel Heatter, news | Sunset to Broadway | *6pm* |
| Elmer Davis, news | | The Mutual Newsreel | | *6:15* |
| Boston Blackie | Yours Truly, Johnny Dollar | The Answer Man | Pete Kelly's Blues | *6:30* |
| | | Sam Hayes, news | | *6:45* |
| The Lone Ranger | The Wednesday Night Fights | The Mysterious Traveler | The Big Story | *7pm* |
| | | | | *7:15* |
| American Agent | Dance Orchestra | The Cisco Kid | The Private Files of Rex Saunders | *7:30* |
| | | | | *7:45* |
| The Fat Man | Lowell Thomas, news | What's the Name of That Song | One Man's Family | *8pm* |
| | Dance Orchestra | | World News | *8:15* |
| Rogue's Gallery | Dr. Christian | The Family Theater | The Falcon | *8:30* |
| | | | | *8:45* |
| Mr. President | Rocky Jordan | Glenn Hardy, news | It Pays to Be Ignorant | *9pm* |
| | | Robert Hurleigh, news | | *9:15* |
| Lawrence Welk Orchestra | Dance Orchestra | International Airport | Mr. District Attorney | *9:30* |
| | | Five Minute Final (9:55PM) | | *9:45* |
| News | The Ten o'Clock Wire | I Love a Mystery | The Richfield Reporter | *10pm* |
| Science of the Mind | Tom Harmon, sports | Frank Edwards, news | Michael Hinn, news | *10:15* |
| Sports | The Phil Norman Show | Lonesome Gal | The Passing Parade | *10:30* |
| Dream Harbor | | | At Home With Lionel Barrymore | *10:45* |

## EVENING — SUMMER, 1951

*Thursday*

| | ABC | CBS | MBS | NBC |
|---|---|---|---|---|
| *5pm* | News | Don Hollenbeck, news | Challenge of the Yukon | Feature Wire |
| *5:15* | Erwin Howard, news | Tom Harmon, sports | | Ted Meyers, news |
| *5:30* | Chet Huntley, news | The World Today | Bobby Benson | Casa Cugat |
| *5:45* | Robert Garred, news | Frank Goss, news | | Elmer Patterson, news |
| *6pm* | Main Street to Malibu | Suspense | Gabriel Heatter, news | Dangerous Assignment |
| *6:15* | Elmer Davis, news | | The Mutual Newsreel | |
| *6:30* | Philo Vance | The Hallmark Playhouse | The Answer Man | Bold Venture |
| *6:45* | | | Sam Hayes, news | |
| *7pm* | The Silver Eagle | The Longines Symphonette | Murder By Experts | The Screen Director's Playhouse |
| *7:15* | | | | |
| *7:30* | I Fly Anything | Sammy Kaye Orchestra | The Singing Marshall | |
| *7:45* | | | | |
| *8pm* | Ted Mack's Original Amateur Hour | Lowell Thomas, news | Tarzan | One Man's Family |
| *8:15* | | Dance Orchestra | | World News |
| *8:30* | | The Nation's Nightmare | Reporter's Roundup | The Truitts |
| *8:45* | Foreign Reporter | | | |
| *9pm* | Operation Dixie | The FBI in Peace and War | Glenn Hardy, news | Dragnet |
| *9:15* | | | Robert Hurleigh, news | |
| *9:30* | The New Frontier | Robert Q. Lewis's Waxworks | The Rod and Gun Club | We Call It Jazz |
| *9:45* | | | News (9:55PM) | |
| *10pm* | News | The Ten o'Clock Wire | I Love a Mystery | The Richfield Reporter |
| *10:15* | Science of the Mind | Tom Harmon, sports | Frank Edwards, news | Michael Hinn, news |
| *10:30* | Sports | The Phil Norman Show | Lonesome Gal | The Passing Parade |
| *10:45* | Dream Harbor | | | At Home With Lionel Barrymore |

# EVENING — SUMMER, 1951

*Friday*

| ABC | CBS | MBS | NBC | |
|---|---|---|---|---|
| News | Don Hollenbeck, news | Mert's Record Adventure | Feature Wire | *5pm* |
| Erwin Howard, news | Tom Harmon, sports | | Ted Meyers, news | *5:15* |
| Chet Huntley, news | The World Today | The Singing Marshall | Casa Cugat | *5:30* |
| Robert Garred, news | Frank Goss, news | Mel Allen's Popsicle Clubhouse (5:55PM) | Elmer Patterson, news | *5:45* |
| Main Street to Malibu | Capitol Cloak Room | Gabriel Heatter, news | Vacation Serenade | *6pm* |
| Elmer Davis, news | | The Mutual Newsreel | | *6:15* |
| Boston Blackie | Summer Cruise | The Answer Man | Mr. Keen, Tracer of Lost Persons | *6:30* |
| | | Sam Hayes, news | | *6:45* |
| Dance Orchestra | Command Theater | The Hidden Truth | Roy Shields and Company | *7pm* |
| | | | | *7:15* |
| Sophisticated Rhythm | The Women's Forum | The Cisco Kid | The Colgate Sports Newsreel, Bill Stern | *7:30* |
| | | | Pro and Con | *7:45* |
| Defense Attorney | Lowell Thomas, news | Magazine Theater | One Man's Family | *8pm* |
| | Dance Orchestra | | World News | *8:15* |
| This is Your FBI | Music from Catalina | True or False | Dimension X | *8:30* |
| | | | | *8:45* |
| A Life in Your Hands | Robert Q. Lewis's Waxworks | Glenn Hardy, news | The NBC Theater | *9pm* |
| | | Robert Hurleigh, news | | *9:15* |
| Newstand Theater | Music | Crime Fighters | | *9:30* |
| | | Five Minute Final (9:55PM) | | *9:45* |
| News | The Ten o'Clock Wire | I Love a Mystery | The Richfield Reporter | *10pm* |
| Science of the Mind | Tom Harmon, sports | Frank Edwards, news | Michael Hinn, news | *10:15* |
| Leighton Noble Orchetra | The Phil Norman Show | Lonesome Gal | The Passing Parade | *10:30* |
| The New Yorkers | | | At Home With Lionel Barrymore | *10:45* |

## EVENING — SUMMER, 1951

*Saturday*

| | ABC | CBS | MBS | NBC |
|---|---|---|---|---|
| *5pm* | Robert Nathan, news | Gaston Fisher, news | The Air Force Hour | The Marine Corps Show |
| *5:15* | It's Your Business | Tom Harmon, sports | | |
| *5:30* | Ira Blue, news | The World Today | Mert's Record Adventure | The Record Album Review |
| *5:45* | News | Frank Goss, news | | Elmer Patterson, news |
| *6pm* | World Opinion | The Rayburn and Finch Show | Hawaii Calls | Maisie |
| *6:15* | | | | |
| *6:30* | Bert Andrews, news | | Caribbean Crossroads | Bob and Ray |
| *6:45* | Report to the People | | | |
| *7pm* | Saturday at the Shamrock | Songs for Sale | Music | |
| *7:15* | | | | |
| *7:30* | | | Salute to the Reservists | Grand Ole Opry |
| *7:45* | | | | |
| *8pm* | The Lone Ranger | The Camel Caravan, Vaughn Monroe | Dude Ranch Roundup | The Musical Merry-Go-Round |
| *8:15* | | | | |
| *8:30* | The Sheriff | Rate Your Mate | Lombardoland USA | The Magnificent Montague |
| *8:45* | | | | |
| *9pm* | Marines in Review | Gangbusters | Newspaper of the Air | Riverside Rancho |
| *9:15* | | | The Jerry Shard Trio | |
| *9:30* | Dance Party | Dance Orchestra | Dance Orchestra | Crime Does Not Pay |
| *9:45* | | | | |
| *10pm* | | The Ten o'Clock Wire | Monica Sings | The Night Reporter |
| *10:15* | | George Fisher, gossip | Music | Supervisor Ray Darby, comment |
| *10:30* | Leighton Noble Orchestra | The Phil Norman Show | The Arthur Van Show | Charlene Hawkes and Company |
| *10:45* | | | | |

## DAYTIME — SUMMER, 1951

*Sunday*

| | ABC | CBS | MBS | NBC |
|---|---|---|---|---|
| *8am* | Music (7:00AM) | The Salt Lake Tabernacle Choir | The Hour of Triumph | Grandpa Reads the Funnies |
| *8:15* | | | | |
| *8:30* | Flying Feet | Invitation to Learning | The Back to God Hour | The U. N. is My Beat |
| *8:45* | | | | Hometown Happenings |
| *9am* | The Sunday School Hour | The People's Platform | The Radio Bible Class | News |
| *9:15* | | | | The Christian Science Monitor |
| *9:30* | Sunday with Bill Davidson | Howard K. Smith, news | The Voice of Prophecy | The Eternal Light |
| *9:45* | | Charles Collingwood, news | | |
| *10am* | | Your Invitation to Music | Glenn Hardy, news | Herbert J. Mann, sports |
| *10:15* | | | Real Estate | Crime is Your Problem |
| *10:30* | | | The Lutheran Hour | The University of Chicago Round Table |
| *10:45* | | | | |
| *11am* | | | Frank and Ernest, songs | The Catholic Hour |
| *11:15* | Alvin Wilder, news | | William Hillman, news | |
| *11:30* | National Vespers | String Serenade | Your Science Reporter | Bob Considine, sports |
| *11:45* | | | Hazel Markel, news | The World of Books |
| *12pm* | Christian in Action | News | Broadway News | Yesterday, Today and Tomorrow |
| *12:15* | | Larry Leseuer, news | Bill Cunningham, news | |
| *12:30* | Message of Israel | The University Explorer | California Caravan | David Lawrence, news |
| *12:45* | | Callifornia Holiday | | John Cameron Swayze, news |
| *1pm* | The Old Fashioned Revival Hour | Your Tropical Trip | Wild Bill Hickock | The Saint |
| *1:15* | | | | |
| *1:30* | | Here's Frank Sinatra | Hashknife Hartley and Sleepy Stevens | The Story of Dr. Kildare |

## DAYTIME — SUMMER, 1951

*Monday-Friday*

| ABC | CBS | MBS | NBC | |
|---|---|---|---|---|
| The Breakfast Club | The Ralph Story Show | Cecil Brown, news | Behind the Headlines | *8am* |
| | News | Robert Greene, news | The Johnny Murray Show | *8:15* |
| | Grand Slam | Bible Institute | The Jack Berch Show | *8:30* |
| | Rosemary | | Dial Dave Garroway | *8:45* |
| Johnny Olsen's Luncheon Club | Wendy Warren and the News | Kate Smith Speaks | Coffee Time | *9am* |
| Edwin C. Hill, news | Aunt Jenny's True Life Stories | The Gospel Singer | Meyers Goes to the Market | *9:15* |
| The Strange Romance of Evelyn Winters | The Romance of Helen Trent | Nancy Young, talk | Ladies' Day | *9:30* |
| When a Girl Marries | Our Gal Sunday | | | *9:45* |
| Lone Journey | Big Sister | Glenn Hardy, news | All Around Town | *10am* |
| Yesterday on Broadway | Ma Perkins | Tello-Test Quiz | | *10:15* |
| My True Story | Young Dr. Malone | The Answer Man | Break the Bank | *10:30* |
| | The Guiding Light | In the Morgan Manner | | *10:45* |
| The Magazine of the Air | The Second Mrs. Burton | Ladies Fair | Double or Nothing | *11am* |
| Easy Aces | Perry Mason | | | *11:15* |
| Quiz Program / On Strings of Song | This is Nora Drake | Queen for a Day | Live Like a Millionaire | *11:30* |
| Paul Harvey, news | The Brighter Day | | | *11:45* |
| Hank Weaver, gossip | Bill Keneelly, news | Broadway News | The Farm Reporter | *12pm* |
| Altar Bound | Wendell Noble, news | Cedric Foster, news | The Road of Life | *12:15* |
| Modern Romances | House Party | Norma Dixon, talk | Pepper Young's Family | *12:30* |
| Peace of Mind | | The Bell Ringer | The Right to Happiness | *12:45* |
| The France Scully Show | Hilltop House | The Jack Kirkwood Show | Mary Noble, Backstage Wife | *1pm* |
| Ira Cook, talk | King's Row | | Stella Dallas | *1:15* |
| | The Phil Norman Show | Double or Nothing | Young Widder Brown | *1:30* |

## DAYTIME — SUMMER, 1951

*Sunday*

| | ABC | CBS | MBS | NBC |
|---|---|---|---|---|
| *1:45* | | | | |
| *2pm* | The Voice of Prophecy | The Main Street Music Hall | The Shadow | The Whisperer |
| *2:15* | | | | |
| *2:30* | Soul Clinic | The Phil Regan Show | True Detective Mysteries | Music from Hollywood |
| *2:45* | | | | |
| *3pm* | The Hour of Decision | Tapestries of Melody | Challenge of the Yukon | Martin Kane, Private Detective |
| *3:15* | | | | |
| *3:30* | Back to the Bible | Memo from Molly | Nick Carter, Master Detective | You Can't Take It With You |
| *3:45* | | | | |
| *4pm* | This Thing Called Life | Guy Lombardo Orchestra | Bandstand USA | The Quiz KIds |
| *4:15* | | | | |
| *4:30* | The Layman's Hour | The Peggy Lee Show | Whispering Strings | The New Theater |
| *4:45* | | | | |

# DAYTIME — SUMMER, 1951

*Monday-Friday*

| ABC | CBS | MBS | NBC | |
|---|---|---|---|---|
| | | | The Woman in My House | *1:45* |
| Mary Margaret McBride, talk | Paul Masterson, talk | News | Just Plain Bill | *2pm* |
| | Mr. Information (2:25PM) | Luncheon with Lopez | Front Page Farrell | *2:15* |
| Variety Fare | Jack Owens, news | Club 930 | Lorenzo Jones | *2:30* |
| | George Fisher, gossip | | Bob and Ray | *2:45* |
| Family Circle | Arthur Godfrey Time | | Welcome, Travelers | *3pm* |
| | | | | *3:15* |
| | | | Aunt Mary | *3:30* |
| | | Lynn at Hollywood | News | *3:45* |
| Perfect Husband | Curt Massey, songs | Robert Hurleigh, news | Dr. Paul | *4pm* |
| | Strike It Rich | Frank Hemingway, news | Life Can Be Beautiful | *4:15* |
| Songs of Another Season | | Behind the Story | Burritt and Wheeler, talk | *4:30* |
| The Hollywood Park Races | The Johnny Dugan Show | Sam Hayes, news | | *4:45* |

## DAYTIME — SUMMER, 1951

*Saturday*

| | ABC | CBS | MBS | NBC |
|---|---|---|---|---|
| *8am* | No School Today (7:45AM) | Let's Pretend | Leslie Nichols, news | The Hollywood Love Story |
| *8:15* | | | Robert Greene, news | |
| *8:30* | | Make Believe Town | Flying Feet | Secret Story |
| *8:45* | Mirandy | | | |
| *9am* | No School Today | The Armstrong Theater of Today | | It's Higgins, Sir |
| *9:15* | Ira Cook's Beach Party | | | |
| *9:30* | | Grand Central Station | Here's to Veterans | The US Marine Band |
| *9:45* | | Cedric Adams, news (9:55AM) | Extra Time | |
| *10am* | | Stars Over Hollywood | Newspaper of the Air | Jackie Robinson, sports |
| *10:15* | | | Land of the Free | |
| *10:30* | | Alias Jane Doe | Helen Hall, songs | Rio Rhythm |
| *10:45* | | | Guest Star | |
| *11am* | | Music with the Hormel Girls | Dunn on Discs | Mary Lee Taylor, cooking |
| *11:15* | | | | |
| *11:30* | | Meet the Missus | | The National Farm and Home Hour |
| *11:45* | | | | |
| *12pm* | Pan-American Union Concert | Fun to Be Young | Sid Fuller, news | The Farm Reporter |
| *12:15* | | | Music | Quick, What's the Answer |
| *12:30* | San Francisco Sketchbook | Motor City Melodies | The Man on the Farm | |
| *12:45* | | | | |
| *1pm* | Horse Racing | Chicagoans Orchestra | Sports Parade | |
| *1:15* | News | | | Are You from Dixie |
| *1:30* | Saturday Afternoon with Bill Davidson | Mr. Information | Jack Ross Campus | |
| *1:45* | | George Fisher, gossip | | |

## DAYTIME — SUMMER, 1951

*Saturday*

| | ABC | CBS | MBS | NBC |
|---|---|---|---|---|
| *2pm* | | The Phil Norman Show | The Armed Forces Review | |
| *2:15* | | | | Harmony and Home |
| *2:30* | | This is Living | Georgia Crackers | |
| *2:45* | | | | |
| *3pm* | | Cross-Section USA | Bands for Bonds | |
| *3:15* | | | | |
| *3:30* | Harry Wismer, sports | This is Los Angeles | The US Marine Band | |
| *3:45* | Vacationland, USA | | | |
| *4pm* | Junior Junction | CBS Farm News | John Flynn, news | |
| *4:15* | | Paul Masterson, talk | Frank Hemingway, news | |
| *4:30* | Music of Today | | Mark Rogers, news | Living 1951 |
| *4:45* | | Tom Harmon, sports | Twin Views of the News | |

| EVENING — FALL, 1951 | | | | |
|---|---|---|---|---|
| *Sunday* | | | | |
| | ABC | CBS | MBS | NBC |
| *5pm* | Stop the Music | The Charlie McCarthy Show | The Northwestern Reviewing Stand | The Phil Harris - Alice Faye Show |
| *5:15* | | | | |
| *5:30* | | Dick Joy, news | The Enchanted Hour | The Theater Guild of the Air |
| *5:45* | | Tom Harmon, sports | | |
| *6pm* | Walter Winchell, gossip | Meet Corliss Archer | News | |
| *6:15* | Louella Parsons, gossip | | Music | |
| *6:30* | Hollywood Stars on Stage | The Carnation Contented Hour | James MacCaffray, news | The Eddie Cantor Show |
| *6:45* | | | Major George Elliott, comment | |
| *7pm* | Paul Harvey, news | O'Hara | Take a Number | The Silent Men |
| *7:15* | Matt Weinstock, news | | | |
| *7:30* | The Ted Mack Family Hour | The Whistler | Comedy of Errors | Music with the Hormel Girls |
| *7:45* | | | | |
| *8pm* | Drew Pearson, news | Our Miss Brooks | Twenty Questions | Charlene Hawkes and Company |
| *8:15* | Don Gardiner, news | | | |
| *8:30* | Walter Winchell, gossip | The Youth Opportunity Program | Top Tunes with Tendler | The Standard Symphony Hour |
| *8:45* | Chet Huntley, news | | | |
| *9pm* | This Week Around the World | The Charlie McCarrthy Show | Glenn Hardy, news | |
| *9:15* | | | Report from the Pentagon | |
| *9:30* | Canaan Caravan | The Lucky Strike Program, Jack Benny | The Chicago Theater of the Air | Senators Report |
| *9:45* | | | | Services Unlimited |
| *10pm* | | The Ten o'Clock Wire | | The Richfield Reporter |
| *10:15* | | George Fisher, gossip | | Mayor Bowron, comment |
| *10:30* | Career Theater | Dance Orchestra | The Arthur Van Show | The Jubilee Show |
| *10:45* | | | | |

# EVENING — FALL, 1951

*Monday*

| ABC | CBS | MBS | NBC | |
|---|---|---|---|---|
| Mark Trail | Edward R. Murrow, news | Bobby Benson | Feature Wire | *5pm* |
| Victor Borge piano (5:25PM) | Tom Harmon, sports | | Ted Meyers, news | *5:15* |
| Chet Huntley, news | The World Today | Clyde Beatty Adventures | The Voice of Firestone | *5:30* |
| Robert Garred, news | Frank Goss, news | Tex Fletcher, news (5:55PM) | | *5:45* |
| Hank Weaver, news | The Lux Radio Theater | Gabriel Heatter, news | America Speaks | *6pm* |
| Elmer Davis, news | | The Mutual Newsreel | | *6:15* |
| Boston Blackie | | The Answer Man | The American Way | *6:30* |
| | | Sam Hayes, news | | *6:45* |
| The Lone Ranger | The Bob Hawk Show | The Affairs of Peter Salem | The Mario Lanza Show | *7pm* |
| | | | | *7:15* |
| The Big Hand | The Choraliers | The Cisco Kid | Music for Tired Businessmen | *7:30* |
| | | | | *7:45* |
| Public Affairs | Lowell Thomas, news | Let George Do It | One Man's Family | *8pm* |
| | The Jack Smith Show | | World News | *8:15* |
| Henry J. Taylor, news | Arthur Godfrey's Talent Scouts | Under Arrest | The Railroad Hour | *8:30* |
| World News | | | | *8:45* |
| Stage 52 | Suspense | Glenn Hardy, news | The Bell Telephone Hour | *9pm* |
| | | Fulton Lewis Jr., news | | *9:15* |
| | The Beulah Show | War Front, Home Front | KFI Calling | *9:30* |
| | Club Fifteen | | | *9:45* |
| Hank Weaver, news | The Ten o'Clock Wire | I Love a Mystery | The Richfield Reporter | *10pm* |
| Science of the Mind | Carroll Alcott, news | Frank Edwards, news | The Passing Parade | *10:15* |
| Between the Bookends | The Phil Harmon Show | Lonesome Gal | At Home With Lionel Barrymore | *10:30* |
| Dream Harbor | This I Believe (10:55PM) | | Repeat Performance | *10:45* |

# EVENING — FALL, 1951

*Tuesday*

| | ABC | CBS | MBS | NBC |
|---|---|---|---|---|
| *5pm* | Fun Factory | Edward R. Murrow, news | Challenge of the Yukon | Feature Wire |
| *5:15* | | Tom Harmon, sports | | Ted Meyers, news |
| *5:30* | Chet Huntley, news | The World Today | Sky King | Casa Cugat |
| *5:45* | Robert Garred, news | Frank Goss, news | Tex Fletcher, news (5:55PM) | Elmer Patterson, news |
| *6pm* | Hank Weaver, news | Life with Luigi | Gabriel Heatter, news | The Hardy Family |
| *6:15* | Elmer Davis, news | | The Mutual Newsreel | |
| *6:30* | Philo Vance | Pursuit | The Answer Man | Fibber McGee and Molly |
| *6:45* | | | Sam Hayes, news | |
| *7pm* | Mr. Mercury | People Are Funny | John Steele, Adventure | Big Town |
| *7:15* | | | | |
| *7:30* | Mr. President | The Hollywood Music Hall | The Count of Monte Cristo | The Phillip Morris Playhouse on Broadway |
| *7:45* | | | | |
| *8pm* | Public Affairs | Lowell Thomas, news | Song of Liberty | One Man's Family |
| *8:15* | | The Jack Smith Show | | World News |
| *8:30* | United or Not | Mr. and Mrs. North | Two-Thousand Plus | The Cavalcade of America |
| *8:45* | | | | |
| *9pm* | America's Town Meeting of the Air | Visiting Time | Glenn Hardy, news | The Bob Hope Show |
| *9:15* | | | Fulton Lewis Jr., news | |
| *9:30* | | The Beulah Show | Official Detective | The Tums Hollywood Theater |
| *9:45* | Twin Views of the News | Club Fifteen | | |
| *10pm* | Hank Weaver, news | The Ten o'Clock Wire | I Love a Mystery | The Richfield Reporter |
| *10:15* | Science of the Mind | Carroll Alcott, news | Frank Edwards, news | The Passing Parade |
| *10:30* | Between the Bookends | The Phil Norman Show | Lonesome Gal | At Home With Lionel Barrymore |
| *10:45* | Dream Harbor | This I Believe (10:55PM) | | Repeat Performance |

## EVENING — FALL, 1951

*Wednesday*

| ABC | CBS | MBS | NBC | |
|---|---|---|---|---|
| Mark Trail | Edward R. Murrow, news | Bobby Benson | Feature Wire | *5pm* |
| Victor Borge, piano (5:25PM) | Tom Harmon, sports | | Ted Meyers, news | *5:15* |
| Chet Huntley, news | The World Today | Clyde Beatty Adventures | Casa Cugat | *5:30* |
| Robert Garred, news | Frank Goss, news | Tex Fletcher, news (5:55PM) | Elmer Patterson, news | *5:45* |
| Hank Weaver, news | The Red Skelton Show | Gabriel Heatter, news | Tales of the Texas Rangers | *6pm* |
| Elmer Davis, news | | The Mutual Newsreel | | *6:15* |
| Boston Blackie | The Bing Crosby Chesterfield Show | The Answer Man | The Halls of Ivt | *6:30* |
| | | Sam Hayes, news | | *6:45* |
| The Lone Ranger | The Wednesday Night Fights | The Mysterious Traveler | Barry Craig, Confidential Investigator | *7pm* |
| | | | | *7:15* |
| Mystery Theater | | The Cisco Kid | Meredith Wilson's Music Room | *7:30* |
| | | | | *7:45* |
| The Top Guy | Lowell Thomas, news | What's the Name of That Song | One Man's Family | *8pm* |
| | The Jack Smith Show | | World News | *8:15* |
| Rogue's Gallery | Dr. Christian | The Family Theater | The Great Gildersleeve | *8:30* |
| | | | | *8:45* |
| Music By Adlam | The Bank Party | Glenn Hardy, news | You Bet Your Life | *9pm* |
| | | Fulton Lewis Jr., news | | *9:15* |
| | The Beulah Show | International Airport | The Big Story | *9:30* |
| | Club Fifteen | | | *9:45* |
| Hank Weaver, news | The Ten o'Clock Wire | I Love a Mystery | The Richfield Reporter | *10pm* |
| Science of the Mind | Carroll Alcott, news | Frank Edwards, news | The Passing Parade | *10:15* |
| Between the Bookends | The Phil Norman Show | Lonesome Gal | At Home With Lionel Barrymore | *10:30* |
| Dream Harbor | This I Believe (10:55PM) | | Repeat Performance | *10:45* |

| EVENING — FALL, 1951 | | | | |
|---|---|---|---|---|
| *Thursday* | | | | |
| | ABC | CBS | MBS | NBC |
| *5pm* | Fun Factory | Edward R. Murrow, news | Challenge of the Yukon | Feature Wire |
| *5:15* | | Tom Harmon, sports | | Ted Meyers, news |
| *5:30* | Chet Huntley, news | The World Today | Sky King | Casa Cugat |
| *5:45* | Robert Garred, news | Frank Goss, news | Tex Fletcher, news (5:55PM) | Elmer Patterson, news |
| *6pm* | Hank Weaver, news | Hearthstone of the Death Squad | Gabriel Heatter, news | Maisie |
| *6:15* | Elmer Davis, news | | The Mutual Newsreel | |
| *6:30* | Philo Vance | Operation Underground | The Answer Man | Bold Venture |
| *6:45* | | | Sam Hayes, news | |
| *7pm* | The Silver Eagle | The Lineup | Murder By Experts | Your Hit Parade |
| *7:15* | | | | |
| *7:30* | The Hollywood Star Playhouse | Robert Q. Lewis's Waxworks | The Singing Marshall | The Marine Corps Show |
| *7:45* | | | | |
| *8pm* | Ted Mack's Original Amateur Hour | Lowell Thomas, news | Tarzan | One Man's Family |
| *8:15* | | The Jack Smith Show | | World News |
| *8:30* | | The Hallmark Playhouse | Price of Peace | Father Knows Best |
| *8:45* | Time for Defense | | | |
| *9pm* | | The FBI in Peace and War | Glenn Hardy, news | Dragnet |
| *9:15* | Foreign Reporter | | Fulton Lewis Jr., news | |
| *9:30* | Music | The Beulah Show | The Rod and Gun Club | Mr. Keen, Tracer of Lost Persons |
| *9:45* | Academic Nutrition | Club Fifteen | | |
| *10pm* | Hank Weaver, news | The Ten o'Clock Wire | I Love a Mystery | The Richfield Reporter |
| *10:15* | Science of the Mind | Carroll Alcott, news | Frank Edwards, news | The Passing Parade |
| *10:30* | Between the Bookends | The Phil Norman Show | Lonesome Gal | At Home With Lionel Barrymore |
| *10:45* | Dream Harbor | This I Believe (10:55PM) | | Repeat Performance |

| EVENING — FALL, 1951 | | | | |
|---|---|---|---|---|
| *Friday* | | | | |
| ABC | CBS | MBS | NBC | |
| Mark Trail | Edward R. Murrow, news | Bobby Benson | Feature Wire | *5pm* |
| Victor Borge, piano (5:25PM) | Tom Harmon, sports | | Ted Meyers, news | *5:15* |
| Chet Huntley, news | The World Today | Clyde Beatty Adventures | Casa Cugat | *5:30* |
| Robert Garred, news | Frank Goss, news | Tex Fletcher, news (5:55PM) | Elmer Patterson, news | *5:45* |
| Hank Weaver, news | Pigskin Predictions | Gabriel Heatter, news | Duffy's Tavern | *6pm* |
| Elmer Davis, news | The American Legion | The Mutual Newsreel | | *6:15* |
| Boston Blackie | Command Theater | The Answer Man | The NBC Theater | *6:30* |
| | | Sam Hayes, news | | *6:45* |
| Madison Square Garden Boxing | Capitol Cloak Room | The Hidden Truth | | *7pm* |
| | | | | *7:15* |
| Joe Hasel's Sports Page | The Women's Forum | The Cisco Kid | Melody Time | *7:30* |
| | | | Sports | *7:45* |
| Richard Diamond, Private Detective | Lowell Thomas, news | Touchdown Tips | One Man's Family | *8pm* |
| | The Jack Smith Show | Guest Star | World News | *8:15* |
| This is Your FBI | The Big Time, Georgie Price | True or False | The Roy Rogers Show | *8:30* |
| | | | | *8:45* |
| The Adventures of Ozzie and Harriet | The P. Weston Show | Glenn Hardy, news | The Martin and Lewis Show | *9pm* |
| | | Fulton Lewis Jr., news | | *9:15* |
| Mr. District Attorney | The Beulah Show | Crime Fighters | You Can't Take It With You | *9:30* |
| | Club Fifteen | | | *9:45* |
| Hank Weaver, news | The Ten o'Clock Wire | I Love a Mystery | The Richfield Reporter | *10pm* |
| Science of the Mind | Carroll Alcott, news | Frank Edwards, news | The Passing Parade | *10:15* |
| Music | The Phil Norman Show | Lonesome Gal | At Home With Lionel Barrymore | *10:30* |
| The New Yorkers | This I Believe (10:55PM) | | Repeat Performance | *10:45* |

# EVENING — FALL, 1951

*Saturday*

| | ABC | CBS | MBS | NBC |
|---|---|---|---|---|
| *5pm* | Quick, What's the Answer | Hanlon's Press Box | The Air Force Hour | Here Comes the Band (4:45PM) |
| *5:15* | | Tom Harmon, sports | | Hal Wolf, sports |
| *5:30* | Ira Blue, news | The World Today | The US Army Band | Les Paul Orchestra |
| *5:45* | Robert Garred, news | Frank Goss, news | | Bob Considine, sports |
| *6pm* | World Opinion | Hopalong Cassidy | Hawaii Calls | Talent Search |
| *6:15* | | | | |
| *6:30* | Science Editor | Yours Truly, Johnny Dollar | Caribbean Crossroads | Grand Ole Opry |
| *6:45* | Report to the People | | | |
| *7pm* | As We See It | How To | The Drexel Institute Choir | Dangerous Assignment |
| *7:15* | Talking It Over | | | |
| *7:30* | The All WAC Band | Meet Millie | Salute to the Reservists | The Magnificent Montague |
| *7:45* | | | | |
| *8pm* | The Lone Ranger | The Camel Caravan, Vaughn Monroe | Dude Ranch Roundup | Nightbeat |
| *8:15* | | | | |
| *8:30* | Defense Attorney | Gene Autry's Melody Ranch | Lombardoland USA | Jane Ace, Disc Jockey |
| *8:45* | | | | |
| *9pm* | The Navy Hour | Gangbusters | Newspaper of the Air | Bob and Ray |
| *9:15* | | | The California National Guard | |
| *9:30* | The Layman's Hour | Broadway is My Beat | Dance Orchestra | Music |
| *9:45* | | | Cecil Brown, news (9:55PM) | Sunday Previews (9:55PM) |
| *10pm* | Hank Weaver, news | The Ten o'Clock Wire | Monica Sings | The Night Reporter |
| *10:15* | ABC Dancing Party | Carroll Alcott, news | Music | Supervisor Ray Darby, comment |
| *10:30* | Dance Orchestra | The Phil Norman Show | The Arthur Van Show | The Old Barn Frolics |
| *10:45* | | This I Believe (10:55PM) | | |

| DAYTIME — FALL, 1951 | | | | |
|---|---|---|---|---|
| *Sunday* | | | | |
| | ABC | CBS | MBS | NBC |
| *8am* | The Morning Chapter | The Salt Lake Tabernacle Choir | The Hour of Triumph | Grandpa Reads the Funnies |
| *8:15* | | | | |
| *8:30* | Flying Feet | Invitation to Learning | The Back to God Hour | The Boy Scout Jamboree |
| *8:45* | | | | Hometown Happenings |
| *9am* | The Sunday School Hour | The People's Platform | The Radio Bible Class | News |
| *9:15* | | | | The Christian Science Monitor |
| *9:30* | Sunday with Bill Davidson | Howard K. Smith, news | The Voice of Prophecy | The Eternal Light |
| *9:45* | | Charles Collingwood, news | | |
| *10am* | | String Serenade | Glenn Hardy, news | Herbert J. Mann, sports |
| *10:15* | | The University Explorer | Mark Rogers, news | Crime is Your Problem |
| *10:30* | | Starlight Melodies | The Lutheran Hour | The University of Chicago Round Table |
| *10:45* | | | | |
| *11am* | | The Longines Symphonette | Frank and Ernest, songs | The Catholic Hour |
| *11:15* | Alvin Wilder, news | | William Hillman, news | |
| *11:30* | National Vespers | New York Philharmonic Orchestra | Your Science Reporter | Bob Considine, sports |
| *11:45* | | | The Canary Pet Shop | The World of Books |
| *12pm* | Christian in Action | | Broadway News | Yesterday, Today and Tomorrow |
| *12:15* | | | Bill Cunningham, news | |
| *12:30* | Message of Israel | The Magic of Believing | California Caravan | David Lawrence, news |
| *12:45* | | | | John Cameron Swayze, news |
| *1pm* | The Old Fashioned Revival Hour | Fan Book | Hashknife Hartley and Sleepy Stevens | The Saint |
| *1:15* | | World News | | |
| *1:30* | | The Frankie Laine Show | Wild Bill Hickock | Martin Kane, Private Detective |

## DAYTIME — FALL, 1951

*Monday-Friday*

| ABC | CBS | MBS | NBC | |
|---|---|---|---|---|
| The Breakfast Club | The Ralph Story Show | Cecil Brown, news | Behind the Headlines | *8am* |
| | News | Robert Greene, news | The Johnny Murray Show | *8:15* |
| | Grand Slam | Bible Institute | Spotlight Serenade | *8:30* |
| | Rosemary | | Dial Dave Garroway | *8:45* |
| Victor Lindlahr, health | Wendy Warren and the News | Popular Music | Coffee Time | *9am* |
| Chet Huntley, news | Aunt Jenny's True Life Stories | | | *9:15* |
| Break the Bank | The Romance of Helen Trent | Nancy Young, talk | Ladies' Day | *9:30* |
| | Our Gal Sunday | | | *9:45* |
| The Jack Berch Show | Big Sister | Glenn Hardy, news | News | *10am* |
| Lone Journey | Ma Perkins | Tello-Test Quiz | King's Row | *10:15* |
| My True Story | Young Dr. Malone | The Answer Man | Strike It Rich | *10:30* |
| | The Guiding Light | In the Morgan Manner | | *10:45* |
| The Magazine of the Air | The Second Mrs. Burton | Ladies Fair | Double or Nothing | *11am* |
| When a Girl Marries | Perry Mason | | | *11:15* |
| Against the Storm | This is Nora Drake | Queen for a Day | Live Like a Millionaire | *11:30* |
| Easy Aces | The Brighter Day | | | *11:45* |
| News | Bill Keneelly, news | Broadway News | The Farm Reporter | *12pm* |
| Paul Harvey, news | Wendell Noble, news | Cedric Foster, news | The Road of Life | *12:15* |
| Tom Owens' Cowboys | House Party | Take a Number | Pepper Young's Family | *12:30* |
| | | | The Right to Happiness | *12:45* |
| The France Scully Show | Hilltop House | The Jack Kirkwood Show | Mary Noble, Backstage Wife | *1pm* |
| Ira Cook, talk | Hawthorne's Mailbag | | Stella Dallas | *1:15* |
| | The Phil Norman Show | Double or Nothing | Young Widder Brown | *1:30* |

## DAYTIME — FALL, 1951

*Sunday*

| | ABC | CBS | MBS | NBC |
|---|---|---|---|---|
| *1:45* | | | | |
| *2pm* | The Voice of Prophecy | Arthur Godfrey's Digest | The Shadow | The American Forum of the Air |
| *2:15* | | | | |
| *2:30* | The Greatest Story Ever Told | Tapestries of Melody | True Detective Mysteries | Music from Hollywood |
| *2:45* | | | | |
| *3pm* | The Hour of Decision | My Friend Irma | Challenge of the Yukon | The Story of Dr. Kildare |
| *3:15* | | | | |
| *3:30* | Marines in Review | The Famous Radio Players | Nick Carter, Master Detective | The Big Show |
| *3:45* | | | | |
| *4pm* | This Thing Called Life | The Lucky Strike Program, Jack Benny | News | |
| *4:15* | | | Music | |
| *4:30* | Sammy Kaye's Sylvania Serenade | Amos 'n' Andy | The Armed Forces Review | |
| *4:45* | | | | |

## DAYTIME — FALL, 1951

*Monday-Friday*

| ABC | CBS | MBS | NBC | |
|---|---|---|---|---|
| | | | The Woman in My House | *1:45* |
| Variety Fare | Paul Masterson, talk | Larry Chatterton, news | Just Plain Bill | *2pm* |
| | | Club 930 | Front Page Farrell | *2:15* |
| The Story of Mary Marlin | Jack Owens, news | | Lorenzo Jones | *2:30* |
| The Strange Romance of Evelyn Winters | George Fisher, gossip | | News | *2:45* |
| Valiant Lady | Arthur Godfrey Time | | Welcome, Travelers | *3pm* |
| Marriage for Two | | | | *3:15* |
| Perfect Husband | | Talk Back with Happy Felton | Aunt Mary | *3:30* |
| | | Lynn at Hollywood | Dr. Paul | *3:45* |
| Erwin Howard, news | Curt Massey, songs | Fulton Lewis Jr., news | Life Can Be Beautiful | *4pm* |
| Main Street to Malibu | Winner Take All | Frank Hemingway, news | Bob and Ray | *4:15* |
| Big Jon and Sparkie | | Behind the Story | Burritt and Wheeler, talk | *4:30* |
| | The Johnny Dugan Show | Sam Hayes, news | | *4:45* |

## DAYTIME — FALL, 1951

*Saturday*

| | ABC | CBS | MBS | NBC |
|---|---|---|---|---|
| *8am* | Pre-Game Platter Party (7:45AM) | Let's Pretend | Leslie Nichols, news | The Saturday Symphony |
| *8:15* | | | Robert Greene, news | |
| *8:30* | | Give and Take | The Haven of Rest | |
| *8:45* | | | | |
| *9am* | No School Today | The Armstrong Theater of Today | Flying Feet | |
| *9:15* | Ira Cook's Beach Party | | | |
| *9:30* | Space Patrol | Stars Over Hollywood | Here's to Veterans | |
| *9:45* | | | Calfornia Civil Defense | |
| *10am* | Pre-Game Platter Party | Grand Central Station | Newspaper of the Air | |
| *10:15* | | | Pigskin Parley | |
| *10:30* | | City Hospital | Extra Time | |
| *10:45* | | | John Flynn, news | |
| *11am* | | Music with the Hormel Girls | Music | Mary Lee Taylor, cooking |
| *11:15* | | | | |
| *11:30* | | Meet the Missus | Sports Parade | The National Farm and Home Hour |
| *11:45* | Sports | | | |
| *12pm* | | Galen Drake's Football Roundup | Sid Fuller, news | The Farm Reporter |
| *12:15* | | | Bands for Bonds | Coast Guard on Parade |
| *12:30* | | | The Man on the Farm | Coffee in Washington |
| *12:45* | | | | |
| *1pm* | | | Georgia Crackers | Public Affairs |
| *1:15* | | | | |
| *1:30* | | | Music | Salute to Colleges |
| *1:45* | | | Sports | Sports |

## DAYTIME — FALL, 1951

*Saturday*

| | ABC | CBS | MBS | NBC |
|---|---|---|---|---|
| *2pm* | Harry Wismer, sports | | | |
| *2:15* | Saturday Afternoon with Bill Davidson | | | |
| *2:30* | | Fun to Be Young | | |
| *2:45* | | | | |
| *3pm* | | The Phil Norman Show | | |
| *3:15* | | | | |
| *3:30* | | This is Living | | |
| *3:45* | The Memory Book | | | |
| *4pm* | Junior Junction | This is Los Angeles | | |
| *4:15* | | | | |
| *4:30* | San Francisco Sketchbook | Paul Masterson, talk | Frank Hemingway, news | |
| *4:45* | | | Sports | Here Comes the Band |

# LISTINGS FOR 1952

## EVENING — WINTER, 1952

*Sunday*

| | ABC | CBS | MBS | NBC |
|---|---|---|---|---|
| *5pm* | Stop the Music | The Charlie McCarthy Show | The Northwestern Reviewing Stand | The Phil Harris - Alice Faye Show |
| *5:15* | | | | |
| *5:30* | | Dick Joy, news | The Enchanted Hour | The Theater Guild of the Air |
| *5:45* | | Tom Harmon, sports | | |
| *6pm* | Walter Winchell, gossip | Meet Corliss Archer | Comedy Theater | |
| *6:15* | Cafe' Istanbul | | | |
| *6:30* | | Remember the Time | James MacCaffray, news | The $64 Question |
| *6:45* | The Three Suns | | Major George Elliott, comment | |
| *7pm* | Paul Harvey, news | The People Act | The John J. Anthony Program | News |
| *7:15* | Main Street to Malibu | | | Pro and Con |
| *7:30* | The Great Adventure | The Whistler | Comedy of Errors | Tin Pan Valley |
| *7:45* | | | | |
| *8pm* | Drew Pearson, news | Our Miss Brooks | Twenty Questions | The Eileen Christy Show |
| *8:15* | Don Gardiner, news | | | |
| *8:30* | Walter Winchell, gossip | The Phillip Morris Playhouse on Broadway | Top Tunes with Tendler | The Standard Symphony Hour |
| *8:45* | Chet Huntley, news | | | |
| *9pm* | Musical Interlude | The Charlie McCarrthy Show | Glenn Hardy, news | |
| *9:15* | Canaan Caravan | | Report from the Pentagon | |
| *9:30* | | The Lucky Strike Program, Jack Benny | The Chicago Theater of the Air | Income Tax |
| *9:45* | | | | Operation Brotherhood |
| *10pm* | News | The Ten o'Clock Wire | | The Richfield Reporter |
| *10:15* | George Sokolsky, news | George Fisher, gossip | | Mayor Bowron, comment |
| *10:30* | Career Theater | The Book Association | Science of the Mind | Music |
| *10:45* | | Strange Facts | Music | |

## EVENING — WINTER, 1952

*Monday*

| ABC | CBS | MBS | NBC | |
|---|---|---|---|---|
| Fun Factory | Edward R. Murrow, news | Bobby Benson | Feature Wire | *5pm* |
| World Flight Report (5:25PM) | Tom Harmon, sports | | Ted Meyers, news | *5:15* |
| Chet Huntley, news | The World Today | Wild Bill Hickock | The Voice of Firestone | *5:30* |
| Robert Garred, news | Frank Goss, news | Cecil Brown, news (5:55PM) | | *5:45* |
| Hank Weaver, news | The Lux Radio Theater | Gabriel Heatter, news | Sports | *6pm* |
| Elmer Davis, news | | The Mutual Newsreel | The Passing Parade | *6:15* |
| Headline Edition | | The Answer Man | The American Way | *6:30* |
| Music | | Sam Hayes, news | | *6:45* |
| The Lone Ranger | The Bob Hawk Show | Woman of the Year | Nightbeat | *7pm* |
| | | | | *7:15* |
| Henry J. Taylor, news | The Choraliers | The Cisco Kid | Dangerous Assignment | *7:30* |
| World News | | | | *7:45* |
| The Big Hand | Lowell Thomas, news | Let George Do It | One Man's Family | *8pm* |
| | The Jack Smith Show | | World News | *8:15* |
| Time for Defense | Arthur Godfrey's Talent Scouts | The Hollywood Playhouse | The Railroad Hour | *8:30* |
| | | | | *8:45* |
| CBC Symphony Orchestra | Suspense | Glenn Hardy, news | The Bell Telephone Hour | *9pm* |
| | | Fulton Lewis Jr., news | | *9:15* |
| | The Beulah Show | War Front, Home Front | KFI Calling | *9:30* |
| | Club Fifteen | | | *9:45* |
| Hank Weaver, news | The Ten o'Clock Wire | I Love a Mystery | The Richfield Reporter | *10pm* |
| Science of the Mind | Bill Keneelly, news | Frank Edwards, news | Joy Forever | *10:15* |
| Perfect Husband | Starlight Revue | Lonesome Gal | Repeat Performance | *10:30* |
| | This I Believe (10:55PM) | | | *10:45* |

## EVENING — WINTER, 1952

*Tuesday*

| | ABC | CBS | MBS | NBC |
|---|---|---|---|---|
| *5pm* | Tom Corbett, Space Cadet | Edward R. Murrow, news | Sergeant Preston of the Yukon | Feature Wire |
| *5:15* | World Flight Report (5:25PM) | Tom Harmon, sports | | Ted Meyers, news |
| *5:30* | Chet Huntley, news | The World Today | Sky King | Casa Cugat |
| *5:45* | Robert Garred, news | Frank Goss, news | Cecil Brown, news (5:55PM) | Elmer Patterson, news |
| *6pm* | Hank Weaver, news | Life with Luigi | Gabriel Heatter, news | Sports |
| *6:15* | Elmer Davis, news | | The Mutual Newsreel | The Passing Parade |
| *6:30* | Headline Edition | Pursuit | The Answer Man | Fibber McGee and Molly |
| *6:45* | Music | | Sam Hayes, news | |
| *7pm* | The Silver Eagle | People Are Funny | The Black Museum | The Eddie Cantor Show |
| *7:15* | | | | |
| *7:30* | Mr. President | The Hollywood Music Hall | The Affairs of Peter Salem | The Man Called X |
| *7:45* | | | | |
| *8pm* | Newstand Theater | Lowell Thomas, news | The Count of Monte Cristo | One Man's Family |
| *8:15* | | The Jack Smith Show | | World News |
| *8:30* | The Metropolitan Opera Auditions | Mr. and Mrs. North | The Story of Dr. Kildare | The Cavalcade of America |
| *8:45* | | | | |
| *9pm* | America's Town Meeting of the Air | Visiting Time | Glenn Hardy, news | The Bob Hope Show |
| *9:15* | | | Fulton Lewis Jr., news | |
| *9:30* | | The Beulah Show | Official Detective | The Tums Hollywood Theater |
| *9:45* | Twin Views of the News | Peggy Lee, songs | | |
| *10pm* | Hank Weaver, news | The Ten o'Clock Wire | I Love a Mystery | The Richfield Reporter |
| *10:15* | Science of the Mind | Bill Keneelly, news | Frank Edwards, news | Joy Forever |
| *10:30* | Perfect Husband | The Phil Norman Show | Lonesome Gal | Repeat Performance |
| *10:45* | | This I Believe (10:55PM) | | |

## EVENING — WINTER, 1952

*Wednesday*

| ABC | CBS | MBS | NBC | |
|---|---|---|---|---|
| Fun Factory | Edward R. Murrow, news | The Green Hornet | Feature Wire | *5pm* |
| World Flight Report (5:25PM) | Tom Harmon, sports | | Ted Meyers, news | *5:15* |
| Chet Huntley, news | The World Today | Wild Bill Hickock | Casa Cugat | *5:30* |
| Robert Garred, news | Frank Goss, news | Cecil Brown, news (5:55PM) | Elmer Patterson, news | *5:45* |
| Hank Weaver, news | The Red Skelton Show | Gabriel Heatter, news | Sports | *6pm* |
| Elmer Davis, news | | The Mutual Newsreel | The Passing Parade | *6:15* |
| Headline Edition | The Bing Crosby Chesterfield Show | The Answer Man | The Halls of Ivy | *6:30* |
| Music | | Sam Hayes, news | | *6:45* |
| The Lone Ranger | The Wednesday Night Fights | The Family Theater | Barry Craig, Confidential Investigator | *7pm* |
| | | | | *7:15* |
| Mystery Theater | | The Cisco Kid | Meredith Wilson's Music Room | *7:30* |
| | | | | *7:45* |
| The Top Guy | Lowell Thomas, news | What's the Name of That Song | One Man's Family | *8pm* |
| | The Jack Smith Show | | World News | *8:15* |
| Rogue's Gallery | Dr. Christian | The Gracie Fields Show | The Great Gildersleeve | *8:30* |
| | | | | *8:45* |
| The Magic of Believing | Big Town | Glenn Hardy, news | You Bet Your Life | *9pm* |
| | | Fulton Lewis Jr., news | | *9:15* |
| Vine Street Varieties | The Beulah Show | Out of the Thunder | The Big Story | *9:30* |
| | Club Fifteen | | | *9:45* |
| Hank Weaver, news | The Ten o'Clock Wire | I Love a Mystery | The Richfield Reporter | *10pm* |
| Science of the Mind | Bill Keneelly, news | Frank Edwards, news | Joy Forever | *10:15* |
| Perfect Husband | The Phil Norman Show | Lonesome Gal | Repeat Performance | *10:30* |
| | This I Believe (10:55PM) | | | *10:45* |

## EVENING — WINTER, 1952

*Thursday*

| | ABC | CBS | MBS | NBC |
|---|---|---|---|---|
| *5pm* | Tom Corbett, Space Cadet | Edward R. Murrow, news | Sergeant Preston of the Yukon | Feature Wire |
| *5:15* | World Flight Report (5:25PM) | Tom Harmon, sports | | Ted Meyers, news |
| *5:30* | Chet Huntley, news | The World Today | Sky King | Casa Cugat |
| *5:45* | Robert Garred, news | Frank Goss, news | Cecil Brown, news (5:55PM) | Elmer Patterson, news |
| *6pm* | Hank Weaver, news | Mr. Chameleon | Gabriel Heatter, news | Sports |
| *6:15* | Elmer Davis, news | | The Mutual Newsreel | The Passing Parade |
| *6:30* | Headline Edition | Stars in the Air | The Answer Man | Bold Venture |
| *6:45* | Music | | Sam Hayes, news | |
| *7pm* | The Silver Eagle | Hollywood Sound Stage | The Modern Adventures of Casanova | Your Hit Parade |
| *7:15* | | | | |
| *7:30* | Defense Attorney | Public Affairs | Bobby Benson | The Hollywood Music Box |
| *7:45* | | | | |
| *8pm* | Ted Mack's Original Amateur Hour | Lowell Thomas, news | Tarzan | One Man's Family |
| *8:15* | | The Jack Smith Show | | World News |
| *8:30* | | The Hallmark Playhouse | The Hardy Family | Father Knows Best |
| *8:45* | John Carver, news | | | |
| *9pm* | The Redhead | The FBI in Peace and War | Glenn Hardy, news | Dragnet |
| *9:15* | | | Fulton Lewis Jr., news | |
| *9:30* | Foreign Reporter | The Beulah Show | The Rod and Gun Club | Mr. Keen, Tracer of Lost Persons |
| *9:45* | Academic Nutrition | Peggy Lee, songs | | |
| *10pm* | Hank Weaver, news | The Ten o'Clock Wire | I Love a Mystery | The Richfield Reporter |
| *10:15* | Science of the Mind | Bill Keneelly, news | Frank Edwards, news | Joy Forever |
| *10:30* | Perfect Husband | The Phil Norman Show | Lonesome Gal | Repeat Performance |
| *10:45* | | This I Believe (10:55PM) | | |

## EVENING — WINTER, 1952

*Friday*

| ABC | CBS | MBS | NBC | |
|---|---|---|---|---|
| Fun Factory | Edward R. Murrow, news | The Green Hornet | Feature Wire | *5pm* |
| World Flight Report (5:25PM) | Tom Harmon, sports | | Ted Meyers, news | *5:15* |
| Chet Huntley, news | The World Today | Wild Bill Hickock | Casa Cugat | *5:30* |
| Robert Garred, news | Frank Goss, news | Cecil Brown, news (5:55PM) | Elmer Patterson, news | *5:45* |
| Hank Weaver, news | Tom Harmon, sports | Gabriel Heatter, news | Bill Stern Sports | *6pm* |
| Elmer Davis, news | News | The Mutual Newsreel | The Passing Parade | *6:15* |
| Headline Edition | Paul Weston Orchestra | The Answer Man | NBC Presents: Short Story | *6:30* |
| Music | | Sam Hayes, news | | *6:45* |
| Madison Square Garden Boxing | Capitol Cloak Room | Maisie | The Mario Lanza Show | *7pm* |
| | | | | *7:15* |
| Hits and Encores | The Women's Forum | The Cisco Kid | News | *7:30* |
| | | | Melody Time | *7:45* |
| Richard Diamond, Private Detective | Lowell Thomas, news | Reporter's Roundup | One Man's Family | *8pm* |
| | The Jack Smith Show | | World News | *8:15* |
| This is Your FBI | The Lineup | Crime Does Not Pay | The Roy Rogers Show | *8:30* |
| | | | | *8:45* |
| The Adventures of Ozzie and Harriet | Hearthstone of the Death Squad | Glenn Hardy, news | The Martin and Lewis Show | *9pm* |
| | Surprise Theater (9:25PM) | Fulton Lewis Jr., news | | *9:15* |
| Mr. District Attorney | The Beulah Show | Crime Fighters | Call It Jazz | *9:30* |
| | Club Fifteen | | | *9:45* |
| Hank Weaver, news | The Ten o'Clock Wire | I Love a Mystery | The Richfield Reporter | *10pm* |
| Science of the Mind | Bill Keneelly, news | Frank Edwards, news | Joy Forever | *10:15* |
| Perfect Husband | The Phil Norman Show | Lonesome Gal | Repeat Performance | *10:30* |
| | This I Believe (10:55PM) | | | *10:45* |

## EVENING — WINTER, 1952

*Saturday*

| | ABC | CBS | MBS | NBC |
|---|---|---|---|---|
| *5pm* | Quick, What's the Answer | Gaston Fisher, news | Dude Ranch Roundup | Are You from Dixie (4:30PM) |
| *5:15* | | Tom Harmon, sports | | |
| *5:30* | Ira Blue, news | The World Today | Bandstand USA | News |
| *5:45* | Robert Garred, news | Frank Goss, news | | Bob Considine, sports |
| *6pm* | Musical Tintypes | Hopalong Cassidy | Hawaii Calls | The Marine Corps Show |
| *6:15* | | | | |
| *6:30* | Science Editor | The Big Time, Georgie Price | Caribbean Crossroads | The Judy Canova Show |
| *6:45* | Report to the People | Surprise Theater (6:55PM) | | |
| *7pm* | It's Your Business | Robert Q. Lewis's Waxworks | The Drexel Institute Choir | The Camel Caravan, Vaughn Monroe |
| *7:15* | The CIO and You | | | |
| *7:30* | World Mobilization for Peace | | Lombardoland USA | Grand Ole Opry |
| *7:45* | | | | |
| *8pm* | The Lone Ranger | Meet Millie | The MGM Theater of the Air | NBC Symphony Orchestra |
| *8:15* | | | | |
| *8:30* | Concert of Europe | Gene Autry's Melody Ranch | | |
| *8:45* | | | | |
| *9pm* | The Navy Hour | Gangbusters | Newspaper of the Air | Bob and Ray |
| *9:15* | | | Songs for America | |
| *9:30* | The Layman's Hour | Broadway is My Beat | Dance Orchestra | Music |
| *9:45* | | | Cecil Brown, news (9:55PM) | Sunday Previews (9:55PM) |
| *10pm* | Hank Weaver, news | The Ten o'Clock Wire | Monica Sings | The Night Reporter |
| *10:15* | Income Tax | Bill Keneelly, news | Music | Supervisor Ray Darby, comment |
| *10:30* | Alert America | The Phil Norman Show | | Roundup Time |
| *10:45* | Songs | This I Believe (10:55PM) | | |

## DAYTIME — WINTER, 1952

*Sunday*

| | ABC | CBS | MBS | NBC |
|---|---|---|---|---|
| *8am* | News | The Salt Lake Tabernacle Choir | William Hillman, news | Grandpa Reads the Funnies |
| *8:15* | Morning Song | | Music | |
| *8:30* | The Light and Life Hour | Invitation to Learning | The Back to God Hour | The Boy Scout Jamboree |
| *8:45* | | | | |
| *9am* | The Sunday School Hour | The People's Platform | The Radio Bible Class | The Carnival of Books |
| *9:15* | | | | The Christian Science Monitor |
| *9:30* | Flying Feet | Howard K. Smith, news | The Voice of Prophecy | The Eternal Light |
| *9:45* | | Bill Costello, news | | |
| *10am* | Sunday with Bill Davidson | Guide to Good Living | Glenn Hardy, news | Herbert J. Mann, sports |
| *10:15* | | The University Explorer | Mark Rogers, news | Crime is Your Problem |
| *10:30* | | Music | The Lutheran Hour | The University of Chicago Round Table |
| *10:45* | | | | |
| *11am* | | The Longines Symphonette | Frank and Ernest, songs | The Catholic Hour |
| *11:15* | Alvin Wilder, news | | William Hillman, news | |
| *11:30* | National Vespers | New York Philharmonic Orchestra | Science Reporter | Hometown Happenings |
| *11:45* | | | The Canary Pet Shop | The World of Books |
| *12pm* | Christian in Action | | Broadway News | Critic at Large |
| *12:15* | | | Bill Cunningham, news | Stranger from the Sea |
| *12:30* | Message of Israel | | The Air Force Hour | Earl Godwin, news |
| *12:45* | | | | John Cameron Swayze, news |
| *1pm* | The Old Fashioned Revival Hour | Fan Book | The Mysterious Traveler | The Falcon |
| *1:15* | | World News | | |
| *1:30* | | It's Always Sunday | Under Arrest | Martin Kane, Private Detective |
| *1:45* | | | Bobby Benson (1:55PM) | |

## DAYTIME — WINTER, 1952

*Monday-Friday*

| ABC | CBS | MBS | NBC | |
|---|---|---|---|---|
| The Breakfast Club | The Ralph Story Show | Cecil Brown, news | The Johnny Murray Show | *8am* |
| | News | Robert Greene, news | Spotlight Serenade | *8:15* |
| | Grand Slam | Bible Institute | News | *8:30* |
| | Rosemary | | Coffee Time | *8:45* |
| Victor Lindlahr, health | Wendy Warren and the News | The Garden Guide | | *9am* |
| Chet Huntley, news | Aunt Jenny's True Life Stories | Capitol Commentary | Victor Lindlahr, health | *9:15* |
| Break the Bank | The Romance of Helen Trent | Nancy Young, talk | Ladies' Day | *9:30* |
| | Our Gal Sunday | | | *9:45* |
| The Jack Berch Show | Big Sister | Glenn Hardy, news | News | *10am* |
| Lone Journey | Ma Perkins | Tello-Test Quiz | King's Row | *10:15* |
| My True Story | Young Dr. Malone | The Answer Man | Strike It Rich | *10:30* |
| | The Guiding Light | In the Morgan Manner | | *10:45* |
| The Magazine of the Air | The Second Mrs. Burton | Ladies Fair | Double or Nothing | *11am* |
| When a Girl Marries | Perry Mason | | | *11:15* |
| Against the Storm | This is Nora Drake | Queen for a Day | Live Like a Millionaire | *11:30* |
| Paul Harvey, news | The Brighter Day | | | *11:45* |
| News | Bill Keneelly, news | Broadway News | The Farm Reporter | *12pm* |
| Tom Owens' Cowboys | Wendell Noble, news | Cedric Foster, news | The Road of Life | *12:15* |
| The Sons of the Pioneers | House Party | Behind the Story | Pepper Young's Family | *12:30* |
| | | Music | The Right to Happiness | *12:45* |
| The France Scully Show | Hilltop House | The Jack Kirkwood Show | Mary Noble, Backstage Wife | *1pm* |
| Ira Cook, talk | The Protam Quiz | | Stella Dallas | *1:15* |
| | The Phil Norman Show | Take a Number | Young Widder Brown | *1:30* |
| | | | The Woman in My House | *1:45* |

| DAYTIME — WINTER, 1952 | | | | |
|---|---|---|---|---|
| *Sunday* | | | | |
| | ABC | CBS | MBS | NBC |
| *2pm* | The Voice of Prophecy | Arthur Godfrey's Digest | The Shadow | The American Forum of the Air |
| *2:15* | | | | |
| *2:30* | The Greatest Story Ever Told | Tapestries of Melody | True Detective Mysteries | The Silent Men |
| *2:45* | | | | |
| *3pm* | The Hour of Decision | My Friend Irma | The Gabby Hayes Show | Tales of the Texas Rangers |
| *3:15* | | | | |
| *3:30* | Marines in Review | The Famous Radio Players | Nick Carter, Master Detective | The Big Show |
| *3:45* | | | | |
| *4pm* | This Thing Called Life | The Lucky Strike Program, Jack Benny | News | |
| *4:15* | | | Mark Rogers, news | |
| *4:30* | Sammy Kaye's Sylvania Serenade | Amos 'n' Andy | Little Symphonies | |
| *4:45* | | | | |

# DAYTIME — WINTER, 1952

*Monday-Friday*

| ABC | CBS | MBS | NBC | |
|---|---|---|---|---|
| Variety Fare | Mr. Information | Larry Chatterton, news | Just Plain Bill | *2pm* |
| | The Johnny Dugan Show | Ray Block Orchestra | Front Page Farrell | *2:15* |
| Joyce Jordan, MD | The Women's News Desk | Dick Haymes, songs | Lorenzo Jones | *2:30* |
| The Strange Romance of Evelyn Winters | George Fisher, gossip | Lyn Murray Orchestra | Aunt Mary | *2:45* |
| Valiant Lady | Arthur Godfrey Time | Club 930 | Welcome, Travelers | *3pm* |
| Marriage for Two | | | | *3:15* |
| The Story of Mary Marlin | | | Dr. Paul | *3:30* |
| Between the Bookends | | Lynn at Hollywood | Dial Dave Garroway | *3:45* |
| Mary Margaret McBride, talk | Curt Massey, songs | Fulton Lewis Jr., news | Life Can Be Beautiful | *4pm* |
| | The Jack Owens Show | Frank Hemingway, news | At Home With Lionel Barrymore | *4:15* |
| Big Jon and Sparkie | | Curt Massey, songs | Burritt and Wheeler, talk | *4:30* |
| Mark Trail | Hawthorne's Mailbag | Sam Hayes, news | | *4:45* |

## DAYTIME — WINTER, 1952

*Saturday*

| | ABC | CBS | MBS | NBC |
|---|---|---|---|---|
| *8am* | Weekend Platter Party (7:45AM) | Let's Pretend | Bruce McFarlane, news | Casa Latina (7:30AM) |
| *8:15* | | | Robert Greene, news | |
| *8:30* | | Give and Take | The Haven of Rest | The Saturday Symphony |
| *8:45* | | | | |
| *9am* | No School Today | The Armstrong Theater of Today | Flying Feet | |
| *9:15* | | | | |
| *9:30* | Space Patrol | Stars Over Hollywood | Your Income Tax | |
| *9:45* | | | Calfornia Civil Defense | |
| *10am* | Weekend Platter Party | Grand Central Station | Newspaper of the Air | News |
| *10:15* | | | Land of the Free | The Pursuit to Happiness |
| *10:30* | | City Hospital | Symphonies for Youth | Young America Speaks |
| *10:45* | | | | |
| *11am* | The Metropolitan Opera | Music with the Hormel Girls | | Mary Lee Taylor, cooking |
| *11:15* | | | | |
| *11:30* | | Meet the Missus | Sports | The National Farm and Home Hour |
| *11:45* | | | The Radio Singer | |
| *12pm* | | News | Sid Fuller, news | The Farm Reporter |
| *12:15* | | Galen Drake's Guide to Good Living | Mark Rogers, news | The Down Homers |
| *12:30* | | Paul Masterson, talk | The Man on the Farm | My Secret Story |
| *12:45* | | | | |
| *1pm* | | Fun to Be Young | Georgia Crackers | The Saturday Symphony |
| *1:15* | | | | |
| *1:30* | | The Phil Norman Show | News | |
| *1:45* | | | Sports | |

# DAYTIME — WINTER, 1952

*Saturday*

| | ABC | CBS | MBS | NBC |
|---|---|---|---|---|
| *2pm* | | Mr. Information | Music | |
| *2:15* | | CBS Farm News | | |
| *2:30* | Saturday Afternoon with Bill Davidson | This is Living | Bands for Bonds | |
| *2:45* | | | | |
| *3pm* | | This is Los Angeles | Oklahoma Symphony Orchestra | |
| *3:15* | | | | |
| *3:30* | Harry Wismer, sports | Cross-Section USA | | |
| *3:45* | Una Mae Carlisle, songs | | | |
| *4pm* | Junior Junction | News | John Flynn, news | |
| *4:15* | | Horse Racing | Frank Hemingway, news | |
| *4:30* | San Francisco Sketchbook | | Mark Rogers, news | Are You from Dixie |
| *4:45* | | Income Tax | News | |

# EVENING — SPRING, 1952

*Sunday*

| | ABC | CBS | MBS | NBC |
|---|---|---|---|---|
| *5pm* | Stop the Music | The Charlie McCarthy Show | The Northwestern Reviewing Stand | What's the Score |
| *5:15* | | | | |
| *5:30* | | Dick Joy, news | The Enchanted Hour | The Theater Guild of the Air |
| *5:45* | | Tom Harmon, sports | | |
| *6pm* | Walter Winchell, gossip | The Screen Guild Theater | Comedy Theater | |
| *6:15* | Meet Corliss Archer | | | |
| *6:30* | | Stars in the Air | James MacCaffray, news | The $64 Question |
| *6:45* | The Three Suns | | Major George Elliott, comment | |
| *7pm* | Paul Harvey, news | The People Act | The John J. Anthony Program | The Phil Harris - Alice Faye Show |
| *7:15* | Main Street to Malibu | | | |
| *7:30* | The Great Adventure | The Whistler | Down You Go | Tales of the Texas Rangers |
| *7:45* | | | | |
| *8pm* | Chet Huntley, news | Our Miss Brooks | Twenty Questions | Charlene Hawkes and Company |
| *8:15* | Don Gardiner, news | | | |
| *8:30* | William Tusher in Hollywood | The Phillip Morris Playhouse on Broadway | Information, Please | The Standard Symphony Hour |
| *8:45* | Stars for Defense | | | |
| *9pm* | George Sokolsky, news | The Charlie McCarrthy Show | Glenn Hardy, news | |
| *9:15* | Canaan Caravan | | Report from the Pentagon | |
| *9:30* | | The Lucky Strike Program, Jack Benny | The Chicago Theater of the Air | Stranger from the Sea |
| *9:45* | | | | Senators Report |
| *10pm* | George Sokolsky, news | The Ten o'Clock Wire | | The Richfield Reporter |
| *10:15* | Science of the Mind | George Fisher, gossip | | Mayor Bowron, comment |
| *10:30* | Career Theater | The Protam Quiz | Music | Record Session |
| *10:45* | | Talk | | |

# EVENING — SPRING, 1952

*Monday*

| ABC | CBS | MBS | NBC | |
|---|---|---|---|---|
| Fun Factory | Edward R. Murrow, news | Bobby Benson | Feature Wire | *5pm* |
| Today in Baseball (5:25PM) | Tom Harmon, sports | | Ted Meyers, news | *5:15* |
| Chet Huntley, news | The World Today | Wild Bill Hickock | The Voice of Firestone | *5:30* |
| Robert Garred, news | Frank Goss, news | Cecil Brown, news (5:55PM) | | *5:45* |
| Hank Weaver, news | The Lux Radio Theater | Gabriel Heatter, news | At Home With Lionel Barrymore | *6pm* |
| Elmer Davis, news | | The Mutual Newsreel | The Passing Parade | *6:15* |
| Headline Edition | | The Answer Man | The American Way | *6:30* |
| Music | | Sam Hayes, news | | *6:45* |
| The Lone Ranger | The Bob Hawk Show | Woman of the Year | Nightbeat | *7pm* |
| | | | | *7:15* |
| Henry J. Taylor, news | The Choraliers | The Mysterious Traveler | Dangerous Assignment | *7:30* |
| World News | | | | *7:45* |
| The Big Hand | Lowell Thomas, news | Let George Do It | One Man's Family | *8pm* |
| | The Jack Smith Show | | World News | *8:15* |
| Flying Feet | Arthur Godfrey's Talent Scouts | The Hollywood Playhouse | The Railroad Hour | *8:30* |
| | | | | *8:45* |
| Lives in the Making | Suspense | Glenn Hardy, news | The Bell Telephone Hour | *9pm* |
| | | Fulton Lewis Jr., news | | *9:15* |
| Musical Tintype | The Beulah Show | War Front, Home Front | KFI Calling | *9:30* |
| | Club Fifteen | | | *9:45* |
| Hank Weaver, news | The Ten o'Clock Wire | I Love a Mystery | The Richfield Reporter | *10pm* |
| Science of the Mind | Bill Keneelly, news | Frank Edwards, news | Joy Forever | *10:15* |
| Music from the Moon | Starlight Revue | Lonesome Gal | Repeat Performance | *10:30* |
| | | | | *10:45* |

# EVENING — SPRING, 1952

*Tuesday*

| | ABC | CBS | MBS | NBC |
|---|---|---|---|---|
| *5pm* | Tom Corbett, Space Cadet | Edward R. Murrow, news | Sergeant Preston of the Yukon | Feature Wire |
| *5:15* | Today in Baseball (5:25PM) | Tom Harmon, sports | | Ted Meyers, news |
| *5:30* | Chet Huntley, news | The World Today | Sky King | The Barry Wood Show |
| *5:45* | Robert Garred, news | Frank Goss, news | Cecil Brown, news (5:55PM) | Elmer Patterson, news |
| *6pm* | Hank Weaver, news | Life with Luigi | Gabriel Heatter, news | At Home With Lionel Barrymore |
| *6:15* | Elmer Davis, news | | The Mutual Newsreel | The Passing Parade |
| *6:30* | Headline Edition | Remember the Time | The Answer Man | Fibber McGee and Molly |
| *6:45* | Music | | Sam Hayes, news | |
| *7pm* | The Silver Eagle | People Are Funny | The Black Museum | The Eddie Cantor Show |
| *7:15* | | | | |
| *7:30* | Mr. President | The Hollywood Music Hall | The Affairs of Peter Salem | The Man Called X |
| *7:45* | | | | |
| *8pm* | Newstand Theater | Lowell Thomas, news | The Count of Monte Cristo | One Man's Family |
| *8:15* | | The Jack Smith Show | | World News |
| *8:30* | Escape with Me | Mr. and Mrs. North | The Story of Dr. Kildare | The Cavalcade of America |
| *8:45* | | | | |
| *9pm* | America's Town Meeting of the Air | Candidates and Issues | Glenn Hardy, news | The Bob Hope Show |
| *9:15* | | | Fulton Lewis Jr., news | |
| *9:30* | | The Beulah Show | Official Detective | Barry Craig, Confidential Investigator |
| *9:45* | Twin Views of the News | Peggy Lee, songs | | |
| *10pm* | Hank Weaver, news | The Ten o'Clock Wire | I Love a Mystery | The Richfield Reporter |
| *10:15* | Science of the Mind | Bill Keneelly, news | Frank Edwards, news | Joy Forever |
| *10:30* | Music from the Moon | The Phil Norman Show | Lonesome Gal | Repeat Performance |
| *10:45* | | | | |

# EVENING — SPRING, 1952

*Wednesday*

| ABC | CBS | MBS | NBC | |
|---|---|---|---|---|
| Fun Factory | Edward R. Murrow, news | The Green Hornet | Feature Wire | *5pm* |
| Today in Baseball (5:25PM) | Tom Harmon, sports | | Ted Meyers, news | *5:15* |
| Chet Huntley, news | The World Today | Wild Bill Hickock | The Barry Wood Show | *5:30* |
| Robert Garred, news | Frank Goss, news | Cecil Brown, news (5:55PM) | Elmer Patterson, news | *5:45* |
| Hank Weaver, news | The Red Skelton Show | Gabriel Heatter, news | At Home With Lionel Barrymore | *6pm* |
| Elmer Davis, news | | The Mutual Newsreel | The Passing Parade | *6:15* |
| Headline Edition | The Bing Crosby Chesterfield Show | The Answer Man | The Silent Men | *6:30* |
| Music | | Sam Hayes, news | | *6:45* |
| The Lone Ranger | The Wednesday Night Fights | The Family Theater | The Halls of Ivy | *7pm* |
| | | | | *7:15* |
| Mystery Theater | | The Cisco Kid | Meredith Wilson's Music Room | *7:30* |
| | | | | *7:45* |
| The Top Guy | Lowell Thomas, news | What's the Name of That Song | One Man's Family | *8pm* |
| | The Jack Smith Show | | World News | *8:15* |
| Crossfire | Dr. Christian | The Gracie Fields Show | The Great Gildersleeve | *8:30* |
| | | | | *8:45* |
| Vine Street Varieties | Big Town | Glenn Hardy, news | You Bet Your Life | *9pm* |
| | | Fulton Lewis Jr., news | | *9:15* |
| Time for Defense | The Beulah Show | Out of the Thunder | The Big Story | *9:30* |
| | Club Fifteen | | | *9:45* |
| Hank Weaver, news | The Ten o'Clock Wire | I Love a Mystery | The Richfield Reporter | *10pm* |
| Science of the Mind | Bill Keneelly, news | Frank Edwards, news | Joy Forever | *10:15* |
| Music from the Moon | The Phil Norman Show | Lonesome Gal | Repeat Performance | *10:30* |
| | | | | *10:45* |

## EVENING — SPRING, 1952

*Thursday*

| | ABC | CBS | MBS | NBC |
|---|---|---|---|---|
| *5pm* | Tom Corbett, Space Cadet | Edward R. Murrow, news | Sergeant Preston of the Yukon | Feature Wire |
| *5:15* | Today in Baseball (5:25PM) | Tom Harmon, sports | | Ted Meyers, news |
| *5:30* | Chet Huntley, news | The World Today | Sky King | The Barry Wood Show |
| *5:45* | Robert Garred, news | Frank Goss, news | Cecil Brown, news (5:55PM) | Elmer Patterson, news |
| *6pm* | Hank Weaver, news | Mr. Chameleon | Gabriel Heatter, news | At Home With Lionel Barrymore |
| *6:15* | Elmer Davis, news | | The Mutual Newsreel | The Passing Parade |
| *6:30* | Headline Edition | Hearthstone of the Death Squad | The Answer Man | The Marine Corps Show |
| *6:45* | Music | | Sam Hayes, news | |
| *7pm* | The Silver Eagle | Operation Underground | The Modern Adventures of Casanova | Your Hit Parade |
| *7:15* | | | | |
| *7:30* | Defense Attorney | The Lineup | This is for Europe | Citizen View of 1952 |
| *7:45* | | | | |
| *8pm* | Ted Mack's Original Amateur Hour | Lowell Thomas, news | Clyde Beatty Adventures | One Man's Family |
| *8:15* | | The Jack Smith Show | | World News |
| *8:30* | | The Hallmark Playhouse | The Hardy Family | Father Knows Best |
| *8:45* | John Carver, news | | | |
| *9pm* | Cafe' Istanbul | The FBI in Peace and War | Glenn Hardy, news | Dragnet |
| *9:15* | | | Fulton Lewis Jr., news | |
| *9:30* | Foreign Reporter | The Beulah Show | The Rod and Gun Club | Mr. Keen, Tracer of Lost Persons |
| *9:45* | Academic Nutrition | Peggy Lee, songs | | |
| *10pm* | Hank Weaver, news | The Ten o'Clock Wire | I Love a Mystery | The Richfield Reporter |
| *10:15* | Science of the Mind | Bill Keneelly, news | Frank Edwards, news | Joy Forever |
| *10:30* | Music from the Moon | The Phil Norman Show | Lonesome Gal | Repeat Performance |
| *10:45* | | | | |

## EVENING — SPRING, 1952

*Friday*

| ABC | CBS | MBS | NBC | |
|---|---|---|---|---|
| Fun Factory | Edward R. Murrow, news | The Green Hornet | Feature Wire | *5pm* |
| Today in Baseball (5:25PM) | Tom Harmon, sports | | Ted Meyers, news | *5:15* |
| Chet Huntley, news | The World Today | Wild Bill Hickock | The Barry Wood Show | *5:30* |
| Robert Garred, news | Frank Goss, news | Cecil Brown, news (5:55PM) | Elmer Patterson, news | *5:45* |
| Hank Weaver, news | Paul Masterson, talk | Gabriel Heatter, news | At Home With Lionel Barrymore | *6pm* |
| Elmer Davis, news | | The Mutual Newsreel | The Passing Parade | *6:15* |
| Headline Edition | | The Answer Man | NBC Presents: Short Story | *6:30* |
| Music | | Sam Hayes, news | | *6:45* |
| Madison Square Garden Boxing | Presidential Profiles | Maisie | The Mario Lanza Show | *7pm* |
| | | | | *7:15* |
| Hits and Encores | The Women's Forum | The Cisco Kid | Portrait in Sports | *7:30* |
| | | | Melody Time | *7:45* |
| Richard Diamond, Private Detective | Lowell Thomas, news | Reporter's Roundup | One Man's Family | *8pm* |
| | The Jack Smith Show | | World News | *8:15* |
| This is Your FBI | The Doris Day Show | Crime Does Not Pay | The Roy Rogers Show | *8:30* |
| | | | | *8:45* |
| The Adventures of Ozzie and Harriet | The Big Time, Georgie Price | Glenn Hardy, news | The Martin and Lewis Show | *9pm* |
| | | Fulton Lewis Jr., news | | *9:15* |
| Mr. District Attorney | The Beulah Show | Crime Fighters | The Town Hall Party | *9:30* |
| Musical Interlude (9:55PM) | Club Fifteen | | | *9:45* |
| Hank Weaver, news | The Ten o'Clock Wire | I Love a Mystery | The Richfield Reporter | *10pm* |
| Science of the Mind | Bill Keneelly, news | Frank Edwards, news | Joy Forever | *10:15* |
| Music from the Moon | The Phil Norman Show | Lonesome Gal | Repeat Performance | *10:30* |
| | | | | *10:45* |

## EVENING — SPRING, 1952

*Saturday*

| | ABC | CBS | MBS | NBC |
|---|---|---|---|---|
| *5pm* | The Navy Hour | Horse Racing (4:45PM) | Western Serenade | Medicine USA |
| *5:15* | | Tom Harmon, sports | | |
| *5:30* | Robert Garred, news | The World Today | Bandstand USA | News |
| *5:45* | Stewart Craig, news | Frank Goss, news | | Record Album Review |
| *6pm* | Musical Tintypes | Tarzan | Hawaii Calls | NBC Symphony Orchestra |
| *6:15* | | | | |
| *6:30* | Science Editor | Hopalong Cassidy | Latin Rhythms | |
| *6:45* | Report to the People | | | |
| *7pm* | Talking It Over | Robert Q. Lewis's Waxworks | The Drexel Institute Choir | The Camel Caravan, Vaughn Monroe |
| *7:15* | As We See It | | | |
| *7:30* | Marines in Review | | Lombardoland USA | Grand Ole Opry |
| *7:45* | | | | |
| *8pm* | The Lone Ranger | Meet Millie | The MGM Theater of the Air | The Town Hall Party |
| *8:15* | | | | |
| *8:30* | Campfire Serenade | Gene Autry's Melody Ranch | | |
| *8:45* | | | | |
| *9pm* | San Francisco Sketchbook | Gangbusters | Newspaper of the Air | The Judy Canova Show |
| *9:15* | | | Mr. Mystery | |
| *9:30* | The Layman's Hour | Broadway is My Beat | Dance Orchestra | The Chamber Music Society of Lower Basin Street |
| *9:45* | | | Cecil Brown, news (9:55PM) | |
| *10pm* | News | The Ten o'Clock Wire | Monica Sings | The Night Reporter |
| *10:15* | The American Cancer Society | Bill Keneelly, news | Music | Supervisor Ray Darby, comment |
| *10:30* | Lawrence Welk Orchestra | The Phil Norman Show | | Roundup Time |
| *10:45* | | | | |

## DAYTIME — SPRING, 1952

*Sunday*

| | ABC | CBS | MBS | NBC |
|---|---|---|---|---|
| *8am* | The Clem Davies Show | The Salt Lake Tabernacle Choir | William Hillman, news | Grandpa Reads the Funnies |
| *8:15* | | | Music | |
| *8:30* | The Light and Life Hour | Invitation to Learning | The Back to God Hour | The Boy Scout Jamboree |
| *8:45* | | | | |
| *9am* | The Sunday School Hour | The People's Platform | The Radio Bible Class | The Carnival of Books |
| *9:15* | | | | The Christian Science Monitor |
| *9:30* | Sunday with Bill Davidson | Howard K. Smith, news | The Voice of Prophecy | The Eternal Light |
| *9:45* | | Stewart Craig, news | | |
| *10am* | | Bill Costello, news | Glenn Hardy, news | Herbert J. Mann, sports |
| *10:15* | | Better Eyesight | Mark Rogers, news | Crime is Your Problem |
| *10:30* | | The University Explorer | The Lutheran Hour | The University of Chicago Round Table |
| *10:45* | | The Garden Gate | | |
| *11am* | Message of Israel | The Longines Symphonette | Frank and Ernest, songs | The Catholic Hour |
| *11:15* | | | Science Reporter | |
| *11:30* | National Vespers | New York Philharmonic Orchestra | Land of the Free | Hometown Happenings |
| *11:45* | | | Music | The World of Books |
| *12pm* | Christian in Action | | Broadway News | Critic at Large |
| *12:15* | | | Bill Cunningham, news | Mike 95 |
| *12:30* | Church in Home | | The Robert Montgomery Show | Bob Considine, sports |
| *12:45* | | | | John Cameron Swayze, news |
| *1pm* | The Old Fashioned Revival Hour | Mr. Information | Guy Lombardo Orchestra | The Falcon |
| *1:15* | | News | | |
| *1:30* | | Command Theater | Crime Fighters | Martin Kane, Private Detective |
| *1:45* | | | Bobby Benson (1:55PM) | |

# DAYTIME — SPRING, 1952

*Monday-Friday*

| ABC | CBS | MBS | NBC | |
|---|---|---|---|---|
| The Breakfast Club | The Ralph Story Show | Cecil Brown, news | The Johnny Murray Show | *8am* |
| | News | Robert Greene, news | Spotlight Serenade | *8:15* |
| | Grand Slam | Bible Institute | News | *8:30* |
| | Rosemary | | The Protam Quiz | *8:45* |
| Victor Lindlahr, health | Wendy Warren and the News | The Garden Guide | Coffee Time | *9am* |
| Chet Huntley, news | Aunt Jenny's True Life Stories | Capitol Commentary | Victor Lindlahr, health | *9:15* |
| Break the Bank | The Romance of Helen Trent | Nancy Young, talk | Ladies' Day | *9:30* |
| | Our Gal Sunday | | | *9:45* |
| The Jack Berch Show | Big Sister | Glenn Hardy, news | News | *10am* |
| Lone Journey | Ma Perkins | Tello-Test Quiz | King's Row | *10:15* |
| My True Story | Young Dr. Malone | The Answer Man | Strike It Rich | *10:30* |
| | The Guiding Light | In the Morgan Manner | | *10:45* |
| Whispering Streets | The Second Mrs. Burton | Ladies Fair | Double or Nothing | *11am* |
| When a Girl Marries | Perry Mason | | | *11:15* |
| Against the Storm | This is Nora Drake | Queen for a Day | Live Like a Millionaire | *11:30* |
| Paul Harvey, news | The Brighter Day | | | *11:45* |
| News | Bill Keneelly, news | Broadway News | The Farm Reporter | *12pm* |
| Quizzicale | Hilltop House | Cedric Foster, news | The Road of Life | *12:15* |
| The Sons of the Pioneers | House Party | Behind the Story | Pepper Young's Family | *12:30* |
| | | Music | The Right to Happiness | *12:45* |
| The Al Jarvis Show | Wendell Noble, news | The Jack Kirkwood Show | Mary Noble, Backstage Wife | *1pm* |
| | Mr. Information | | Stella Dallas | *1:15* |
| | The Phil Norman Show | Take a Number | Young Widder Brown | *1:30* |
| | | | The Woman in My House | *1:45* |

## DAYTIME — SPRING, 1952

*Sunday*

| | ABC | CBS | MBS | NBC |
|---|---|---|---|---|
| *2pm* | The Voice of Prophecy | Arthur Godfrey's Digest | The Shadow | The Hollywood Star Playhouse |
| *2:15* | | | | |
| *2:30* | The Greatest Story Ever Told | World News | True Detective Mysteries | The American Forum of the Air |
| *2:45* | | | | |
| *3pm* | The Hour of Decision | My Friend Irma | The Gabby Hayes Show | Terrea Lea, songs |
| *3:15* | | | | News |
| *3:30* | The Herald of Truth | The Famous Radio Players | Nick Carter, Master Detective | The Chase |
| *3:45* | | | | |
| *4pm* | This Thing Called Life | The Lucky Strike Program, Jack Benny | News | Best Plays |
| *4:15* | | | Mark Rogers, news | |
| *4:30* | Sammy Kaye's Sylvania Serenade | Amos 'n' Andy | Little Symphonies | |
| *4:45* | | | | |

## DAYTIME — SPRING, 1952

*Monday-Friday*

| ABC | CBS | MBS | NBC | |
|---|---|---|---|---|
| The Ronnie Kemper Show | Ruth Ashton Reports | Larry Chatterton, news | Just Plain Bill | *2pm* |
| | George Fisher, gossip | Club 930 / Guest Star | Front Page Farrell | *2:15* |
| The Story of Mary Marlin | The Women's News Desk | Club 930 | Lorenzo Jones | *2:30* |
| The Strange Romance of Evelyn Winters | George Fisher, gossip | | The Doctor's Wife | *2:45* |
| The Magazine of the Air | Arthur Godfrey Time | | Welcome, Travelers | *3pm* |
| Between the Bookends | | | | *3:15* |
| Ladies Be Seated | | | Dr. Paul | *3:30* |
| | | Lynn at Hollywood | Dial Dave Garroway | *3:45* |
| Mary Margaret McBride, talk | Curt Massey, songs | Fulton Lewis Jr., news | Life Can Be Beautiful | *4pm* |
| | The Jack Owens Show | Frank Hemingway, news | News | *4:15* |
| Ira Cook, talk | | Curt Massey, songs | Burritt and Wheeler, talk | *4:30* |
| Mark Trail | Hawthorne's Mailbag | Sam Hayes, news | | *4:45* |

## DAYTIME — SPRING, 1952

*Saturday*

| | ABC | CBS | MBS | NBC |
|---|---|---|---|---|
| *8am* | Ira Cook's Beach Party (7:40AM) | Let's Pretend | Bruce McFarlane, news | Turn Back the Clock |
| *8:15* | | | Robert Greene, news | |
| *8:30* | | Give and Take | The Haven of Rest | The Saturday Symphony |
| *8:45* | | | | |
| *9am* | No School Today | The Armstrong Theater of Today | The US Marine Band | |
| *9:15* | | | | |
| *9:30* | Space Patrol | Stars Over Hollywood | Songs for America | |
| *9:45* | | | Calfornia Civil Defense | |
| *10am* | Ira Cook's Beach Party | Grand Central Station | Newspaper of the Air | |
| *10:15* | | | Mark Rogers, news | Guest Star |
| *10:30* | | City Hospital | Dunn on Discs | Young America Speaks |
| *10:45* | | | | |
| *11am* | | Music with the Hormel Girls | | Mary Lee Taylor, cooking |
| *11:15* | | | | |
| *11:30* | | Meet the Missus | The Air Force Hour | The National Farm and Home Hour |
| *11:45* | | | | |
| *12pm* | | News | Sid Fuller, news | The Farm Reporter |
| *12:15* | | Galen Drake's Guide to Good Living | Mark Rogers, news | News |
| *12:30* | | Family Fun | The Man on the Farm | The US Army Band |
| *12:45* | | | | |
| *1pm* | News | Stewart Craig, news | Georgia Crackers | The Saturday Symphony |
| *1:15* | Saturday Afternoon with Bill Davidson | Paul Masterson, talk | | 1:15 |
| *1:30* | | The Phil Norman Show | Armed Forces in Review | |
| *1:45* | | | | |

## DAYTIME — SPRING, 1952

*Saturday*

| | ABC | CBS | MBS | NBC |
|---|---|---|---|---|
| *2pm* | | Mr. Information | The Fifth Army Band | |
| *2:15* | | CBS Farm News | | |
| *2:30* | | This is Living | Bands for Bonds | |
| *2:45* | | | | |
| *3pm* | Ira Cook's Beach Party | This is Los Angeles | Music | |
| *3:15* | | | | |
| *3:30* | | Cross-Section USA | The Men's Corner | |
| *3:45* | | | The Rukeyser Report | |
| *4pm* | | News | John Flynn, news | Are You from Dixie |
| *4:15* | | Stewart Craig, news | Frank Hemingway, news | |
| *4:30* | Junior Junction | George Fisher, gossip | Mark Rogers, news | |
| *4:45* | | Horse Racing | News | |

## EVENING — SUMMER, 1952

*Sunday*

| | ABC | CBS | MBS | NBC |
|---|---|---|---|---|
| *5pm* | Stop the Music | America Calling | The Northwestern Reviewing Stand | The Marie Wilson Show |
| *5:15* | | | | |
| *5:30* | | Dick Joy, news | The Enchanted Hour | Best Plays |
| *5:45* | | Tom Harmon, sports | | |
| *6pm* | Drew Pearson, news | Meet Millie | Music | |
| *6:15* | Melody Highway | | | |
| *6:30* | | Inner Sanctum Mysteries | The Great Day | Hats in the Ring |
| *6:45* | Main Street to Malibu | | | |
| *7pm* | Paul Harvey, news | Rocky Jordan | Little Symphonies | Meet the Press |
| *7:15* | William Tusher in Hollywood | | | |
| *7:30* | Time Capsule | The Whistler | Down You Go | Tales of the Texas Rangers |
| *7:45* | | | | |
| *8pm* | Chet Huntley, news | Horatio Hornblower | Twenty Questions | Charlene Hawkes and Company |
| *8:15* | Don Gardiner, news | | | |
| *8:30* | Stewart Craig, news | The Phillip Morris Playhouse on Broadway | Information, Please | The Hour of Music |
| *8:45* | George Sokolsky, news | | | |
| *9pm* | Chautauqua Symphony Orchestra | The Frank Fontaine Show | Newspaper of the Air | |
| *9:15* | | | Report from the Pentagon | |
| *9:30* | The Hour Approaches | Dance Orchestra | The Chicago Theater of the Air | Stranger from the Sea |
| *9:45* | | | | Melody Time |
| *10pm* | George Sokolsky, news | The Ten o'Clock Wire | | The Richfield Reporter |
| *10:15* | Science of the Mind | George Fisher, gossip | | Mayor Bowron, comment |
| *10:30* | Career Theater | Stewart Craig, news | Romance Music | Music |
| *10:45* | | Beauty Aid | | |

| EVENING — SUMMER, 1952 | | | | |
|---|---|---|---|---|
| *Monday* | | | | |
| ABC | CBS | MBS | NBC | |
| Ira Cook, talk (4:30PM) | Edward R. Murrow, news | The Merry Mailman | Feature Wire | *5pm* |
| Today in Baseball (5:25PM) | Tom Harmon, sports | | Ted Meyers, news | *5:15* |
| Chet Huntley, news | The World Today | Songs of the B-Bar-B | The Voice of Firestone | *5:30* |
| Robert Garred, news | Frank Goss, news | Cecil Brown, news (5:55PM) | | *5:45* |
| Hank Weaver, news | Theater of Romance | Gabriel Heatter, news | Virgil Pinkley, news | *6pm* |
| Elmer Davis, news | | The Mutual Newsreel | The Passing Parade | *6:15* |
| Headline Edition | The Steve Allen Show | The Answer Man | The American Way | *6:30* |
| Music | | Sam Hayes, news | | *6:45* |
| The Lone Ranger | Walk a Mile | Concerto Festival | Music | *7pm* |
| | | | | *7:15* |
| Henry J. Taylor, news | Command Theater | The Mysterious Traveler | Dangerous Assignment | *7:30* |
| World News | | | | *7:45* |
| Chicago Signature | Lowell Thomas, news | Let George Do It | One Man's Family | *8pm* |
| | Calling All Stars | | World News | *8:15* |
| Guy Lombardo Orchestra | Arthur Godfrey's Talent Scouts | War Front, Home Front | The Railroad Hour | *8:30* |
| | | | | *8:45* |
| The Bill Balance Show | The Quiz Kids | Newspaper of the Air | The Bell Telephone Hour | *9pm* |
| | | Fulton Lewis Jr., news | | *9:15* |
| | Hawthorne's Mailbag | Music | KFI Calling | *9:30* |
| | Peggy Lee, songs | | | *9:45* |
| Hank Weaver, news | The Ten o'Clock Wire | I Love a Mystery | The Richfield Reporter | *10pm* |
| Science of the Mind | Bill Keneelly, news | Frank Edwards, news | Joy Forever | *10:15* |
| Music from the Moon | Starlight Revue | Crowell's Nest | Repeat Performance | *10:30* |
| | | | | *10:45* |

## EVENING — SUMMER, 1952

*Tuesday*

| | ABC | CBS | MBS | NBC |
|---|---|---|---|---|
| *5pm* | Ira Cook, talk (4:30PM) | Edward R. Murrow, news | The Merry Mailman | Feature Wire |
| *5:15* | Today in Baseball (5:25PM) | Tom Harmon, sports | | Ted Meyers, news |
| *5:30* | Chet Huntley, news | The World Today | Songs of the B-Bar-B | The Barry Wood Show |
| *5:45* | Robert Garred, news | Frank Goss, news | Cecil Brown, news (5:55PM) | Elmer Patterson, news |
| *6pm* | Hank Weaver, news | The Lineup | Gabriel Heatter, news | Virgil Pinkley, news |
| *6:15* | Elmer Davis, news | | The Mutual Newsreel | The Passing Parade |
| *6:30* | Headline Edition | The Steve Allen Show | The Answer Man | Truth or Consequences |
| *6:45* | Music | | Sam Hayes, news | |
| *7pm* | The Silver Eagle | People Are Funny | The Jimmie Carroll Show | The Capitol Concert |
| *7:15* | | | | |
| *7:30* | Mr. President | The Hollywood Music Hall | The Affairs of Peter Salem | Stan Kenton Orchestra |
| *7:45* | | | | |
| *8pm* | America's Town Meeting of the Air | Lowell Thomas, news | The Count of Monte Cristo | One Man's Family |
| *8:15* | | Calling All Stars | | World News |
| *8:30* | | Mr. and Mrs. North | The Story of Dr. Kildare | The Scarlet Pimpernel |
| *8:45* | | | | |
| *9pm* | The Bill Balance Show | The Straw Hat Concert | Newspaper of the Air | Meet Your Match |
| *9:15* | | | Fulton Lewis Jr., news | |
| *9:30* | | Hawthorne's Mailbag | Official Detective | Barry Craig, Confidential Investigator |
| *9:45* | | Peggy Lee, songs | | |
| *10pm* | Hank Weaver, news | The Ten o'Clock Wire | I Love a Mystery | The Richfield Reporter |
| *10:15* | Science of the Mind | Bill Keneelly, news | Frank Edwards, news | Joy Forever |
| *10:30* | Music from the Moon | The Phil Norman Show | Crowell's Nest | Repeat Performance |
| *10:45* | | | | |

## EVENING — SUMMER, 1952

*Wednesday*

| ABC | CBS | MBS | NBC | |
|---|---|---|---|---|
| Ira Cook, talk (4:30PM) | Edward R. Murrow, news | The Merry Mailman | Feature Wire | *5pm* |
| Today in Baseball (5:25PM) | Tom Harmon, sports | | Ted Meyers, news | *5:15* |
| Chet Huntley, news | The World Today | Songs of the B-Bar-B | The Barry Wood Show | *5:30* |
| Robert Garred, news | Frank Goss, news | Cecil Brown, news (5:55PM) | Elmer Patterson, news | *5:45* |
| Hank Weaver, news | Yours Truly, Johnny Dollar | Gabriel Heatter, news | Virgil Pinkley, news | *6pm* |
| Elmer Davis, news | | The Mutual Newsreel | The Passing Parade | *6:15* |
| Headline Edition | The Steve Alen Show | The Answer Man | What's the Score | *6:30* |
| Music | | Sam Hayes, news | | *6:45* |
| The Lone Ranger | The Wednesday Night Fights | The Family Theater | What's My Line | *7pm* |
| | | | | *7:15* |
| Postmark USA | | The Cisco Kid | Portrait of a City | *7:30* |
| | Tom Harmon, sports | | | *7:45* |
| Parlour Politics | Lowell Thomas, news | What's the Name of That Song | One Man's Family | *8pm* |
| | Calling All Stars | | World News | *8:15* |
| Crossfire | Dr. Christian | The Gracie Fields Show | The Great Gildersleeve | *8:30* |
| | | | | *8:45* |
| The Bill Balance Show | Hearthstone of the Death Squad | Newspaper of the Air | You Bet Your Life | *9pm* |
| | | Fulton Lewis Jr., news | | *9:15* |
| | Hawthorne's Mailbag | Out of the Thunder | The Hollywood Music Box | *9:30* |
| | Peggy Lee, songs | | | *9:45* |
| Hank Weaver, news | The Ten o'Clock Wire | I Love a Mystery | The Richfield Reporter | *10pm* |
| Science of the Mind | Bill Keneelly, news | Frank Edwards, news | Joy Forever | *10:15* |
| Music from the Moon | The Phil Norman Show | Crowell's Nest | Repeat Performance | *10:30* |
| | | | | *10:45* |

## EVENING — SUMMER, 1952

*Thursday*

| | ABC | CBS | MBS | NBC |
|---|---|---|---|---|
| *5pm* | Ira Cook, talk (4:30PM) | Edward R. Murrow, news | The Merry Mailman | Feature Wire |
| *5:15* | Today in Baseball (5:25PM) | Tom Harmon, sports | | Ted Meyers, news |
| *5:30* | Chet Huntley, news | The World Today | Songs of the B-Bar-B | The Barry Wood Show |
| *5:45* | Robert Garred, news | Frank Goss, news | Cecil Brown, news (5:55PM) | Elmer Patterson, news |
| *6pm* | Hank Weaver, news | Mr. Chameleon | Gabriel Heatter, news | Virgil Pinkley, news |
| *6:15* | Elmer Davis, news | | The Mutual Newsreel | The Passing Parade |
| *6:30* | Headline Edition | The Steve Allen Show | The Answer Man | The Marine Corps Show |
| *6:45* | Music | | Sam Hayes, news | |
| *7pm* | The Silver Eagle | Dance Orchestra | Jazz Nocturne | The First Nighter Program |
| *7:15* | | | | |
| *7:30* | Defense Attorney | The Big Time, Georgie Price | This is for Europe | Music |
| *7:45* | | | | |
| *8pm* | Ted Mack's Original Amateur Hour | Lowell Thomas, news | Crime Fighters | One Man's Family |
| *8:15* | | Calling All Stars | | World News |
| *8:30* | | Mr. Keen, Tracer of Lost Persons | The Hardy Family | A Life in Your Hands |
| *8:45* | Stewart Craig, news | | | |
| *9pm* | The Bill Balance Show | The FBI in Peace and War | Newspaper of the Air | Dragnet |
| *9:15* | | | Fulton Lewis Jr., news | |
| *9:30* | | Hawthorne's Mailbag | The Rod and Gun Club | The Chase |
| *9:45* | | Peggy Lee, songs | | |
| *10pm* | Hank Weaver, news | The Ten o'Clock Wire | I Love a Mystery | The Richfield Reporter |
| *10:15* | Science of the Mind | Bill Keneelly, news | Frank Edwards, news | Joy Forever |
| *10:30* | Music from the Moon | The Phil Norman Show | Crowell's Nest | Repeat Performance |
| *10:45* | | | | |

## EVENING — SUMMER, 1952

*Friday*

| ABC | CBS | MBS | NBC | |
|---|---|---|---|---|
| Ira Cook, talk (4:30PM) | Edward R. Murrow, news | The Merry Mailman | Feature Wire | *5pm* |
| Today in Baseball (5:25PM) | Tom Harmon, sports | | Ted Meyers, news | *5:15* |
| Chet Huntley, news | The World Today | Songs of the B-Bar-B | The Barry Wood Show | *5:30* |
| Robert Garred, news | Frank Goss, news | Cecil Brown, news (5:55PM) | Elmer Patterson, news | *5:45* |
| Hank Weaver, news | Paul Masterson, talk | Gabriel Heatter, news | Virgil Pinkley, news | *6pm* |
| Elmer Davis, news | | The Mutual Newsreel | The Passing Parade | *6:15* |
| Headline Edition | The Steve Allen Show | The Answer Man | Music By Mantovani | *6:30* |
| Music | | Sam Hayes, news | | *6:45* |
| The KECA Pops Concert | Capitol Cloak Room | Symphonic Strings | The Mario Lanza Show | *7pm* |
| | | | | *7:15* |
| | The Women's Forum | The Cisco Kid | Portrait in Sports | *7:30* |
| | | | At the Hollywood Bowl | *7:45* |
| The Top Guy | Lowell Thomas, news | Reporter's Roundup | One Man's Family | *8pm* |
| | Calling All Stars | | World News | *8:15* |
| This is Your FBI | Musicland USA | Crime Does Not Pay | The Roy Shield Revue | *8:30* |
| | | | | *8:45* |
| The Bill Balance Show | The Big Time, Georgie Price | Newspaper of the Air | Dance Party | *9pm* |
| | | Fulton Lewis Jr., news | | *9:15* |
| | Hawthorne's Mailbag | Magazine Theater | Bob and Ray | *9:30* |
| | Peggy Lee, songs | | | *9:45* |
| Hank Weaver, news | The Ten o'Clock Wire | I Love a Mystery | The Richfield Reporter | *10pm* |
| Science of the Mind | Bill Keneelly, news | Frank Edwards, news | Joy Forever | *10:15* |
| Music from the Moon | The Phil Norman Show | Crowell's Nest | Repeat Performance | *10:30* |
| | | | | *10:45* |

## EVENING — SUMMER, 1952

*Saturday*

| | ABC | CBS | MBS | NBC |
|---|---|---|---|---|
| *5pm* | The Navy Hour | Larry LeSueur, news | Western Serenade | Are You from Dixie (4:45PM) |
| *5:15* | | Tom Harmon, sports | | |
| *5:30* | Robert Garred, news | The World Today | Music | |
| *5:45* | Stewart Craig, news | Frank Goss, news | Pee Wee Reese Orchestra | Public Affairs |
| *6pm* | Musical Tintypes | Tarzan | Hawaii Calls | The Ohio River Jamboree |
| *6:15* | | | | |
| *6:30* | Science Editor | Hopalong Cassidy | Latin Rhythms | Hollywood Varieties |
| *6:45* | Report to the People | | | |
| *7pm* | It's Your Business | Gunsmoke | The US Military Band | Tin Pan Valley |
| *7:15* | The CIO and You | | | |
| *7:30* | Marines in Review | Robert Q. Lewis's Waxworks | Lombardoland USA | Grand Ole Opry |
| *7:45* | | | | |
| *8pm* | The Lone Ranger | Broadway is My Beat | The MGM Theater of the Air | The Town Hall Party |
| *8:15* | | | | |
| *8:30* | Newstand Theater | Gene Autry's Melody Ranch | | |
| *8:45* | | | | |
| *9pm* | Summer Cruise | Gangbusters | Newspaper of the Air | News |
| *9:15* | | | Monica Sings | Alex Drier, news |
| *9:30* | The Layman's Hour | I Was a Communist for the FBI | Dance Orchestra | Music |
| *9:45* | | | Cecil Brown, news (9:55PM) | |
| *10pm* | The Garden of Eden | The Ten o'Clock Wire | The Game of the Day | The Night Reporter |
| *10:15* | I Covered the Story | Bill Keneelly, news | | Supervisor Ray Darby, comment |
| *10:30* | Lawrence Welk Orchestra | The Phil Norman Show | | Commercial |
| *10:45* | | | | Guest Star |

| DAYTIME — SUMMER, 1952 | | | | |
|---|---|---|---|---|
| *Sunday* | | | | |
| | ABC | CBS | MBS | NBC |
| *8am* | The Clem Davies Show | The Salt Lake Tabernacle Choir | This Thing Called Life | Grandpa Reads the Funnies |
| *8:15* | | | The Voice of China | |
| *8:30* | The Light and Life Hour | Invitation to Learning | Back to God | The U.N. is My Beat |
| *8:45* | | | | Songs of the Wild |
| *9am* | The Sunday School Hour | The People's Platform | The Radio Bible Class | Carnival of Books |
| *9:15* | | | | The Christian Science Monitor |
| *9:30* | Sunday with Bill Davidson | Howard K. Smith, news | The Voice of Prophecy | The Eternal Light |
| *9:45* | | Stewart Craig, news | | |
| *10am* | | Bill Costello, news | Glenn Hardy, news | Herbert J. Mann, sports |
| *10:15* | | St. Louis Matinee | Music | Crime is Your Problem |
| *10:30* | | The University Explorer | The Lutheran Hour | The University of Chicago Round Table |
| *10:45* | | The Garden Gate | | |
| *11am* | Message of Israel | Your Invitation to Music | Frank and Ernest, songs | The Catholic Hour |
| *11:15* | | | Land of the Free | |
| *11:30* | National Vespers | | Children's Bible Stories | Hometown Happenings |
| *11:45* | | | Sunday Favorites | The World of Books |
| *12pm* | Christian in Action | | Broadway News | Critic at Large |
| *12:15* | | | Bill Cunningham, news | Mike 95 |
| *12:30* | Wings of Healing | Music for You | The Robert Montgomery Show | Bob Considine, sports |
| *12:45* | | | | John Cameron Swayze, news |
| *1pm* | The Old Fashioned Revival Hour | News | The Green Hornet | The Falcon |
| *1:15* | | News | | |
| *1:30* | | The Main Street Music Hall | Clyde Beatty Adventures | Martin Kane, Private Detective |
| *1:45* | | | | |

## DAYTIME — SUMMER, 1952

*Monday-Friday*

| ABC | CBS | MBS | NBC | |
|---|---|---|---|---|
| The Breakfast Club | The Ralph Story Show | Cecil Brown, news | The Johnny Murray Show | *8am* |
| | News | Gabriel Heatter, news | Spotlight Serenade | *8:15* |
| | Grand Slam | Bible Institute | News | *8:30* |
| | Rosemary | | Coffee Time | *8:45* |
| Sing with Bing | Wendy Warren and the News | Paula Stone, talk | Andy and Virginia, songs | *9am* |
| Chet Huntley, news | Aunt Jenny's True Life Stories | Capitol Commentary | | *9:15* |
| Break the Bank | The Romance of Helen Trent | Nancy Young, talk | Ladies' Day | *9:30* |
| | Our Gal Sunday | | | *9:45* |
| The Jack Berch Show | Big Sister | John Holbrook, news | News | *10am* |
| Lone Journey | Ma Perkins | Tello-Test Quiz | Bob and Ray | *10:15* |
| My True Story | Young Dr. Malone | The Answer Man | Strike It Rich | *10:30* |
| | The Guiding Light | In the Morgan Manner | | *10:45* |
| Whispering Streets | The Second Mrs. Burton | Ladies Fair | Double or Nothing | *11am* |
| Friendly Philosopher | Perry Mason | | | *11:15* |
| Bill Davidson, talk | This is Nora Drake | Queen for a Day | The Brighter Day | *11:30* |
| | The Brighter Day | | Young Dr. Malone | *11:45* |
| News | Bill Keneelly, news | Broadway News | The Farm Reporter | *12pm* |
| Paul Harvey, news | Hilltop House | Cedric Foster, news | The Road of Life | *12:15* |
| The Sons of the Pioneers | House Party | Behind the Story | Pepper Young's Family | *12:30* |
| | | Music | The Right to Happiness | *12:45* |
| Bill Ring, talk | Wendell Noble, news | The Jack Kirkwood Show | Mary Noble, Backstage Wife | *1pm* |
| Al Jarvis, talk | It Happens Every Day | | Stella Dallas | *1:15* |
| | The Phil Norman Show | Take a Number | Young Widder Brown | *1:30* |
| | | | The Woman in My House | *1:45* |

# DAYTIME — SUMMER, 1952

*Sunday*

| | ABC | CBS | MBS | NBC |
|---|---|---|---|---|
| *2pm* | The Voice of Prophecy | Arthur Godfrey's Digest | The Shadow | The Hollywood Star Playhouse |
| *2:15* | | | | |
| *2:30* | Church in Home | World News | True Detective Mysteries | Whitehall 1212 |
| *2:45* | | | | |
| *3pm* | The Hour of Decision | Treasury Bandstand | Sergeant Preston of the Yukon | Terrea Lea, songs |
| *3:15* | | | | Bylines |
| *3:30* | The Herald of Truth | Syncopation Piece | Nick Carter, Master Detective | Top Story |
| *3:45* | | | | At this Hour |
| *4pm* | Here Comes the Band | December Bride | News | The Hollywood Bowl Concert |
| *4:15* | | | Music | |
| *4:30* | Sammy Kaye's Sylvania Serenade | The Doris Day Show | The Concert Band | |
| *4:45* | | | | |

## DAYTIME — SUMMER, 1952

*Monday-Friday*

| ABC | CBS | MBS | NBC | |
|---|---|---|---|---|
| The Ronnie Kemper Show | Ruth Ashton Reports | Larry Chatterton, news | Just Plain Bill | *2pm* |
| | News | Club 930 / Guest Star | Front Page Farrell | *2:15* |
| The Tennessee Ernie Ford Show | Arthur Godfrey Time | Club 930 | Lorenzo Jones | *2:30* |
| | | | The Doctor's Wife | *2:45* |
| Cal Tinney, talk | | | Welcome, Travelers | *3pm* |
| | | | | *3:15* |
| Between the Bookends | | | Dr. Paul | *3:30* |
| Life is Your Business | | Lynn at Hollywood | Dial Dave Garroway | *3:45* |
| Mary Margaret McBride, talk | Curt Massey, songs | Fulton Lewis Jr., news | Life Can Be Beautiful | *4pm* |
| | The Jack Owens Show | Frank Hemingway, news | News | *4:15* |
| Ira Cook, talk | | Curt Massey, songs | Burritt and Wheeler, talk | *4:30* |
| | Hawthorne's Mailbag | Sam Hayes, news | | *4:45* |

## DAYTIME — SUMMER, 1952

*Saturday*

| | ABC | CBS | MBS | NBC |
|---|---|---|---|---|
| *8am* | Flying Feet | Let's Pretend | Bruce McFarlane, news | The Saturday Symphony |
| *8:15* | | | Robert Greene, news | |
| *8:30* | The Eddie Fisher Show | Give and Take | The Haven of Rest | |
| *8:45* | | | | |
| *9am* | No School Today | The Armstrong Theater of Today | The US Marine Band | |
| *9:15* | | | | |
| *9:30* | Space Patrol | Stars Over Hollywood | Public Affairs | |
| *9:45* | | | Calfornia Civil Defense | |
| *10am* | Ira Cook's Beach Party | Grand Central Station | Newspaper of the Air | |
| *10:15* | | | Music | |
| *10:30* | | City Hospital | Dunn on Discs | |
| *10:45* | | | | |
| *11am* | | Music with the Hormel Girls | | Mary Lee Taylor, cooking |
| *11:15* | | | | |
| *11:30* | | Meet the Missus | Bands for Bonds | The National Farm and Home Hour |
| *11:45* | | | | |
| *12pm* | | News | Sid Fuller, news | The Farm Reporter |
| *12:15* | | Gillespie's Garden Guide | Music | News |
| *12:30* | | Chicagoans Orchestra | The Man on the Farm | The US Army Band |
| *12:45* | | | | |
| *1pm* | | Wendell Noble, news | Georgia Crackers | The Saturday Symphony |
| *1:15* | | Stewart Craig, news | | |
| *1:30* | | The Phil Norman Show | Music | |
| *1:45* | | | | |

| DAYTIME — SUMMER, 1952 | | | | |
|---|---|---|---|---|
| *Saturday* | | | | |
| | ABC | CBS | MBS | NBC |
| *2pm* | | Mr. Information | The Fifth Army Band | |
| *2:15* | | Stewart Craig, news | | |
| *2:30* | | This is Living | Dixieland | The Author Speaks |
| *2:45* | | | | The Key to Health |
| *3pm* | | This is Los Angeles | Music | Public Affairs |
| *3:15* | | | | H. V. Kaltenborn, news |
| *3:30* | | The Eddie Fisher Show | The Men's Corner | NBC Summer Symphony |
| *3:45* | | | The Rukeyser Report | |
| *4pm* | Frank and Jackson, songs | News | John Flynn, news | |
| *4:15* | | CBS Farm News | Frank Hemingway, news | |
| *4:30* | Student Symphony | This I Believe | Music | |
| *4:45* | | Horse Racing | Report from the Pentagon | Are You from Dixie |

## EVENING — FALL, 1952

*Sunday*

| | ABC | CBS | MBS | NBC |
|---|---|---|---|---|
| *5pm* | Mickey Katz Orchestra | The Charlie McCarthy Show | The Northwestern Reviewing Stand | Top Story |
| *5:15* | | | | Bylines |
| *5:30* | | Dick Joy, news | The Enchanted Hour | The Theater Guild of the Air |
| *5:45* | | Tom Harmon, sports | | |
| *6pm* | Walter Winchell, gossip | The Hallmark Playhouse | Comedy Theater | |
| *6:15* | Taylor Grant, news | | | |
| *6:30* | Melody Highway | December Bride | | Dragnet |
| *6:45* | Main Street to Malibu | | | |
| *7pm* | Paul Harvey, news | The Choraliers | The John J. Anthony Program | Meet the Press |
| *7:15* | William Tusher in Hollywood | | | |
| *7:30* | Time Capsule | The Whistler | Down You Go | The Phil Harris- Alice Faye Show |
| *7:45* | | | | |
| *8pm* | Drew Pearson, news | Our Miss Brooks | Twenty Questions | Opera for Everyone |
| *8:15* | Don Gardiner, news | | | |
| *8:30* | Chet Huntley, news | The Phillip Morris Playhouse on Broadway | Top Tunes with Tendler | The Hour of Music |
| *8:45* | Stewart Craig, news | | | |
| *9pm* | The Bill Balance Show | The Charlie McCarthy Show | Newspaper of the Air | |
| *9:15* | | | Music | |
| *9:30* | | The Lucky Strike Program, Jack Benny | The Chicago Theater of the Air | Stranger from the Sea |
| *9:45* | | | | Trouble is My Business |
| *10pm* | George Sokolsky, news | The Ten o'Clock Wire | | The Richfield Reporter |
| *10:15* | Science of the Mind | George Fisher, gossip | | Mayor Bowron, comment |
| *10:30* | Career Theater | Stewart Craig, news | Romance Music | Music |
| *10:45* | | Beauty Aid | | |

## EVENING — FALL, 1952

*Monday*

| ABC | CBS | MBS | NBC | |
|---|---|---|---|---|
| Elroy Hirsch, sports | Edward R. Murrow, news | Bobby Benson | Feature Wire | *5pm* |
| Virgil Pinkley, news | Tom Harmon, sports | | The Passing Parade | *5:15* |
| Chet Huntley, news | The World Today | Wild Bill Hickock | The Voice of Firestone | *5:30* |
| Robert Garred, news | Frank Goss, news | Cecil Brown, news (5:55PM) | | *5:45* |
| Hank Weaver, news | The Lux Radio Theater | Gabriel Heatter, news | H. V. Kaltenborn, news | *6pm* |
| Elmer Davis, news | | The Mutual Newsreel | Bill Hayworth, news | *6:15* |
| Headline Edition | | The Answer Man | The American Way | *6:30* |
| Music | | Sam Hayes, news | | *6:45* |
| The Lone Ranger | The Bob Hawk Show | Woman of the Year | Eleanor Roosevelt, talk | *7pm* |
| | | | | *7:15* |
| Henry J. Taylor, news | Rocky Jordan | Under Arrest | Al Goodman's Musical Album | *7:30* |
| World News | | | | *7:45* |
| Life Begins at Eighty | Lowell Thomas, news | Let George Do It | One Man's Family | *8pm* |
| | Charles Collingwood, news | | World News | *8:15* |
| Cafe' Istanbul | Arthur Godfrey's Talent Scouts | Crime Fighters | The Railroad Hour | *8:30* |
| | | | | *8:45* |
| The Bill Balance Show | Suspense | Newspaper of the Air | The Bell Telephone Hour | *9pm* |
| | | Fulton Lewis Jr., news | | *9:15* |
| | Club Fifteen | Reporter's Roundup | KFI Calling | *9:30* |
| | Armchair Adventures | | | *9:45* |
| News | The Ten o'Clock Wire | I Love a Mystery | The Richfield Reporter | *10pm* |
| Science of the Mind | Bill Keneelly, news | Frank Edwards, news | Joy Forever | *10:15* |
| Drama | The Phil Norman Show | Crowell's Nest | Repeat Performance | *10:30* |
| Music from the Moon | | | | *10:45* |

## EVENING — FALL, 1952

*Tuesday*

| | ABC | CBS | MBS | NBC |
|---|---|---|---|---|
| *5pm* | Elroy Hirsch, sports | Edward R. Murrow, news | Sergeant Preston of the Yukon | Feature Wire |
| *5:15* | Virgil Pinkley, news | Tom Harmon, sports | | The Passing Parade |
| *5:30* | Chet Huntley, news | The World Today | Sky King | The Barry Wood Show |
| *5:45* | Robert Garred, news | Frank Goss, news | Cecil Brown, news (5:55PM) | Elmer Patterson, news |
| *6pm* | Hank Weaver, news | Life with Luigi | Gabriel Heatter, news | H. V. Kaltenborn, news |
| *6:15* | Elmer Davis, news | | The Mutual Newsreel | Bill Hayworth, news |
| *6:30* | Headline Edition | My Friend Irma | The Answer Man | Fibber McGee and Molly |
| *6:45* | Music | | Sam Hayes, news | |
| *7pm* | The Silver Eagle | People Are Funny | The Black Museum | Two for the Money |
| *7:15* | | | | |
| *7:30* | Mr. President | The Hollywood Music Hall | The Affairs of Peter Salem | Frances Farwell and Music |
| *7:45* | | | | |
| *8pm* | America's Town Meeting of the Air | Lowell Thomas, news | The Count of Monte Cristo | One Man's Family |
| *8:15* | | Charles Collingwood, news | | World News |
| *8:30* | | Mr. and Mrs. North | The Story of Dr. Kildare | The Cavalcade of America |
| *8:45* | | | | |
| *9pm* | The Bill Balance Show | Public Affairs | Newspaper of the Air | The Martin and Lewis Show |
| *9:15* | | | Fulton Lewis Jr., news | |
| *9:30* | | Peggy Lee, songs | The Search That Never Ends | The Red Skelton Show |
| *9:45* | | Armchair Adventures | | |
| *10pm* | News | The Ten o'Clock Wire | I Love a Mystery | The Richfield Reporter |
| *10:15* | Science of the Mind | Bill Keneelly, news | Frank Edwards, news | Joy Forever |
| *10:30* | The N.Y. Herald Tribune Forum | The Phil Norman Show | Crowell's Nest | Repeat Performance |
| *10:45* | Music from the Moon | | | |

## EVENING — FALL, 1952

*Wednesday*

| ABC | CBS | MBS | NBC | |
|---|---|---|---|---|
| Elroy Hirsch, sports | Edward R. Murrow, news | The Green Hornet | Feature Wire | *5pm* |
| Virgil Pinkley, news | Tom Harmon, sports | | The Passing Parade | *5:15* |
| Chet Huntley, news | The World Today | Wild Bill Hickok | The Barry Wood Show | *5:30* |
| Robert Garred, news | Frank Goss, news | Cecil Brown, news (5:55PM) | Elmer Patterson, news | *5:45* |
| Hank Weaver, news | The Lineup | Gabriel Heatter, news | H. V. Kaltenborn, news | *6pm* |
| Elmer Davis, news | | The Mutual Newsreel | Bill Hayworth, news | *6:15* |
| Headline Edition | What's My Line | The Answer Man | Robert Armbruster Orchestra | *6:30* |
| Music | | Sam Hayes, news | | *6:45* |
| The Lone Ranger | The Wednesday Night Fights | The Family Theater | Public Affairs | *7pm* |
| | | | | *7:15* |
| Mystery Theater | | The Cisco Kid | Walk a Mile | *7:30* |
| | Tom Harmon, sports | | | *7:45* |
| Parlour Politics | Lowell Thomas, news | What's the Name of That Song | One Man's Family | *8pm* |
| | Charles Collingwood, news | | World News | *8:15* |
| Crossfire | Dr. Christian | The Gracie Fields Show | The Great Gildersleeve | *8:30* |
| | | | | *8:45* |
| The Bill Balance Show | The FBI in Peace and War | Newspaper of the Air | You Bet Your Life | *9pm* |
| | | Fulton Lewis Jr., news | | *9:15* |
| | Club Fifteen | Matthew Bell | The Big Story | *9:30* |
| | Armchair Adventures | | | *9:45* |
| News | The Ten o'Clock Wire | I Love a Mystery | The Richfield Reporter | *10pm* |
| Science of the Mind | Bill Keneelly, news | Frank Edwards, news | Joy Forever | *10:15* |
| Drama | The Phil Norman Show | Crowell's Nest | Repeat Performance | *10:30* |
| Music from the Moon | | | | *10:45* |

# EVENING — FALL, 1952

*Thursday*

| | ABC | CBS | MBS | NBC |
|---|---|---|---|---|
| *5pm* | Elroy Hirsch, sports | Edward R. Murrow, news | Sergeant Preston of the Yukon | You and American Unity |
| *5:15* | Virgil Pinkley, news | Tom Harmon, sports | | The Passing Parade |
| *5:30* | Chet Huntley, news | The World Today | Sky King | The Barry Wood Show |
| *5:45* | Robert Garred, news | Frank Goss, news | Cecil Brown, news (5:55PM) | Elmer Patterson, news |
| *6pm* | Hank Weaver, news | The Hollywood Playhouse | Gabriel Heatter, news | H. V. Kaltenborn, news |
| *6:15* | Elmer Davis, news | | The Mutual Newsreel | Bill Hayworth, news |
| *6:30* | Headline Edition | The General Electric Show, Bing Crosby | The Answer Man | The Eddie Cantor Show |
| *6:45* | Music | | Sam Hayes, news | |
| *7pm* | The Silver Eagle | Visiting Time | The Modern Adventures of Casanova | The Judy Canova Show |
| *7:15* | | | | |
| *7:30* | Defense Attorney | Public Affairs | This is for Europe | Truth or Consequences |
| *7:45* | | | | |
| *8pm* | Michael Shayne, Private Detective | Lowell Thomas, news | Distinguished Artists | One Man's Family |
| *8:15* | | Charles Collingwood, news | | World News |
| *8:30* | Remember | The Doris Day Show | The Hardy Family | The Roy Rogers Show |
| *8:45* | Charles Collingwood, news | | | |
| *9pm* | The Bill Balance Show | Meet Millie | Newspaper of the Air | Father Knows Best |
| *9:15* | | | Fulton Lewis Jr., news | |
| *9:30* | | Peggy Lee, songs | The Rod and Gun Club | Musical Americana |
| *9:45* | | Armchair Adventures | | |
| *10pm* | News | The Ten o'Clock Wire | I Love a Mystery | The Richfield Reporter |
| *10:15* | Science of the Mind | Bill Keneelly, news | Frank Edwards, news | Joy Forever |
| *10:30* | Music from the Moon | The Phil Norman Show | Crowell's Nest | Repeat Performance |
| *10:45* | | | | |

# EVENING — FALL, 1952

*Friday*

| ABC | CBS | MBS | NBC | |
|---|---|---|---|---|
| Elroy Hirsch, sports | Edward R. Murrow, news | The Green Hornet | Feature Wire | *5pm* |
| Virgil Pinkley, news | Tom Harmon, sports | | The Passing Parade | *5:15* |
| Chet Huntley, news | The World Today | Wild Bill Hickok | The Barry Wood Show | *5:30* |
| Robert Garred, news | Frank Goss, news | Cecil Brown, news (5:55PM) | Elmer Patterson, news | *5:45* |
| Hank Weaver, news | Ballot Box, 1952 | Gabriel Heatter, news | H. V. Kaltenborn, news | *6pm* |
| Elmer Davis, news | | The Mutual Newsreel | Bill Hayworth, news | *6:15* |
| Headline Edition | | The Answer Man | Music By Mantovani | *6:30* |
| Music | | Sam Hayes, news | | *6:45* |
| Madison Square Garden Boxing | Capitol Cloak Room | Maisie | Hy Gardner Calling | *7pm* |
| | | | Words in the Night | *7:15* |
| Hits and Encores | The Women's Forum | The Cisco Kid | Los Angeles: Fifty Years Ago | *7:30* |
| | | | Melody Time | *7:45* |
| Crime Letter from Dan Dodge | Lowell Thomas, news | Touchdown Tips | One Man's Family | *8pm* |
| | Charles Collingwood, news | | World News | *8:15* |
| This is Your FBI | Gunsmoke | Crime Does Not Pay | Your Hit Parade | *8:30* |
| | | | | *8:45* |
| The Adventures of Ozzie and Harriet | Mr. Keen, Tracer of Lost Persons | Newspaper of the Air | Western Music | *9pm* |
| | | Fulton Lewis Jr., news | | *9:15* |
| Meet Corliss Archer | Club Fifteen | Magazine Theater | Frances Farwell Sings | *9:30* |
| | Armchair Adventures | | Serenade in Blue | *9:45* |
| News | The Ten o'Clock Wire | I Love a Mystery | The Richfield Reporter | *10pm* |
| Science of the Mind | Bill Keneelly, news | Frank Edwards, news | Joy Forever | *10:15* |
| Drama | The Phil Norman Show | Crowell's Nest | Repeat Performance | *10:30* |
| Music from the Moon | | | | *10:45* |

| EVENING — FALL, 1952 | | | | |
|---|---|---|---|---|
| *Saturday* | | | | |
| | ABC | CBS | MBS | NBC |
| *5pm* | The Navy Hour | Gaston Fisher, news | Western Serenade | Are You from Dixie (4:45PM) |
| *5:15* | | Tom Harmon, sports | Report from the Pentagon | |
| *5:30* | Robert Garred, news | The World Today | The California National Guard | |
| *5:45* | Stewart Craig, news | Frank Goss, news | H. R. Baukhage, news | Earl Godwin, news |
| *6pm* | Musical Tintypes | Tarzan | Hawaii Calls | NBC Symphony Orchestra |
| *6:15* | | | | |
| *6:30* | Science Editor | Hopalong Cassidy | Latin Rhythms | |
| *6:45* | Report to the People | | | |
| *7pm* | Speaking for Business | The Camel Caravan, Vaughn Monroe | The US Military Band | Pee Wee King Orchestra |
| *7:15* | As We See It | | | |
| *7:30* | Escape with Me | Broadway is My Beat | Lombardoland USA | Grand Ole Opry |
| *7:45* | | | | |
| *8pm* | The Lone Ranger | The Steve Allen Show | The MGM Theater of the Air | Western Music |
| *8:15* | | | | |
| *8:30* | Newstand Theater | Gene Autry's Melody Ranch | | |
| *8:45* | | | | |
| *9pm* | Marines in Review | Gangbusters | Newspaper of the Air | Terrea Lee, songs |
| *9:15* | | | The Rukeyser Report | Melody Time |
| *9:30* | The Layman's Hour | I Was a Communist for the FBI | Dance Orchestra | Dude Martin's Sunday Preview |
| *9:45* | | | Cecil Brown, news (9:55PM) | |
| *10pm* | The Garden of Eden | The Ten o'Clock Wire | Monica Sings | The Night Reporter |
| *10:15* | The Sextette from Hunger | Bill Keneelly, news | Dance Time | Supervisor Ray Darby, comment |
| *10:30* | Lawrence Welk Orchestra | The Phil Norman Show | Music | Dude Ranch Jamboree |
| *10:45* | | | | |

## DAYTIME — FALL, 1952

*Sunday*

| | ABC | CBS | MBS | NBC |
|---|---|---|---|---|
| *8am* | The Clem Davies Show | The Salt Lake Tabernacle Choir | Journey to Melody (7:30AM) | Grandpa Reads the Funnies |
| *8:15* | | | | |
| *8:30* | The Light and Life Hour | Invitation to Learning | The Back to God Hour | The U.N. is My Beat |
| *8:45* | | | | News |
| *9am* | The Sunday School Hour | The Asia Story | The Radio Bible Class | The Carnival of Books |
| *9:15* | | | | The Christian Science Monitor |
| *9:30* | Sunday with Bill Davidson | Howard K. Smith, news | The Voice of Prophecy | The Eternal Light |
| *9:45* | | Stewart Craig, news | | |
| *10am* | | Bill Costello, news | Newspaper of the Air | Herbert J. Mann, sports |
| *10:15* | | St. Louis Matinee | Sunday Favorites | Crime is Your Problem |
| *10:30* | | The University Explorer | The Lutheran Hour | The University of Chicago Round Table |
| *10:45* | | The U.N. Record | | |
| *11am* | Message of Israel | The Longines Symphonette | Frank and Ernest, songs | The Catholic Hour |
| *11:15* | | | Land of the Free | |
| *11:30* | National Vespers | New York Philharmonic Orchestra | Your Science Reporter | Hometown Happenings |
| *11:45* | | | The Canary Pet Shop | The Garden Guide |
| *12pm* | Christian in Action | | Broadway News | Elmo Roper, news |
| *12:15* | | | Bill Cunningham, news | The World of Books |
| *12:30* | Wings of Healing | Your Invitation to Music | Bands for Bonds | Bob Considine, news |
| *12:45* | | | | Critic at Large |
| *1pm* | The Old Fashioned Revival Hour | News | | The Chase |
| *1:15* | | George Fisher, gossip | Guy Lombardo Orchestra | |
| *1:30* | | Pick the Winner | Clyde Beatty Adventures | Martin Kane, Private Detective |
| *1:45* | | | | |

## DAYTIME — FALL, 1952

*Monday-Friday*

| ABC | CBS | MBS | NBC | |
|---|---|---|---|---|
| The Breakfast Club | The Ralph Story Show | Cecil Brown, news | The Johnny Murray Show | *8am* |
| | News | Gabriel Heatter, news | Coffee Time | *8:15* |
| | Grand Slam | Bible Institute | Pat Bishop, news | *8:30* |
| | Rosemary | | Andy and Virginia, songs | *8:45* |
| Sing with Bing | Wendy Warren and the News | Record Rhapsody | | *9am* |
| Chet Huntley, news | Aunt Jenny's True Life Stories | Capitol Commentary | Victor Lindlahr, health | *9:15* |
| Break the Bank | The Romance of Helen Trent | Nancy Young, talk | Ladies' Day | *9:30* |
| | Our Gal Sunday | | | *9:45* |
| The Jack Berch Show | Big Sister | Newspaper of the Air | News | *10am* |
| Friendly Philosopher | Ma Perkins | Tello-Test Quiz | Bob and Ray | *10:15* |
| My True Story | Young Dr. Malone | The Answer Man | Strike It Rich | *10:30* |
| | The Guiding Light | In the Morgan Manner | | *10:45* |
| Whispering Streets | The Second Mrs. Burton | Ladies Fair | Double or Nothing | *11am* |
| When a Girl Marries | Perry Mason | | | *11:15* |
| The Jack Owens Show | This is Nora Drake | Queen for a Day | The Brighter Day | *11:30* |
| | The Brighter Day | | Neighbor's Voice | *11:45* |
| News | Bill Keneelly, news | Broadway News | The Farm Reporter | *12pm* |
| Paul Harvey, news | Hilltop House | Cedric Foster, news | The Road of Life | *12:15* |
| Play It Again | House Party | The Bell Ringer | Pepper Young's Family | *12:30* |
| | | Behind the Story | The Right to Happiness | *12:45* |
| Bill Ring, talk | Wendell Noble, news | The Jack Kirkwood Show | Mary Noble, Backstage Wife | *1pm* |
| Al Jarvis, talk | It Happens Every Day | | Stella Dallas | *1:15* |
| | The Phil Norman Show | The Lucky U Ranch | Young Widder Brown | *1:30* |
| | | | The Woman in My House | *1:45* |

| DAYTIME — FALL, 1952 | | | | |
|---|---|---|---|---|
| *Sunday* | | | | |
| | ABC | CBS | MBS | NBC |
| *2pm* | The Voice of Prophecy | Arthur Godfrey's Digest | The Shadow | The Hollywood Star Playhouse |
| *2:15* | | | | |
| *2:30* | The Greatest Story Ever Told | World News | True Detective Mysteries | Music |
| *2:45* | | | | Drama |
| *3pm* | The Hour of Decision | America Calling | Nick Carter, Master Detective | Best Plays |
| *3:15* | | | | |
| *3:30* | The Herald of Truth | The Hollywood Barn Dance | Official Detective | |
| *3:45* | | | | |
| *4pm* | Church in Home | The Lucky Strike Program, Jack Benny | News | Meet Your Match |
| *4:15* | | | Music | |
| *4:30* | Politics on Trial | Amos 'n' Andy | Little Symphonies | The Aldrich Family |
| *4:45* | | | | |

## DAYTIME — FALL, 1952

*Monday-Friday*

| ABC | CBS | MBS | NBC | |
|---|---|---|---|---|
| The Ronnie Kemper Show | George Fisher, gossip | Larry Chatterton, news | Just Plain Bill | *2pm* |
| | Arthur Godfrey Time | Club 930 / Guest Star | Front Page Farrell | *2:15* |
| The Tennessee Ernie Ford Show | | Club 930 / Take a Number | Lorenzo Jones | *2:30* |
| | | | The Doctor's Wife | *2:45* |
| | | Club 930 | Welcome, Travelers | *3pm* |
| The Storyteller | | | | *3:15* |
| Cal Tinney, talk | | Lynn at Hollywood | Dr. Paul | *3:30* |
| | Curt Massey, songs | Paula Stone, news | Dial Dave Garroway | *3:45* |
| Mary Margaret McBride, talk | The Beulah Show | Fulton Lewis Jr., news | Life Can Be Beautiful | *4pm* |
| | The Jack Smith Show | Frank Hemingway, news | Pat Bishop, news | *4:15* |
| Nancy Holmes, home talk | Home Folks | Curt Massey, songs | Burritt and Wheeler, talk | *4:30* |
| News | Hawthorne's Mailbag | Sam Hayes, news | | *4:45* |

## DAYTIME — FALL, 1952

*Saturday*

| | ABC | CBS | MBS | NBC |
|---|---|---|---|---|
| *8am* | Flying Feet | Let's Pretend | Bruce McFarlane, news | Morning Music |
| *8:15* | | | Robert Greene, news | |
| *8:30* | A Man and His Music | Give and Take | The Haven of Rest | |
| *8:45* | | | | |
| *9am* | | The Armstrong Theater of Today | The US Marine Band | |
| *9:15* | | | | |
| *9:30* | Space Patrol | Stars Over Hollywood | News | |
| *9:45* | | | Calfornia Civil Defense | |
| *10am* | Ira Cook's Beach Party | Fun for All, Arlene Francis | Newspaper of the Air | On the Scouting Trail |
| *10:15* | | | News | |
| *10:30* | | City Hospital | Strictly Dixie | The Marine Corps Show |
| *10:45* | | | | |
| *11am* | | Music with the Hormel Girls | | Mary Lee Taylor, cooking |
| *11:15* | | | | |
| *11:30* | Sports | Meet the Missus | Music | The National Farm and Home Hour |
| *11:45* | | | | |
| *12pm* | | News | Sid Fuller, news | The Farm Reporter |
| *12:15* | | Gillespie's Garden Guide | Music | Hollywood Varieites |
| *12:30* | | The Space Adventures of Super Noodle | The Man on the Farm | |
| *12:45* | | Stewart Craig, news | | |
| *1pm* | | Galen Drake's Football Roundup | The Men's Corner | Pigskin Parade |
| *1:15* | | | Music | Sports |
| *1:30* | | | College Salute | |
| *1:45* | | | Sports | |

| DAYTIME — FALL, 1952 | | | | |
|---|---|---|---|---|
| *Saturday* | | | | |
| | ABC | CBS | MBS | NBC |
| *2pm* | | | | |
| *2:15* | | | | |
| *2:30* | Ira Cook's Beach Party | News and Views | | |
| *2:45* | | | | |
| *3pm* | | This is Living | | |
| *3:15* | | | | |
| *3:30* | | The Phil Norman Show | | |
| *3:45* | | | | |
| *4pm* | | The Well at Work | | |
| *4:15* | | Wendell Noble, news | | |
| *4:30* | Junior Junction | Stewart Craig, news | Frank Hemingway, news | Musical Scoreboard |
| *4:45* | | Tom Harmon, sports | Music | Are You from Dixie |

# LISTINGS FOR 1953

# EVENING — WINTER, 1953

*Sunday*

| | ABC | CBS | MBS | NBC |
|---|---|---|---|---|
| *5pm* | Mickey Katz Orchestra | The Charlie McCarthy Show | Oklahoma City Symphony Orchestra | Top Story |
| *5:15* | | | | Bylines |
| *5:30* | | Dick Joy, news | | The Theater Guild of the Air |
| *5:45* | | Tom Harmon, sports | | |
| *6pm* | Walter Winchell, gossip | The Hallmark Hall of Fame | | |
| *6:15* | Taylor Grant, news | | Broadway Melodies | |
| *6:30* | Hit Records | Escape | Bandstand USA | Dragnet |
| *6:45* | Presenting Paulena Carter | | | |
| *7pm* | Paul Harvey, news | Broadway is My Beat | The John J. Anthony Program | Barrie Craig, Confidential Investigator |
| *7:15* | Main Street to Malibu | | | |
| *7:30* | Time Capsule | The Whistler | Down You Go | The Phil Harris- Alice Faye Show |
| *7:45* | | | | |
| *8pm* | Drew Pearson, news | Our Miss Brooks | Twenty Questions | Charlene Hawkes and Company |
| *8:15* | Don Gardiner, news | | | |
| *8:30* | Chet Huntley, news | My Little Margie | The Enchanted Hour | The Hour of Music |
| *8:45* | Stewart Craig, news | | | |
| *9pm* | Meditation for Moderns | The Charlie McCarthy Show | Newspaper of the Air | |
| *9:15* | The Sunday Symphony | | Music | |
| *9:30* | | The Lucky Strike Program, Jack Benny | The Chicago Theater of the Air | Stranger from the Sea |
| *9:45* | | | | Mayor Bowron, comment |
| *10pm* | George Sokolsky, news | The Ten o'Clock Wire | | The Richfield Reporter |
| *10:15* | Science of the Mind | George Fisher, gossip | | This Thing Called Life |
| *10:30* | Career Theater | Stewart Craig, news | Music | Meet the Press |
| *10:45* | | Beauty Aid | | |

# EVENING — WINTER, 1953

*Monday*

| ABC | CBS | MBS | NBC | |
|---|---|---|---|---|
| Elroy Hirsch, sports | Edward R. Murrow, news | Bobby Benson | Feature Wire | *5pm* |
| Virgil Pinkley, news | Tom Harmon, sports | | News | *5:15* |
| Chet Huntley, news | The World Today | Wild Bill Hickock | The Voice of Firestone | *5:30* |
| Robert Garred, news | Frank Goss, news | Cecil Brown, news (5:55PM) | | *5:45* |
| Hank Weaver, news | The Lux Radio Theater | Gabriel Heatter, news | H. V. Kaltenborn, news | *6pm* |
| Elmer Davis, news | | The Mutual Newsreel | Bill Hayworth, news | *6:15* |
| Headline Edition | | Behind the Story | The American Way | *6:30* |
| Music | | Sam Hayes, news | | *6:45* |
| The Lone Ranger | The Bob Hawk Show | The Falcon | Hits and Encores | *7pm* |
| | | | | *7:15* |
| Henry J. Taylor, news | Command Theater | The Hall of Fantasy | Al Goodman's Musical Album | *7:30* |
| Alistaire Cooke, comment | | | | *7:45* |
| Life Begins at Eighty | Lowell Thomas, news | Let George Do It | One Man's Family | *8pm* |
| | Charles Collingwood, news | | World News | *8:15* |
| Sparring Partners | Arthur Godfrey's Talent Scouts | Under Arrest | The Railroad Hour | *8:30* |
| | | | | *8:45* |
| Guy Lombardo Records | Suspense | Newspaper of the Air | The Bell Telephone Hour | *9pm* |
| | | Fulton Lewis Jr., news | | *9:15* |
| Footnotes and Music | Club Fifteen | Could This Be You | KFI Calling | *9:30* |
| | Junior Miss | | | *9:45* |
| News | The Ten o'Clock Wire | The Answer Man | The Richfield Reporter | *10pm* |
| Science of the Mind | Bill Keneelly, news | Frank Edwards, news | Joy Forever | *10:15* |
| Music from the Moon | The Phil Norman Show | Crowell's Nest | Repeat Performance | *10:30* |
| | | | | *10:45* |

## EVENING — WINTER, 1953

*Tuesday*

| | ABC | CBS | MBS | NBC |
|---|---|---|---|---|
| *5pm* | Elroy Hirsch, sports | Edward R. Murrow, news | Sergeant Preston of the Yukon | Feature Wire |
| *5:15* | Virgil Pinkley, news | Tom Harmon, sports | | News |
| *5:30* | Chet Huntley, news | The World Today | Sky King | The World We Live In |
| *5:45* | Robert Garred, news | Frank Goss, news | Cecil Brown, news (5:55PM) | Elmer Patterson, news |
| *6pm* | Hank Weaver, news | Life with Luigi | Gabriel Heatter, news | H. V. Kaltenborn, news |
| *6:15* | Elmer Davis, news | | The Mutual Newsreel | Bill Hayworth, news |
| *6:30* | Headline Edition | My Friend Irma | Behind the Story | Fibber McGee and Molly |
| *6:45* | Music | | Sam Hayes, news | |
| *7pm* | The Silver Eagle | People Are Funny | That Hammer Guy | Two for the Money |
| *7:15* | | | | |
| *7:30* | Mr. President | The Hollywood Music Hall | The MBS Roundtable | Frances Farwell and Music |
| *7:45* | | | | |
| *8pm* | America's Town Meeting of the Air | Lowell Thomas, news | The Count of Monte Cristo | One Man's Family |
| *8:15* | | Charles Collingwood, news | | World News |
| *8:30* | | Mr. and Mrs. North | The Story of Dr. Kildare | The Cavalcade of America |
| *8:45* | | | | |
| *9pm* | Perspective | The Doris Day Show | Newspaper of the Air | The Martin and Lewis Show |
| *9:15* | | | Fulton Lewis Jr., news | |
| *9:30* | Report to the People | Club Fifteen | The Search That Never Ends | The Red Skelton Show |
| *9:45* | Science Editor | Junior Miss | | |
| *10pm* | News | The Ten o'Clock Wire | The Answer Man | The Richfield Reporter |
| *10:15* | Science of the Mind | Bill Keneelly, news | Frank Edwards, news | Joy Forever |
| *10:30* | Music from the Moon | The Phil Norman Show | Crowell's Nest | Repeat Performance |
| *10:45* | The Playboys | | | |

# EVENING — WINTER, 1953

*Wednesday*

| ABC | CBS | MBS | NBC | |
|---|---|---|---|---|
| Elroy Hirsch, sports | Edward R. Murrow, news | Songs of the B-Bar-B | Feature Wire | *5pm* |
| Virgil Pinkley, news | Tom Harmon, sports | | News | *5:15* |
| Chet Huntley, news | The World Today | Wild Bill Hickok | The World We Live In | *5:30* |
| Robert Garred, news | Frank Goss, news | Cecil Brown, news (5:55PM) | Elmer Patterson, news | *5:45* |
| Hank Weaver, news | The Lineup | Gabriel Heatter, news | H. V. Kaltenborn, news | *6pm* |
| Elmer Davis, news | | The Mutual Newsreel | Bill Hayworth, news | *6:15* |
| Headline Edition | What's My Line | Behind the Story | Hollywood Varieties | *6:30* |
| Music | | Sam Hayes, news | | *6:45* |
| The Lone Ranger | The Lineup | Music | The Bob Hope Show | *7pm* |
| | | | | *7:15* |
| Mystery Theater | On Stage | The Cisco Kid | Walk a Mile | *7:30* |
| | | | | *7:45* |
| The American Music Hall | Lowell Thomas, news | What's the Name of That Song | One Man's Family | *8pm* |
| | Charles Collingwood, news | | World News | *8:15* |
| Crossfire | Dr. Christian | The Music Hall | The Great Gildersleeve | *8:30* |
| | | | | *8:45* |
| Tales of Tomorrow | The FBI in Peace and War | Newspaper of the Air | You Bet Your Life | *9pm* |
| | | Fulton Lewis Jr., news | | *9:15* |
| Heritage | Club Fifteen | Dear Margie, It's Murder | The Big Story | *9:30* |
| | Junior Miss | | | *9:45* |
| News | The Ten o'Clock Wire | The Answer Man | The Richfield Reporter | *10pm* |
| Science of the Mind | Bill Keneelly, news | Frank Edwards, news | Joy Forever | *10:15* |
| Music from the Moon | The Phil Norman Show | Crowell's Nest | Repeat Performance | *10:30* |
| | | | | *10:45* |

## EVENING — WINTER, 1953

*Thursday*

| | ABC | CBS | MBS | NBC |
|---|---|---|---|---|
| *5pm* | Elroy Hirsch, sports | Edward R. Murrow, news | Sergeant Preston of the Yukon | The Passing Parade |
| *5:15* | Virgil Pinkley, news | Tom Harmon, sports | | News |
| *5:30* | Chet Huntley, news | The World Today | Sky King | The World We Live In |
| *5:45* | Robert Garred, news | Frank Goss, news | Cecil Brown, news (5:55PM) | Elmer Patterson, news |
| *6pm* | Hank Weaver, news | Time for Love | Gabriel Heatter, news | H. V. Kaltenborn, news |
| *6:15* | Elmer Davis, news | | The Mutual Newsreel | Bill Hayworth, news |
| *6:30* | Headline Edition | The General Electric Show, Bing Crosby | Behind the Story | The Eddie Cantor Show |
| *6:45* | Music | | Sam Hayes, news | |
| *7pm* | The Silver Eagle | The Youth Opportunity Program | The Crime Files of Flamond | The Judy Canova Show |
| *7:15* | | | | |
| *7:30* | The Metropolitan Opera Auditions | Visiting Time | Jazz Nocturne | Truth or Consequences |
| *7:45* | | | | |
| *8pm* | Magic Melodies | Lowell Thomas, news | Crime Fighters | One Man's Family |
| *8:15* | | Charles Collingwood, news | | World News |
| *8:30* | | December Bride | Top Tunes with Tendler | The Roy Rogers Show |
| *8:45* | Stewart Craig, news | | | |
| *9pm* | The KECA Pops Concert | Meet Millie | Newspaper of the Air | Father Knows Best |
| *9:15* | | | Fulton Lewis Jr., news | |
| *9:30* | Strike Up the Band | Club Fifteen | The Rod and Gun Club | Musical Americana |
| *9:45* | | Junior Miss | | |
| *10pm* | News | The Ten o'Clock Wire | The Answer Man | The Richfield Reporter |
| *10:15* | Science of the Mind | Bill Keneelly, news | Frank Edwards, news | Joy Forever |
| *10:30* | Music from the Moon | The Phil Norman Show | Crowell's Nest | Repeat Performance |
| *10:45* | The Playboys | | | |

# EVENING — WINTER, 1953

*Friday*

| ABC | CBS | MBS | NBC | |
|---|---|---|---|---|
| Elroy Hirsch, sports | Edward R. Murrow, news | Songs of the B-Bar-B | Feature Wire | *5pm* |
| Virgil Pinkley, news | Tom Harmon, sports | | News | *5:15* |
| Chet Huntley, news | The World Today | Wild Bill Hickok | The World We Live In | *5:30* |
| Robert Garred, news | Frank Goss, news | Cecil Brown, news (5:55PM) | Elmer Patterson, news | *5:45* |
| Hank Weaver, news | Rocky Jordan | Gabriel Heatter, news | H. V. Kaltenborn, news | *6pm* |
| Elmer Davis, news | | The Mutual Newsreel | Bill Hayworth, news | *6:15* |
| Headline Edition | Yours Truly, Johnny Dollar | Behind the Story | Showtime | *6:30* |
| Music | | Sam Hayes, news | | *6:45* |
| Madison Square Garden Boxing | Capitol Cloak Room | Official Detective | Your Income Tax | *7pm* |
| | | | Melody Time | *7:15* |
| Hits and Encores | News on the Record | The Cisco Kid | Los Angeles: Fifty Years Ago | *7:30* |
| | | | Melody Time | *7:45* |
| Crime Letter from Dan Dodge | Lowell Thomas, news | John Steele, Adventurer | One Man's Family | *8pm* |
| | Charles Collingwood, news | | World News | *8:15* |
| This is Your FBI | There's Music in the Air | The Music Hall | The All-Star Bands for Bonds | *8:30* |
| | | | | *8:45* |
| The Adventures of Ozzie and Harriet | Mr. Keen, Tracer of Lost Persons | Newspaper of the Air | Western Music | *9pm* |
| | | Fulton Lewis Jr., news | | *9:15* |
| Meet Corliss Archer | Club Fifteen | The Great Day | Frances Farwell Sings | *9:30* |
| | Junior Miss | | Serenade in Blue | *9:45* |
| News | The Ten o'Clock Wire | The Answer Man | The Richfield Reporter | *10pm* |
| Science of the Mind | Bill Keneelly, news | Frank Edwards, news | Joy Forever | *10:15* |
| The Music School | The Phil Norman Show | Crowell's Nest | Repeat Performance | *10:30* |
| Music from the Moon | | | | *10:45* |

## EVENING — WINTER, 1953

*Saturday*

| | ABC | CBS | MBS | NBC |
|---|---|---|---|---|
| *5pm* | The Navy Hour | Tom Harmon, sports | Report from the Pentagon | Are You from Dixie (4:30PM) |
| *5:15* | | The World Today | Western Serenade | |
| *5:30* | Robert Garred, news | Tom Harmon, sports | Al Helfer, news | Reuben, Reuben |
| *5:45* | Stewart Craig, news | Frank Goss, news | H. R. Baukhage, news | |
| *6pm* | The Garden of Eden | Tarzan | Hawaii Calls | NBC Symphony Orchestra |
| *6:15* | Music | | | |
| *6:30* | Presenting Paulena Carter | Gunsmoke | Take a Number | |
| *6:45* | Your Child and You | | | |
| *7pm* | The CIO and You | The Camel Caravan, Vaughn Monroe | Movie Quiz | Tonight in Hollywood |
| *7:15* | Industry Reports | | | |
| *7:30* | Marines in Review | Dance Orchestra | True or False | Grand Ole Opry |
| *7:45* | | | | |
| *8pm* | The Lone Ranger | Saturday Night, Country Style | College Choir | The Town Hall Party |
| *8:15* | | | | |
| *8:30* | ABC Dancing Party | Gene Autry's Melody Ranch | Lombardoland USA | |
| *8:45* | | | | |
| *9pm* | | Gangbusters | Newspaper of the Air | Terrea Lee, songs |
| *9:15* | | | Record Hits | Supervisor Ray Darby, comment |
| *9:30* | The Layman's Hour | I Was a Communist for the FBI | Radio Free Europe | Meredith Wilson's Music Hall |
| *9:45* | | | Music | |
| *10pm* | News | The Ten o'Clock Wire | The New England Barn Dance | The Night Reporter |
| *10:15* | Income Tax | Bill Keneelly, news | | This Thing Called Love |
| *10:30* | The Music School | The Phil Norman Show | Music | Music |
| *10:45* | Music from the Moon | | Monica Sings | |

## DAYTIME — WINTER, 1953

*Sunday*

| | ABC | CBS | MBS | NBC |
|---|---|---|---|---|
| *8am* | The Clem Davies Show | The Salt Lake Tabernacle Choir | Journey to Melody (7:30AM) | Grandpa Reads the Funnies |
| *8:15* | | | | |
| *8:30* | The Light and Life Hour | Invitation to Learning | The Back to God Hour | The U.N. is My Beat |
| *8:45* | | | | News |
| *9am* | The Sunday School Hour | The Middle East Story | The Radio Bible Class | Carnival of Books |
| *9:15* | | | | The Christian Science Monitor |
| *9:30* | Sunday with Bill Davidson | Howard K. Smith, news | The Voice of Prophecy | The Eternal Light |
| *9:45* | | Stewart Craig, news | | |
| *10am* | | Bill Costello, news | Newspaper of the Air | Herbert J. Mann, sports |
| *10:15* | | The Garden Guild | Sunday Favorites | Bob Crosby Orchestra |
| *10:30* | | The University Explorer | The Lutheran Hour | Investment Information |
| *10:45* | Drama | Treasury Bandstand | | Concert in Miniature |
| *11am* | Message of Israel | The Longines Symphonette | Frank and Ernest, songs | The Catholic Hour |
| *11:15* | | | Land of the Free | |
| *11:30* | National Vespers | New York Philharmonic Orchestra | Your Science Reporter | Hometown Happenings |
| *11:45* | | | The Canary Pet Shop | The Garden Guide |
| *12pm* | Christian in Action | | Broadway News | Elmo Roper, news |
| *12:15* | | | Bill Cunningham, news | The World of Books |
| *12:30* | News | | The US Military Academy Band | Bob Considine, news |
| *12:45* | Drama | | | Critic at Large |
| *1pm* | The Old Fashioned Revival Hour | The Hollywood Story | | The Chase |
| *1:15* | | | Guy Lombardo Orchestra | |
| *1:30* | | The Quiz Kids | Music for You | Jason and the Golden Fleece |
| *1:45* | | | | |

## DAYTIME — WINTER, 1953

*Monday-Friday*

| ABC | CBS | MBS | NBC | |
|---|---|---|---|---|
| The Breakfast Club | The Ralph Story Show | Cecil Brown, news | The Johnny Murray Show | *8am* |
| | News | Gabriel Heatter, news | Coffee Time | *8:15* |
| | Grand Slam | Bible Institute | Pat Bishop, news | *8:30* |
| | Rosemary | | Andy and Virginia, songs | *8:45* |
| The Garden Guide | Wendy Warren and the News | Record Rhapsody | | *9am* |
| Chet Huntley, news | Aunt Jenny's True Life Stories | Capitol Commentary | Victor Lindlahr, health | *9:15* |
| Break the Bank | The Romance of Helen Trent | Nancy Young, talk | Ladies' Day | *9:30* |
| | Our Gal Sunday | | | *9:45* |
| The Jack Berch Show | The Road of Life | Newspaper of the Air | News | *10am* |
| The Hall of Musical Fame | Ma Perkins | Tello-Test Quiz | Bob and Ray | *10:15* |
| My True Story | Young Dr. Malone | The Answer Man | Strike It Rich | *10:30* |
| | The Guiding Light | In the Morgan Manner | | *10:45* |
| Whispering Streets | The Second Mrs. Burton | Ladies Fair | Double or Nothing | *11am* |
| When a Girl Marries | Perry Mason | | | *11:15* |
| Hits and Encores | This is Nora Drake | Queen for a Day | Every Day | *11:30* |
| | The Brighter Day | | The Bob Hope Show | *11:45* |
| News | Bill Keneelly, news | Broadway News | The Farm Reporter | *12pm* |
| Paul Harvey, news | Hilltop House | Cedric Foster, news | The Road of Life | *12:15* |
| The Jack Owens Show | House Party | Music | Pepper Young's Family | *12:30* |
| | | | The Right to Happiness | *12:45* |
| Bill Ring, talk | Wendell Noble, news | The Jack Kirkwood Show | Mary Noble, Backstage Wife | *1pm* |
| Al Jarvis, talk | Home Folks | | Stella Dallas | *1:15* |
| | The Phil Norman Show | The Lucky U Ranch | Young Widder Brown | *1:30* |
| | | | The Woman in My House | *1:45* |

# DAYTIME — WINTER, 1953

*Sunday*

| | ABC | CBS | MBS | NBC |
|---|---|---|---|---|
| *2pm* | The Voice of Prophecy | Arthur Godfrey's Digest | The Shadow | The Hollywood Star Playhouse |
| *2:15* | | | | |
| *2:30* | The Greatest Story Ever Told | World News | True Detective Mysteries | News |
| *2:45* | | | | Pro and Con |
| *3pm* | The Hour of Decision | America Calling | Nick Carter, Master Detective | Best Plays |
| *3:15* | | | | |
| *3:30* | The Herald of Truth | The Hollywood Barn Dance | The Squad Room | |
| *3:45* | | | | |
| *4pm* | Church in Home | The Lucky Strike Program, Jack Benny | News | Meet Your Match |
| *4:15* | | | Music | |
| *4:30* | Wings of Healing | Amos 'n' Andy | The Northwestern Reviewing Stand | The Aldrich Family |
| *4:45* | The Eddie Fisher Show | | Music | |

## DAYTIME — WINTER, 1953

*Monday-Friday*

| ABC | CBS | MBS | NBC | |
|---|---|---|---|---|
| The Ronnie Kemper Show | George Fisher, gossip | Larry Chatterton, news | Just Plain Bill | *2pm* |
| | Arthur Godfrey Time | Talk and Music | Front Page Farrell | *2:15* |
| | | Take a Number | Lorenzo Jones | *2:30* |
| Drama | | | The Doctor's Wife | *2:45* |
| Play It Again | | Club 930 | Welcome, Travelers | *3pm* |
| | | | | *3:15* |
| Cal Tinney, talk | | Lynn at Hollywood | Dr. Paul | *3:30* |
| | Curt Massey, songs | The Mac McGuire Show | Dial Dave Garroway | *3:45* |
| Mary Margaret McBride, talk | Ruth Ashton Reports | Fulton Lewis Jr., news | Life Can Be Beautiful | *4pm* |
| | | Frank Hemingway, news | Pat Bishop, news | *4:15* |
| Nancy Holmes, home talk | The Untold Story | Curt Massey, songs | Burritt and Wheeler, talk | *4:30* |
| News | Hawthorne's Mailbag | Sam Hayes, news | | *4:45* |

## DAYTIME — WINTER, 1953

*Saturday*

| | ABC | CBS | MBS | NBC |
|---|---|---|---|---|
| *8am* | Flying Feet | Grand Central Station | Helen Hall, news | Morning Music |
| *8:15* | | | Robert Greene, news | |
| *8:30* | A Man and His Music | Give and Take | The Haven of Rest | |
| *8:45* | | | | |
| *9am* | Drama | The Armstrong Theater of Today | Strictly Dixie | On the Scouting Trail |
| *9:15* | Mirandy's Garden Patch | | | |
| *9:30* | Space Patrol | Stars Over Hollywood | Here's to Veterans | |
| *9:45* | | | Calfornia Civil Defense | |
| *10am* | Ira Cook's Beach Party | Fun for All, Arlene Francis | Newspaper of the Air | Young America Speaks |
| *10:15* | | | Music | |
| *10:30* | | City Hospital | Symphonies for Youth | Breakfast in Hollywood |
| *10:45* | | | | |
| *11am* | The Metropolitan Opera | Music with the Hormel Girls | | Mary Lee Taylor, cooking |
| *11:15* | | | | |
| *11:30* | | Meet the Missus | Farm Quiz | The National Farm and Home Hour |
| *11:45* | | | | |
| *12pm* | | News | Sid Fuller, news | The Farm Reporter |
| *12:15* | | Gillespie's Garden Guide | Music | Melody Time |
| *12:30* | | Stewart Craig, news | The Man on the Farm | |
| *12:45* | | Gillespie's Garden Guide | | |
| *1pm* | | Let's Pretend | The Men's Corner | The Treasury of Music |
| *1:15* | | | Your Income Tax | |
| *1:30* | | The Phil Norman Show | The Mac McGuire Show | Robert Armbruster Orchestra |
| *1:45* | | | | |

| DAYTIME — WINTER, 1953 | | | | |
|---|---|---|---|---|
| *Saturday* | | | | |
| | ABC | CBS | MBS | NBC |
| *2pm* | | This is Living | The Walter Preston Show | Big City Serenade |
| *2:15* | | | | |
| *2:30* | Drama | This is Los Angeles | | The Marine Corps Show |
| *2:45* | Ira Cook's Beach Party | | | |
| *3pm* | | Income Tax Report | Salute to the Nation | News |
| *3:15* | | Gillespie's Garden Guide | | H. V. Kaltenborn, news |
| *3:30* | | Washington, USA | The 101 Ranch Boys | The Chuck Cecil Show |
| *3:45* | | Larry LeSueur, news | | |
| *4pm* | | Gaston Fisher, news | John Flynn, news | Saturday Segue |
| *4:15* | | Horse Racing | Frank Hemingway, news | |
| *4:30* | The Garden of Eden | | Record Hits | Are You from Dixie |
| *4:45* | The March of Dimes | CBS Farm News | | |

## EVENING — SPRING, 1953

*Sunday*

| | ABC | CBS | MBS | NBC |
|---|---|---|---|---|
| *5pm* | Mickey Katz Orchestra | The Charlie McCarthy Show | Little Symphonies | Bob Considine, news |
| *5:15* | | | | Top Story |
| *5:30* | | Dick Joy, news | | The Theater Guild of the Air |
| *5:45* | Your Telegram (5:55PM) | Tom Harmon, sports | | |
| *6pm* | Walter Winchell, gossip | The Hallmark Hall of Fame | News | |
| *6:15* | Taylor Grant, news | | Report from the Pentagon | |
| *6:30* | Cinema Music | Choral Symphony | Bandstand USA | Dragnet |
| *6:45* | | The International Music Man | | |
| *7pm* | Memory Music | Broadway is My Beat | Little Symphonies | Barrie Craig, Confidential Investigator |
| *7:15* | | | | |
| *7:30* | This Week Around the World | The Whistler | Down You Go | The Phil Harris- Alice Faye Show |
| *7:45* | | | | |
| *8pm* | Don Gardiner, news | Our Miss Brooks | Twenty Questions | Charlene Hawkes and Company |
| *8:15* | Chet Huntley, news | | | |
| *8:30* | Stewart Craig, news | My Little Margie | Treasury Varieties | The Hour of Music |
| *8:45* | Paul Harvey, news | | | |
| *9pm* | Meditation for Moderns | The Charlie McCarthy Show | Newspaper of the Air | |
| *9:15* | Benny Strong Orchestra | | Music | |
| *9:30* | Cathedral Vespers | The Lucky Strike Program, Jack Benny | The Chicago Theater of the Air | Stranger from the Sea |
| *9:45* | | | | Mayor Bowron, comment |
| *10pm* | George Sokolsky, news | The Ten o'Clock Wire | | The Richfield Reporter |
| *10:15* | Science of the Mind | George Fisher, gossip | | This Thing Called Life |
| *10:30* | Career Theater | Music | Music | Meet the Press |
| *10:45* | | | | |

# EVENING — SPRING, 1953

*Monday*

| ABC | CBS | MBS | NBC | |
|---|---|---|---|---|
| Elroy Hirsch, sports | Edward R. Murrow, news | Bobby Benson | Feature Wire | *5pm* |
| Virgil Pinkley, news | Tom Harmon, sports | | News | *5:15* |
| Chet Huntley, news | The World Today | Wild Bill Hickock | The Voice of Firestone | *5:30* |
| Robert Garred, news | Frank Goss, news | Cecil Brown, news (5:55PM) | | *5:45* |
| Len Beardsley, news | The Lux Radio Theater | Gabriel Heatter, news | The Record Album Review | *6pm* |
| Elmer Davis, news | | The Mutual Newsreel | Bill Hayworth, news | *6:15* |
| Headline Edition | | Behind the Story | The American Way | *6:30* |
| Lum and Abner | | Sam Hayes, news | | *6:45* |
| The Lone Ranger | The Bob Hawk Show | The Falcon | The Dinah Shore Show | *7pm* |
| | | | Your Hostess | *7:15* |
| Henry J. Taylor, news | Command Theater | The Hall of Fantasy | Melody Time | *7:30* |
| Alistaire Cooke, comment | | | Institutional Program | *7:45* |
| Life Begins at Eighty | Lowell Thomas, news | Let George Do It | One Man's Family | *8pm* |
| | Robert Trout, news | | World News | *8:15* |
| Standing Room Only | Arthur Godfrey's Talent Scouts | Under Arrest | The Railroad Hour | *8:30* |
| | | | | *8:45* |
| News of Tomorrow | Suspense | Newspaper of the Air | The Bell Telephone Hour | *9pm* |
| The Judy Lynn Trio | | Fulton Lewis Jr., news | | *9:15* |
| Guy Lombardo Orchestra | Club Fifteen | Could This Be You | KFI Calling | *9:30* |
| | Junior Miss | | | *9:45* |
| News | The Ten o'Clock Wire | Elton Britt, news | The Richfield Reporter | *10pm* |
| Science of the Mind | Bill Keneelly, news | Frank Edwards, news | Joy Forever | *10:15* |
| Music from the Moon | The Phil Norman Show | Music | Repeat Performance | *10:30* |
| | | | | *10:45* |

## EVENING — SPRING, 1953

*Tuesday*

| | ABC | CBS | MBS | NBC |
|---|---|---|---|---|
| *5pm* | Elroy Hirsch, sports | Edward R. Murrow, news | Sergeant Preston of the Yukon | Feature Wire |
| *5:15* | Virgil Pinkley, news | Tom Harmon, sports | | News |
| *5:30* | Chet Huntley, news | The World Today | Sky King | The World We Live In |
| *5:45* | Robert Garred, news | Frank Goss, news | Cecil Brown, news (5:55PM) | Elmer Patterson, news |
| *6pm* | Len Beardsley, news | Yours Truly, Johnny Dollar | Gabriel Heatter, news | The Record Album Review |
| *6:15* | Elmer Davis, news | | The Mutual Newsreel | Bill Hayworth, news |
| *6:30* | Headline Edition | My Friend Irma | Behind the Story | Fibber McGee and Molly |
| *6:45* | Lum and Abner | | Sam Hayes, news | |
| *7pm* | The Silver Eagle | People Are Funny | That Hammer Guy | Two for the Money |
| *7:15* | | | | |
| *7:30* | Mr. President | The Hollywood Music Hall | The Affairs of Peter Salem | Melody Time |
| *7:45* | | | | |
| *8pm* | America's Town Meeting of the Air | Lowell Thomas, news | High Adventure | One Man's Family |
| *8:15* | | Robert Trout, news | | World News |
| *8:30* | | Mr. and Mrs. North | The Count of Monte Cristo | Stars from Paris |
| *8:45* | | | | |
| *9pm* | News of Tomorrow | The Doris Day Show | Newspaper of the Air | The Martin and Lewis Show |
| *9:15* | Benny Strong Orchestra | Louella Parsons, gossip | Fulton Lewis Jr., news | |
| *9:30* | Report to the People | Club Fifteen | The Search That Never Ends | The Red Skelton Show |
| *9:45* | Science Editor | Junior Miss | | |
| *10pm* | News | The Ten o'Clock Wire | H. R. Baukhage, news | The Richfield Reporter |
| *10:15* | Science of the Mind | Bill Keneelly, news | Frank Edwards, news | Joy Forever |
| *10:30* | Music from the Moon | The Phil Norman Show | Crowell's Nest | Repeat Performance |
| *10:45* | The Playboys | | | |

# EVENING — SPRING, 1953

*Wednesday*

| ABC | CBS | MBS | NBC | |
|---|---|---|---|---|
| Elroy Hirsch, sports | Edward R. Murrow, news | Songs of the B-Bar-B | Feature Wire | *5pm* |
| Virgil Pinkley, news | Tom Harmon, sports | | News | *5:15* |
| Chet Huntley, news | The World Today | Wild Bill Hickok | The World We Live In | *5:30* |
| Robert Garred, news | Frank Goss, news | Cecil Brown, news (5:55PM) | Elmer Patterson, news | *5:45* |
| Len Beardsley, news | The Phillip Morris Playhouse on Broadway | Gabriel Heatter, news | The Record Album Review | *6pm* |
| Elmer Davis, news | | The Mutual Newsreel | Bill Hayworth, news | *6:15* |
| Headline Edition | What's My Line | Behind the Story | Hollywood Varieties | *6:30* |
| Lum and Abner | | Sam Hayes, news | | *6:45* |
| The Lone Ranger | On Stage | The Family Theater | The Bob Hope Show | *7pm* |
| | | | | *7:15* |
| Mystery Theater | Hawthorne: City Editor | The Cisco Kid | Walk a Mile | *7:30* |
| | | | | *7:45* |
| The Top Guy | Lowell Thomas, news | What's the Name of That Song | One Man's Family | *8pm* |
| | Robert Trout, news | | World News | *8:15* |
| The Adventurer | Dr. Christian | Answers for Americans | The Great Gildersleeve | *8:30* |
| | | | | *8:45* |
| News of Tomorrow | The FBI in Peace and War | Newspaper of the Air | You Bet Your Life | *9pm* |
| Benny Strong Orchestra | | Fulton Lewis Jr., news | | *9:15* |
| Crossfire | Club Fifteen | Dear Margie, It's Murder | The Big Story | *9:30* |
| | Junior Miss | | | *9:45* |
| News | The Ten o'Clock Wire | H. R. Baukhage, news | The Richfield Reporter | *10pm* |
| Science of the Mind | Bill Keneelly, news | Frank Edwards, news | Joy Forever | *10:15* |
| Music from the Moon | The Phil Norman Show | Crowell's Nest | Repeat Performance | *10:30* |
| | | | | *10:45* |

# EVENING — SPRING, 1953

*Thursday*

| | ABC | CBS | MBS | NBC |
|---|---|---|---|---|
| *5pm* | Elroy Hirsch, sports | Edward R. Murrow, news | Sergeant Preston of the Yukon | The Passing Parade |
| *5:15* | Virgil Pinkley, news | Tom Harmon, sports | | News |
| *5:30* | Chet Huntley, news | The World Today | Sky King | The World We Live In |
| *5:45* | Robert Garred, news | Frank Goss, news | Cecil Brown, news (5:55PM) | Elmer Patterson, news |
| *6pm* | Len Beardsley, news | Time for Love | Gabriel Heatter, news | The Record Album Review |
| *6:15* | Elmer Davis, news | | The Mutual Newsreel | Bill Hayworth, news |
| *6:30* | Headline Edition | The General Electric Show, Bing Crosby | Behind the Story | The Eddie Cantor Show |
| *6:45* | Lum and Abner | | Sam Hayes, news | |
| *7pm* | The Silver Eagle | The Youth Opportunity Program | The Crime Files of Flamond | The Judy Canova Show |
| *7:15* | | | | |
| *7:30* | Time Capsule | International Music | The Enchanted Hour | Truth or Consequences |
| *7:45* | | | | |
| *8pm* | Heritage | Lowell Thomas, news | Crime Fighters | One Man's Family |
| *8:15* | | Robert Trout, news | | World News |
| *8:30* | The ABC Radio Workshop | December Bride | Music of the People | The Roy Rogers Show |
| *8:45* | | | | |
| *9pm* | News of Tomorrow | Meet Millie | Newspaper of the Air | Father Knows Best |
| *9:15* | Benny Strong Orchestra | | Fulton Lewis Jr., news | |
| *9:30* | Strike Up the Band | Club Fifteen | Life is Worth Living | Songs That Never Die |
| *9:45* | | Junior Miss | | |
| *10pm* | News | The Ten o'Clock Wire | H. R. Baukhage, news | The Richfield Reporter |
| *10:15* | Science of the Mind | Bill Keneelly, news | Frank Edwards, news | Joy Forever |
| *10:30* | Music from the Moon | The Phil Norman Show | Crowell's Nest | Repeat Performance |
| *10:45* | The Playboys | | | |

## EVENING — SPRING, 1953

*Friday*

| ABC | CBS | MBS | NBC | |
|---|---|---|---|---|
| Elroy Hirsch, sports | Edward R. Murrow, news | Songs of the B-Bar-B | Feature Wire | *5pm* |
| Virgil Pinkley, news | Tom Harmon, sports | | News | *5:15* |
| Chet Huntley, news | The World Today | Wild Bill Hickok | The World We Live In | *5:30* |
| Robert Garred, news | Frank Goss, news | Cecil Brown, news (5:55PM) | Elmer Patterson, news | *5:45* |
| Len Beardsley, news | Rocky Jordan | Gabriel Heatter, news | The Record Album Review | *6pm* |
| Elmer Davis, news | | The Mutual Newsreel | Bill Hayworth, news | *6:15* |
| Headline Edition | Mr. Chameleon | Behind the Story | Showtime | *6:30* |
| Lum and Abner | | Sam Hayes, news | | *6:45* |
| Madison Square Garden Boxing | Capitol Cloak Room | Official Detective | The Dinah Shore Show | *7pm* |
| | | | Words in the Night | *7:15* |
| Hits and Encores | News on the Record | The Cisco Kid | Polka Party | *7:30* |
| | | | Pro and Con | *7:45* |
| Michael Shayne, Private Detective | Lowell Thomas, news | John Steele, Adventurer | One Man's Family | *8pm* |
| | Robert Trout, news | | World News | *8:15* |
| This is Your FBI | Escape | The Music Hall | The All-Star Bands for Bonds | *8:30* |
| | | | | *8:45* |
| The Adventures of Ozzie and Harriet | Mr. Keen, Tracer of Lost Persons | Newspaper of the Air | Western Music | *9pm* |
| | | Fulton Lewis Jr., news | | *9:15* |
| Meet Corliss Archer | Club Fifteen | The Rod and Gun Club | Melody Time | *9:30* |
| | Junior Miss | | Serenade in Blue | *9:45* |
| News | The Ten o'Clock Wire | H. R. Baukhage, news | The Richfield Reporter | *10pm* |
| Science of the Mind | Bill Keneelly, news | Frank Edwards, news | Joy Forever | *10:15* |
| Music from the Moon | The Phil Norman Show | Crowell's Nest | Repeat Performance | *10:30* |
| | | | | *10:45* |

## EVENING — SPRING, 1953

*Saturday*

| | ABC | CBS | MBS | NBC |
|---|---|---|---|---|
| *5pm* | The Navy Hour | Gaston Fischer, news | The Men's Corner | Are You from Dixie (4:30PM) |
| *5:15* | | Tom Harmon, sports | Western Serenade | |
| *5:30* | Robert Garred, news | The World Today | Al Helfer, news | Medicine, USA |
| *5:45* | Stewart Craig, news | Frank Goss, news | H. R. Baukhage, news | News |
| *6pm* | Music | Tarzan | Hawaii Calls | NBC Symphony Orchestra |
| *6:15* | | | | |
| *6:30* | Your Child and You | Gunsmoke | Latin Rhythms | |
| *6:45* | Call to Colors | | | |
| *7pm* | As We See It | The Camel Caravan, Vaughn Monroe | Take a Number | Tex Williams Orchestra |
| *7:15* | Business Voice | | | |
| *7:30* | Marines in Review | Good News: Country Style | True or False | Grand Ole Opry |
| *7:45* | | | | |
| *8pm* | The Lone Ranger | News | College Choir | The Town Hall Party |
| *8:15* | | Music | | |
| *8:30* | ABC Dancing Party | Gene Autry's Melody Ranch | Lombardoland USA | |
| *8:45* | | | | |
| *9pm* | | Gangbusters | Newspaper of the Air | Terrea Lee, songs |
| *9:15* | | | Paul Carter, news | Supervisor Ray Darby, comment |
| *9:30* | The Layman's Hour | I Was a Communist for the FBI | Monica Sings | Meredith Wilson's Music Hall |
| *9:45* | | | Music | |
| *10pm* | News | The Ten o'Clock Wire | Sports | The Night Reporter |
| *10:15* | The American Cancer Socieity | Bill Keneelly, news | | This Thing Called Love |
| *10:30* | Lawrence Welk Orchestra | The Phil Norman Show | | Dangerous Assignment |
| *10:45* | | | | |

| DAYTIME — SPRING, 1953 | | | | |
|---|---|---|---|---|
| *Sunday* | | | | |
| | ABC | CBS | MBS | NBC |
| *8am* | The Clem Davies Show | The Salt Lake Tabernacle Choir | Journey to Melody (7:30AM) | Grandpa Reads the Funnies |
| *8:15* | | | | |
| *8:30* | The Light and Life Hour | Invitation to Learning | The Back to God Hour | The U.N. is My Beat |
| *8:45* | | | | News |
| *9am* | The Sunday School Hour | The Europe Story | The Radio Bible Class | Carnival of Books |
| *9:15* | | | | The Christian Science Monitor |
| *9:30* | Sunday with Bill Davidson | Howard K. Smith, news | The Voice of Prophecy | The Eternal Light |
| *9:45* | | Stewart Craig, news | | |
| *10am* | | Bill Costello, news | Newspaper of the Air | Herbert J. Mann, sports |
| *10:15* | | Treasury Bandstand | Paul Carter, news | Bob Crosby Orchestra |
| *10:30* | | The University Explorer | The Lutheran Hour | Investment Information |
| *10:45* | | Treasury Bandstand | | Senator's Report |
| *11am* | Message of Israel | The Longines Symphonette | Frank and Ernest, songs | The Catholic Hour |
| *11:15* | | | Land of the Free | |
| *11:30* | National Vespers | New York Philharmonic Orchestra | Science Reporter | The American Forum of the Air |
| *11:45* | | | Across the Pacific | |
| *12pm* | Christian in Action | | Broadway News | Hometown Happenings |
| *12:15* | | | Bill Cunningham, news | The World of Books |
| *12:30* | News | | Music | Bob Considine, news |
| *12:45* | Presenting Paulena Carter | | | Critic at Large |
| *1pm* | The Old Fashioned Revival Hour | Music for You | The Lanny Ross Show | The Story of G. I. Joe |
| *1:15* | | | Guy Lombardo Orchestra | |
| *1:30* | | Arthur Godfrey's Digest | Clyde Beatty Adventures | Jason and the Golden Fleece |
| *1:45* | | | | |

| DAYTIME — SPRING, 1953 | | | | |
|---|---|---|---|---|
| *Monday-Friday* | | | | |
| ABC | CBS | MBS | NBC | |
| The Breakfast Club | The Ralph Story Show | Cecil Brown, news | Golden Gags | *8am* |
| | News | Gabriel Heatter, news | The Johnny Murray Show | *8:15* |
| | Grand Slam | Bible Institute | Pat Bishop, news | *8:30* |
| | Rosemary | | Andy and Virginia, songs | *8:45* |
| The Garden Guide | Wendy Warren and the News | Record Rhapsody | | *9am* |
| Chet Huntley, news | Aunt Jenny's True Life Stories | Capitol Commentary | Ladies' Day | *9:15* |
| Turn to a Friend | The Romance of Helen Trent | Nancy Young, talk | | *9:30* |
| | Our Gal Sunday | | News | *9:45* |
| The Jack Berch Show | The Road of Life | Newspaper of the Air | Victor Lindlahr, health | *10am* |
| The Hall of Musical Fame | Ma Perkins | Tello-Test Quiz | The Phrase That Pays | *10:15* |
| My True Story | Young Dr. Malone | The Jack Wagner Show | Strike It Rich | *10:30* |
| | The Guiding Light | | | *10:45* |
| Whispering Streets | The Second Mrs. Burton | Ladies Fair | Double or Nothing | *11am* |
| When a Girl Marries | Perry Mason | | | *11:15* |
| Hits and Encores | This is Nora Drake | Queen for a Day | The Garden Guide | *11:30* |
| | The Brighter Day | | The Bob Hope Show | *11:45* |
| News | Bill Keneelly, news | Broadway News | The Farm Reporter | *12pm* |
| Paul Harvey, news | Hilltop House | Cedric Foster, news | The Road of Life | *12:15* |
| The Jack Owens Show | House Party | Music | Pepper Young's Family | *12:30* |
| | | | The Right to Happiness | *12:45* |
| Bill Ring, talk | Wendell Noble, news | The Jack Kirkwood Show | Mary Noble, Backstage Wife | *1pm* |
| Bill Davidson, talk | Home Folks | | Stella Dallas | *1:15* |
| | The Phil Norman Show | The Lucky U Ranch | Young Widder Brown | *1:30* |
| | | | The Woman in My House | *1:45* |

## DAYTIME — SPRING, 1953

*Sunday*

| | ABC | CBS | MBS | NBC |
|---|---|---|---|---|
| *2pm* | The Voice of Prophecy | | The Shadow | The Chase |
| *2:15* | | | | |
| *2:30* | The Greatest Story Ever Told | Hollywood Story | True Detective Mysteries | The University of Chicago Round Table |
| *2:45* | | | | Pro and Con |
| *3pm* | The Hour of Decision | Baker's Theater of Stars | Nick Carter, Master Detective | Best Plays |
| *3:15* | | | | |
| *3:30* | The Herald of Truth | The Hollywood Barn Dance | The Squad Room | |
| *3:45* | | | | |
| *4pm* | Church in Home | The Lucky Strike Program, Jack Benny | News | My Son Jeep |
| *4:15* | | | Paul Carter, news | |
| *4:30* | Wings of Healing | Amos 'n' Andy | The Northwestern Reviewing Stand | The Aldrich Family |
| *4:45* | | | | |

## DAYTIME — SPRING, 1953

*Monday-Friday*

| ABC | CBS | MBS | NBC | |
|---|---|---|---|---|
| The Todds | George Fisher, gossip | Quick, What's the Answer / Sagebrush Jamboree | Just Plain Bill | *2pm* |
| | Arthur Godfrey Time | | Front Page Farrell | *2:15* |
| The Ronnie Kemper Show | | Fearless Follies | Lorenzo Jones | *2:30* |
| | | | The Doctor's Wife | *2:45* |
| Beat the Record | | | Welcome, Travelers | *3pm* |
| | | | | *3:15* |
| Cal Tinney, talk | | Lynn at Hollywood | Dr. Paul | *3:30* |
| | Curt Massey, songs | The Mac McGuire Show | Dial Dave Garroway | *3:45* |
| Mary Margaret McBride, talk | Ruth Ashton Reports | Fulton Lewis Jr., news | Life Can Be Beautiful | *4pm* |
| | | Frank Hemingway, news | Burritt and Wheeler, talk | *4:15* |
| Nancy Holmes, home talk | Hawthorne: City Editor | Curt Massey, songs | | *4:30* |
| News | | Sam Hayes, news | | *4:45* |

## DAYTIME — SPRING, 1953

*Saturday*

| | ABC | CBS | MBS | NBC |
|---|---|---|---|---|
| *8am* | Flying Feet | Grand Central Station | Paul Carter, news | Golden Gags |
| *8:15* | | | Robert Greene, news | Morning Music |
| *8:30* | A Man and His Music | Give and Take | The Haven of Rest | |
| *8:45* | The Garden of Eden | | | |
| *9am* | A Man and His Music | The Armstrong Theater of Today | Strictly Dixie | Jump Jump and the Ice Queen |
| *9:15* | Mirandy's Garden Patch | | | |
| *9:30* | Space Patrol | Stars Over Hollywood | Here's to Veterans | On the Scouting Trail |
| *9:45* | | | Calfornia Civil Defense | |
| *10am* | Ira Cook's Platter Party | Fun for All, Arlene Francis | Newspaper of the Air | Young America Speaks |
| *10:15* | | | Paul Carter, news | |
| *10:30* | | City Hospital | Symphonies for Youth | Breakfast in Hollywood |
| *10:45* | | | | |
| *11am* | | Music with the Hormel Girls | | Mary Lee Taylor, cooking |
| *11:15* | | | | |
| *11:30* | | Meet the Missus | Farm Quiz | The National Farm and Home Hour |
| *11:45* | | | | |
| *12pm* | | News | Sid Fuller, news | The Farm Reporter |
| *12:15* | | Gillespie's Garden Guide | Music | Repeat Performance |
| *12:30* | | Stewart Craig, news | The Man on the Farm | |
| *12:45* | | Gillespie's Garden Guide | | |
| *1pm* | Horse Racing | Let's Pretend | Club 930 | |
| *1:15* | | | | Melody Time |
| *1:30* | Ira Cook's Platter Party | The Phil Norman Show | | Club Saturday |
| *1:45* | | | | |

## DAYTIME — SPRING, 1953

*Saturday*

| | ABC | CBS | MBS | NBC |
|---|---|---|---|---|
| *2pm* | | This is Living | | |
| *2:15* | | | | |
| *2:30* | | This is Los Angeles | | |
| *2:45* | | | | |
| *3pm* | | Meet Music | | News |
| *3:15* | | | | H. V. Kaltenborn, news |
| *3:30* | | | The US Marine Band | The Chuck Cecil Show |
| *3:45* | | | | |
| *4pm* | | | John Flynn, news | Saturday Segue |
| *4:15* | | | Frank Hemingway, news | |
| *4:30* | The Eddie Fisher Show | Washington, USA | Paul Carter, news | Are You from Dixie |
| *4:45* | | | Music | |

| EVENING — SUMMER, 1953 | | | | |
|---|---|---|---|---|
| *Sunday* | | | | |
| | ABC | CBS | MBS | NBC |
| *5pm* | Music | Junior Miss | Little Symphonies | Bob Considine, news |
| *5:15* | | | | Top Story |
| *5:30* | Al Donahue Orchestra | Dick Joy, news | | Best Plays |
| *5:45* | | Tom Harmon, sports | | |
| *6pm* | News | December Bride | News | |
| *6:15* | Austin Kiplinger, economics | | Report to the Pentagon | |
| *6:30* | Cinema Music | Escape | Music | Confession |
| *6:45* | | | | |
| *7pm* | Memory Music | Broadway is My Beat | Little Symphonies | Barrie Craig, Confidential Investigator |
| *7:15* | | | | |
| *7:30* | This Week Around the World | The Whistler | Down You Go | The Tony Martin Show |
| *7:45* | | | | |
| *8pm* | Don Gardiner, news | Twenty-First Precinct | Twenty Questions | John Kirby and Company |
| *8:15* | Chet Huntley, news | | | |
| *8:30* | Paul Harvey, news | My Little Margie | The Sounding Board | The Hour of Music |
| *8:45* | News | | | |
| *9pm* | Meditation for Moderns | World Dances | Newspaper of the Air | |
| *9:15* | Guest Star | | Music | |
| *9:30* | Cathedral Vespers | Guy Lombardo Orchestra | The Chicago Theater of the Air | Stranger from the Sea |
| *9:45* | | | | Mayor Bowron, comment |
| *10pm* | George Sokolsky, news | The Ten o'Clock Wire | | The Richfield Reporter |
| *10:15* | Science of the Mind | George Fisher, gossip | | Songs |
| *10:30* | Career Theater | The Robert Q. Lewis Show | Music | Meet the Press |
| *10:45* | | | | |

# EVENING — SUMMER, 1953

| *Monday* | | | | |
|---|---|---|---|---|
| ABC | CBS | MBS | NBC | |
| Elroy Hirsch, sports | Edward R. Murrow, news | Bobby Benson | Feature Wire | *5pm* |
| Virgil Pinkley, news | Tom Harmon, sports | | News | *5:15* |
| Chet Huntley, news | The World Today | The City | The Voice of Firestone | *5:30* |
| Robert Garred, news | Frank Goss, news | Cecil Brown, news (5:55PM) | | *5:45* |
| Len Beardsley, news | The Lux Summer Theater | Gabriel Heatter, news | George Putnam, news | *6pm* |
| Elmer Davis, news | | The Mutual Newsreel | Out of the West | *6:15* |
| Three City By-Line | | Behind the Story | The American Way | *6:30* |
| Music | | Sam Hayes, news | | *6:45* |
| The Lone Ranger | Walk a Mile | The Falcon | The Les Paul - Mary Ford Show | *7pm* |
| | | | Your Hostess | *7:15* |
| Henry J. Taylor, news | Arthur Godfrey's Talent Scouts | The Hall of Fantasy | The World We Live In | *7:30* |
| London Column | | | The Nation's Business | *7:45* |
| Guy Lombardo Orchestra | Cedric Adams,, news | Let George Do It | One Man's Family | *8pm* |
| | Music | | World News | *8:15* |
| Chautauqua Symphony Orchestra | Lowell Thomas, news | Under Arrest | The Railroad Hour | *8:30* |
| | Family Skeleton | | | *8:45* |
| | The Johnny Mercer Show | Newspaper of the Air | The Bell Telephone Hour | *9pm* |
| | | Fulton Lewis Jr., news | | *9:15* |
| | Story | Could This Be You | KFI Calling | *9:30* |
| | Hawthorne's Mailbag | | | *9:45* |
| News | The Ten o'Clock Wire | H. R. Baukhage, news | The Richfield Reporter | *10pm* |
| Science of the Mind | Bill Keneelly, news | Frank Edwards, news | Joy Forever | *10:15* |
| Lonesome Gal | The Phil Norman Show | Music | Repeat Performance | *10:30* |
| | | | Sports | *10:45* |

# EVENING — SUMMER, 1953

*Tuesday*

| | ABC | CBS | MBS | NBC |
|---|---|---|---|---|
| *5pm* | Elroy Hirsch, sports | Edward R. Murrow, news | Bobby Benson | Feature Wire |
| *5:15* | Virgil Pinkley, news | Tom Harmon, sports | | News |
| *5:30* | Chet Huntley, news | The World Today | The City | Guy Lombardo Orchestra |
| *5:45* | Robert Garred, news | Frank Goss, news | Cecil Brown, news (5:55PM) | |
| *6pm* | Len Beardsley, news | Yours Truly, Johnny Dollar | Gabriel Heatter, news | George Putnam, news |
| *6:15* | Elmer Davis, news | | The Mutual Newsreel | Out of the West |
| *6:30* | Three City By-Line | Mr. and Mrs. North | Behind the Story | Cousin Willie |
| *6:45* | Music | | Sam Hayes, news | |
| *7pm* | Captain Starr of Space | People Are Funny | That Hammer Guy | Two for the Money |
| *7:15* | | | | |
| *7:30* | Mr. President | The Hollywood Music Hall | The Affairs of Peter Salem | Stan Kenton Orchestra |
| *7:45* | | | | |
| *8pm* | America's Town Meeting of the Air | Louella Parsons, gossip | High Adventure | One Man's Family |
| *8:15* | | Timeless Tales | | World News |
| *8:30* | | Lowell Thomas, news | The Count of Monte Cristo | The Eddie Fisher Show |
| *8:45* | | Family Skeleton | | Sports Digest |
| *9pm* | Discovery | The Johnny Mercer Show | Newspaper of the Air | The Baron and the Bee |
| *9:15* | Literary Greats | | Fulton Lewis Jr., news | |
| *9:30* | Pocket Operetta | Stars | The Search That Never Ends | The First Nighter Program |
| *9:45* | | Hawthorne's Mailbag | | |
| *10pm* | News | The Ten o'Clock Wire | H. R. Baukhage, news | The Richfield Reporter |
| *10:15* | Science of the Mind | Bill Keneelly, news | Frank Edwards, news | Joy Forever |
| *10:30* | Lonesome Gal | The Phil Norman Show | Crowell's Nest | Music |
| *10:45* | | | | Sports |

## EVENING — SUMMER, 1953

*Wednesday*

| ABC | CBS | MBS | NBC | |
|---|---|---|---|---|
| Elroy Hirsch, sports | Edward R. Murrow, news | Bobby Benson | Feature Wire | *5pm* |
| Virgil Pinkley, news | Tom Harmon, sports | | News | *5:15* |
| Chet Huntley, news | The World Today | The City | Bill Stern, sports | *5:30* |
| Robert Garred, news | Frank Goss, news | Cecil Brown, news (5:55PM) | Elmer Patterson, news | *5:45* |
| Len Beardsley, news | The Phillip Morris Playhouse on Broadway | Gabriel Heatter, news | George Putnam, news | *6pm* |
| Elmer Davis, news | | The Mutual Newsreel | Out of the West | *6:15* |
| Three City By-Line | Guy Lombardo Orchestra | Behind the Story | My Son Jeep | *6:30* |
| Music | | Sam Hayes, news | | *6:45* |
| The Lone Ranger | Dr. Christian | The Family Theater | The Scarlet Pimpernel | *7pm* |
| | | | | *7:15* |
| Mike Malloy, Private Eye | Crime Classics | The Cisco Kid | Cilfton Utley, news | *7:30* |
| | | | Report from Washington | *7:45* |
| The Adventurer | The FBI in Peace and War | Crime Fighters | One Man's Family | *8pm* |
| | | | World News | *8:15* |
| Crossfire | Lowell Thomas, news | Answers for Americans | The Great Gildersleeve | *8:30* |
| | Family Skeleton | | | *8:45* |
| Al Donahue Orchestra | The Johnny Mercer Show | Newspaper of the Air | You Bet Your Life | *9pm* |
| | | Fulton Lewis Jr., news | | *9:15* |
| Lawrence Welk Orchestra | Story | Dear Margie, It's Murder | Truth or Consequences | *9:30* |
| | Hawthorne's Mailbag | | | *9:45* |
| News | The Ten o'Clock Wire | H. R. Baukhage, news | The Richfield Reporter | *10pm* |
| Science of the Mind | Bill Keneelly, news | Frank Edwards, news | Joy Forever | *10:15* |
| Lonesome Gal | The Phil Norman Show | Crowell's Nest | Repeat Performance | *10:30* |
| | | | Sports | *10:45* |

## EVENING — SUMMER, 1953

*Thursday*

| | ABC | CBS | MBS | NBC |
|---|---|---|---|---|
| *5pm* | Elroy Hirsch, sports | Edward R. Murrow, news | Bobby Benson | Feature Wire |
| *5:15* | Virgil Pinkley, news | Tom Harmon, sports | | News |
| *5:30* | Chet Huntley, news | The World Today | The City | Bill Stern, sports |
| *5:45* | Robert Garred, news | Frank Goss, news | Cecil Brown, news (5:55PM) | Elmer Patterson, news |
| *6pm* | Len Beardsley, news | Theater of Romance | Gabriel Heatter, news | George Putnam, news |
| *6:15* | Elmer Davis, news | | The Mutual Newsreel | Out of the West |
| *6:30* | Three City By-Line | On Stage | Behind the Story | The Eddie Cantor Show |
| *6:45* | Music | | Sam Hayes, news | |
| *7pm* | Captain Starr of Space | The Youth Opportunity Program | Deadline | The Judy Canova Show |
| *7:15* | | | | |
| *7:30* | Time Capsule | The Theater of Famous Radio Players | The Enchanted Hour | Clifton Utley, news |
| *7:45* | | | | |
| *8pm* | Heritage | Meet Millie | John Steele, Adventurer | One Man's Family |
| *8:15* | | | | World News |
| *8:30* | Times Square | Lowell Thomas, news | London Melody | The Roy Rogers Show |
| *8:45* | | Family Skeleton | | |
| *9pm* | Music | The Boy Scout Jamboree | Newspaper of the Air | Father Knows Best |
| *9:15* | Al Donahue Orchestra | | Fulton Lewis Jr., news | |
| *9:30* | Lawrence Welk Orchestra | Stars | Music | Songs That Never Die |
| *9:45* | | Hawthorne's Mailbag | | |
| *10pm* | News | The Ten o'Clock Wire | H. R. Baukhage, news | The Richfield Reporter |
| *10:15* | Science of the Mind | Bill Keneelly, news | Frank Edwards, news | Joy Forever |
| *10:30* | Lonesome Gal | The Phil Norman Show | Crowell's Nest | Music |
| *10:45* | | | | Sports |

## EVENING — SUMMER, 1953

*Friday*

| ABC | CBS | MBS | NBC | |
|---|---|---|---|---|
| Elroy Hirsch, sports | Edward R. Murrow, news | Bobby Benson | Feature Wire | *5pm* |
| Virgil Pinkley, news | Tom Harmon, sports | | News | *5:15* |
| Chet Huntley, news | The World Today | The City | Bill Stern, sports | *5:30* |
| Robert Garred, news | Frank Goss, news | Cecil Brown, news (5:55PM) | Elmer Patterson, news | *5:45* |
| Len Beardsley, news | Rogers of the Gazette | Gabriel Heatter, news | George Putnam, news | *6pm* |
| Elmer Davis, news | | The Mutual Newsreel | Out of the West | *6:15* |
| Three City By-Line | Summer in St. Louis | Behind the Story | US Marine Corps Band | *6:30* |
| Music | | Sam Hayes, news | | *6:45* |
| Madison Square Garden Boxing | Mr. Chameleon | Official Detective | The All-American Sports Show | *7pm* |
| | | | | *7:15* |
| Emphrada Park Orchestra | News on the Record | The Cisco Kid | Polka Party | *7:30* |
| | | | Everyday | *7:45* |
| The All-Star Parade | Mr. Keen, Tracer of Lost Persons | True or False | One Man's Family | *8pm* |
| | Robert Trout, news | | World News | *8:15* |
| Platterbrains | Lowell Thomas, news | The Music Hall | The Eddie Fisher Show | *8:30* |
| | Family Skeleton | | The Rosemary Clooney Show | *8:45* |
| What's the Name of That Song | The Johnny Mercer Show | Newspaper of the Air | The Town Hall Party | *9pm* |
| | | Fulton Lewis Jr., news | | *9:15* |
| Lawrence Welk Orchestra | Stars | The Titus Moody Show | Music | *9:30* |
| | Hawthorne's Mailbag | | | *9:45* |
| News | The Ten o'Clock Wire | H. R. Baukhage, news | The Richfield Reporter | *10pm* |
| Science of the Mind | Bill Keneelly, news | Frank Edwards, news | Joy Forever | *10:15* |
| Lonesome Gal | The Phil Norman Show | Crowell's Nest | Repeat Performance | *10:30* |
| | | | Sports | *10:45* |

## EVENING — SUMMER, 1953

*Saturday*

| | ABC | CBS | MBS | NBC |
|---|---|---|---|---|
| *5pm* | News | Gaston Fischer, news | The Men's Corner | Saturday Segue |
| *5:15* | Music | Tom Harmon, sports | Western Serenade | |
| *5:30* | Robert Garred, news | The World Today | Al Helfer, news | Music |
| *5:45* | Una Mae Carlisle, songs | Frank Goss, news | Music | News |
| *6pm* | Music | Gangbusters | Hawaii Calls | NBC Summer Symphony |
| *6:15* | | | | |
| *6:30* | Man of Color | Gunsmoke | Latin Rhythms | |
| *6:45* | Report to the People | | | |
| *7pm* | Marines in Review | Saturday Night, Country Style | Take a Number | Tex Williams Orchestra |
| *7:15* | | | | |
| *7:30* | News | Good News: Country Style | The New England Barn Dance | The Tex Ritter Show |
| *7:45* | It's Your Business | | | |
| *8pm* | The Lone Ranger | The Hollywood Barn Dance | Chamber Music | Grand Ole Opry |
| *8:15* | | | | |
| *8:30* | Lawrence Welk Orchestra | Gene Autry's Melody Ranch | Lombardoland USA | The Town Hall Party |
| *8:45* | | | | |
| *9pm* | Al Donahue Orchestra | The Hollywood Caravan | Newspaper of the Air | |
| *9:15* | | | Paul Carter, news | |
| *9:30* | The Layman's Hour | | Monica Sings | Spade Cooley Orchestra |
| *9:45* | | | Music | |
| *10pm* | News | The Ten o'Clock Wire | Sports | New Talent, USA |
| *10:15* | Town and Country | Bill Keneelly, news | | |
| *10:30* | Lawrence Welk Orchestra | The Phil Norman Show | | |
| *10:45* | | | | |

| DAYTIME — SUMMER, 1953 | | | | |
|---|---|---|---|---|
| *Sunday* | | | | |
| | ABC | CBS | MBS | NBC |
| *8am* | The Clem Davies Show | The Salt Lake Tabernacle Choir | Wings of Healing | Grandpa Reads the Funnies |
| *8:15* | | | | |
| *8:30* | The Light and Life Hour | Invitation to Learning | The Back to God Hour | The Carnival of Books |
| *8:45* | | | | Bible Readings |
| *9am* | The Sunday School Hour | The Europe Story | The Radio Bible Class | |
| *9:15* | | | | The Christian Science Monitor |
| *9:30* | Sunday with Bill Davidson | Howard K. Smith, news | The Voice of Prophecy | Words We Live By |
| *9:45* | | Stewart Craig, news | | |
| *10am* | | Bill Costello, news | The Answer Man | Herbert J. Mann, sports |
| *10:15* | | The U.N. on the Record | Sunday Favorites | Serenade in Blue |
| *10:30* | | The University Explorer | The Lutheran Hour | News |
| *10:45* | | Christy Fox, news | | Senator's Report |
| *11am* | Message of Israel | String Serenade | Frank and Ernest, songs | The Catholic Hour |
| *11:15* | | | Land of the Free | |
| *11:30* | National Vespers | World Music Festivals | Featured Artist | The University of Chicago Round Table |
| *11:45* | | | Across the Pacific | |
| *12pm* | Christian in Action | | Broadway News | Hometown Happenings |
| *12:15* | | | Bill Cunningham, news | The World of Books |
| *12:30* | News | | Bandstand USA | The Facts Forum |
| *12:45* | Presenting Paulena Carter | | | Critic at Large |
| *1pm* | The Old Fashioned Revival Hour | The World Today | Guy Lombardo Orchestra | Opera is for Everyone |
| *1:15* | | | | |
| *1:30* | | On a Sunday Afternoon | Music By Kostelanetz | |
| *1:45* | | | | |

| DAYTIME — SUMMER, 1953 | | | | |
|---|---|---|---|---|
| *Monday-Friday* | | | | |
| ABC | CBS | MBS | NBC | |
| The Breakfast Club | The Ralph Story Show | Cecil Brown, news | Murray Talks | *8am* |
| | News | Gabriel Heatter, news | News | *8:15* |
| | Grand Slam | Bible Institute | Pat Bishop, news | *8:30* |
| | Rosemary | | Andy and Virginia, songs | *8:45* |
| The Garden Guide | Wendy Warren and the News | Record Rhapsody | | *9am* |
| Chet Huntley, news | Aunt Jenny's True Life Stories | Capitol Commentary | Ladies' Day | *9:15* |
| Double or Nothing | The Romance of Helen Trent | Nancy Young, talk | | *9:30* |
| Turn to a Friend (9:55AM) | Our Gal Sunday | | News | *9:45* |
| The Jack Berch Show | The Road of Life | Newspaper of the Air | The Ten o'Clock Date | *10am* |
| | Ma Perkins | Tello-Test Quiz | | *10:15* |
| My True Story | Young Dr. Malone | The Jack Wagner Show | Strike It Rich | *10:30* |
| | The Guiding Light | | | *10:45* |
| Whispering Streets | The Second Mrs. Burton | Ladies Fair | The Bob Hope Show | *11am* |
| When a Girl Marries | Perry Mason | | It Pays to Be Married | *11:15* |
| Hits and Encores | This is Nora Drake | Queen for a Day | The Phrase That Pays | *11:30* |
| | The Brighter Day | | Second Chance | *11:45* |
| News | Bill Keneelly, news | Broadway News | The Farm Reporter | *12pm* |
| Paul Harvey, news | Hilltop House | Cedric Foster, news | The Road of Life | *12:15* |
| The Ronnie Kemper Show | House Party | Hughesreel | Pepper Young's Family | *12:30* |
| | | Music | The Right to Happiness | *12:45* |
| Bill Davidson, talk | Arthur Godfrey Time | The Jack Kirkwood Show | Mary Noble, Backstage Wife | *1pm* |
| | | | Stella Dallas | *1:15* |
| | | The Lucky U Ranch | Young Widder Brown | *1:30* |
| | | | The Woman in My House | *1:45* |

# DAYTIME — SUMMER, 1953

*Sunday*

| | ABC | CBS | MBS | NBC |
|---|---|---|---|---|
| *2pm* | The Voice of Prophecy | | The Shadow | |
| *2:15* | | | | |
| *2:30* | Pan-American Union | Hollywood Story | True Detective Mysteries | |
| *2:45* | | | | |
| *3pm* | The Hour of Decision | Your Music | Nick Carter, Master Detective | |
| *3:15* | | | | |
| *3:30* | The Herald of Truth | The Grant Park Concerts | The Squad Room | Youth Wants to Know |
| *3:45* | | | | |
| *4pm* | Church in Home | | News | Jason and the Golden Fleece |
| *4:15* | | | Paul Carter, news | |
| *4:30* | Wings of Healing | Richard Diamond, Private Detective | The Northwestern Reviewing Stand | I Saw Tomorrow |
| *4:45* | | | | |

## DAYTIME — SUMMER, 1953

*Monday-Friday*

| ABC | CBS | MBS | NBC | |
|---|---|---|---|---|
| The Todds | | Quick, What's the Answer / Sagebrush Jamboree | Just Plain Bill | *2pm* |
| | | | Front Page Farrell | *2:15* |
| Meet the Millionaire | Curt Massey, songs | Fearless Follies | Lorenzo Jones | *2:30* |
| | The Wizard of Odds | | The Doctor's Wife | *2:45* |
| Beat the Record | The Story Backyard | | Welcome, Travelers | *3pm* |
| | | | | *3:15* |
| The Jack Owens Show | Off Balance | | Dr. Paul | *3:30* |
| | | Lynn at Hollywood | Dial Dave Garroway | *3:45* |
| Mary Margaret McBride, talk | The Phil Norman Show | Fulton Lewis Jr., news | Life Can Be Beautiful | *4pm* |
| | | Frank Hemingway, news | Burritt and Wheeler, talk | *4:15* |
| Nancy Holmes, home talk | Wendell Noble, news | Curt Massey, songs | | *4:30* |
| News | Fisher: City Editor | Sam Hayes, news | | *4:45* |

| DAYTIME — SUMMER, 1953 | | | | |
|---|---|---|---|---|
| *Saturday* | | | | |
| | ABC | CBS | MBS | NBC |
| *8am* | Flying Feet | Grand Central Station | Record Hits | Music |
| *8:15* | | | Robert Greene, news | |
| *8:30* | A Man and His Music | Give and Take | The Haven of Rest | |
| *8:45* | | | | |
| *9am* | | The Armstrong Theater of Today | Strictly Dixie | Jump Jump and the Ice Queen |
| *9:15* | Mirandy's Garden Patch | | | |
| *9:30* | Space Patrol | Stars Over Hollywood | Here's to Veterans | Music |
| *9:45* | | | Calfornia Civil Defense | |
| *10am* | Ira Cook's Platter Party | Fun for All, Arlene Francis | Newspaper of the Air | Modern Romances |
| *10:15* | | | Paul Carter, news | |
| *10:30* | | City Hospital | The American South | Breakfast in Hollywood |
| *10:45* | | | | |
| *11am* | | Music with the Hormel Girls | | Mary Lee Taylor, cooking |
| *11:15* | | | | |
| *11:30* | | Meet the Missus | Farm Quiz | The National Farm and Home Hour |
| *11:45* | | | | |
| *12pm* | | News | Sid Fuller, news | The Farm Reporter |
| *12:15* | | Gillespie's Garden Guide | Music | Repeat Performance |
| *12:30* | | CBS Farm News | The Man on the Farm | |
| *12:45* | | Gillespie's Garden Guide | | |
| *1pm* | Horse Racing | This is Los Angeles | Records | |
| *1:15* | | | | Melody Time |
| *1:30* | Ira Cook's Platter Party | The Phil Norman Show | | Club Saturday |
| *1:45* | | | | |

## DAYTIME — SUMMER, 1953

*Saturday*

| | ABC | CBS | MBS | NBC |
|---|---|---|---|---|
| *2pm* | | This is Living | | |
| *2:15* | | | | |
| *2:30* | | Meet Music | The Merry-Go-Round | |
| *2:45* | | | | |
| *3pm* | | | | Easy Listening |
| *3:15* | | | | |
| *3:30* | | | The US Army Band | |
| *3:45* | | | | |
| *4pm* | News | | Music | The Record Album Review |
| *4:15* | Music | | Frank Hemingway, news | |
| *4:30* | The Navy Hour | Capitol Cloak Room | Music | |
| *4:45* | | | Guest Star | |

| EVENING — FALL, 1953 | | | | |
|---|---|---|---|---|
| *Sunday* | | | | |
| | ABC | CBS | MBS | NBC |
| *5pm* | Treasury Bandstand | The Hollywood Music Hall | Sunday Symphonies | Bob Considine, news |
| *5:15* | | | | Ask Hollywood |
| *5:30* | | Dick Joy, news | | The Six Shooter |
| *5:45* | Music | Tom Harmon, sports | | |
| *6pm* | Walter Winchell, gossip | The Hallmark Hall of Fame | Under Arrest | Hollywood Story |
| *6:15* | Taylor Grant, news | | | |
| *6:30* | Cinema Time | The Charlie McCarthy Show | State of the Nation | Theater Royal |
| *6:45* | | | | |
| *7pm* | The American Music Hall | Gene Autry's Melody Ranch | Where in the World | Last Man Out |
| *7:15* | | | | |
| *7:30* | This Week Around the World | The Whistler | Twenty Questions | Meet the Press |
| *7:45* | | | | |
| *8pm* | Don Gardiner, news | Our Miss Brooks | The Sounding Board | The Marriage |
| *8:15* | Paul Harvey, news | | | |
| *8:30* | The NY Herald Tribune Forum | My Little Margie | Mr District Attorney | The Hour of Music |
| *8:45* | | | | |
| *9pm* | Meditation for Moderns | The General Electric Show, Bing Crosby | Newspaper of the Air | |
| *9:15* | Songs by Bob Dini | | Music | |
| *9:30* | Cathedral Vespers | The Lucky Strike Program, Jack Benny | The Chicago Theater of the Air | And for Tomorrow |
| *9:45* | | | | Mayor Poulson, comment |
| *10pm* | George Sokolsky, news | The Ten o'Clock Wire | | The Richfield Reporter |
| *10:15* | Science of the Mind | The Answer Man | | Music |
| *10:30* | Career Theater | The Man of the Week | The Men's Corner | |
| *10:45* | | | The Rukeyser Report | The Sixth Army Band |

## EVENING — FALL, 1953

*Monday*

| ABC | CBS | MBS | NBC | |
|---|---|---|---|---|
| Elroy Hirsch, sports | Edward R. Murrow, news | Bobby Benson | Feature Wire | *5pm* |
| Fleetwood Lawton, news | Tom Harmon, sports | | News | *5:15* |
| Chet Huntley, news | The World Today | Wild Bill Hickock | The Voice of Firestone | *5:30* |
| Robert Garred, news | Frank Goss, news | Cecil Brown, news (5:55PM) | | *5:45* |
| Len Beardsley, news | The Lux Radio Theater | Gabriel Heatter, news | George Putnam, news | *6pm* |
| Bill Stern, sports | | Perry Como, songs | Out of the West | *6:15* |
| Lum and Abner | | Virgil Pinkley, news | The American Way | *6:30* |
| John W. Vandercook, news | | Sam Hayes, news | | *6:45* |
| The Lone Ranger | The Camel Caravan, Vaughn Monroe | The Falcon | Fibber McGee and Molly | *7pm* |
| | | | Man on the Go | *7:15* |
| Henry J. Taylor, news | Arthur Godfrey's Talent Scouts | Reporter's Roundup | The World We Live In | *7:30* |
| Headline Edition | | | The Nation's Business | *7:45* |
| Guy Lombardo Orchestra | Suspense | Counterspy | One Man's Family | *8pm* |
| | | | World News | *8:15* |
| Hollywood Stairway | Lowell Thomas, news | Let George Do It | The Railroad Hour | *8:30* |
| Mike Malloy, Private Eye | Family Skeleton | | | *8:45* |
| Celebrity Table | The Beulah Show | Newspaper of the Air | The Bell Telephone Hour | *9pm* |
| | Junior Miss | The Mutual Newsreel | | *9:15* |
| | The Phil Norman Show | Could This Be You | KFI Calling | *9:30* |
| | Here's Hawthorne | | | *9:45* |
| Edwin C. Hill, news | The Ten o'Clock Wire | Fulton Lewis Jr., news | The Richfield Reporter | *10pm* |
| Science of the Mind | Bill Keneelly, news | Frank Edwards, news | Joy Forever | *10:15* |
| Lonesome Gal | The Phil Norman Show | Crowell's Nest | The Al Poska Show | *10:30* |
| | | | | *10:45* |

## EVENING — FALL, 1953

*Tuesday*

| | ABC | CBS | MBS | NBC |
|---|---|---|---|---|
| *5pm* | Elroy Hirsch, sports | Edward R. Murrow, news | Sergeant Preston of the Yukon | Feature Wire |
| *5:15* | Fleetwood Lawton, news | Tom Harmon, sports | | News |
| *5:30* | Chet Huntley, news | The World Today | Sky King | Guy Lombardo Orchestra |
| *5:45* | Robert Garred, news | Frank Goss, news | Cecil Brown, news (5:55PM) | |
| *6pm* | Len Beardsley, news | Yours Truly, Johnny Dollar | Gabriel Heatter, news | George Putnam, news |
| *6:15* | Bill Stern, sports | | Lou and Her Boys | Out of the West |
| *6:30* | Lum and Abner | The Twenty-First Precinct | Virgil Pinkley, news | Rocky Fortune |
| *6:45* | John W. Vandercook, news | | Sam Hayes, news | |
| *7pm* | Captain Starr of Space | People Are Funny | Mickey Spillane Mystery | Fibber McGee and Molly |
| *7:15* | | | | Man on the Go |
| *7:30* | Three City By-Line | Mr. and Mrs. North | The Search That Never Ends | Your Hostess |
| *7:45* | Headline Edition | | | Here's to Veterans |
| *8pm* | Science Editor | Louella Parsons, gossip | High Adventure | One Man's Family |
| *8:15* | Report to the People | Grandma Moses | | World News |
| *8:30* | Hollywood Stairway | Lowell Thomas, news | The Count of Monte Cristo | Coke Time, Eddie Fisher |
| *8:45* | Mike Malloy, Private Eye | Family Skeleton | | The Dinah Shore Show |
| *9pm* | America's Town Meeting of the Air | The Beulah Show | Newspaper of the Air | Dragnet |
| *9:15* | | The Bill Balance Show | The Mutual Newsreel | |
| *9:30* | | Hear the Stars | Betty Clooney and Three Sons | Barrie Craig, Confidential Investigator |
| *9:45* | Music | | Music | |
| *10pm* | Edwin C. Hill, news | The Ten o'Clock Wire | Fulton Lewis Jr., news | The Richfield Reporter |
| *10:15* | Science of the Mind | Bill Keneelly, news | Frank Edwards, news | Joy Forever |
| *10:30* | Lonesome Gal | The Phil Norman Show | Crowell's Nest | The Al Poska Show |
| *10:45* | | | | |

# EVENING — FALL, 1953

*Wednesday*

| ABC | CBS | MBS | NBC | |
|---|---|---|---|---|
| Elroy Hirsch, sports | Edward R. Murrow, news | Songs of the B-Bar-B | Feature Wire | *5pm* |
| Fleetwood Lawton, news | Tom Harmon, sports | | News | *5:15* |
| Chet Huntley, news | The World Today | Wild Bill Hickok | Sports | *5:30* |
| Robert Garred, news | Frank Goss, news | Cecil Brown, news (5:55PM) | Elmer Patterson, news | *5:45* |
| Len Beardsley, news | Dr. Christian | Gabriel Heatter, news | George Putnam, news | *6pm* |
| Bill Stern, sports | | Perry Como, songs | Out of the West | *6:15* |
| Lum and Abner | The Longines Symphonette | Virgil Pinkley, news | Hollywood Searchlight | *6:30* |
| John W. Vandercook, news | | Sam Hayes, news | | *6:45* |
| The Lone Ranger | The Wednesday Night Fights | Deadline | Fibber McGee and Molly | *7pm* |
| | | | Man on the Go | *7:15* |
| Three City By-Line | | The Cisco Kid | Walk a Mile | *7:30* |
| Headline Edition | | | | *7:45* |
| The Philco Radio Playhouse | The FBI in Peace and War | Bulldog Drummond | One Man's Family | *8pm* |
| | | | World News | *8:15* |
| Hollywood Stairway | Lowell Thomas, news | The Family Theater | The Great Gildersleeve | *8:30* |
| Mike Malloy, Private Eye | Family Skeleton | | | *8:45* |
| Mystery Theater | The Beulah Show | Newspaper of the Air | You Bet Your Life | *9pm* |
| | Guy Lombardo Orchestra | The Mutual Newsreel | | *9:15* |
| The NY Herald Tribune Forum | The Phil Norman Show | Betty Clooney and Three Sons | The Big Story | *9:30* |
| | Here's Hawthorne | Music | | *9:45* |
| Edwin C. Hill, news | The Ten o'Clock Wire | Fulton Lewis Jr., news | The Richfield Reporter | *10pm* |
| Science of the Mind | Bill Keneelly, news | Frank Edwards, news | Joy Forever | *10:15* |
| Lonesome Gal | The Phil Norman Show | Crowell's Nest | The Al Poska Show | *10:30* |
| | | | | *10:45* |

## EVENING — FALL, 1953

*Thursday*

| | ABC | CBS | MBS | NBC |
|---|---|---|---|---|
| *5pm* | Elroy Hirsch, sports | Edward R. Murrow, news | Sergeant Preston of the Yukon | Feature Wire |
| *5:15* | Fleetwood Lawton, news | Tom Harmon, sports | | News |
| *5:30* | Chet Huntley, news | The World Today | Sky King | Sports |
| *5:45* | Robert Garred, news | Frank Goss, news | Cecil Brown, news (5:55PM) | Elmer Patterson, news |
| *6pm* | Len Beardsley, news | Meet Mr. McNutley | Gabriel Heatter, news | George Putnam, news |
| *6:15* | Bill Stern, sports | | Lou and Her Boys | Out of the West |
| *6:30* | Lum and Abner | Time for Love | Virgil Pinkley, news | The Eddie Cantor Show |
| *6:45* | John W. Vandercook, news | | Sam Hayes, news | |
| *7pm* | Captain Starr of Space | The Youth Opportunity Program | Official Detective | Fibber McGee and Molly |
| *7:15* | | | | Man on the Go |
| *7:30* | Three City By-Line | The Choraliers | The Rod and Gun Club | Truth or Consequences |
| *7:45* | Headline Edition | | | |
| *8pm* | George Jessel Salutes | Meet Millie | Nightmare | One Man's Family |
| *8:15* | | | | World News |
| *8:30* | Hollywood Stairway | Lowell Thomas, news | The Enchanted Hour | The Roy Rogers Show |
| *8:45* | Mike Malloy, Private Eye | Family Skeleton | | |
| *9pm* | Horatio Hornblower | The Beulah Show | Newspaper of the Air | Father Knows Best |
| *9:15* | | The Bill Balance Show | The Mutual Newsreel | |
| *9:30* | Lawrence Welk Orchestra | Here's Hawthorne | Betty Clooney and Three Sons | Songs That Never Die |
| *9:45* | | | Music | |
| *10pm* | Edwin C. Hill, news | The Ten o'Clock Wire | Fulton Lewis Jr., news | The Richfield Reporter |
| *10:15* | Science of the Mind | Bill Keneelly, news | Frank Edwards, news | Joy Forever |
| *10:30* | Lonesome Gal | The Phil Norman Show | Crowell's Nest | The Al Poska Show |
| *10:45* | | | | |

| EVENING — FALL, 1953 | | | | |
|---|---|---|---|---|
| *Friday* | | | | |
| ABC | CBS | MBS | NBC | |
| Elroy Hirsch, sports | Edward R. Murrow, news | Songs of the B-Bar-B | Feature Wire | *5pm* |
| Fleetwood Lawton, news | Tom Harmon, sports | | News | *5:15* |
| Chet Huntley, news | The World Today | Wild Bill Hickok | Sports | *5:30* |
| Robert Garred, news | Frank Goss, news | Cecil Brown, news (5:55PM) | Elmer Patterson, news | *5:45* |
| Len Beardsley, news | On Stage | Gabriel Heatter, news | George Putnam, news | *6pm* |
| Bill Stern, sports | | Perry Como, songs | Out of the West | *6:15* |
| Lum and Abner | Pigskin Predictions | Virgil Pinkley, news | Rocky Fortune | *6:30* |
| John W. Vandercook, news | News | Sam Hayes, news | | *6:45* |
| Madison Square Garden Boxing | Stagestruck | Take a Number | Fibber McGee and Molly | *7pm* |
| | | | Man on the Go | *7:15* |
| Three City By-Line | | The Cisco Kid | Sound Stage | *7:30* |
| Hits and Encores | | | | *7:45* |
| What's the Name of That Song | Mr. Keen, Tracer of Lost Persons | Starlight Theater | One Man's Family | *8pm* |
| | | | World News | *8:15* |
| Hollywood Stairway | Lowell Thomas, news | Great Day | Coke Time, Eddie Fisher | *8:30* |
| Mike Malloy, Private Eye | Family Skeleton | | The Dinah Shore Show | *8:45* |
| The Adventures of Ozzie and Harriet | The Beulah Show | Newspaper of the Air | The Bob Hope Show | *9pm* |
| | Junior Miss | The Mutual Newsreel | | *9:15* |
| Meet Corliss Archer | The Phil Norman Show | Betty Clooney and Three Sons | The Phil Harris - Alice Faye Show | *9:30* |
| | Here's Hawthorne | Music | | *9:45* |
| Edwin C. Hill, news | The Ten o'Clock Wire | Fulton Lewis Jr., news | The Richfield Reporter | *10pm* |
| Science of the Mind | Bill Keneelly, news | Frank Edwards, news | Joy Forever | *10:15* |
| Lonesome Gal | The Phil Norman Show | Crowell's Nest | The Al Poska Show | *10:30* |
| | | | | *10:45* |

| EVENING — FALL, 1953 | | | | |
|---|---|---|---|---|
| *Saturday* | | | | |
| | ABC | CBS | MBS | NBC |
| *5pm* | The Navy Hour | Gaston Fischer, news | Salute to the Nation | Sports |
| *5:15* | | Tom Harmon, sports | | News |
| *5:30* | Robert Garred, news | The World Today | Report to the Pentagon | The Marine Corp Band |
| *5:45* | Fascinating Rhythm | Frank Goss, news | Music | |
| *6pm* | Music | Gangbusters | Hawaii Calls | The Polka Party |
| *6:15* | | | | |
| *6:30* | Man of Color | Gunsmoke | European Assignment | |
| *6:45* | Your Child and You | | Crowell's Nest | |
| *7pm* | Marines in Review | Two for the Money | | Tex Williams Orchestra |
| *7:15* | | | | |
| *7:30* | As We See It | The Jimmy Wakely Show | Chamber Music | The Tex Ritter Show |
| *7:45* | It's Your Business | | | |
| *8pm* | The Lone Ranger | Saturday Night, Country Style | College Choir | Grand Ole Opry |
| *8:15* | | | | |
| *8:30* | Lawrence Welk Orchestra | | Lombardoland USA | The Town Hall Party |
| *8:45* | | | | |
| *9pm* | Music | Dude Martin's Sunday Preview | Newspaper of the Air | |
| *9:15* | | | Music | |
| *9:30* | The Layman's Hour | Crime Classics | Monica Sings | America's Pop Music |
| *9:45* | | | Music | |
| *10pm* | News | The Ten o'Clock Wire | The Barn Dance Jamboree | |
| *10:15* | Town and Country | Bill Keneelly, news | | |
| *10:30* | Lawrence Welk Orchestra | The Phil Norman Show | | |
| *10:45* | | | | |

## DAYTIME — FALL, 1953

*Sunday*

| | ABC | CBS | MBS | NBC |
|---|---|---|---|---|
| *8am* | The Clem Davies Show | The Salt Lake Tabernacle Choir | Wings of Healing | Grandpa Reads the Funnies |
| *8:15* | | | | |
| *8:30* | The Light and Life Hour | Invitation to Learning | The Back to God Hour | On the Scouting Trail |
| *8:45* | | | | |
| *9am* | The Sunday School Hour | Washington, USA | The Radio Bible Class | Bible Readings |
| *9:15* | | | | The Christian Science Monitor |
| *9:30* | Sunday with Bill Davidson | Howard K. Smith, news | The Voice of Prophecy | The Eternal Light |
| *9:45* | | Stewart Craig, news | | |
| *10am* | | The Answer Man | Newspaper of the Air | Herbert J. Mann, sports |
| *10:15* | | The U.N. on the Record | Frank and Ernest, songs | Agriculture, USA |
| *10:30* | | The University Explorer | The Lutheran Hour | Young America Sings |
| *10:45* | | Christy Fox, news | | |
| *11am* | Message of Israel | The Longines Symphonette | Sunday Favorites | The Catholic Hour |
| *11:15* | | | | |
| *11:30* | National Vespers | New York Philharmonic Orchestra | Featured Artist | Jump Jump and the Ice Queen |
| *11:45* | | | Record Pets of the Week | |
| *12pm* | Christian in Action | | Broadway News | Hometown Happenings |
| *12:15* | Temple Knesseth | | Bill Cunningham, news | The World of Books |
| *12:30* | Religious Lecture | | BBC Bandstand | The Facts Forum |
| *12:45* | | | | News |
| *1pm* | The Old Fashioned Revival Hour | The World Today | Guy Lombardo Orchestra | NBC Symphony Orchestra |
| *1:15* | | | The Lanny Ross Show | |
| *1:30* | | Rogers of the Gazette | Crime Fighters | |
| *1:45* | | | | |

## DAYTIME — FALL, 1953

*Monday-Friday*

| ABC | CBS | MBS | NBC | |
|---|---|---|---|---|
| The Breakfast Club | The Ralph Story Show | Cecil Brown, news | Murray Talks | *8am* |
| | News | Gabriel Heatter, news | | *8:15* |
| | Make Up Your Mind | Bible Institute | Pat Bishop, news | *8:30* |
| | Rosemary | | Andy and Virginia, songs | *8:45* |
| The Garden Guide | Wendy Warren and the News | Record Rhapsody | | *9am* |
| Chet Huntley, news | Aunt Jenny's True Life Stories | Capitol Commentary | Ladies' Day | *9:15* |
| Double or Nothing | The Romance of Helen Trent | Nancy Young, talk | | *9:30* |
| Turn to a Friend (9:55AM) | Our Gal Sunday | | News | *9:45* |
| The Jack Berch Show | The Road of Life | Newspaper of the Air | The Ten o'Clock Date | *10am* |
| | Ma Perkins | Tello-Test Quiz | Second Chance | *10:15* |
| My True Story | Young Dr. Malone | The Jack Wagner Show | Strike It Rich | *10:30* |
| | The Guiding Light | | | *10:45* |
| Whispering Streets | The Second Mrs. Burton | Ladies Fair | The Bob Hope Show | *11am* |
| When a Girl Marries | Perry Mason | | News | *11:15* |
| Modern Romances | This is Nora Drake | Queen for a Day | The Phrase That Pays | *11:30* |
| Hits and Encores | The Brighter Day | | Two Boys and a Girl | *11:45* |
| News | Bill Keneelly, news | Broadway News | The Farm Reporter | *12pm* |
| Paul Harvey, news | Hilltop House | Cedric Foster, news | The Road of Life | *12:15* |
| News | House Party | Fearless Follies | Pepper Young's Family | *12:30* |
| The Ronnie Kemper Show | | | The Right to Happiness | *12:45* |
| Bill Davidson, talk | Arthur Godfrey Time | | Mary Noble, Backstage Wife | *1pm* |
| | | | Stella Dallas | *1:15* |
| | | The Lucky U Ranch | Young Widder Brown | *1:30* |
| | | | The Woman in My House | *1:45* |

## DAYTIME — FALL, 1953

*Sunday*

| | ABC | CBS | MBS | NBC |
|---|---|---|---|---|
| *2pm* | The Voice of Prophecy | Arthur Godfrey's Digest | The Shadow | Opera is for Everyone |
| *2:15* | | | | |
| *2:30* | The Greatest Story Ever Told | Hollywood Story | True Detective Mysteries | |
| *2:45* | | | | |
| *3pm* | The Hour of Decision | The Johnny Mercer Show | Nick Carter, Master Detective | |
| *3:15* | | | | |
| *3:30* | The Herald of Truth | | The Squad Room | |
| *3:45* | | | | |
| *4pm* | Church in Home | The Lucky Strike Program, Jack Benny | News | |
| *4:15* | | | Record Hits | |
| *4:30* | Wings of Healing | Amos 'n' Andy | The Northwestern Reviewing Stand | Waltz Time |
| *4:45* | | | | |

## DAYTIME — FALL, 1953

*Monday-Friday*

| ABC | CBS | MBS | NBC | |
|---|---|---|---|---|
| The Todds | | Quick, What's the Answer / Sagebrush Jamboree | Just Plain Bill | *2pm* |
| | | | Front Page Farrell | *2:15* |
| Jack's Place | Curt Massey, songs | Behind the Story | Lorenzo Jones | *2:30* |
| | The Wizard of Odds | Lynn at Hollywood | It Pays to Be Married | *2:45* |
| Beat the Record | Ruth Ashton Reports | Hughesreel | Welcome, Travelers | *3pm* |
| | The Story's Background | Tello-Test Quiz | | *3:15* |
| The Jack Owen Show | Off Balance | The Jack Kirkwood Show | News | *3:30* |
| | | | Dial Dave Garroway | *3:45* |
| Mary Margaret McBride, talk | The Phil Norman Show | Fulton Lewis Jr., news | Life Can Be Beautiful | *4pm* |
| | | Frank Hemingway, news | Burritt and Wheeler, talk | *4:15* |
| Nancy Holmes, home talk | Wendell Noble, news | Curt Massey, songs | | *4:30* |
| Elmer Davis, news | Fisher: City Editor | Sam Hayes, news | | *4:45* |

## DAYTIME — FALL, 1953

*Saturday*

| | ABC | CBS | MBS | NBC |
|---|---|---|---|---|
| *8am* | Flying Feet | Theater of Romance | Record Hits | The Bass Harris Show |
| *8:15* | | | Frank Singiser, news | |
| *8:30* | A Man and His Music | Give and Take | The Haven of Rest | |
| *8:45* | | | | |
| *9am* | | The Armstrong Theater of Today | Farm Quiz | The Don Otis Show |
| *9:15* | Mirandy's Garden Patch | | | |
| *9:30* | The World Tomorrow | Stars Over Hollywood | The Saturday Notebook | |
| *9:45* | | | Here's to Veterans | |
| *10am* | Ira Cook's Platter Party | Fun for All, Arlene Francis | Newspaper of the Air | |
| *10:15* | | | The Saturday Notebook | |
| *10:30* | | Music with the Hormel Girls | Woody Woodpecker | |
| *10:45* | | | | |
| *11am* | | Meet the Missus | | Mary Lee Taylor, cooking |
| *11:15* | | | | |
| *11:30* | | The Robert Q. Lewis Show | The Saturday Notebook | The National Farm and Home Hour |
| *11:45* | | Galen Drake's Football Roundup | Strictly Dixie | |
| *12pm* | | News | Sid Fuller, news | The Farm Reporter |
| *12:15* | | Gillespie's Garden Guide | Music | |
| *12:30* | | Galen Drake's Football Roundup | The Man on the Farm | Melody Time |
| *12:45* | | | | Song 'n' Dance |
| *1pm* | | | Records | Sports |
| *1:15* | | | The Saturday Notebook | |
| *1:30* | | | College Salute | |
| *1:45* | Sports | | Sports | |

## DAYTIME — FALL, 1953

*Saturday*

| | ABC | CBS | MBS | NBC |
|---|---|---|---|---|
| *2pm* | | | | |
| *2:15* | | | | |
| *2:30* | | This is Los Angeles | | |
| *2:45* | | | | |
| *3pm* | | Do It Yourself | | |
| *3:15* | | | | |
| *3:30* | | The Phil Norman Show | | The Record Album Review |
| *3:45* | | | | |
| *4pm* | | Capitol Cloak Room | | |
| *4:15* | Music | | Frank Hemingway, news | |
| *4:30* | | Meet the Music | The American South | |
| *4:45* | | Press Box | | |

# LISTINGS FOR 1954

# EVENING — WINTER, 1954

*Sunday*

| | ABC | CBS | MBS | NBC |
|---|---|---|---|---|
| *5pm* | Evening Comes | The Hollywood Music Hall | Symphony for Youth | Bob Considine, news |
| *5:15* | | | | News |
| *5:30* | Music By Mantovani | Dick Joy, news | | Sunday at Home, Jan Murray |
| *5:45* | Private Wire | Tom Harmon, sports | | |
| *6pm* | Walter Winchell, gossip | The Hallmark Hall of Fame | Author Meets the Critics | The NBC Star Playhouse |
| *6:15* | Taylor Grant, news | | | |
| *6:30* | Mickey Katz Orchestra | The Charlie McCarthy Show | The Northwestern Reviewing Stand | |
| *6:45* | | | | |
| *7pm* | The American Music Hall | Gene Autry's Melody Ranch | Report to the Pentagon | The Six Shooter |
| *7:15* | | | Hazel Markel, news | |
| *7:30* | This Week Around the World | The Whistler | Twenty Questions | The Phil Harris - Alice Faye Show |
| *7:45* | | | | |
| *8pm* | Don Gardiner, news | Our Miss Brooks | The Sounding Board | Meet the Press |
| *8:15* | Paul Harvey, news | | | |
| *8:30* | Career Theater | My Little Margie | State of the Nation | The Hour of Music |
| *8:45* | | | | |
| *9pm* | Meditation for Moderns | The General Electric Show, Bing Crosby | Newspaper of the Air | |
| *9:15* | Robert Pierce, news | | The Rukeyser Report | |
| *9:30* | Elmer Davis, news | The Lucky Strike Program, Jack Benny | The Chicago Theater of the Air | Last Man Out |
| *9:45* | Presenting Paulena Carter | | | |
| *10pm* | George Sokolsky, news | The Ten o'Clock Wire | | The Richfield Reporter |
| *10:15* | Science of the Mind | The Answer Man | | Mayor Poulson, comment |
| *10:30* | The Old Fashioned Revival Hour | Leading Question | The Men's Corner | Songs That Never Die |
| *10:45* | | | Music | |

## EVENING — WINTER, 1954

*Monday*

| ABC | CBS | MBS | NBC | |
|---|---|---|---|---|
| Elroy Hirsch, sports | Edward R. Murrow, news | Bobby Benson | Feature Wire | *5pm* |
| Fleetwood Lawton, news | Tom Harmon, sports | | News | *5:15* |
| Chet Huntley, news | The World Today | Wild Bill Hickock | The Voice of Firestone | *5:30* |
| Robert Garred, news | Frank Goss, news | Cecil Brown, news (5:55PM) | | *5:45* |
| Len Beardsley, news | The Lux Radio Theater | Gabriel Heatter, news | George Putnam, news | *6pm* |
| Bill Stern, sports | | Music By Kostelanetz | Out of the West | *6:15* |
| Lum and Abner | | Virgil Pinkley, news | The American Way | *6:30* |
| John W. Vandercook, news | | Sam Hayes, news | | *6:45* |
| The Lone Ranger | The Camel Caravan, Vaughn Monroe | The Falcon | Fibber McGee and Molly | *7pm* |
| | | | Man on the Go | *7:15* |
| Henry J. Taylor, news | Arthur Godfrey's Talent Scouts | Could This Be You | The World We Live In | *7:30* |
| Headline Edition | | | The Nation's Business | *7:45* |
| The Metropolitan Opera Auditions | Suspense | Under Arrest | One Man's Family | *8pm* |
| | | | World News | *8:15* |
| Hollywood Stairway | Lowell Thomas, news | Let George Do It | The Railroad Hour | *8:30* |
| Mike Malloy, Private Eye | Family Skeleton | | | *8:45* |
| Brotherhood at Work | The Beulah Show | Newspaper of the Air | The Bell Telephone Hour | *9pm* |
| | The Les Paul - Mary Ford Show | The Mutual Newsreel | | *9:15* |
| Decision | The Bill Balance Show | Reporter's Roundup | The Bergie Music Box | *9:30* |
| | | | | *9:45* |
| Edwin C. Hill, news | The Ten o'Clock Wire | Fulton Lewis Jr., news | The Richfield Reporter | *10pm* |
| Science of the Mind | Bill Keneelly, news | Frank Edwards, news | Joy Forever | *10:15* |
| Lonesome Gal | The Phil Norman Show | The Deems Taylor Show | The Al Poska Show | *10:30* |
| | | | | *10:45* |

## EVENING — WINTER, 1954

*Tuesday*

| | ABC | CBS | MBS | NBC |
|---|---|---|---|---|
| *5pm* | Elroy Hirsch, sports | Edward R. Murrow, news | Sergeant Preston of the Yukon | Feature Wire |
| *5:15* | Fleetwood Lawton, news | Tom Harmon, sports | | News |
| *5:30* | Chet Huntley, news | The World Today | Sky King | Guy Lombardo Orchestra |
| *5:45* | Robert Garred, news | Frank Goss, news | Cecil Brown, news (5:55PM) | |
| *6pm* | Len Beardsley, news | Yours Truly, Johnny Dollar | Gabriel Heatter, news | George Putnam, news |
| *6:15* | Bill Stern, sports | | Bing Crosby Sings | Out of the West |
| *6:30* | Lum and Abner | My Friend Irma | Virgil Pinkley, news | Rocky Fortune |
| *6:45* | John W. Vandercook, news | | Sam Hayes, news | |
| *7pm* | Captain Starr of Space | People Are Funny | Mickey Spillane Mystery | Fibber McGee and Molly |
| *7:15* | | | | Man on the Go |
| *7:30* | Three City By-Line | Mr. and Mrs. North | The Search That Never Ends | KFI Calling |
| *7:45* | Headline Edition | | | |
| *8pm* | Science Editor | Louella Parsons, gossip | High Adventure | One Man's Family |
| *8:15* | Report to the People | Galen Drake, talk | | World News |
| *8:30* | Hollywood Stairway | Lowell Thomas, news | The Count of Monte Cristo | The Dinah Shore Show |
| *8:45* | Mike Malloy, Private Eye | Family Skeleton | | Your Hostess |
| *9pm* | America's Town Meeting of the Air | The Beulah Show | Newspaper of the Air | Dragnet |
| *9:15* | | The Bill Balance Show | The Mutual Newsreel | |
| *9:30* | | | Musical Memories | The Burgie Music Box |
| *9:45* | Monitor News | | | |
| *10pm* | Edwin C. Hill, news | The Ten o'Clock Wire | Fulton Lewis Jr., news | The Richfield Reporter |
| *10:15* | Science of the Mind | Bill Keneelly, news | Frank Edwards, news | Joy Forever |
| *10:30* | Lonesome Gal | The Phil Norman Show | Crowell's Nest | The Al Poska Show |
| *10:45* | | | | |

# EVENING — WINTER, 1954

*Wednesday*

| ABC | CBS | MBS | NBC | |
|---|---|---|---|---|
| Elroy Hirsch, sports | Edward R. Murrow, news | Songs of the B-Bar-B | Feature Wire | *5pm* |
| Fleetwood Lawton, news | Tom Harmon, sports | | News | *5:15* |
| Chet Huntley, news | The World Today | Wild Bill Hickok | Sports | *5:30* |
| Robert Garred, news | Frank Goss, news | Cecil Brown, news (5:55PM) | Elmer Patterson, news | *5:45* |
| Len Beardsley, news | Casey, Crime Photographer | Gabriel Heatter, news | George Putnam, news | *6pm* |
| Bill Stern, sports | | Perry Como, songs | Out of the West | *6:15* |
| Lum and Abner | Guy Lombardo Orchestra | Virgil Pinkley, news | Stars from Paris | *6:30* |
| John W. Vandercook, news | | Sam Hayes, news | | *6:45* |
| The Lone Ranger | Syncopation Piece | Nightmare | Fibber McGee and Molly | *7pm* |
| | | | Man on the Go | *7:15* |
| Three City By-Line | The Longines Symphonette | The Cisco Kid | Walk a Mile | *7:30* |
| Headline Edition | | | | *7:45* |
| The Philco Radio Playhouse | The FBI in Peace and War | Deadline | One Man's Family | *8pm* |
| | | | World News | *8:15* |
| Hollywood Stairway | Lowell Thomas, news | The Family Theater | The Great Gildersleeve | *8:30* |
| Mike Malloy, Private Eye | Family Skeleton | | | *8:45* |
| Mystery Theater | The Beulah Show | Newspaper of the Air | You Bet Your Life | *9pm* |
| | The Les Paul - Mary Ford Show | The Mutual Newsreel | | *9:15* |
| Lawrence Welk Orchestra | The Bill Balance Show | Musical Memories | The Burgie Music Box | *9:30* |
| | | | | *9:45* |
| Edwin C. Hill, news | The Ten o'Clock Wire | Fulton Lewis Jr., news | The Richfield Reporter | *10pm* |
| Science of the Mind | Bill Keneelly, news | Frank Edwards, news | Joy Forever | *10:15* |
| Lonesome Gal | The Phil Norman Show | Crowell's Nest | The Al Poska Show | *10:30* |
| | | | | *10:45* |

| EVENING — WINTER, 1954 | | | | |
|---|---|---|---|---|
| *Thursday* | | | | |
| | ABC | CBS | MBS | NBC |
| *5pm* | Elroy Hirsch, sports | Edward R. Murrow, news | Sergeant Preston of the Yukon | Feature Wire |
| *5:15* | Fleetwood Lawton, news | Tom Harmon, sports | | News |
| *5:30* | Chet Huntley, news | The World Today | Sky King | Sports |
| *5:45* | Robert Garred, news | Frank Goss, news | Cecil Brown, news (5:55PM) | Elmer Patterson, news |
| *6pm* | Len Beardsley, news | Meet Mr. McNutley | Gabriel Heatter, news | George Putnam, news |
| *6:15* | Bill Stern, sports | | Music By Kostelanetz | Out of the West |
| *6:30* | Lum and Abner | Time for Love | Virgil Pinkley, news | The Eddie Cantor Show |
| *6:45* | John W. Vandercook, news | | Sam Hayes, news | |
| *7pm* | Captain Starr of Space | The Twenty-First Precinct | Official Detective | Fibber McGee and Molly |
| *7:15* | | | | Man on the Go |
| *7:30* | Three City By-Line | The Choraliers | The Rod and Gun Club | Truth or Consequences |
| *7:45* | Headline Edition | | | |
| *8pm* | Parade of Music | Meet Millie | Crime Fighters | One Man's Family |
| *8:15* | | | | World News |
| *8:30* | Hollywood Stairway | Lowell Thomas, news | The Enchanted Hour | The Roy Rogers Show |
| *8:45* | Mike Malloy, Private Eye | Family Skeleton | | |
| *9pm* | Horatio Hornblower | The Beulah Show | Newspaper of the Air | Father Knows Best |
| *9:15* | | The Bill Balance Show | The Mutual Newsreel | |
| *9:30* | Hamish Melodies | | Musical Memories | The Burgie Music Box |
| *9:45* | | | | |
| *10pm* | Edwin C. Hill, news | The Ten o'Clock Wire | Fulton Lewis Jr., news | The Richfield Reporter |
| *10:15* | Science of the Mind | Bill Keneelly, news | Frank Edwards, news | Joy Forever |
| *10:30* | Lonesome Gal | The Phil Norman Show | The Deems Taylor Show | The Al Poska Show |
| *10:45* | | | | |

# EVENING — WINTER, 1954

*Friday*

| ABC | CBS | MBS | NBC | |
|---|---|---|---|---|
| Elroy Hirsch, sports | Edward R. Murrow, news | Songs of the B-Bar-B | Feature Wire | *5pm* |
| Fleetwood Lawton, news | Tom Harmon, sports | | News | *5:15* |
| Chet Huntley, news | The World Today | Wild Bill Hickok | Sports | *5:30* |
| Robert Garred, news | Frank Goss, news | Cecil Brown, news (5:55PM) | Elmer Patterson, news | *5:45* |
| Len Beardsley, news | Junior Miss | Gabriel Heatter, news | George Putnam, news | *6pm* |
| Bill Stern, sports | | Perry Como, songs | Out of the West | *6:15* |
| Lum and Abner | That's Rich | Virgil Pinkley, news | The House of Glass | *6:30* |
| John W. Vandercook, news | | Sam Hayes, news | | *6:45* |
| Madison Square Garden Boxing | Arthur Godfrey's Digest | Take a Number | Fibber McGee and Molly | *7pm* |
| | | | Man on the Go | *7:15* |
| Three City By-Line | | The Cisco Kid | Sound Stage | *7:30* |
| Hits and Encores | | | | *7:45* |
| Guy Lombardo Orchestra | Mr. Keen, Tracer of Lost Persons | Take a Number | One Man's Family | *8pm* |
| | | | World News | *8:15* |
| Hollywood Stairway | Lowell Thomas, news | Have a Heart | The Dinah Shore Show | *8:30* |
| Mike Malloy, Private Eye | Family Skeleton | | Income Tax | *8:45* |
| The Adventures of Ozzie and Harriet | The Beulah Show | Newspaper of the Air | The Bob Hope Show | *9pm* |
| | The Les Paul - Mary Ford Show | The Mutual Newsreel | | *9:15* |
| What's the Name of That Song | The Bill Balance Show | Musical Memories | The Burgie Music Box | *9:30* |
| | | | | *9:45* |
| Edwin C. Hill, news | The Ten o'Clock Wire | Fulton Lewis Jr., news | The Richfield Reporter | *10pm* |
| Science of the Mind | Bill Keneelly, news | Frank Edwards, news | Joy Forever | *10:15* |
| Lonesome Gal | The Phil Norman Show | Crowell's Nest | The Big Story | *10:30* |
| | | | | *10:45* |

## EVENING — WINTER, 1954

*Saturday*

| | ABC | CBS | MBS | NBC |
|---|---|---|---|---|
| *5pm* | Science Editor | Gaston Fischer, news | Woody Woodpecker | Melody Time |
| *5:15* | Income Tax | Tom Harmon, sports | | News |
| *5:30* | Robert Garred, news | The World Today | | Saturday Segue |
| *5:45* | Know Your Schools | Frank Goss, news | | |
| *6pm* | Anonymous | Gangbusters | Hawaii Calls | The Polka Party |
| *6:15* | | | | |
| *6:30* | Man of Color | Gunsmoke | Dinner Melodies | |
| *6:45* | Your Child and You | | | |
| *7pm* | Marines in Review | Two for the Money | Farm Quiz | The Tex Williams Show |
| *7:15* | | | | |
| *7:30* | It's Your Business | The Jimmy Wakely Show | Chamber Music | The Tex Ritter Show |
| *7:45* | Crowley Reports | | | |
| *8pm* | The Lone Ranger | Saturday Night, Country Style | College Choir | Grand Ole Opry |
| *8:15* | | | | |
| *8:30* | Lawrence Welk Orchestra | | Lombardoland USA | The Town Hall Party |
| *8:45* | | | | |
| *9pm* | | Dude Martin Orchestra | Newspaper of the Air | |
| *9:15* | | | TheNational Guard | |
| *9:30* | The Layman's Hour | Crime Classics | Monica Sings | The Burgie Music Box |
| *9:45* | | | The Mel Hinke Trio | |
| *10pm* | News | The Ten o'Clock Wire | The Barn Dance Jamboree | America's Pop Music |
| *10:15* | Church Service | Bill Keneelly, news | | |
| *10:30* | Lawrence Welk Orchestra | The Phil Norman Show | | |
| *10:45* | | | | |

## DAYTIME — WINTER, 1954

*Sunday*

| | ABC | CBS | MBS | NBC |
|---|---|---|---|---|
| *8am* | The Clem Davies Show | The Salt Lake Tabernacle Choir | Wings of Healing | Grandpa Reads the Funnies |
| *8:15* | | | | |
| *8:30* | The Light and Life Hour | Invitation to Learning | The Back to God Hour | On the Scouting Trail |
| *8:45* | | | | |
| *9am* | The Sunday School Hour | Capitol Cloak Room | The Radio Bible Class | Bible Readings |
| *9:15* | | | | The Christian Science Monitor |
| *9:30* | The World Tomorrow | Howard K. Smith, news | The Voice of Prophecy | The Eternal Light |
| *9:45* | | The Answer Man | | |
| *10am* | Sunday with Bill Davidson | Man's Right to Knowledge | Newspaper of the Air | Herbert J. Mann, sports |
| *10:15* | | | Frank and Ernest, songs | Hometown Happenings |
| *10:30* | | The University Explorer | The Lutheran Hour | Sunday Report |
| *10:45* | | Christy Fox, news | | Senator's Report |
| *11am* | Message of Israel | The Longines Symphonette | Keep Healthy | The Catholic Hour |
| *11:15* | | | Land of the Free | |
| *11:30* | National Vespers | New York Philharmonic Orchestra | Across the Blue Pacific | Young America Sings |
| *11:45* | | | Record Pets of the Week | |
| *12pm* | Christian in Action | | Broadway News | The Shirley Thomas Show |
| *12:15* | | | Bill Cunningham, news | |
| *12:30* | Religious Lecture | | Sunday Serenade | The Facts Forum |
| *12:45* | | | | The World of Books |
| *1pm* | The Old Fashioned Revival Hour | The Twentieth Century Concert Hall | Counterspy | Opera is for Everyone |
| *1:15* | | | | |
| *1:30* | | The World Today | Nick Carter, Master Detective | |
| *1:45* | | | | |

## DAYTIME — WINTER, 1954

*Monday-Friday*

| ABC | CBS | MBS | NBC | |
|---|---|---|---|---|
| The Breakfast Club | The Ralph Story Show | Historical Footnotes | Murray Talks | *8am* |
| | News | Gabriel Heatter, news | | *8:15* |
| | Make Up Your Mind | Bible Institute | Pat Bishop, news | *8:30* |
| | Rosemary | | Andy and Virginia, songs | *8:45* |
| The Garden Guide | Wendy Warren and the News | Record Rhapsody | | *9am* |
| Chet Huntley, news | Aunt Jenny's True Life Stories | Capitol Commentary | Ladies' Day | *9:15* |
| Modern Romances | The Romance of Helen Trent | Nancy Young, talk | | *9:30* |
| | Our Gal Sunday | | News | *9:45* |
| The Jack Berch Show | The Road of Life | Newspaper of the Air | Art Baker's Notebook | *10am* |
| | Ma Perkins | Tello-Test Quiz | Second Chance | *10:15* |
| My True Story | Young Dr. Malone | The Jack Wagner Show | Strike It Rich | *10:30* |
| | The Guiding Light | | | *10:45* |
| Whispering Streets | The Second Mrs. Burton | Wonderful City | The Bob Hope Show | *11am* |
| When a Girl Marries | Perry Mason | | News | *11:15* |
| Grand Central Station | This is Nora Drake | Queen for a Day | The Phrase That Pays | *11:30* |
| | The Brighter Day | | Two Boys and a Girl | *11:45* |
| News | Bill Keneelly, news | Broadway News | The Farm Reporter | *12pm* |
| Paul Harvey, news | Hilltop House | Cedric Foster, news | The Road of Life | *12:15* |
| News | House Party | Tapestiries of Life | Pepper Young's Family | *12:30* |
| The Todds | | The Jack Wagner Show | The Right to Happiness | *12:45* |
| Bill Davidson, talk | Arthur Godfrey Time | | Mary Noble, Backstage Wife | *1pm* |
| | | | Stella Dallas | *1:15* |
| | | Ladies Fair | Young Widder Brown | *1:30* |
| | | | The Woman in My House | *1:45* |

## DAYTIME — WINTER, 1954

*Sunday*

| | ABC | CBS | MBS | NBC |
|---|---|---|---|---|
| *2pm* | The Voice of Prophecy | Rogers of the Gazette | The Shadow | |
| *2:15* | | | | |
| *2:30* | The Greatest Story Ever Told | Stagestruck | True Detective Mysteries | |
| *2:45* | | | | |
| *3pm* | The Hour of Decision | The Johnny Mercer Show | Bulldog Drummond | |
| *3:15* | | | | |
| *3:30* | The Herald of Truth | | The Squad Room | NBC Symphony Orchestra |
| *3:45* | | | | |
| *4pm* | Church in Home | The Lucky Strike Program, Jack Benny | Oklahoma City Symphony Orchestra | |
| *4:15* | | | | |
| *4:30* | Wings of Healing | Amos 'n' Andy | | The Marriage |
| *4:45* | | | | |

## DAYTIME — WINTER, 1954

*Monday-Friday*

| ABC | CBS | MBS | NBC | |
|---|---|---|---|---|
| The Ronnie Kemper Show | | Quick, What's the Answer / The Johnny Olsen Show | Just Plain Bill | *2pm* |
| Romance in Music | | | Front Page Farrell | *2:15* |
| | Curt Massey, songs | Behind the Story | Lorenzo Jones | *2:30* |
| | The Wizard of Odds | Lynn at Hollywood | It Pays to Be Married | *2:45* |
| Beat the Record | Ruth Ashton Reports | Hughesreel | Welcome, Travelers | *3pm* |
| | The Story's Background | Tello-Test Quiz | | *3:15* |
| The Jack Owen Show | Off Balance | The Jack Kirkwood Show | Dr. Paul | *3:30* |
| | | | News | *3:45* |
| Mary Margaret McBride, talk | The Phil Norman Show | Fulton Lewis Jr., news | Life Can Be Beautiful | *4pm* |
| | | Frank Hemingway, news | Burritt and Wheeler, talk | *4:15* |
| Nancy Holmes, home talk | Fisher: City Editor | Curt Massey, songs | | *4:30* |
| Elmer Davis, news | | Sam Hayes, news | | *4:45* |

| DAYTIME — WINTER, 1954 | | | | |
|---|---|---|---|---|
| *Saturday* | | | | |
| | ABC | CBS | MBS | NBC |
| *8am* | A Man and His Music | The Robert Q. Lewis Show | The Basil DeSoto Show | The Bass Harris Show |
| *8:15* | | | Frank Singiser, news | |
| *8:30* | | | The Haven of Rest | |
| *8:45* | | | | |
| *9am* | | The Armstrong Theater of Today | Flying Feet | Jump Jump and the Ice Queen |
| *9:15* | Mirandy's Garden Patch | | | |
| *9:30* | Space Patrol | Stars Over Hollywood | The Basil DeSoto Show | Song and Dance |
| *9:45* | | | Here's to Veterans | |
| *10am* | Ira Cook's Platter Party | City Hospital | Newspaper of the Air | |
| *10:15* | | | The Basil DeSoto Show | |
| *10:30* | | Music with the Hormel Girls | The Don Otis Show | |
| *10:45* | | | | |
| *11am* | The Metropolitan Opera | Galen Drake, talk | | Mary Lee Taylor, cooking |
| *11:15* | | | | |
| *11:30* | | | The Basil DeSoto Show | The National Farm and Home Hour |
| *11:45* | | | Strictly Dixie | |
| *12pm* | | News | Sid Fuller, news | The Farm Reporter |
| *12:15* | | Gillespie's Garden Guide | Music | The Farmland Party Line |
| *12:30* | | CBS Farm News | The Man on the Farm | |
| *12:45* | | The Les Paul - Mary Ford Show | | |
| *1pm* | | This is Los Angeles | The Frank Evans Show | Now Hear This |
| *1:15* | | | | |
| *1:30* | | The Phil Norman Show | | |
| *1:45* | | | | |

| DAYTIME — WINTER, 1954 | | | | |
|---|---|---|---|---|
| *Saturday* | | | | |
| | ABC | CBS | MBS | NBC |
| *2pm* | | Do It Yourself | | |
| *2:15* | | | | |
| *2:30* | Ira Cook's Platter Party | Gardening is Fun | | |
| *2:45* | | Meet the Music | | |
| *3pm* | | | | The Record Album Review |
| *3:15* | | | | |
| *3:30* | | | | |
| *3:45* | | | | |
| *4pm* | Platterbrains | | | |
| *4:15* | | Horse Racing | Frank Hemingway, news | |
| *4:30* | The Navy Hour | | Your Income Tax | |
| *4:45* | | Income Tax Report | | |

## EVENING — SPRING, 1954

*Sunday*

| | ABC | CBS | MBS | NBC |
|---|---|---|---|---|
| *5pm* | Evening Comes | The Charlie McCartny Show | News | Theater Royal |
| *5:15* | | | The Globetrotters | |
| *5:30* | | Dick Joy, news | The Enchanted Hour | The Shirley Thomas Show |
| *5:45* | Private Wire | Tom Harmon, sports | | |
| *6pm* | Walter Winchell, gossip | The Hallmark Hall of Fame | The Triumphant Hour | Quiet Mood |
| *6:15* | Taylor Grant, news | | | |
| *6:30* | Mickey Katz Orchestra | The Northwestern Reviewing Stand | The Northwestern Reviewing Stand | The Golden Hour |
| *6:45* | | | | |
| *7pm* | The American Music Hall | Gene Autry's Melody Ranch | Alan Helfer, news | |
| *7:15* | | | Hazel Markel, news | |
| *7:30* | This Week Around the World | The Whistler | The Army Show | The Phil Harris - Alice Faye Show |
| *7:45* | | | | |
| *8pm* | Don Gardiner, news | Our Miss Brooks | The Sounding Board | Inheritance |
| *8:15* | Paul Harvey, news | | | |
| *8:30* | Career Theater | My Little Margie | State of the Nation | The Hour of Music |
| *8:45* | | | | |
| *9pm* | Meditation for Moderns | The General Electric Show, Bing Crosby | Newspaper of the Air | |
| *9:15* | Elmer Davis, news | | The Rukeyser Report | |
| *9:30* | Reverand Fritchman, religion | The Lucky Strike Program, Jack Benny | The Chicago Theater of the Air | Meet the Press |
| *9:45* | Camp Meeting | | | |
| *10pm* | | The Ten o'Clock Wire | | The Richfield Reporter |
| *10:15* | Science of the Mind | The Answer Man | | Mayor Poulson, comment |
| *10:30* | The Old Fashioned Revival Hour | Leading Question | The Garden Show | Songs That Never Die |
| *10:45* | | | Music | |

## EVENING — SPRING, 1954

*Monday*

| ABC | CBS | MBS | NBC | |
|---|---|---|---|---|
| Elroy Hirsch, sports | Edward R. Murrow, news | Bobby Benson | Feature Wire | *5pm* |
| Len Beardsley, news | Today in Los Angeles | | News | *5:15* |
| Chet Huntley, news | Tom Harmon, sports | Wild Bill Hickock | The Voice of Firestone | *5:30* |
| Robert Garred, news | Frank Goss, news | Cecil Brown, news (5:55PM) | | *5:45* |
| Quincy Howe, news | The Lux Radio Theater | Gabriel Heatter, news | George Putnam, news | *6pm* |
| Bill Stern, sports | | Music By Kostelanetz | Sports | *6:15* |
| Music By Mantovani | | Virgil Pinkley, news | The American Way | *6:30* |
| John W. Vandercook, news | | Sam Hayes, news | | *6:45* |
| The Lone Ranger | Night Watch | The Falcon | Fibber McGee and Molly | *7pm* |
| | | | Out of the West | *7:15* |
| Henry J. Taylor, news | Arthur Godfrey's Talent Scouts | Could This Be You | The World We Live In | *7:30* |
| Headline Edition | | | The Nation's Business | *7:45* |
| Back to the Bible | Suspense | Under Arrest | One Man's Family | *8pm* |
| | | | World News | *8:15* |
| Lum and Abner | Lowell Thomas, news | Let George Do It | The Railroad Hour | *8:30* |
| Hollywood Stairway | The Tennessee Ernie Ford Show | | | *8:45* |
| Brotherhood at Work | The Beulah Show | Newspaper of the Air | The Bell Telephone Hour | *9pm* |
| | The Julius LaRosa Show | Guy Lombardo Orchestra | | *9:15* |
| Doorway to the Future | The Bergie Music Box | Reporter's Roundup | American Bandstand | *9:30* |
| | | | | *9:45* |
| Edwin C. Hill, news | The Ten o'Clock Wire | Fulton Lewis Jr., news | The Richfield Reporter | *10pm* |
| Science of the Mind | Carroll Alcott, news | Frank Edwards, news | Joy Forever | *10:15* |
| Lonesome Gal | The Phil Norman Show | Sports | The Al Poska Show | *10:30* |
| | | | | *10:45* |

## EVENING — SPRING, 1954

*Tuesday*

| | ABC | CBS | MBS | NBC |
|---|---|---|---|---|
| *5pm* | Elroy Hirsch, sports | Edward R. Murrow, news | Bobby Benson | Feature Wire |
| *5:15* | Len Beardsley, news | Today in Los Angeles | | News |
| *5:30* | Chet Huntley, news | Tom Harmon, sports | Sky King | Guy Lombardo Orchestra |
| *5:45* | Robert Garred, news | Frank Goss, news | Cecil Brown, news (5:55PM) | |
| *6pm* | Quincy Howe, news | Yours Truly, Johnny Dollar | Gabriel Heatter, news | George Putnam, news |
| *6:15* | Bill Stern, sports | | The Answer Man | Sports |
| *6:30* | Music By Mantovani | My Friend Irma | Virgil Pinkley, news | Elmer Patterson, news |
| *6:45* | John W. Vandercook, news | | Sam Hayes, news | Melody Time |
| *7pm* | Captain Starr of Space | People Are Funny | Mickey Spillane Mystery | Fibber McGee and Molly |
| *7:15* | | | | Out of the West |
| *7:30* | Three City By-Line | Mr. and Mrs. North | The Search That Never Ends | KFI Calling |
| *7:45* | Headline Edition | | | |
| *8pm* | Back to the Bible | Louella Parsons, gossip | High Adventure | One Man's Family |
| *8:15* | | News | | World News |
| *8:30* | Lum and Abner | Lowell Thomas, news | Author Meets the Critics | The Dinah Shore Show |
| *8:45* | Hollywood Stairway | The Tennessee Ernie Ford Show | | Your Hostess |
| *9pm* | America's Town Meeting of the Air | The Beulah Show | Newspaper of the Air | Dragnet |
| *9:15* | | The Bill Balance Show | Guy Lombardo Orchestra | |
| *9:30* | | The Bergie Music Box | Manhattan Crossroads | American Bandstand |
| *9:45* | Monitor News | | Edward Arnold, comment | |
| *10pm* | Edwin C. Hill, news | The Ten o'Clock Wire | Fulton Lewis Jr., news | The Richfield Reporter |
| *10:15* | Science of the Mind | Carroll Alcott, news | Frank Edwards, news | Joy Forever |
| *10:30* | Lonesome Gal | The Phil Norman Show | Sports | The Al Poska Show |
| *10:45* | | | | |

# EVENING — SPRING, 1954

*Wednesday*

| ABC | CBS | MBS | NBC | |
|---|---|---|---|---|
| Elroy Hirsch, sports | Edward R. Murrow, news | Songs of the B-Bar-B | Feature Wire | *5pm* |
| Len Beardsley, news | Today in Los Angeles | | News | *5:15* |
| Chet Huntley, news | Tom Harmon, sports | Wild Bill Hickok | The Record Album Review | *5:30* |
| Robert Garred, news | Frank Goss, news | Cecil Brown, news (5:55PM) | Elmer Patterson, news | *5:45* |
| Quincy Howe, news | Casey, Crime Photographer | Gabriel Heatter, news | George Putnam, news | *6pm* |
| Bill Stern, sports | | Perry Como, songs | Sports | *6:15* |
| Music By Mantovani | Guy Lombardo Orchestra | Virgil Pinkley, news | Barry Craig, Confidential Investigator | *6:30* |
| John W. Vandercook, news | | Sam Hayes, news | | *6:45* |
| The Lone Ranger | The Twenty-First Precinct | The Squad Room | Fibber McGee and Molly | *7pm* |
| | | | Out of the West | *7:15* |
| Three City By-Line | The Longines Symphonette | The Cisco Kid | Walk a Mile | *7:30* |
| Headline Edition | | | | *7:45* |
| Back to the Bible | The FBI in Peace and War | Nightmare | One Man's Family | *8pm* |
| | | | World News | *8:15* |
| Lum and Abner | Lowell Thomas, news | The Family Theater | The Great Gildersleeve | *8:30* |
| Hollywood Stairway | The Tennessee Ernie Ford Show | | | *8:45* |
| Mystery Theater | The Beulah Show | Newspaper of the Air | You Bet Your Life | *9pm* |
| | The Julius LaRosa Show | Guy Lombardo Orchestra | | *9:15* |
| Beautiful to See | The Bergie Music Box | Manhattan Crossroads | American Bandstand | *9:30* |
| | | Robert Hurleigh, news | | *9:45* |
| Edwin C. Hill, news | The Ten o'Clock Wire | Fulton Lewis Jr., news | The Richfield Reporter | *10pm* |
| Science of the Mind | Carroll Alcott, news | Frank Edwards, news | Joy Forever | *10:15* |
| Lonesome Gal | The Phil Norman Show | Sports | The Al Poska Show | *10:30* |
| | | | | *10:45* |

| EVENING — SPRING, 1954 | | | | |
|---|---|---|---|---|
| *Thursday* | | | | |
| | ABC | CBS | MBS | NBC |
| *5pm* | Elroy Hirsch, sports | Edward R. Murrow, news | Sergeant Preston of the Yukon | Feature Wire |
| *5:15* | Len Beardsley, news | Today in Los Angeles | | News |
| *5:30* | Chet Huntley, news | Tom Harmon, sports | Sky King | The Record Album Review |
| *5:45* | Robert Garred, news | Frank Goss, news | Cecil Brown, news (5:55PM) | Elmer Patterson, news |
| *6pm* | Quincy Howe, news | Meet Mr. McNutley | Gabriel Heatter, news | George Putnam, news |
| *6:15* | Bill Stern, sports | | The Answer Man | Sports |
| *6:30* | Music By Mantovani | Time for Love | Virgil Pinkley, news | The Eddie Cantor Show |
| *6:45* | John W. Vandercook, news | | Sam Hayes, news | |
| *7pm* | Captain Starr of Space | On Stage | Official Detective | Fibber McGee and Molly |
| *7:15* | | | | Out of the West |
| *7:30* | Three City By-Line | The Choraliers | The Rod and Gun Club | Truth or Consequences |
| *7:45* | Headline Edition | | | |
| *8pm* | Back to the Bible | Meet Millie | Crime Fighters | One Man's Family |
| *8:15* | | | | World News |
| *8:30* | Lum and Abner | Lowell Thomas, news | London Melodies | The Roy Rogers Show |
| *8:45* | Hollywood Stairway | The Tennessee Ernie Ford Show | | |
| *9pm* | The World We Live In | The Beulah Show | Newspaper of the Air | The Six Shooter |
| *9:15* | | The Bill Balance Show | Guy Lombardo Orchestra | |
| *9:30* | The All-Star Review | The Bergie Music Box | Manhattan Crossroads | American Bandstand |
| *9:45* | | | Edward Arnold, comment | |
| *10pm* | Edwin C. Hill, news | The Ten o'Clock Wire | Fulton Lewis Jr., news | The Richfield Reporter |
| *10:15* | Science of the Mind | Carroll Alcott, news | Frank Edwards, news | Joy Forever |
| *10:30* | Lonesome Gal | The Phil Norman Show | Sports | The Al Poska Show |
| *10:45* | | | | |

## EVENING — SPRING, 1954

*Friday*

| ABC | CBS | MBS | NBC | |
|---|---|---|---|---|
| Elroy Hirsch, sports | Edward R. Murrow, news | Songs of the B-Bar-B | Feature Wire | *5pm* |
| Len Beardsley, news | Today in Los Angeles | | News | *5:15* |
| Chet Huntley, news | Tom Harmon, sports | Wild Bill Hickok | The Record Album Review | *5:30* |
| Robert Garred, news | Frank Goss, news | Cecil Brown, news (5:55PM) | Elmer Patterson, news | *5:45* |
| Quincy Howe, news | Junior Miss | Gabriel Heatter, news | George Putnam, news | *6pm* |
| Bill Stern, sports | | Perry Como, songs | Sports | *6:15* |
| Music By Mantovani | That's Rich | Virgil Pinkley, news | Can You Top This | *6:30* |
| John W. Vandercook, news | | Sam Hayes, news | | *6:45* |
| Madison Square Garden Boxing | Arthur Godfrey's Digest | Starlight Theater | Fibber McGee and Molly | *7pm* |
| | | | Out of the West | *7:15* |
| Three City By-Line | | The Cisco Kid | Sound Stage | *7:30* |
| Hits and Encores | | | | *7:45* |
| Back to the Bible | Mr. Keen, Tracer of Lost Persons | Take a Number | One Man's Family | *8pm* |
| | | | World News | *8:15* |
| Lum and Abner | Lowell Thomas, news | Have a Heart | The Dinah Shore Show | *8:30* |
| Hollywood Stairway | The Tennessee Ernie Ford Show | | To Be Perfectly Frank | *8:45* |
| The Adventures of Ozzie and Harriet | The Beulah Show | Newspaper of the Air | The Bob Hope Show | *9pm* |
| | The Julius LaRosa Show | Think | | *9:15* |
| What's the Name of That Song | The Bergie Music Box | Manhattan Crossroads | American Bandstand | *9:30* |
| | | Robert Hurleigh, news | | *9:45* |
| Edwin C. Hill, news | The Ten o'Clock Wire | Fulton Lewis Jr., news | The Richfield Reporter | *10pm* |
| Science of the Mind | Carroll Alcott, news | Frank Edwards, news | Joy Forever | *10:15* |
| Lonesome Gal | The Phil Norman Show | Sports | The Big Story | *10:30* |
| | | | | *10:45* |

# EVENING — SPRING, 1954

*Saturday*

| | ABC | CBS | MBS | NBC |
|---|---|---|---|---|
| *5pm* | Science Editor | Gaston Fischer, news | Music | Motorist Melody |
| *5:15* | Army Reserve | Today in Los Angeles | Al Helfer, news | H. C. McClellan, news |
| *5:30* | Robert Garred, news | Tom Harmon, sports | Guest Star | Saturday Segue |
| *5:45* | Know Your Schools | Frank Goss, news | Sports | |
| *6pm* | Presenting Paulena Carter | Gangbusters | Hawaii Calls | The Polka Party |
| *6:15* | Rex Koury, news | | | |
| *6:30* | Man of Color | Gunsmoke | The Garden Show | |
| *6:45* | Your Child and You | | Dinner Melodies | |
| *7pm* | Marines in Review | Two for the Money | Farm Quiz | Tex Williams Orchestra |
| *7:15* | | | | |
| *7:30* | In Washington | The Jimmy Wakely Show | Music By Kostelanetz | The Tex Ritter Show |
| *7:45* | As We See It | | | |
| *8pm* | The Lone Ranger | Saturday Night, Country Style | College Choir | Grand Ole Opry |
| *8:15* | | | | |
| *8:30* | News and Views | Crime Classics | Lombardoland USA | The Town Hall Party |
| *8:45* | | | | |
| *9pm* | Lawrence Welk Orchestra | The Jimmy Wakely Show | Newspaper of the Air | |
| *9:15* | | | Forward March | |
| *9:30* | The Layman's Hour | The Burgie Music Box | Monica Sings | American Bandstand |
| *9:45* | | | The Mel Hinke Trio | |
| *10pm* | News | The Ten o'Clock Wire | Sports | America's Pop Music |
| *10:15* | Reserve | Carroll Alcott, news | | |
| *10:30* | Lawrence Welk Orchestra | The Phil Norman Show | | |
| *10:45* | | | | |

## DAYTIME — SPRING, 1954

*Sunday*

| | ABC | CBS | MBS | NBC |
|---|---|---|---|---|
| *8am* | The Clem Davies Show | The Salt Lake Tabernacle Choir | Wings of Healing | Grandpa Reads the Funnies |
| *8:15* | | | | |
| *8:30* | The Light and Life Hour | Invitation to Learning | The Back to God Hour | On the Scouting Trail |
| *8:45* | | | | |
| *9am* | The Sunday School Hour | Capitol Cloak Room | The Radio Bible Class | Bible Readings |
| *9:15* | | | | The Christian Science Monitor |
| *9:30* | The World Tomorrow | Howard K. Smith, news | The Voice of Prophecy | The Eternal Light |
| *9:45* | | The Answer Man | | |
| *10am* | Sunday with Bill Davidson | Galen Drake, talk | Newspaper of the Air | Herbert J. Mann, sports |
| *10:15* | | | Frank and Ernest, songs | Hometown Happenings |
| *10:30* | | The University Explorer | The Lutheran Hour | The California Sportsman |
| *10:45* | | Christy Fox, news | | Senators Report |
| *11am* | Message of Israel | The Longines Symphonette | The Garden Show | The Catholic Hour |
| *11:15* | | | Land of the Free | |
| *11:30* | National Vespers | New York Philharmonic Orchestra | Sunday Favorites | Young America Sings |
| *11:45* | | | Across the Blue Pacific | |
| *12pm* | Christian in Action | | Broadway News | The University of Chicago Round Table |
| *12:15* | | | Bill Cunningham, news | |
| *12:30* | Religious Lecture | | Sunday Serenade | The Facts Forum |
| *12:45* | | | The Garden Show | The World of Books |
| *1pm* | The Old Fashoined Revival Hour | The Twentieth Century Concert Hall | Guy Lombardo Orchestra | Opera is for Everyone |
| *1:15* | | | | |
| *1:30* | | The World Today | Flight in the Blue | |
| *1:45* | | | | |

# DAYTIME — SPRING, 1954

*Monday-Friday*

| ABC | CBS | MBS | NBC | |
|---|---|---|---|---|
| The Breakfast Club | The Ralph Story Show | Historical Footnotes | Murray Talks | *8am* |
| | News | Gabriel Heatter, news | | *8:15* |
| | Make Up Your Mind | Bible Institute | Pat Bishop, news | *8:30* |
| | Rosemary | | Andy and Virginia, songs | *8:45* |
| The Garden Guide | Wendy Warren and the News | Melody Manor | | *9am* |
| Chet Huntley, news | Aunt Jenny's True Life Stories | Capitol Commentary | Ladies' Day | *9:15* |
| Beat the Record | The Romance of Helen Trent | Nancy Young, talk | | *9:30* |
| Ever Since Eve | Our Gal Sunday | | News | *9:45* |
| The Todds | The Road of Life | Newspaper of the Air | Art Baker's Notebook | *10am* |
| | Ma Perkins | Tello-Test Quiz | Second Chance | *10:15* |
| My True Story | Young Dr. Malone | The Jack Wagner Show | Strike It Rich | *10:30* |
| | The Guiding Light | | | *10:45* |
| Whispering Streets | The Second Mrs. Burton | The Madeleine Carroll Show | The Bob Hope Show | *11am* |
| When a Girl Marries | Perry Mason | | News | *11:15* |
| Modern Romances | This is Nora Drake | Queen for a Day | The Phrase That Pays | *11:30* |
| Songs of Love | The Brighter Day | | Lady's Book | *11:45* |
| News | Bill Keneelly, news | Broadway News | The Farm Reporter | *12pm* |
| Paul Harvey, news | Hilltop House | Cedric Foster, news | The Road of Life | *12:15* |
| News | House Party | Tapestiries of Life | Pepper Young's Family | *12:30* |
| Your Town | | The Jack Wagner Show | The Right to Happiness | *12:45* |
| Bill Davidson, talk | Arthur Godfrey Time | | Mary Noble, Backstage Wife | *1pm* |
| | | | Stella Dallas | *1:15* |
| | | | Young Widder Brown | *1:30* |
| | | | The Woman in My House | *1:45* |

## DAYTIME — SPRING, 1954

*Sunday*

| | ABC | CBS | MBS | NBC |
|---|---|---|---|---|
| *2pm* | The Voice of Prophecy | Stagestruck | The Shadow | |
| *2:15* | | | | |
| *2:30* | The Greatest Story Ever Told | | True Detective Mysteries | |
| *2:45* | | | | |
| *3pm* | The Hour of Decision | The Johnny Mercer Show | Nick Carter, Master Detective | |
| *3:15* | | | | |
| *3:30* | The Herald of Truth | | Bob Considine, news | NBC Spring Symphony |
| *3:45* | | | Alan Wismer, sports | |
| *4pm* | Church in Home | The Lucky Strike Program, Jack Benny | Oklahoma City Symphony Orchestra | |
| *4:15* | | | | |
| *4:30* | Wings of Healing | Amos 'n' Andy | | The American Forum of the Air |
| *4:45* | | | | |

## DAYTIME — SPRING, 1954

*Monday-Friday*

| ABC | CBS | MBS | NBC | |
|---|---|---|---|---|
| Murder in the Afternoon | | Quick, What's the Answer / The Johnny Olsen Show | Just Plain Bill | *2pm* |
| | | | Front Page Farrell | *2:15* |
| | Curt Massey, songs | Let's Go to Town | Lorenzo Jones | *2:30* |
| | The Wizard of Odds | Lynn at Hollywood | It Pays to Be Married | *2:45* |
| Beat the Record / Mike Malloy, Private Eye | Ruth Ashton Reports | Crowell's Nest | Welcome, Travelers | *3pm* |
| Ever Since Eve | Off Balance | | | *3:15* |
| Make Believe Ballroom | | Behind the Story | Dr. Paul | *3:30* |
| | | Tello-Test Quiz | News | *3:45* |
| Mary Margaret McBride, talk | The Phil Norman Show | Fulton Lewis Jr., news | Life Can Be Beautiful | *4pm* |
| | | Frank Hemingway, news | Burritt and Wheeler, talk | *4:15* |
| Nancy Holmes, home talk | Fisher: City Editor | Curt Massey, songs | | *4:30* |
| Elmer Davis, news | | Sam Hayes, news | | *4:45* |

## DAYTIME — SPRING, 1954

*Saturday*

| | ABC | CBS | MBS | NBC |
|---|---|---|---|---|
| *8am* | A Man and His Music | The Robert Q. Lewis Show | The Basil DeSoto Show | The Bass Harris Show |
| *8:15* | | | Frank Singiser, news | |
| *8:30* | | | The Haven of Rest | |
| *8:45* | | | | |
| *9am* | | The Armstrong Theater of Today | Flying Feet | Jump Jump and the Ice Queen |
| *9:15* | Mirandy's Garden Patch | | | |
| *9:30* | Space Patrol | Stars Over Hollywood | The Basil DeSoto Show | Song and Dance |
| *9:45* | | | The Garden Show | |
| *10am* | Ira Cook's Platter Party | City Hospital | Newspaper of the Air | |
| *10:15* | | | The Basil DeSoto Show | |
| *10:30* | | The P. L. Hayes Show | Woody Woodpecker | |
| *10:45* | | | | |
| *11am* | | Galen Drake, talk | | Mary Lee Taylor, cooking |
| *11:15* | | | | |
| *11:30* | | The Robert Q. Lewis Show | The Basil DeSoto Show | The National Farm and Home Hour |
| *11:45* | | | Fixit and Make It | |
| *12pm* | | News | Sid Fuller, news | The Farm Reporter |
| *12:15* | | Science Adventures | The Answer Man | The Farmland Party Line |
| *12:30* | | The Answer Man | The Man on the Farm | |
| *12:45* | | The Garden Gate | | |
| *1pm* | Horse Racing | This is Los Angeles | The Frank Evans Show | Now Hear This |
| *1:15* | | | | |
| *1:30* | Ira Cook's Platter Party | The Phil Norman Show | | |
| *1:45* | | | | |

| DAYTIME — SPRING, 1954 | | | | |
|---|---|---|---|---|
| *Saturday* | | | | |
| | ABC | CBS | MBS | NBC |
| *2pm* | The Metropolitan Opera | Do It Yourself | | |
| *2:15* | | | | |
| *2:30* | | The Longines Symphonette | | |
| *2:45* | | | | |
| *3pm* | | Meet the Music | | The Record Album Review |
| *3:15* | | | | |
| *3:30* | | | | |
| *3:45* | | | | |
| *4pm* | Platterbrains | | | |
| *4:15* | | | Frank Hemingway, news | |
| *4:30* | The Navy Hour | | The Garden Show | |
| *4:45* | | | Music | |

| EVENING — SUMMER, 1954 | | | | |
|---|---|---|---|---|
| *Sunday* | | | | |
| | ABC | CBS | MBS | NBC |
| *5pm* | Highway Frolics, Jimmy Nelson | Escape | The Winnipeg Concert | Conversation |
| *5:15* | | | | |
| *5:30* | George Sokolsky, news | Dick Joy, news | | The Shirley Thomas Show |
| *5:45* | Private Wire | Tom Harmon, sports | The Globetrotters | |
| *6pm* | Taylor Grant, news | The Cobbs | Wonderful City | Quiet Mood |
| *6:15* | Frank Coniff, news | | | |
| *6:30* | Mickey Katz Orchestra | The Music Hall | The Northwestern Reviewing Stand | We Saw Tomorrow |
| *6:45* | | | | |
| *7pm* | Highway Frolics, Jimmy Nelson | Broadway is My Beat | Global Frontiers | |
| *7:15* | | | Hazel Markel, news | |
| *7:30* | | The Whistler | The Army Hour | Meet the Press |
| *7:45* | | | | |
| *8pm* | Don Gardiner, news | Suspense | The Sounding Board | Inheritance |
| *8:15* | Paul Harvey, news | | | |
| *8:30* | Beyond the Stars | My Little Margie | State of the Nation | Pacific Festival |
| *8:45* | | | | |
| *9pm* | Meditation for Moderns | The Gary Crosby Show | Newspaper of the Air | |
| *9:15* | Reverend Fitchman, religion | | The Men's Corner | |
| *9:30* | Music By Mantovani | The Best of Bill Ballance | The Chicago Theater of the Air | Songs That Never Die |
| *9:45* | | | | |
| *10pm* | George Hamilton, news | The Ten o'Clock Wire | | The Richfield Reporter |
| *10:15* | Science of the Mind | Flight by Night | | Mayor Poulson, comment |
| *10:30* | The Old Fashioned Revival Hour | Crossroads in Asia | Little Symphonies | Career Theater |
| *10:45* | | I Believe | | |

# EVENING — SUMMER, 1954

*Monday*

| ABC | CBS | MBS | NBC | |
|---|---|---|---|---|
| News | Edward R. Murrow, news | Think | Feature Wire | *5pm* |
| Bill Stern, sports | Today in Los Angeles | Music | News | *5:15* |
| Chet Huntley, news | Tom Harmon, sports | News | Art Baker's Notebook | *5:30* |
| Robert Garred, news | Frank Goss, news | Sports | Elmer Patterson, news | *5:45* |
| John W. Vandercook, news | Gunsmoke | Gabriel Heatter, news | George Putnam, news | *6pm* |
| Dinner Music | | In the Mood | Sports | *6:15* |
| | Gangbusters | Virgil Pinkley, news | The American Way | *6:30* |
| | | Sam Hayes, news | | *6:45* |
| | Mr. Keen, Tracer of Lost Persons | The Falcon | Fibber McGee and Molly | *7pm* |
| | Hill Songs | | Out of the West | *7:15* |
| The Lone Ranger | Arthur Godfrey's Talent Scouts | Could This Be You | The World We Live In | *7:30* |
| | | | The Nation's Business | *7:45* |
| Back to the Bible | My Friend Irma | Under Arrest | World News | *8pm* |
| | | | One Man's Family | *8:15* |
| Music | Lowell Thomas, news | Let George Do It | Best of All | *8:30* |
| | The Tennessee Ernie Ford Show | | | *8:45* |
| | The P. L. Hayes Show | Newspaper of the Air | The Bell Telephone Hour | *9pm* |
| | | Think | | *9:15* |
| Doorway to the Future | The Bergie Music Box | Reporter's Roundup | American Bandstand | *9:30* |
| | | | | *9:45* |
| Edwin C. Hill, news | The Ten o'Clock Wire | Fulton Lewis, Jr., news | The Richfield Reporter | *10pm* |
| Science of the Mind | Carroll Alcott, news | Frank Edwards, news | Joy Forever | *10:15* |
| Lonesome Gal | The Phil Norman Show | Sports | The Al Poska Show | *10:30* |
| | | | | *10:45* |

# EVENING — SUMMER, 1954

*Tuesday*

| | ABC | CBS | MBS | NBC |
|---|---|---|---|---|
| *5pm* | News | Edward R. Murrow, news | News | Feature Wire |
| *5:15* | Bill Stern, sports | Today in Los Angeles | Music | News |
| *5:30* | Chet Huntley, news | Tom Harmon, sports | News | Art Baker's Notebook |
| *5:45* | Robert Garred, news | Frank Goss, news | Sports | Elmer Patterson, news |
| *6pm* | John W. Vandercook, news | Yours Truly, Johnny Dollar | Gabriel Heatter, news | George Putnam, news |
| *6:15* | Dinner Music | | Bing Crosby Records | Sports |
| *6:30* | | The Jack Carson Show | Virgil Pinkley, news | Crime and Peter Chambers |
| *6:45* | | | Sam Hayes, news | |
| *7pm* | | Mr. Keen, Tracer of Lost Persons | Mickey Spillane Mystery | Fibber McGee and Molly |
| *7:15* | | Hill Songs | | Out of the West |
| *7:30* | The Silver Eagle | People Are Funny | The Search That Never Ends | Spotlight on Paris |
| *7:45* | | | | |
| *8pm* | Back to the Bible | Night Watch | High Adventure | World News |
| *8:15* | | | | One Man's Family |
| *8:30* | Doorway to the Future | Lowell Thomas, news | Author Meets the Critics | KFI Calling |
| *8:45* | | The Tennessee Ernie Ford Show | | |
| *9pm* | America's Town Meeting of the Air | The P. L. Hayes Show | Newspaper of the Air | Dragnet |
| *9:15* | | | Names in the News | |
| *9:30* | | The Bergie Music Box | Manhattan Crossroads | American Bandstand |
| *9:45* | Monitor News | | Edward Arnold, comment | |
| *10pm* | Edwin C. Hill, news | The Ten o'Clock Wire | Fulton Lewis, Jr., news | The Richfield Reporter |
| *10:15* | Science of the Mind | Carroll Alcott, news | Frank Edwards, news | Joy Forever |
| *10:30* | Lonesome Gal | The Phil Norman Show | Sports | The Al Poska Show |
| *10:45* | | | | |

## EVENING — SUMMER, 1954

*Wednesday*

| ABC | CBS | MBS | NBC | |
|---|---|---|---|---|
| News | Edward R. Murrow, news | News | Feature Wire | *5pm* |
| Bill Stern, sports | Today in Los Angeles | Music | News | *5:15* |
| Chet Huntley, news | Tom Harmon, sports | News | Art Baker's Notebook | *5:30* |
| Robert Garred, news | Frank Goss, news | Sports | Elmer Patterson, news | *5:45* |
| John W. Vandercook, news | Casey, Crime Photographer | Gabriel Heatter, news | George Putnam, news | *6pm* |
| Dinner Music | | In the Mood | Sports | *6:15* |
| | The Jack Carson Show | Virgil Pinkley, news | Barrie Craig, Confidential Investigator | *6:30* |
| | | Sam Hayes, news | | *6:45* |
| Paul Whiteman Varieties | Mr. Keen, Tracer of Lost Persons | The Squad Room | Fibber McGee and Molly | *7pm* |
| | Hill Songs | | Out of the West | *7:15* |
| The Lone Ranger | TheTwenty-First Precinct | The Cisco Kid | The News Game | *7:30* |
| | | | | *7:45* |
| Back to the Bible | The FBI in Peace and War | Nightmare | World News | *8pm* |
| | | | One Man's Family | *8:15* |
| The ABC Workshop | Lowell Thomas, news | The Family Theater | Spend a Million | *8:30* |
| | The Tennessee Ernie Ford Show | | | *8:45* |
| Lawrence Welk Orchestra | The P. L. Hayes Show | Newspaper of the Air | You Bet Your Life | *9pm* |
| | | Think | | *9:15* |
| Dance Orchestra | The Bergie Music Box | Manhattan Crossroads | American Bandstand | *9:30* |
| | | Edward Arnold, comment | | *9:45* |
| Edwin C. Hill, news | The Ten o'Clock Wire | Fulton Lewis, Jr., news | The Richfield Reporter | *10pm* |
| Science of the Mind | Carroll Alcott, news | Frank Edwards, news | Joy Forever | *10:15* |
| Lonesome Gal | The Phil Norman Show | Sports | The Al Poska Show | *10:30* |
| | | | | *10:45* |

# EVENING — SUMMER, 1954

*Thursday*

| | ABC | CBS | MBS | NBC |
|---|---|---|---|---|
| *5pm* | News | Edward R. Murrow, news | News | Feature Wire |
| *5:15* | Bill Stern, sports | Today in Los Angeles | Music | News |
| *5:30* | Chet Huntley, news | Tom Harmon, sports | News | Art Baker's Notebook |
| *5:45* | Robert Garred, news | Frank Goss, news | Sports | Elmer Patterson, news |
| *6pm* | John W. Vandercook, news | Meet Mr. McNutley | Gabriel Heatter, news | George Putnam, news |
| *6:15* | Dinner Music | | Bing Crosby Records | Sports |
| *6:30* | | The Jack Carson Show | Virgil Pinkley, news | Senor Ben |
| *6:45* | | | Sam Hayes, news | |
| *7pm* | | Mr. Keen, Tracer of Lost Persons | Official Detective | Fibber McGee and Molly |
| *7:15* | | Hill Songs | | Out of the West |
| *7:30* | The Silver Eagle | That's Rich | Music | The Adventures of the Scarlet Pimpernel |
| *7:45* | | | | |
| *8pm* | Back to the Bible | Meet Millie | Crime Fighters | World News |
| *8:15* | | | | One Man's Family |
| *8:30* | Romance Music | Lowell Thomas, news | London Melodies | The Roy Rogers Show |
| *8:45* | | The Tennessee Ernie Ford Show | | |
| *9pm* | The World We Live In | The P. L. Hayes Show | Newspaper of the Air | Dr. Six Gun |
| *9:15* | | | Names in the News | |
| *9:30* | The Treasury Show | The Bergie Music Box | Manhattan Crossroads | American Bandstand |
| *9:45* | | | Edward Arnold, comment | |
| *10pm* | Edwin C. Hill, news | The Ten o'Clock Wire | Fulton Lewis, Jr., news | The Richfield Reporter |
| *10:15* | Science of the Mind | Carroll Alcott, news | Frank Edwards, news | Joy Forever |
| *10:30* | Lonesome Gal | The Phil Norman Show | Sports | The Al Poska Show |
| *10:45* | | | | |

# EVENING — SUMMER, 1954

*Friday*

| ABC | CBS | MBS | NBC | |
|---|---|---|---|---|
| News | Edward R. Murrow, news | News | Feature Wire | *5pm* |
| Bill Stern, sports | Today in Los Angeles | Music | News | *5:15* |
| Chet Huntley, news | Tom Harmon, sports | News | Art Baker's Notebook | *5:30* |
| Robert Garred, news | Frank Goss, news | Sports | Elmer Patterson, news | *5:45* |
| John W. Vandercook, news | Do It Yourself | Gabriel Heatter, news | George Putnam, news | *6pm* |
| Dinner Music | | In the Mood | Sports | *6:15* |
| | The Jack Carson Show | Virgil Pinkley, news | Hear America Swingin' | *6:30* |
| | | Sam Hayes, news | | *6:45* |
| | Mr. Keen, Tracer of Lost Persons | Counterspy | Fibber McGee and Molly | *7pm* |
| | Hill Songs | | Out of the West | *7:15* |
| The Lone Ranger | Arthur Godfrey's Digest | The Cisco Kid | Sound Stage | *7:30* |
| | | | | *7:45* |
| Back to the Bible | | Take a Number | World News | *8pm* |
| | | | One Man's Family | *8:15* |
| Music | Lowell Thomas, news | Have a Heart | The 1960 Town Hall Party | *8:30* |
| | The Tennessee Ernie Ford Show | | | *8:45* |
| | The P. L. Hayes Show | Newspaper of the Air | | *9pm* |
| | | Think | | *9:15* |
| Football Forecast | The Bergie Music Box | Manhattan Crossroads | American Bandstand | *9:30* |
| | | Edward Arnold, comment | | *9:45* |
| Edwin C. Hill, news | The Ten o'Clock Wire | Fulton Lewis, Jr., news | The Richfield Reporter | *10pm* |
| Science of the Mind | Carroll Alcott, news | Frank Edwards, news | Joy Forever | *10:15* |
| Lonesome Gal | The Phil Norman Show | Sports | The Al Poska Show | *10:30* |
| | | | | *10:45* |

## EVENING — SUMMER, 1954

*Saturday*

| | ABC | CBS | MBS | NBC |
|---|---|---|---|---|
| *5pm* | News | Carroll Alcott, news | Music | Motorist Melody |
| *5:15* | The Three Suns | Today in Los Angeles | Guest Star | News |
| *5:30* | Robert Garred, news | Tom Harmon, sports | Bowling Today | Saturday Segue |
| *5:45* | Know Your Schools | Frank Goss, news | Sports | |
| *6pm* | Marines in Review | Freddy Martin Orchestra | Hawaii Calls | The Polka Party |
| *6:15* | | | | |
| *6:30* | Man of Color | Sammy Kaye Orchestra | The Brevard Festival | |
| *6:45* | Sports | | | |
| *7pm* | Concerts | Two for the Money | Farm Quiz | Tex Williams Orchestra |
| *7:15* | | | | |
| *7:30* | Dr. Bartlett, heatlh | Dance Orchestra | Music By Kostelanetz | The Tex Ritter Show |
| *7:45* | Ballads | | | |
| *8pm* | Back to the Bible | Saturday Night, Country Style | The Enchanted Hour | Grand Ole Opry |
| *8:15* | | | | |
| *8:30* | Dr. Fifeld, health | | Lombardoland USA | The Town Hall Party |
| *8:45* | | | | |
| *9pm* | Lawrence Welk Orchestra | Hometown Jamboree | Newspaper of the Air | |
| *9:15* | | | Forward March | |
| *9:30* | The Layman's Hour | The Burgie Music Box | Monica Sings | American Bandstand |
| *9:45* | | | Helen O'Connell, songs | |
| *10pm* | News | The Ten o'Clock Wire | Sports | America's Pop Music |
| *10:15* | Martha Harp, songs | Carroll Alcott, news | | |
| *10:30* | Lawrence Welk Orchestra | The Phil Norman Show | The Frank Carroll Show | |
| *10:45* | | | | |

## DAYTIME — SUMMER, 1954

*Sunday*

| | ABC | CBS | MBS | NBC |
|---|---|---|---|---|
| *8am* | Morning Song | The Salt Lake Tabernacle Choir | Wings of Healing | Grandpa Reads the Funnies |
| *8:15* | Shower Blessings | | | |
| *8:30* | The Light and Life Hour | Invitation to Learning | The Back to God Hour | Collector's Item |
| *8:45* | | | | |
| *9am* | The World Tomorrow | Capitol Cloak Room | The Radio Bible Class | News |
| *9:15* | | | | The Christian Science Monitor |
| *9:30* | Message of Israel | Howard K. Smith, news | The Voice of Prophecy | The Eternal Light |
| *9:45* | | Better Gardens | | |
| *10am* | Christian in Action | Leading Question | Newspaper of the Air | Herbert J. Mann, sports |
| *10:15* | | | Frank and Ernest, songs | Hometown Happenings |
| *10:30* | | The University Explorer | The Lutheran Hour | The California Sportsman |
| *10:45* | | Christy Fox, news | | Senators Report |
| *11am* | Church in Home | Your Invitation to Music | Keep Healthy | The Catholic Hour |
| *11:15* | | | Land of the Free | |
| *11:30* | Romance Music | | Sunday Favorites | The Howard University Choir |
| *11:45* | | | Across the Blue Pacific | |
| *12pm* | | | Broadway News | The University of Chicago Round Table |
| *12:15* | | | Bill Cunningham, news | |
| *12:30* | Religious Lecture | Sunday Afternoon | Music By Manotvani | The Facts Forum |
| *12:45* | | | | The World of Books |
| *1pm* | The Old Fashioned Revival Hour | | Guy Lombardo Orchestra | Opera is for Everyone |
| *1:15* | | | | |
| *1:30* | | | Flight in the Blue | |
| *1:45* | | | | |

| DAYTIME — SUMMER, 1954 | | | | |
|---|---|---|---|---|
| *Monday-Friday* | | | | |
| ABC | CBS | MBS | NBC | |
| The Breakfast Club | The Ralph Story Show | Cecil Brown, news | Murray Talks | *8am* |
| | News | Gabriel Heatter, news | | *8:15* |
| | Make Up Your Mind | Bible Institute | Pat Bishop, news | *8:30* |
| | Rosemary | | Andy and Virginia, songs | *8:45* |
| The Garden Guide | Wendy Warren and the News | The Wife Saver | | *9am* |
| Chet Huntley, news | Aunt Jenny's True Life Stories | Capitol Commentary | Ladies' Day | *9:15* |
| My True Story | The Romance of Helen Trent | Nancy Young, talk | | *9:30* |
| | Our Gal Sunday | | News | *9:45* |
| Whispering Streets | The Road of Life | Newspaper of the Air | Art Baker's Notebook | *10am* |
| When a Girl Marries | Ma Perkins | Tello-Test Quiz | Second Chance | *10:15* |
| Modern Romances | Young Dr. Malone | The Jack Wagner Show | Strike It Rich | *10:30* |
| Shopper's Special | The Guiding Light | | | *10:45* |
| Beat the Record | The Second Mrs. Burton | Florida Calling | The Phrase That Pays | *11am* |
| | Perry Mason | | News | *11:15* |
| The Todds | This is Nora Drake | Queen for a Day | The Record Album Review | *11:30* |
| | The Brighter Day | | Lady's Book | *11:45* |
| News | Bill Keneelly, news | Broadway News | The Farm Reporter | *12pm* |
| Paul Harvey, news | Hilltop House | Cedric Foster, news | The Feminine Touch | *12:15* |
| News | House Party | The Jack Wagner Show | Pepper Young's Family | *12:30* |
| Nancy Holmes, home talk | | | The Right to Happiness | *12:45* |
| Bill Davidson, talk | Arthur Godfrey Time | | Mary Noble, Backstage Wife | *1pm* |
| | | | Stella Dallas | *1:15* |
| | | | Young Widder Brown | *1:30* |
| | | | The Woman in My House | *1:45* |

## DAYTIME — SUMMER, 1954

*Sunday*

| | ABC | CBS | MBS | NBC |
|---|---|---|---|---|
| *2pm* | The Voice of Prophecy | | The Shadow | |
| *2:15* | | | | |
| *2:30* | Sammy Kaye Orchestra | The World Today | True Detective Mysteries | |
| *2:45* | | | | |
| *3pm* | The Hour of Decision | Hollywood Today | Nick Carter, Master Detective | |
| *3:15* | | | | |
| *3:30* | The Herald of Truth | Summer in St. Louis | Bob Considine, news | NBC Summer Symphony |
| *3:45* | | | Alan Wismer, sports | |
| *4pm* | Melodies | Juke Box Jury | British Music | |
| *4:15* | | | | |
| *4:30* | Wings of Healing | | Promenade Symphony of Toronto | The American Forum of the Air |
| *4:45* | | | | |

# DAYTIME — SUMMER, 1954

*Monday-Friday*

| ABC | CBS | MBS | NBC | |
|---|---|---|---|---|
| Murder in the Afternoon | | Quick, What's the Answer / The Johnny Olsen Show | Just Plain Bill | *2pm* |
| | | | Lorenzo Jones | *2:15* |
| | Curt Massey, songs | Star Time | Front Page Farrell | *2:30* |
| | Mike and Buff's Mail | Lynn at Hollywood | It Pays to Be Married | *2:45* |
| Make Believe Ballroom | Ruth Ashton Reports | Crowell's Nest | Welcome, Travelers | *3pm* |
| | The Phil Norman Show | | | *3:15* |
| The H. Weaver Show | | Behind the Story | Dr. Paul | *3:30* |
| | The Matinee Editor | Tello-Test Quiz | The Little Concert | *3:45* |
| | | Fulton Lewis, Jr., news | News | *4pm* |
| | | Frank Hemingway, news | Burritt and Wheeler, talk | *4:15* |
| | | Here's the Answer | | *4:30* |
| Elroy Hirsch, sports | | Sam Hayes, news | | *4:45* |

## DAYTIME — SUMMER, 1954

*Saturday*

| | ABC | CBS | MBS | NBC |
|---|---|---|---|---|
| *8am* | A Man and His Music | The Robert Q. Lewis Show | The Basil DeSoto Show | The Bass Harris Show |
| *8:15* | | | Frank Singiser, news | |
| *8:30* | | | The Haven of Rest | |
| *8:45* | Mirandy's Garden Patch | | | |
| *9am* | No School Today | Theater of Romance | Flying Feet | Jump Jump and the Ice Queen |
| *9:15* | | | | |
| *9:30* | Space Patrol | Stars Over Hollywood | The Basil DeSoto Show | The Book Carnival |
| *9:45* | | | Here's to Veterans | The Chuck Cecil Show |
| *10am* | Ira Cook's Platter Party | City Hospital | Newspaper of the Air | |
| *10:15* | | | The Basil DeSoto Show | |
| *10:30* | | Meet the Missus | The Carroll Show | |
| *10:45* | | | | |
| *11am* | | Galen Drake, talk | | Mary Lee Taylor, cooking |
| *11:15* | | | | |
| *11:30* | | | The Basil DeSoto Show | The National Farm and Home Hour |
| *11:45* | | | Fixit and Make It | |
| *12pm* | | News | Sid Fuller, news | The Farm Reporter |
| *12:15* | | Overseas Report | The Frank Evans Show | The Farmland Party Line |
| *12:30* | | Farm News | | |
| *12:45* | | The Garden Gate | | |
| *1pm* | | This is Los Angeles | | Now Hear This |
| *1:15* | | | | |
| *1:30* | | The Phil Norman Show | | |
| *1:45* | | | | |

## DAYTIME — SUMMER, 1954

*Saturday*

| | ABC | CBS | MBS | NBC |
|---|---|---|---|---|
| *2pm* | The Metropolitan Opera | Do It Yourself | | |
| *2:15* | | | | |
| *2:30* | | Meet the Music | | |
| *2:45* | | | | |
| *3pm* | | | | The Record Album Review |
| *3:15* | | | | |
| *3:30* | | | | |
| *3:45* | | | | |
| *4pm* | | | | |
| *4:15* | | | Frank Hemingway, news | |
| *4:30* | Platterbrains | | Musical Almanac | |
| *4:45* | | | | |

Affectionately, Jayne Mansfield
Richard Koper

Captain Midnight's
Post-War Radio Years
Radio's High-Tech Adventure Thrills!
by Leonard Zane

THE NEW YORK
OLD-TIME RADIO
SCHEDULE BOOK
VOLUME
3
1946-1954
KEITH D. LEE

ALSO
STARRING...
FORTY BIOGRAPHICAL ESSAYS ON THE GREATEST CHARACTER ACTORS OF HOLLYWOOD'S GOLDEN ERA, 1930-1965
CYNTHIA AND SARA BRIDESON

FOREVER AMBER
FROM NOVEL TO FILM

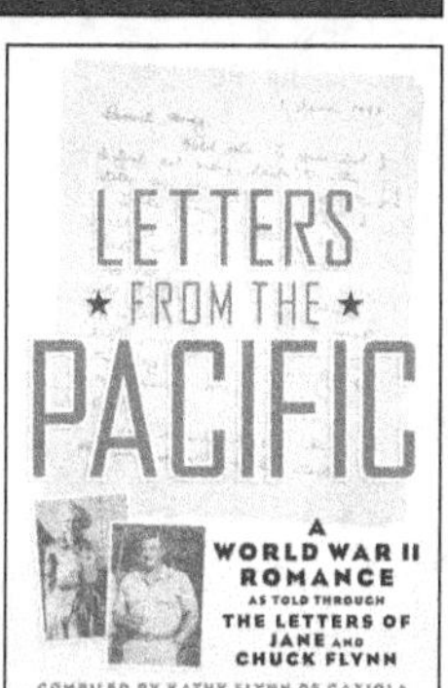

LETTERS
FROM THE
PACIFIC
A WORLD WAR II ROMANCE
AS TOLD THROUGH THE LETTERS OF JANE AND CHUCK FLYNN
COMPILED BY KATHY FLYNN DE GAXIOLA
WITH LUZ GAXIOLA FLYNN AND MICA GAXIOLA FLYNN

WILD WILD WESTERNERS
A Roundup of Interviews with Western Movie and TV Veterans
BY TOM WEAVER

THE SILVER AGE OF COMICS
Fantastic Four
WILLIAM SCHOELL

www.ingramcontent.com/pod-product-compliance
Lightning Source LLC
Chambersburg PA
CBHW051332230426
43668CB00010B/1243